# Leipziger Altorientalistische Studien

Herausgegeben von
Michael P. Streck

Band 4

2016
Harrassowitz Verlag · Wiesbaden

Nathan Wasserman

# Akkadian Love Literature
## of the Third and Second Millennium BCE

2016
Harrassowitz Verlag · Wiesbaden

Bibliografische Information der Deutschen Nationalbibliothek
Die Deutsche Nationalbibliothek verzeichnet diese Publikation in der Deutschen Nationalbibliografie; detaillierte bibliografische Daten sind im Internet über http://dnb.dnb.de abrufbar.

Bibliographic information published by the Deutsche Nationalbibliothek
The Deutsche Nationalbibliothek lists this publication in the Deutsche Nationalbibliografie; detailed bibliographic data are available in the Internet at http://dnb.dnb.de .

For further information about our publishing program consult our website http://www.harrassowitz-verlag.de


Printed on permanent/durable paper.
Printing and binding: Hubert & Co., Göttingen
Printed in Germany

ISSN 2193-4436
ISBN 978-3-447-10726-6

To Ada Manuela

*asmat kī illūr ṣēri*

# Contents

The Corpus

# Preface

The present monograph is an offshoot of the project *Sources of Early Akkadian Literature* (SEAL),[1] headed by the present author and Michael P. Streck (Leipzig University). From the inception of the joint work on SEAL it was clear that the extensive corpus of Akk. literary texts should be presented in two different and complementary modes: an online database followed by a printed publication. Each of these media has inherent advantages. The internet allows for regular additions, modifications and updates which are unavoidable in the preliminary work on large textual corpora. It is also more open and accessible to the public than printed books. But the ephemeral nature of online databases renders them less suitable for the final publication.

Initiated in 2005, SEAL now (Spring 2016) contains almost 690 literary texts of all genres, from the third to the mid-second mill. BCE. Without interrupting the online posting of the texts, it is now time to present the corpus, section by section, in book form. The compositions that deal with love and sex were chosen as the first group of SEAL texts to be published in this way. Other sections of the corpus will follow.

Though the product of a single author, this book owes much to different people. Michael Streck, a colleague with whom I had the luck to start the SEAL project and who has subsequently become a true friend, offered much good advice. His mastery of all aspects of Mesopotamian culture proved crucial. His most important suggestions are mentioned in the text as (MPS). Dominique Charpin, Sophie Démare-Lafont, Eckart Frahm, Stefan Jakob, Leonid Kogan, Jana Matuszak, Piotr Michalowski, and Rony Weinstein, have all contributed to my work and I wish to thank them cordially. Special thanks go to four colleagues. Marten Stol turned my attention to the Chicago text A 7478, sent me his preliminary transliteration of the obverse, and offered valuable comments on my edition. Jakob Klein sent me the photos of the Moussaieff Love Song and made it possible for me to publish this tablet. Andrew George shared his unpublished edition of the love incantation MS 3062 and other relevant material with me. Uri Gabbay discussed the Sumerian incipits in the catalogue KAR 158 and other texts in the book with me. Warm thanks also go to Jon Taylor, Béatrice André-Salvini, Joachim Marzahn, and Walter Farber – the keepers of the cuneiform tablets at the British Museum, the Louvre, the Vorderasiatisches Museum and the Oriental Institute in Chicago, respectively – for their readiness to open their collections to me. Yigal Bloch, Melanie Christina Mohr, Sivan Kedar, Svetlana Matskėvich, Juyoung Oh and Shlomit Bechar assisted me in technical matters and deserve my thanks too.

Anastasia Keshman walked by me through these years. I am grateful to her. On the 30th of November 2012 our daughter Ada Manuela was born. I dedicate this book to our daughter, with love.

Jerusalem, October 2016 Nathan Wasserman

1 The SEAL project (http://www.seal.uni-leipzig.de/) was financed by two consecutive three-year grants by the German-Israeli Foundation for Scientific Research and Development (2007–2009 and 2010–2012).

# Akkadian Love Literature: An Overview

# 1. The Scope of This Study

This study aims to present all Akk. literary texts dealing with love and sex from the third to the second mill. BCE. Surprisingly, unlike Sum. love songs which have been collected and discussed,[2] the corpus of Akk. literary texts dealing with love and sex, though treated separately by various scholars,[3] was not collected systematically or addressed as a whole. This monograph aims to fill this gap and to provide a modern edition accompanied by a comprehensive discussion of the corpus.

My approach is philological and literary. While general aspects of love and sexuality in ancient Mesopotamia are treated *en passant*, this monograph does not tackle these topics from the gender or cultural studies perspective.[4] Although Biblical parallels[5] and references from Classical sources are occasionally included, this is not a comparative study. Material artifacts and visual representations which bear witness to love and sex in ancient Mesopotamia, best left to sociologists, archaeologists and art historians, are also beyond the scope of this study. Epic and mythic episodes which refer to love (like the encounter between Enkidu and Šamḫat in Gilg. II and Ištar's attempt to seduce Gilgameš in Gilg. VI, the amatory relationship between Nergal and Ereškigal in the myth bearing this name, or the scene of copulation between the husband and the wife described in Atraḫasīs I 300[6]) are omitted or referred to only indirectly. Later texts from the first mill. which concern love and sex – notably the love dialogue of Nabû and Tašmētu (SAA 3, 14), the love ritual mentioning Marduk and his consort Ištar of Babylon (Lambert 1975[7]), the ŠÀ.ZI.GA incantations (Biggs 1967), and the Egalkurra texts (Stadhouders 2013, esp. 309–311) – are referred to briefly in the commentary and discussion, but not treated separately. The omen series which predicts the prospects of a marriage, or how fertile a woman is,[8] are also not discussed at any length.

Two factors determined the definition of the corpus. The first relates to the project *Sources of Early Akkadian Literature* (SEAL) which provides the foundation for this study. SEAL presently covers the third and second mill. BCE, but not the first (c. 690 compositions). Since I am convinced that any group of texts (e.g. hymns, laments, incantations, etc.) should be treated only after thorough analysis of its entire literary system, it would have been incorrect to go beyond the present scope of SEAL and treat a group within the corpus in isolation. In addition, many of the first mill. texts which thematically belong to the

---

2 See esp. Sefati 1998 and shortly also Hecker 2005, 167–168.

3 Klein/Sefati's (2008) article offers a succinct summary of the more recent studies on this corpus.

4 The literature on love and sexuality in ancient Mesopotamia is extensive. Wiggermann's 2010 article "Sexualität" in the RlA offers an excellent summary of the subject with a detailed bibliographical survey.

5 All Biblical references lean on the English translation of the New Jewish Publication Society of America Tanakh.

6 Lambert/Millard 1969, 64–65.

7 See also Fincke 2013.

8 See esp. Böck 2000, 59 and passim.

literary corpus treated here (ŠÀ.ZI.GA and the Egalkurra texts) come very close to rituals[9] and medical compendia, which require different treatment than the corpus of third and second mill. texts. In order to avoid further delay in the publication of this monograph, I decided against the inclusion of first mill. material.

## 1.1 The Corpus[10]

The group of Akk. texts dealing with sexual attraction and emotional connection from the third and second mill. BCE contains a few dozen different compositions, comprised of three sub-groups:

Table (1): The core group of some twenty non-homogenous texts: monologues, dialogues, hymnal compositions, as well as descriptive texts:[11]

| Publication | Period (Provenance) | Description |
|---|---|---|
| № 1. A 7478 | OB | Monologue/Descriptive: ♀ yearning ♂ absent |
| № 2. CUSAS 10, 8 | OB | Monologue: ♂ yearning ♀ absent |
| № 3. CUSAS 10, 9 | OB | Monologue: ♀ yearning ♂ indifferent |
| № 4. CUSAS 10, 10 | OB | Monologue: ♂ scorning ♀ yearning |
| № 5. CUSAS 10, 13 | OB | Prayer → Descriptive: ♂ + ♀uniting |
| № 6. Fs. Renger 192–193 | Late OB | Monologue: ♀ yearning ♂ absent |
| № 7. JAOS 103, 26–27 | Late OB - MB | Descriptive: ♂ + ♀ uniting → ♂ absent |
| № 8. KAL 3, 75 | MA (Assur) | Monologue/Descriptive |
| № 9. LKA 15 | MA (Assur) | Descriptive: ♀ yearning ♂ absent |
| № 10. MIO 12, 52–53 | Late OB | Descriptive: ♂ + ♀ uniting |

9 On the question of the dependence of love-related compositions on rituals, see Hecker 2005, 176 and Klein/Sefati 2008 (esp. p. 624).

10 The texts are referred to by their name (publication place) and their sequel number in the study (№). These numbers are internal and do not correspond to the number of the texts in the SEAL database.

11 The text MIO 12, 53–54, published by Lambert in 1966 as love lyric, is better defined as a lament (similarly Hecker 2005, 169).

| Publication | Period (Provenance) | Description |
|---|---|---|
| № 11. Moussaieff Love Song | MB - OB origin (Nippur?) | Descriptive: ♂ + ♀ uniting |
| № 12. Or. 60, 340 | MB (Nippur) | Descriptive: ♂ + ♀ uniting |
| № 13. PRAK 1 B 472 | Early OB (Ur III?) (Kiš) | Monologue/Descriptive: ♂ + ♀ uniting |
| № 14a. PRAK 2 C 3 | Early OB (Ur III?) (Kiš) | Descriptive (fragmentary) |
| № 14b. PRAK 2 C 30 | Early OB (Ur III?) (Kiš) | Monologue/Descriptive (fragmentary) |
| № 14c. PRAK 2 C 41 | Early OB (Ur III?) (Kiš) | Descriptive? (fragmentary) |
| № 14d. PRAK 2 C 125 | Early OB (Ur III?) (Kiš) | Monologue/Descriptive (fragmentary) |
| № 14e. PRAK 2 C 134 | Early OB (Ur III?) (Kiš) | Monologue/Descriptive (fragmentary) |
| № 14f. PRAK 2 C 135 | Early OB (Ur III?) (Kiš) | Monologue/Descriptive (fragmentary) |
| № 15. YOS 11, 24 | OB (Larsa) | Descriptive: ♂ + ♀ uniting |
| № 16. ZA 49, 168–169 | OB (Sippar) | Dialogue: ♂ scorning ♀ yearning → ♂ + ♀ uniting |

Table (2): Ancient catalogues listing incipits of love songs, virtually all now lost:

| Publication | Period (Provenance) | Description |
|---|---|---|
| № 17. ASJ 10, 18 | Late OB | Different incipits |
| № 18. CUSAS 10, 12 | OB | Different incipits |
| № 19. KAR 158 | MB/MA (Assur) | Different incipits |

Table (3): A dozen incantations which aim to manipulate the will of the beloved and to win over a stubborn or disdainful lover:

| Publication | Period (Provenance) | Description |
|---|---|---|
| № 20. CUSAS 10, 11 | OB | Historiola; ♂ manipulating ♀ |
| № 21. KBo 36, 27 | MB (Hattuša) | ♂ self-encouraging → ♂ + ♀ uniting |

| Publication | Period (Provenance) | Description |
|---|---|---|
| № 22. MAD 5, 8 | OAkk (Kiš) | Historiola; ♂ manipulating ♀ |
| № 23. MS 3062 | OB | ♀ manipulating ♂ |
| № 24. VS 17, 23 | OB | ♂ manipulating ♀ |
| № 25. YOS 11, 21c | OB (Larsa?) | ♀ manipulating ♂ |
| № 26. YOS 11, 87 | OB (Larsa?) | Historiola; ♂ manipulating ♀ |
| № 27. ZA 75, 198–204a | OB (Isin) | ♀ manipulating ♂ |
| № 28. ZA 75, 198–204b | OB (Isin) | ♀ manipulating ♀ |
| № 29. ZA 75, 198–204c | OB (Isin) | ♀ manipulating ♂ ; ♀ manipulating ♀ |
| № 30. ZA 75, 198–204d | OB (Isin) | ♀ manipulating ♂ |
| № 31. ZA 75, 198–204e | OB (Isin) | ♀ manipulating ♂ |
| № 32. ZA 75, 198–204g | OB (Isin) | ♀ manipulating ♂ |
| № 33. ZA 75, 198–204h | OB (Isin) | ♀ manipulating ♂ |
| № 34. ZA 75, 198–204i | OB (Isin) | ♀ manipulating ♂ → ♂ + ♀ uniting(?) |

The data above makes it clear that the textual corpus of Akk. Love Literature is non-homogenous.[12] Furthermore, the present corpus is considerably larger than previously assumed,[13] not only because it includes the group of love incantations, but also because new texts were added, notably the monologue A 7478 (№ 1) and the dialogue of the Moussaieff Love Song (№ 11), as well as the incantation MS 3062 (№ 23), and the hymnic fragments from Kiš (PRAK 2 C 3; PRAK 2 C 30; PRAK 2 C 41; PRAK 2 C 125; PRAK 2 C 134, and PRAK 2 C 135 = № 14a–f). Another MB love incantation, accompanied by a ritual, was recently discovered by Elyze Zomer (Leipzig) in the Vorderasiatisches Museum in Berlin. The text, VAT 13226, will be published in Zomer's forthcoming dissertation. It was kindly sent to me by her but will not be included in the present study.

The relation between any literary corpus and actual sexual practices in a given society is tricky. Literature is never a direct or impartial mirror of social reality – not where sexual norms and habits are concerned, and certainly not when ancient society is at stake. One must avoid the temptation of writing a history of sexuality based on literary sources alone.

12 On the non-homogeneity of the Akk. corpus of love-related compositions, see also Hecker 2005, 167. See further Klein/Sefati 2008, 618–619: "Compared with the large corpus of Sumerian Dumuzi-Inana love songs, the number of Akkadian love songs preserved is small, and their type and character is rather diverse".

13 Significantly larger than presented in Hecker 2005 and in Klein/Sefati 2008, 618–619, but similar to that outlined in Wiggermann 2010.

As Ormand (2009, 22) put it in relation to ancient Greek love poetry: "We must take care when using poetry as an indication of sexual practice in the real world", but he continues "[n]onetheless, this is the evidence that exists, and my strategy is to make the most of it". This study tries to follow this carefully measured stand.

# 2. Thematic and Temporal Classification of the Corpus

## 2.1 The Problem of the Love Lyrics

*The Problem of the Love Lyrics* was the title of W. G. Lambert's study of an enigmatic first mill. ritual whose divine protagonists are Marduk, Ṣarpanītum and Ištar of Babylon (Lambert 1975). The problem, as Lambert put it, was in the philological difficulties presented by the text itself and its general interpretation: "The results, when these problems have been overcome, are often most baffling. In places there is something like the work of those modern poets who try to create word pictures without grammar. Imagery of the boldest kind is commonplace, and the eroticism is the most explicit for ancient Mesopotamia. Parallels are hard to find" (Lambert 1975, 99). For me, the problem of love lyrics resides in the fact that in quite a number of cases the corpus contained in this book does not correspond to the definition "lyric". Or, in the neat wording of D. O. Edzard (1987, 58): "Ich fürchte, die 'Love Lyrics' sind weder sehr lieblich noch sehr lyrisch". The language of incantations about love and sex, though rich in metaphor and imagery, is straightforward, audacious and rarely refers to emotions; the term "lyric" is accordingly not fitting. In other texts from the core group there are blunt, even caustic phrases, that certainly do not merit the title "lyric": "You were born the daughter of a substitute, with no dowry! You have a mole on (your) forehead! As long as you show no respect, putting yourself to shame, I shall tell you where your (right) place is! You do not listen to me, you. (By) following your heart, mounting the clouds, you keep chasing lovers away!",[14] or "I despise the girl who does not worship (me). I do not desire for the girl who does not [fawn]. I shall not give her [my love-charm]. Talking in order to disagree why [does it exist?]"[15] Of course, counter-examples exist, as the following expressive descriptions indicate: "The daughters of Anu, the lights of heaven, [*in day-ti*]*me*(?) purified the sky of Anu. Love came about, twittering over the people; May Love twitter over me!"[16] But the corpus as a whole cannot be labeled "lyric", unless the term is loosely applied.

Consequently, the neutral header *Akkadian Love Literature* (henceforth ALL) was chosen to define the corpus treated here.

---

14 CUSAS 10, 10: 17–25 (№ 4).
15 ZA 49, 168–169 ii 10–14 (№ 16).
16 CUSAS 10, 11: 2–6 (№ 20).

## 2.2 Akkadian Love Literature: a Genre?

Given the diversity of the corpus, the question whether ALL really constitutes a genre is pertinent. The problem becomes more complex when we consider that ancient catalogues present a variety of generic terms, like *zamārum*, *elēlum*, *irtum*, *nūrum* and more (see Groneberg 2003 and Shehata 2009), many of which refer to what we somewhat simplistically call "love lyrics" – although no generic subscript which defines ALL exists. This situation differs from Sum. love lyrics, where many, if not all love songs carry the subscript bal-bal-e, mostly related to Inanna.[17] In other words, more than in any other area of Akk. literature, emic and etic generic definitions do not apply to ALL.

When looking for internal criteria, one encounters similar difficulties defining texts which belong to ALL by style or by a fixed set of literary devices. In fact ALL is not connected stylistically but purely thematically: texts pertaining to the human or divine realm, whose main topic is emotional connection and sexual desire. Indeed, the corpus of Akk. love-related compositions tends to employ a set of key words and stock phrases (see §§ 5, 6 below), but this is not, in my opinion, sufficient to warrant its being labeled a "genre". Love-related literature, which extends across the Akk. literary system, cannot be reduced to one specific genre.[18]

## 2.3 Akkadian Love Literature – between Official Cult and Private Context

Klein and Sefati's conclusion of their important article *'Secular' Love Songs in Mesopotamian Literature* (2008, 624) is worth citing *in extenso*:

> From the above survey of Mesopotamian love songs, it follows that both in the Sumerian period and later, the scribes did not deem it worthy or important to copy and transmit to future generations popular and "secular" love songs, which were no doubt circulating orally and were commonly sung at weddings and banquets. Thus, all types of love songs known to the present day are connected in one way or another to gods and goddesses, rooted in the cult; or at least they center around the personality of the king and were written down and copied by the scribes for him and his courtly circle.

Although focusing more on Sum. love poetry, the authors also discuss some Akk. love-related compositions (especially the catalogue KAR 158 and the OB dialogue ZA 49, 168–169). Their conclusion, therefore, refers to both Sum. and Akk. literatures, and as such is relevant to this study.

The key terminological distinction employed by Klein and Sefati in their study is between popular or secular (in fact, the authors keep using "secular" with quotation marks) and cultic or cultic-mythological. To my mind, this dichotomy is not applicable to the corpora under discussion. What is the meaning of the adjective secular when referring to

---

17 Klein/Sefati 2008, 614.

18 I am aware that my present position on the matter has changed since my *Style and Form in Old-Babylonian Literary Texts* (Wasserman 2003, 176–179).

ancient Mesopotamian culture? Can one propose a sphere in ancient Mesopotamia which was detached from divine rules, free of religious practice? Can one say with confidence that a love song, sung in the familial setting of a private wedding, is devoid of cultic and even mythological background? The answer to my mind is negative. The difference which is relevant to the material is between texts which were composed for, and performed in, an *official* cult (most likely the royal court), and texts whose inception, impetus, and eventually performance or audience, was *private*.[19] Furthermore, the two types of text are not mutually exclusive. In principle, a text which at first was composed for, and presented at, some official ceremony, could later be used in a private context; inversely, a text whose origin was private could later be re-worked and used in an official setting.

Examining the core group of the corpus of ALL and the catalogues (that is, excluding love incantations which were most probably used in magical circumstances), one can identify a group of texts which belongs to the private sphere: CUSAS 10, 8 (№ 2); CUSAS 10, 9 (№ 3); CUSAS 10, 10 (№ 4); ZA 49, 168–169 (№ 16); and perhaps also A 7478 (№1) and the Moussaieff Love Song (№ 11). On the background of everyday situations, these texts describe different amorous wishes, memories and expectations between ordinary men and women. It is hard to see how these texts could have a function in a public or an official setting. The rest of the core group – CUSAS 10, 13 (№ 5); Fs. Renger 192–193 (№ 6); JAOS 103, 26–27 (№ 7); KAL 3, 75 (№ 8); LKA 15 (№ 9); MIO 12, 52–53 (№ 10); Or. 60, 340 (№ 12); PRAK 1 B 472 (№ 13); the Kiš fragments (№ 14a–f) and YOS 11, 24 (№ 15) – may well have been part of a public cultic event.

As for the catalogues, it stands to reason that the compositions listed in ASJ 10, 18 (№ 17) and KAR 158 (№ 19) were mainly composed for, and perhaps performed in, the cultic or palatial context. The catalogue CUSAS 10, 12 (№ 18), however, contains incipits which do not seem to fit an official cult. This Babylonian catalogue collected compositions whose incipits refer predominantly to the private context.

In summation, the corpus of ALL appears to be less homogenous than Klein and Sefati assumed. Unlike the parallel Sum. corpus, Akk. love-related texts are comprised of compositions whose setting is personal and private, and other which seem to be at home in the public and official context.

## 2.4 Old Babylonian Texts vs. Middle Babylonian/Assyrian Texts

Leaving aside incantations and catalogues pertaining to ALL, OB texts and MB/MA texts can be distinguished by a simple scribal parameter: all four MB/MA texts end with a colophon,[20] while only one OB text ends with a colophon – Fs. Renger 192–193 (№ 6), a text which dates to the time of Ammī-ditāna, i.e. to the late OB period. Based on the corpus

19 Even this terminological distinction is not free of problems, as one could rightly claim that there were no truly private arrangements in ancient Mesopotamian society in matters of love and copulation, since these matters were in fact embedded in familial or communal situations.

20 JAOS 103, 26–27 (№ 7), KAL 3, 75 (№ 8), LKA 15 (№ 9), Or. 60, 340 (№ 12). The case of the Moussaieff Love Song (№ 11) is somewhat different. According to my analysis, it is an MB copy of an OB text. It does not contain a colophon.

at hand it seems safe to conclude that this MB/MA group of texts was copied, or composed, by trained scribes and incorporated into the official scribal tradition. The fact that the MB/MA texts, more than those of OB, refer to the court and to royal settings, reinforces this notion.

The OB group of texts, by contrast, is characterized by inventiveness and creativity. Some of the OB texts appear "half-baked": drafts or exercises at a non-final stage of composition (see YOS 11, 24 = № 15 and perhaps also A 7478 = № 1). Other OB texts, however, are well-structured and carefully written (see MIO 12, 52–53 = № 10), and were no doubt the final products of trained scribes designed to be put down in writing and used on official occasions.

# 3. Characterization of the Corpus

## 3.1 The Style of Akkadian Love Literature

The style of ALL cannot be described in a general manner. Given the absence of a clear set of stylistic or extra-linguistic criteria (see above), the corpus was instead defined according to theme, that of love and sex. Consequently ALL consists of different sorts of text – monologues, dialogues, hymnal compositions, and incantations – in different styles.

Some literary devices, known from other Akk. literary texts, can be elucidated. MIO 12, 52–53: 9–10 (№ 10) shows repetitions and *parallelismus membrorum*, as e.g.: *Muʾati duššupū dādūka | dišpa iš[ebbe kuz]ub râmika*, "Muʾati, so sweet is your passion, the appeal of your love is sated with honey". Chiastic constructions are found in CUSAS 10, 8: 7–9 (№ 2): *kīma dišpim ṭābat | ana appim | kīma karānim eššet*, "She is sweet as honey, she is fresh like wine to the nose". Other cases of chiasm are in PRAK 1 B 472: i 6'–i 7' (№ 13): *dādūka ṭābū | muḫtanbū inbūka*, "How sweet is your lovemaking, your fruits are profuse!" and in MAD 5, 8: 8–9 (№ 22): *kirīšum turdā | turdāma ana kirîm*, "To the garden you came down, indeed came down to the garden!" Alliteration is found, e.g. in the monologue CUSAS 10, 8 (№ 2), where *nāṭil šunātim* (l. 14) and *rigim šinūnūtim* (l. 20) echo each other, and in the love incantation CUSAS 10, 11 (№ 20), where *ḫasāsum*, "to think on, to remember" (l. 8) is echoed by *ḫašāšum*, "to rejoice" (l. 9). More such ornamental literary devices can be found.

But what stylistically singles out a number of texts pertaining to ALL is an unexpected assortment of lyric expressions with vulgarisms. The following example comes not from one composition, but from a sequence of incipits: "Big one(m.), big one, do not arise!",[21] "Let me look at you by the light of the window!",[22] "Let us complete the deed of lovemaking!",[23] and "Let me grow long for the girl!".[24] The first and last incipits in this

21 CUSAS 10, 12: 5 (№ 18): *rabûm rabûm lā tetebbēma.*

22 CUSAS 10, 12: 6 (№ 18): *luppalsakka innūr apātim.*

23 CUSAS 10, 12: 7 (№ 18): *i nuštaqti nēpeštu râmimma.*

24 CUSAS 10, 12: 8 (№ 18): *abbunti luštuḫma.*

sequence refer in a straightforward manner to the erect male member, while the second and the third are sentimental, offering a poetic vision of a romantic meeting.

Another, closely related characteristic of ALL are passages of natural flow of speech. A fine example are the opening lines of the love dialogue ZA 49, 168–169 (№ 16), where the man tells the woman: "Yell! Do not bother to reply! Not so much talking! My decision is made, I will not change for you a word, anything I said".[25] Another example is found in dialogue CUSAS 10, 10 (№ 4), where the man speaks in disdain to the woman who loves him: "To your canal – no one will come near it!"[26] (where "canal" stands for the female sex organ). And he goes on: "Do not place (me?) in the salt, your field is all too well known!"[27] (again, a disparaging allusion to her sex organ). The continuation is difficult due to the informal and highly idiomatic nature of the speech: "The (fact) that you did not bring for me (good) news from your womb, as a baby of men – should I swallow (that) potsherd? I will release the bitch! One who bolts down a stone in order to release you when would he have his word?"[28] It is hard to find such sharp and vivid colloquialisms in other kinds of Akk. text, even epistolary texts. Finally, the corpus of ALL shows a high incidence of hapax legomena[29] and rarely used words.[30]

## 3.2 The Human Realm and the Divine Realm

The actors in ALL may be human or divine. In contrast to Sum. love lyrics,[31] in Akk. the two realms are usually kept apart, and only rarely do humans and deities interact amorously with each other. The clearest case for such interaction is Or. 60, 340 (№ 12), where the young men of the city gather by the city-wall and copulate with the insatiable goddess Ištar.[32] In KBo 36, 27 (№ 21), an MB love incantation from Hattuša, the male speaker declares that he wants to make love to the goddesses Nanāya and Kilili. In another text, a man is deemed so beautiful that he is *compared* to a god by his admiring female lover: "I

---

25 ZA 49, 168–169 i 1–4 (№ 16): *ṣurpī tūrki ezbī lā magal dabābum qabê qabûmma ul enniakkim.*

26 CUSAS 10, 10: 36 (№ 4): *ana pattiki mamman ul iṭeḫḫēši.*

27 CUSAS 10, 10: 38–39 (№ 4): *ina ṭābtim lā tašakkani<ni?> eqelki ḫukkum.*

28 CUSAS 10, 10: 40–45 (№ 4): *ša lā tublīm ina sassūriki kīma šīr nišī ṭēmam anāku išḫilṣam alât kalbatam uššar lāʾim abnim ana wašāriki mati qabāšu liškun.*

29 Newly attested words (not including verb stems attested for the first time): *baZkum*, "quacking (of ducks)", Moussaieff Love Song rev. 5 (№ 11); *duššuptum*, "sweetness", CUSAS 10, 9: 8 (№ 3); *emṣūtum*, "hunger", ZA 75, 198–204a: 9 (№ 27); *garāḫum*, "to copulate", KBo. 36, 27: 15f. (№ 21); *ḫubūšum*, "bulge", ZA 75, 198–204a: 36 (№ 27); *ḫuttutum*, "to infest", CUSAS 10, 8: 4–6 (№ 2); *inṣabum*, "earring", PRAK 1 B 472 i 9 (№ 13); *mukazzibtum*, "one who fawns", CUSAS 10, 10: 2 (№ 4); *muppirum*, "provider", YOS 11, 87: 9 (№ 26); *nawārtum*, "brightness", Moussaieff Love Song: 1 (№ 11); *nikurrûm*, "what is denied", Moussaieff Love Song rev. 11 (№ 11); *piṭirtum*, "loosening", ZA 75, 198–204d: 61 (№ 30); *šupuktum*, "heap (of grain)", A 7478 i 15 (№ 1); *taw/mṣītum*, "opening(?)", Moussaieff Love Song obv. 3 (№ 11). (MPS).

30 Words hitherto only attested lexically: *indūrum*, "waterskin", KAR 158 ii 53 (№ 19); *mašûm*, "to spend the night", JAOS 103, 26–27: 1f. (№ 7); *munûm*, "(a type of bed)", PRAK 1 B 472 i 8 (№ 13).

31 See Klein/Sefati 2008, 615–617 discussion of the love dialogues mentioning Šu-Sîn.

32 Ištar is the goddess who is most open, even eager, to engage in sexual rapports with (special) men, as seen in the opening of SB Gilg. VI.

saw your face: you are a god! I implore you…".[33] But these are exceptions. As a rule, humans fall in love and crave other humans, and gods seek and yearn for gods. Ištar and Dumuzi are the amatory divine couple *par excellence* (JAOS 103, 26–27 = № 7; LKA 15 = № 9), but another couple, Nanāya and Muʾati (MIO 12, 52–53 = № 10), is also attested in the corpus. As stated above, the separation of the human and the divine is a fundamental difference between Sum. love songs and ALL.

## 3.3 Personal Names

An interesting aspect of the corpus are the personal names attested in it. The fact is that ALL contains more personal and royal names than any other genre in the Akk. literary corpus.[34] If we disregard the names of scribes found in colophons, the *only* two (possibly three) personal, non-royal, names in the entire Akk. literary corpus (not including historiographical texts and literary letters) come from texts which concern love: the Isin tablet of love incantations where a woman addresses two gentlemen, a certain Erra-bāni and a certain Iddin-Damu,[35] and a fragment from Kiš where a woman called Šâti-Enlil is probably found.[36] This tendency towards personalization is complemented by the semantic emphasis on body parts of love-related texts (see below). In fact, this Iddin-Damu is described, perhaps even ridiculed, by his physiognomy: "Big-mouth, curled-ears, Iddin-Damu!...".[37] Love, and especially sexual desire in Akk. literature, is therefore not abstract, but concrete and personalized.

## 3.4 The Royal Presence

No less significant is the royal presence in the corpus. The king holds a special place in ALL: *šarrum* is mentioned explicitly 14 times,[38] and is probably referred to indirectly elsewhere.[39] More importantly, six different kings are mentioned by name in ALL: Rīm-Sîn, Hammurāpi(2x), Abī-ešuḫ, Ammī-ditāna, Ammī-ṣaduqa, and Shalmaneser.

Recently, an intriguing new name was added to this list of monarchs. While working on the literary material from Kiš, copied by de Genouillac a century ago, I identified a

33 CUSAS 10, 9: 17–18 (№ 3): *[p]ānīka āmur ilāt(a) usellēka* (see also l. 12), and cf. SB Gilg I 207, when Šamḫat says to Enkidu: *damqāta Enkidu kī ili tabašši* "You are handsome, Enkidu, you are just like a god!" (Trans. George).

34 As expected, in literary-historiographical compositions, royal names can also be found: Sargon (in OA Sargon Legend), Narām-Sîn (in Erra and Narām-Sîn), Gungunum (in the Gungunum hymn), and Yahdun-līm and Zimrī-līm (in the Zimrī-līm epic). Only two kings are mentioned in non-historiographical compositions that do not belong to love lyrics: Hammurāpi (in the hymn of Agušaya) and Samsu-iluna (in the Nanāya hymn VS 10, 215).

35 ZA 75, 198–204a 30 (№ 27), ZA 75, 198–204h 100 (№ 33), ZA 75, 198–204i 117 (№ 34).

36 PRAK 2 C 3: 3 (№ 14a).

37 ZA 75, 198–204h 100 (№ 33): *rapšam pîm lāwiam uznīn Iddin-Damu*.

38 CUSAS 10, 12: 33 (№ 18), JAOS 103, 26–27: 19 (№ 7), KAL 3, 75 iii 8' (№ 8), KAR 158 i 32', ii 24', ii 43', iii 5', iii 40', iii 42' (№ 19), MIO 12, 52–53: 14, 5', 6' (№ 10), ZA 49, 168–169 iv 6 (№ 16).

39 Note the summary line in KAR 158 viii 24' (№ 19): "12 hymns (for?/of?) the king, Akk.".

small group of broken fragments as belonging to ALL. Surprisingly, the protagonist in three of these fragments is none other than Šu-Sîn, who can only be the King of Ur. The texts are not in Sum. but in Akk., and the king's name is spelled in a unique way, using the sign "30" for the syllabic value sin, unlike virtually all other spellings of this monarch's name which regularly use EN.ZU for Sîn.[40]

One of the fragments from Kiš states: "…Šu-Sîn my beloved";[41] another reads: "Šu-Sîn! *Pla[y with* … As the sun let him *shine* ...";[42] and a third fragment, which also mentions Šu-Sîn, begins: "The[y? ...], To[uch my(?) …], In (my) la[p(?) …]".[43] Another fragment from this group, in which the name of Šu-Sîn does not appear, reads: [...... y]our light(?) … My lord… … *they went far away*… Just like dawn let (*the sun?/light?*) *sh*[*ine on me*(?)]… My lord (*at*) dawn play [with my(?)…], May the boy…, may he […], Let me […] (in my?) *lap* […]"[44] (see the full edition of this group of fragments below).

The appearance of Šu-Sîn in a group of Akk. love-related texts is surprising. OB Akk. literary texts do not usually refer to Ur III kings. The only other similar case I know of is the bilingual text PBS 1/1, 11 where Šulgi is mentioned.[45] But is it in fact so surprising to find Šu-Sîn in an Akk. love-related text? One has to keep in mind that Šu-Sîn has left us three Sum. love compositions in which he in person, and not the divine Dumuzi, is the lover of the goddess Inanna.[46]

Both grammar and orthography of the Kiš fragments are archaic, as can be seen in the syllabic values šà and àm. Epigraphically as well, the fragments show an undisputed archaic hand. I suggest that these fragments come from the earliest layer of OB, or perhaps even earlier, namely that these fragmentary texts are rare remnants of Ur III Akk. literature. The resurfacing of the Akk. tradition of love literature from the Ur III period (be it original, or an OB copy thereof) answers a question which was not adequately addressed: given the rich Sum. love lyric tradition on the one hand and the corpus of Akk. love literature on the other – why do we not have bilingual love-related texts? Or, in other words, was there a textual bridge between the Sum. and Akk. lore of love literature? A partial answer seems possible now: such a bridge did exist, but not – as far as our present data reveals – in the form of bilingual texts, or translation of Sum. texts to Akk., but as parallel traditions: one in Sum. and one in Akk., and that, I venture, already in the Ur III period.

Finally, a word about the place of discovery of these fragments is in order. I do not think that it is mere chance that the Akk. love-related fragments mentioning Šu-Sîn were unearthed in northern Babylonia, in Kiš. It is important to remember that two key pieces of Akk. love lyric also come from Kiš: the OAkk love incantation MAD 5, 8 (№ 22), and the early OB text PRAK 1 B 472 (№ 13).[47] Turning our attention to the later OB period,

---

40 More on this spelling, see below in the commentary to the Kiš fragments.

41 PRAK 2 C 134 i 6' (№ 14e): Šu-Sîn(30) *na-ra?-mi*.

42 PRAK 2 C 3 obv. 8'–9' (№ 14a): Šu-Sîn(30) *mé-le-e*[*l*? …] / *ki Šamši*([d]UTU-*ši*) *li*-[*ip*?]-[*pu*?]-[*uḫ*?].

43 PRAK 2 C 30: 1'–3' (№14b): *šu-n*[*u*?...] / *lu-pi*-[*it-ma*…] / *i-na su*?-[*ni*?..].

44 PRAK 2 C 125: 1–7 (№ 14d): [… …] x *nu?-úr?-k*[*a* …] / [*be*]-[*li*?] x x *šu*? *hu*? *ir-ti-qù-ma* x …] / *ak-ki-ma še-ri-ma li-p*[*u*?-*ḫa*?-*am*?...] / *be-li*! *še-ri me-le-e*[*l* … / *li*-[x] x (x) *m*]*a*?-*ru-um li*?-[…] / *lu-ul*-[x x x x] x *su*?-*ni* […] / […] x x […].

45 Goodnick Westenholz 2005 (ref. Uri Gabbay).

46 Šu-Sîn A, B, and C (cf. Sefati 1998, 344–352, 353–359, 360–364, respectively).

47 Goodnick Westenholz (1987, 416 n.6) suggested that this fragment could be connected to some of the

Groneberg (1999, 172) has suggested – based on contextual arguments and orthography – that Fs. Renger 192–193 (№ 6), a fragment of a tablet comprising different *irtum* love-related compositions mentioning Ammī-ditāna, was also originally written in Kiš.[48]

Kiš was the center *par excellence* of Akk. culture in the earlier periods of Mesopotamia and the available material reflects this cultural prominence. As such, Kiš seems to have played a crucial role in the development of the Akk. love literature in pre-OB times, deriving directly from its central political position as the birthplace of royal ideology of northern, i.e. "non-Sumerian" kingship.[49]

## 3.5 Gender Relations

Aware of the risk of "forc[ing] ancient literary characters into anachronistic sexual and social identities by classifying them with modern labels such as homosexual, heterosexual, gay, or bisexual" (Walls 2001, 14), I will use the neutral terms same-sex relations vs. opposite-sex relations.[50] Nonetheless, it is hard to avoid the impression that the gender-power paradigm of the texts in the ALL corpus is not that different from the main gender-power paradigm in modern times.[51] In other words, as far as the testimony of ALL goes, the sexual norm (and here I do not mean "norm" in the ethical or moral sense, but in the distributional-statistical meaning of the term) in ancient Mesopotamian society is clearly that of opposite-sex relations. In fact, in sharp contrast to love lyrics in other pre-modern literatures, notably in Archaic Greek poetry and to some extent also in early Arabic love poetry, one finds in the corpus of ALL *only* opposite-sex – he/she or she/he – relations.[52] Reference to homosexual relations in the erotic or amatory context (i.e. not in the legal context, as will be briefly discussed below) are extraordinarily rare in Mesopotamian literature and appear only in the latest phase of this civilization – in texts from the Seleucid

other Kiš fragments treated here.

48 This assumption is accepted by Klein/Sefati 2008, 622.

49 On the central role of Kiš in pre-Sargonic times see recently Steinkeller 2013, 145–151. It appears that its northern location in the Mesopotamian plain spared Kiš from the dramatic political events which took place in the south in the post-Hammurāpi period, and literary texts are written there until the end of the first Babylonian dynasty, when other major cites, such as Nippur, Isin and Larsa, go silent (Groneberg 1999, 172).

50 See also Ormand 2009, 14–20 with more literature on the methodological issues regarding sexuality in the ancient world. In the vast body of literature on sexuality in the ancient world I found Halperin 1998 revealing.

51 A similar opinion regarding ancient Greek myths can be found (Gilhuly apud Holmberg 2009, 316): "There is an implicit assumption that Greek heterosexuality, and the power dynamics that characterized it, were less radically different from our own, less determined by historical factors than homosexuality was".

52 For the relations between Gilgameš and Enkidu, see below.

and Persian periods.[53] These late texts, it is argued persuasively, are infused with Greek and Hellenistic influences, to which homosexual love should be attributed.[54]

Of course, sexual relations between two men are attested in Mesopotamian texts, but not literary ones (with the possible exception of the story of Gilgameš and Enkidu, discussed below).[55] One needs only look at Middle Assyrian Laws §§ 19–20 and the section dealing with sex omens in the series Šumma ālu (Guinan 1997). And still, seen from the perspective of ALL, opposite-sex relations are presented as the only social norm, and same-sex relations are not hinted at in the corpus, not referred to as religiously or socially prohibited, and not even ridiculed. Only once in our corpus does a representative of the "third gender" appear: in one incipit in the catalogue CUSAS 10, 12 (№ 18) we read: "For eternity of years, an eternity, (for) four eons (of years), indeed five (eons of years), I will come out to you(m.), the *kalû*".[56]

Does this allow us to say that since opposite-sex relations were considered the social norm in ancient Mesopotamia, same-sex relations – notably between two men – were seen as *deviating* from the norm? Or put more sharply – following Foucault's influential insights regarding sexuality in the ancient world[57] – was there a sexual *norm* in ancient Mesopotamia at all? Did different sexual practices and preferences *define* a person socially, ethically and morally?

This important and interesting question will have to remain open in this study which is philological by nature. Two remarks, however, will not be out of place. First, one must remember that much of the written evidence in our hands presents the hegemonic view of society, as constructed by scribes who were integrated into the dominant religious and political institutions of ancient Mesopotamia. It is possible that these hegemonic groups purposefully or unintentionally ignored other, non-standard forms of sexuality and silenced them. However, since we are confined by our data, we must accept that very little can be said about the non-hegemonic forms of sexuality. The second remark concerns the way some forms of sexuality were presented by the central cultural mechanisms of ancient Mesopotamia. From the point of view of Mesopotamian hegemony, the otherness of same-sex relations, even their anomaly, as it is perceived through texts, is underscored by the fact that practitioners of same-sex relations are etiologized and mythologized, and are allocated a special role in Mesopotamian hegemonic religion (as the *kalû*,[58] *pilpilû*,[59] *assinnu* and *kurgarrû*[60]). Only after being processed by religious and mythological categorization, and becoming constructs of hegemonic ideology, can such sexual practices and practitioners be

53 KI.ÁG NÍTA *ana* NÍTA "love of a man for a man" in the late magico-astral texts (BRM 4, 20: 6 // STT 300, 9) which are listing the appropriate time for the preformance of different rituals and spells according to day and month, see Scurlock 2005–2006, 131, Geller 2010, 27, 45, and now Geller 2014, 28 and 33 (refs. Avigail Wagschal).

54 See Scurlock 2005–2006, 125, 131 and passim, Geller 2010, 27, 49 and Geller 2014 passim.

55 On homosexuality in ancient Mesopotamia, see briefly Cooper 2006–2008, 20 (with previous bibliography).

56 CUSAS 10, 12: 29–30 (№ 18): *ana dār šanātim dār erbēt šār u ḫamšet lūṣīkum kalû.*

57 On the crucial impact of Foucault's writings on Classical studies, see recently Ormand 2014.

58 See Gabbay 2008.

59 See Peled 2013.

60 See Peled 2014. On the different classes of effeminate males, see Cooper 2006–2008, 20 (with previous bibliography).

part of the official cultural matrix of ancient Mesopotamia. One should be cautious, therefore, and remember that it is possible that the variance of sexual practices in ancient Mesopotamia was actually much wider than presented in our texts.[61]

And still, not only does ALL know virtually only opposite-sex relations, but – as will be discussed – a number of texts in the corpus cannot be understood unless one realizes that their background is formal, legally binding marriage.

The only clear exception to the above are the relations between Gilgameš and Enkidu which come to an emotional climax in Gilgameš's lament over his dead friend. There is no doubt in my mind that the epic depicts the relationship between the two comrades as all-embracing: from suspicious rivalry to official brotherhood (sealed by the adoption of Enkidu by Ninsun), from warrior-like friendship to the intimacy of sharing vulnerabilities, emotions and even corporal love.[62] In Gilgameš's lament the epic beautifully fuses heroic and erotic imagery: "The axe at my side, in which my arm trusted, the sword of my belt, the shield in front of me, my festive garment, the girdle of my delight (*lalû*!)".[63] But note that here too – as in some texts in ALL – the conceptual frame of the powerful relationship between the friends is revealed as legal marriage, for in the first series of dreams Gilgameš sees an axe – Enkidu, of course – to whom he makes love "as to a wife",[64] and when lamenting his dead friend, Gilgameš is described covering the face of his dead body "as a bride".[65]

What becomes evident, when returning to the texts in our corpus, is that interestingly the dynamic between the sexes in ALL does not focus entirely, nor even primarily, on masculine desire. No less than male, female sexuality and emotional needs find their place in ALL. Another point worth making is the absence of masculine sexual violence, or even threat, as means to attain sexual gratification.[66] Remarkably, the only direct references to physical violence in the corpus are that of women towards men. In one love incantation the woman addresses a resisting male lover: "I have hit (*maḫāṣum*) your head; you keep crawling on the ground like ....",[67] and similarly "I have hit your head, I have changed your mood".[68] A mythical precursor to these aggressive statements can be found. Ištar, the archetypal female figure in Mesopotamian culture is said to have hit (again, *maḫāṣum*) her resisting lovers (SB Gilg. VI 76). Clearly, the woman's threat in the love incantations to hit the man, thus overcoming his resistance, mirrors Ištar's mythological aggression.

---

61 On these questions, from the angle of Hittite texts, see Peled 2010a and 2010b (where further bibliography is found).

62 The literature on this subject is extensive. I will mention only a few discussions which I found interesting and revealing: George 2003, 903, Walls 2001, 17–33, Cooper 2002, and recently also Gadotti 2014, 287.

63 SB Gilg. VIII 46–48 (= George 2003, 655).

64 OB Gilg. II ii 31–33 (= George 2003, 174): *ḫaṣṣinu šani būnūšu āmuršuma aḫtadu anāku arāmšuma kīma aššatim aḫabbub elšu*, "An axe, strange was his appearance; I saw it and was glad (seeing that) I was making love to it as a wife, cuddling it." See also Atraḫasis I 300 (Lambert/Millard 1969: 64–65).

65 SB Gilg. VIII 59: *iktum ibri kīma kallati* [*pānīšu*] (George 2003, 654). (And note also VIII 35–36, regrettably very broken lines).

66 Walls (2001, 25) stresses the "undertones of potential (male) violence".

67 ZA 75, 198–204i 109 (№ 34): *amtaḫaṣ muḫḫaka kīma… taptanaššilam qaqqaram.*

68 ZA 75, 198–204a 11 (№ 27): *amtaḫaṣ muḫḫaka uštanni ṭēmka.*

But these references to female violence must be taken as an upside-down view of Mesopotamian reality, where men dominated women legally and physically. Table XII of Gilgameš offers a good example of the actual power-paradigm in Mesopotamian patriarchal society. One of the regulations in the Netherworld is said to be: "You must not kiss the wife you love, you must not strike the wife you hate".[69] The emotional dependency of the female lover on her man is made plain throughout the dialogue CUSAS 10, 9 (№ 3), and, inversely, in two incipits from the catalogue CUSAS 10, 12 (№ 18): "To slavery I shall not degrade myself before you(m.)",[70] and "I shell not serve before my friend".[71]

## 3.6 Social and Familial Setting

The social background of ALL is not easily defined, as it varies from text to text. One cannot speak of one social setting in this group of texts, each of which has its own *Sitz im Leben.*

In some texts a man is trying to attract an unmarried young woman (YOS 11, 87 = № 26 and perhaps also CUSAS 10, 11 = № 20), perhaps courting a girl in a neighboring area. The backgrounds of other texts, by contrast, seem to be the legally bound conjugal relationship, i.e. the married couple. So, e.g., a man insults his previous lover, saying: "You were born the daughter of a substitute, with no dowry!",[72] proving that the woman's unworthy descent, which prevents her from wedding, is a tenable argument for abandoning her for another woman. In like manner, some texts hint at indirect competition between a female lover and the lawful wife, the *aššatum*. CUSAS 10, 9: 13 (№ 3) reads: "I encircle (you) like a wife, so that (you?) will *not become "stiff"*.[73] As I understand this line, the female lover tries to prevent the wife from gaining access to regular sexual relations with the husband – the lover of the female speaker. A man referring in a pejorative way to his wife, while praising the sexual powers of his female lover, may perhaps be found in the love incantation from Hattuša: "Instead of my 'wailing woman' – your two openings! Instead of my 'wailing woman' – your bed! I will be making love (to you)! oh Kilili! I will have intercourse (with you)! – oh Kilili!".[74]

A passage from a first mill. love ritual brings a rare echo of the growing erotic fatigue in married couples, which had much to do, I presume, with the rivalry between wives and female lovers: "At night there is no housewife, at night there is no housewife, at night the man's wife poses no objection".[75] If correctly understood, these lines express the man's frustration at being repeatedly sexually rejected. According to the ritual, apparently, the wife poses no obstacles to sex with the man. Another text which attests to intra-familial sexual and emotional problems is an OB ritual destined to remedy relations between a man and his wife (*aššatum*, again): "Its ritual: you take clay of a licorice's root, in sun-rise

---

69 SB Gilg. XII 23–24: *aššatka ša tarammu lā tanaššiq aššatka ša tazerru lā tamaḫḫaṣ.*
70 CUSAS 10, 12: 24 (№ 18): *an[a wa]rdūtim ul abâ[š]ka.*
71 CUSAS 10, 12: 25 (№ 18): *ul azzaz maḫar ibriya.*
72 CUSAS 10, 10: 17–18 (№ 4): *mārat pūḫi wa[ldāti] ina [lā] širi[ktim].*
73 CUSAS 10, 9: 13 (№ 3): *asaḫḫur kīma aštim ana [lā] makāki.*
74 KBo 36, 27: 18'–20' (№ 21): *akkū bakkītiya pittāki akkū bakkītiya mayyālki arâm Kilili anâk Kilili.*
75 Lambert 1975, 108: 6–8: *mūšu emūqti lā ibašši mūšu emūqti lā ibašši mūšu alti amēli lā iparrik.*

(or/and) sun-set, you roll pellets (from the clay), seven and seven, you recite the incantation over the seven and seven (pellets). After you have recited the incantation, you will drench them twice (and) you will recite (again) the incantation. You put (the pellets?) in between her breasts and (your) wife will come to you".[76]

On the other side of the gender scale, there might be a rare mention of men rivaling the husband. An incipit from a catalogue reads: "The wild bull is not standing – let the red gazelles come out!".[77] I suggest interpreting this line allegorically: the wild bull represents the husband and the red (male)-gazelles represent the suitors who show up when the husband is not "standing".[78]

What about prostitutes? When comparing our corpus to one of the famous love scenes of Akk. literature, viz. the seduction of Enkidu by Šamḫat in OB Gilg. II, one realizes that there is no direct reference to prostitutes in the corpus.[79] Only one incipit mentions a woman of the social category *laḫannatu*, which may very well be that of a high-ranking courtesan: "My Nippur-girl, a sweet courtesan".[80] Slaves and slave-girls are also not attested (although there are metaphoric descriptions which hint at submissive relationships between a man and a woman).[81] This finding, though negative by nature, bolsters the idea that the social setting of ALL in the wider sense is that of free men and women. I prefer not

76 Wasserman 2010, 332–333: 7–18. It should be pointed out that wisdom texts contain sharp criticism of men betraying their wives, as in the bilingual proverb [l]ú-lal-la [gal$_4$]-la ba-ab-ús [l]ú nu-gi-nagiš šu-kin-bi min-àm // *sarru murteddû ūrī lā kīna šittā niggalāšu*, "A liar, chaser of (woman's) pudenda, is not trustworthy: two are his 'sickles'" (Lambert 1960, 255: 7–10, cf. SP 23.7 [= Alster 1997, 271: 9–10] and SP 1.158 [= Alster 1997, 32] and Wasserman 2008, 76). Westbrook 1984 showed that legal texts too were conscious of the threat which extra-marital affairs posed on the cohesion of married couples (see also Cooper 2006–2008, 17). A first mill. omen furnishes a rare glimpse into the possible dramatic developments which could take place in a triangle of love: Boissier DA 220: 12 (cf. CAD M/2, 287b with vars.): *aššat amēli ana muštarriqiša* (var. *muštarqiša*) *ištanappar mutam dūkma yâši aḫzanni*, "(If…) a man's wife will keep writing to her secret lover: 'kill (my) husband and marry me!". (Ref. Yoram Cohen).

77 CUSAS 10, 12: 12–13 (№ 18): *rīmum ul izzazma armū sāmūtu līṣûnim*.

78 Here as well, wisdom literature is careful to warn men against such behavior: Šimâ milka (= Y. Cohen 2013, 86) 27: *ē tešši īnīka ana aššat amēli*, "Do not covet (another) man's wife!". So also The Instructions of Šurrupag (= ETCSL 5.6.1) 33–34.

79 This surely was not an unimaginable event, as demonstrated by the omen from Šumma ālu: "If someone marries a prostitute (MUNUS.KAR.KID = *ḫarimtum*) – that house will not pros[per]" (Moren 1977, 67: 4 and note to this line on pp. 68–69). Warnings against relationships with prostitutes are found in different wisdom texts. See, again, Šimâ milka (= Y. Cohen 2013, 86) 37: *iḫḫaz* (*ḫarimta*) *ul ibâr* (*āḫissa*) (*ana bīt irrubu*) *iša[ppuḫ]*…, "If he takes (a prostitute) as his wife, he will not live long, being her groom; she will squan[der] (whatever there is in the house she enters)". (As shown by Cohen in his commentary (2013, 106), this wisdom saying can be fully understood only by taking into account its fuller version, found in BWL 102: 72–80. The additions from The Counsels of Wisdom are in brackets). Sum. wisdom literature also expresses similar views, as, e.g., The Instructions of Šuruppag (= ETCSL 5.6.1) 154. An important group of attestations to prostitutes in society and ritual is found in the Sum. (and bilingual) diatribes and dialogues and in texts focusing on the é-éš-dam institution. This body of texts, treated by Matuszak (forthcoming), goes beyond the boundaries of the present study and cannot be dealt with here. On prostitutes in general, see Cooper's (2006–2008) exhaustive summary article.

80 KAR 158 vii 18' (№ 19): $^{uru}$*Nippurītī laḫannatu dašuptu*, and see commentary to this line.

81 CUSAS 10, 12: 24 (№ 18): *an[a wa]rdūtim ul abâ[š]ka*, "To slavery I shall not degrade myself before you(m.)" and also l. 25 in the same catalogue: *ul azzaz maḫar ibriya*, "I shell not serve before my friend".

to stress this point further and suggest that the social milieu of Akk. love-related compositions is necessarily that of the "... highly educated and witty, belonging to the elite of society",[82] or of the wealthy and respected families,[83] but I do subscribe to the idea that the protagonists found in the corpus of ALL are characterized as belonging to the same, homogenous, social stratum of free citizens.

## 3.7 Free Love?

In a number of articles in the 1970s and 1980s, Jean Bottéro developed the idea that ancient Mesopotamians exercised their sexuality in a wide range of ways, with people of different gender and social background, without inhibition, moral constraint or emotional guilt. The only restriction, so Bottéro, was that these diverse sexual activities be consensual and not infringe on the legal rights of fellow citizens.[84] Bottéro called this *L'amour libre*, or "free love" (see Bottéro 1987). In a short but pertinent critique of this thesis, Cooper (2009) has shown that Bottéro's concept of free love cannot be upheld. I will not repeat Cooper's arguments, and restrict myself to the corpus of ALL.

It is clear from the corpus that Mesopotamian culture was neither non-judgmental regarding sexual behaviors nor indifferent to gender or social background. In addition to the fact that the matrimonial relationship forms the backdrop to a number of texts in the corpus (see § 3.6 above), the issue of social boundaries and the morality of specific relationships is frequently voiced in the texts.[85] Are the young men in YOS 11, 87 (№ 26) and in CUSAS 10, 8 (№ 2), desperately looking at the object of their desire, the daughter of a gentleman, not hampered by social restrictions? And isn't the woman in CUSAS 10, 10 (№ 4) rejected by her lover because of her lowly social status? In many cases it is precisely these social obstacles that propel the emotions that the compositions in our corpus describe.

82 Klein/Sefati 2008, 623.
83 Cf. Alster 1993, 16–17 and Klein/Sefati 2008, 617 (stating this regarding Sumerian love lyrics).
84 In his discussion of different attitudes to prostitution, Cooper (2006–2008, 14) remarks: "Sex in itself was not sinful in ancient Mesopotamia (as dishonesty or impiety were), even if it might cause temporary impurity...".
85 See in particular Westbrook 1984.

# 4. Love and Attraction in the Corpus

## 4.1 Love in Akkadian Love Literature

Unsurprisingly, ALL is characterized by the appearance of the semantic field Love (see Appendix 1).[86] First and foremost the verb *râmum* and its derivations – a verb which, as Walls (2001, 31) points out, is semantically indifferent to gender and is not restricted to masculine sexuality (unlike other verbs denoting copulation, as *niākum* and *reḫûm*). Another verb which is common in ALL to describe amorous activity is *ṣiāḫum*, "to laugh, to make merry, to make love" and its derivations.[87] Less common verbs such as *menûm*,[88] and *ḫabābum*,[89] "to be amicable", also appear. The expression *ištāl lamāda*, "he asked to know",[90] probably carries a sexual meaning as well. As to the object of desire, one finds a wide array of terms designating the "beloved": *bēlum, dādum, ḫāwirum, ḫībum, ḫarmum, mārum, naḫšum, narāmum* and *šudād/tum*.[91] Metaphorical appellations are also found, as e.g. *illūrum nasqum*, "a chosen flower".[92] Words designating "love, sexual appeal, or sexual charms" are also typical to the corpus: *lalûm, inbum, dādū, kuzbum*[93] and the still-mysterious *irʾemum/irimmum*.[94] Being attracted can be expressed idiomatically with non-specific verbs. One such case entails the verb *leqûm*, "to take". In a dialogue the woman says to the male lover who ignores her: "The boy is not aware of the (girl) watching him. To you I am very much attracted (lit. "taken").[95]

---

86 This observation is not as trivial as it may at first seem. A comparison with the Hebrew Bible proves that the number of attestations of "love" alone is not what determines whether a text belongs to love literature: in the book of Songs the verb "to love" is attested 17 times. However, it is attested 20 times in Genesis and 50 times in Psalms.

87 See, Groneberg 1999, 185–187. On the amorous and sexual insinuations of the semantically parallel verb √ṣḥq in Heb. cf. Paul 2002, 498.

88 KAR 158 i 37' (№ 19).

89 CUSAS 10, 9: 32 (№ 3). For this verb see Groneberg 1986 and Walls 2001, 24 with n. on 83f. (in the epic of Gilgameš), and commentary to CUSAS 10, 9: 29 and 32 (№ 3) below.

90 CUSAS 10, 12: 36–37 (№ 18).

91 First mill. omen texts supply us with the term for a secret lover of a married woman: *muštarriqu* (CAD M/2, 287b) .

92 Moussaieff Love Song obv. 13 (№ 11).

93 *kuzbum*, "attractiveness, sexual appeal", though found in the corpus (cf. Moussaieff Love Song rev. 7 = № 11), is less typical of ALL. In royal hymns and especially in the epic of Gilgameš this word carries special importance (see Walls 2001, 22–24).

94 A similar list of terms referring to sex and love is found in the first mill. incantations of the type Egalkurra, which aim to help address high authority persons by making these people "love" the one who approaches them (Stadhouders 2013, 311).

95 CUSAS 10, 9: 4–5 (№ 3): *ul īde mārum nāṭilassu akkâšim mādiš* [*le*?]-*qá*-[*ku*!]. The verb *leqûm* is a key-verb in the famous seduction scene of Šamḫat, as shows SB Gilg. I 181–182, 190 (= George 2003, 548): *kuzubki lilqe... liqî napīssu... ilteqe napīssu.*

## 4.2 Physiognomic Signs of Being in Love

In a small number of cases it is possible to find physiognomic signs of falling or being in love. The clearest case is that of the woman in the love dialogue who describes herself as following: "My (ominous) signs trouble me: My upper lip becomes moist, while my lower lip trembles! I shall embrace him, I shall kiss him…".[96] Another such case might be the incipit from the Babylonian catalogue: "My little finger is [bent?] down",[97] and the description of the woman in a difficult line from the text honoring Rīm-Sîn of Larsa: "Indeed, her lips are relaxed; she carries (good) news. She is perfect in her competence!".[98] Interpretation of somatic traits as these are abundant in physiognomic omens, collected and studied by Böck (2000).

Widening our vista to encompass Greek erotic literature, one finds that these physiognomic signs fit well into a genre of technical texts from the Hellenistic period known as "Body Divination". Chandezon et al. (2014, 306–307) is worth citing fully:

> … [These] sources [relate] to the reading of body parts. [They offered] reflections on gender and sexual relations. Two little known treatises on body divination circulated under the name of Melampous, *hierogrammatos*; they offer[ed] individual predictions and moral interpretations based on the detailed observation of body parts, especially the head… These treatises… are each devoted to the reading of specific signs providing omens. The first one, *Peri palmōn mantikē*, deals with predictions that are based on the observation of spontaneous pulsations, tremblings, or convulsions, *palmoi*, which occur in all parts of the body… The second treatise, *Peri elaiōn tou sōmatos*… deals with the interpretation of skin irregularities designated by the generic term *elaia*, describing olive-shaped anomalies, moles, warts, or birthmarks… The interpretation follows the principle that any loss of control of the body is due to divine intervention… The sexual and the social identity of the addressee are detailed. The divinatory value of the tremor varies according to sex, social status, activity, and physical condition.

As Chandezon et al. (2014, 307) note, "the discipline is ancient. In Mesopotamia, manuals dating to the second mill. BCE provide individual prophetic interpretations based on similar body signs, from top to toes…". The rare references in the corpus to physiognomic signs of falling or being in love should therefore be understood not merely as a literary ornament, but as hints of body divination, technical descriptions of somatic signs which foretell the future of the lover and his or her beloved, and of their relationship.

And finally, a more dramatic expression of the love's destabilizing and deleterious potential on the body is attested in the corpus of ALL (see below § 4.3).

96 ZA 49 168–169 ii 20–23 (№ 16): *ittātūya ulap<pa>tāni*[*nni*] *šaptī elītum ila*[*bbik*] *lū šaplītumma irub*[*bam*] *eddiršu anaššiq*[*šu*].

97 CUSAS 10, 12: 27 (№ 18): [*na*]*diat ubānī ṣeḫertum*.

98 YOS 11, 24 ii 7 (№ 15): *mā wašrā šaptāša ublam ṭēma u lē᾿ûtam šuklulat*.

## 4.3 Lovesickness

Lovesickness – a conglomerate of physiognomic and mental symptoms connected to falling or being in love – is a known phenomenon in literary sources and medical compendia.[99] In the medical compendium *šumma ūm ištēn mariṣma* we read: "If (a man) is constantly afflicted with depression, keeps catching his breath (lit. turning to his throat), he is eating bread and drinking beer but not gaining (weight), he says 'woe, my heart!' and wearies himself – this man is sick with lovesickness (*muruṣ râmi*). It is the same for male and female".[100] To this detailed medical description (unique, to the best of my knowledge, in the Mesopotamian medical corpus),[101] we can now add a text from love literature. The beginning of A 7478 (№ 1) presents a woman who is unable to take food, or voluntarily rejects it, because she is in love. Although she has food, she is unable to eat anything despite passing through the pantry. I do not know of any other text in Mesopotamian love literature, indeed in any other literary text in Akk. or Sum., where a person deliberately eshews food because they are in love.

But the deliberate avoidance of food, or the inability to eat, as a sign of falling in love is not just another physical symptom. This description marks a drastic change from the way requited love is normally conceptualized in Akk. love literature, as a joyful state of being. The Dialogue of Pessimism describes this viewpoint: "a man who loves a woman disregards sorrow and gloominess".[102] More importantly, Akk. erotic vocabulary favors sweet substances as *the* way to express passion and desire: honey, ghee, oil, dates, apples, beer and wine – are all typically used in love-related texts. The Chicago text itself starts in this way: "May he give me … and ghee, your passion!".[103] Against this background, the behavior of the woman in A 7478 appears anomalous. How can a woman hungry for love refuse food, which is metaphorically equated with lovemaking? I suggest that the woman is described as being ill, and that love in this text is infused with medical terminology. Simply put, this is an accurate description of lovesickness.

Loss of appetite is a symptom of falling in love in other literatures as well. In *Papyrus Harris* 500 (19th dynasty Egypt, 13th–12th cent. BCE) we find a love poem in which a woman says: "I have departed [from my brother]. [Now when I think of] your love, my

---

99 See the locus classicus: "Sustain me with raisin cakes, refresh me with apples, for I am faint with love" (Songs 2: 5). See further Braungart 1980–1981, Rothaus Caston 2006, Rynearson 2009.

100 Heeßel 2000, 251–252: 8–9: *šumma ašuštu imtanaqqussu napšātišu ittanâr akala ikkal šikara išattīma elīšu lā illak ū'a libbī iqabbi u uštannaḫ muruṣ râmi mariṣ ana zikari u sinništi ištēnma* (ref. Enrique Jiménez).

101 Interestingly, the following entries in this diagnostic text deal with *muruṣ nâki*, "sickness of intercourse" or "veneral disease"). In his discussion of *muruṣ nâki* – translated by Heeßel (2000, 258) as "Erkrankung wegen verbotenen Geschlechtsverkehrs" – Heeßel stresses that, as lovesickness, *muruṣ nâki* is not a real, positively-defined disease, but only a disease which stems from love, or intercourse, respectively. Examining later material (Classical, Late Antiquity, and Medieval) clearly suggest that lovesickness was considered a disease of its own. This medical condition was discussed, in the wider context of melancholy in Mesopotamian sources, by Couto-Ferreira 2010, 33–36

102 Lambert 1960, 146: 48: *amēlu ša sinništa irammu* (var. *iramma*) [*k*]*ūra u nissata imêš*.

103 A 7478 i 1–2 (№ 1), and see also Moussaieff Love Song rev. 6 (№ 11): *ḫimētam lišdam našûkim mārī ummiānim tamarātu našû lalêki*, "The craftsmen carry for you butter and ghee. Audience-gifts – they are carrying for your pleasure".

heart stands still within me. When I behold sw[eet] cakes, [they seem like] salt. Pomegranate wine, [once] sweet in my mouth – It is (now) like the gall of birds".[104] A similar, though not identical description, is found more than two mill. later, in the early 11th cent. AD Arabic treatise of Ibn Hazm, *The Ring of the Dove* which describes different aspects of love: "It can happen that a man sincerely affected by love will start to eat his meal with an excellent appetite; yet the instant the recollection of his loved one is excited, the food sticks in his throat and chokes his gullet".[105]

Defining the woman in love in A 7478 in medical terms, or more generally the pathologization of her love, is evident in the expression *ibbalum akālim*, "without eating", found twice in the opening passage of A 7478 (ll. 4 and 7). It reminds one of the common medical instruction *balum patān* or *lā patān* typically found in medical prescriptions, where the patient is ordered to take a medicine on an empty stomach. What is crucial here is the clear connection between not-eating and being sick,[106] i.e. lovesickness.

The loss of appetite in A 7478 helps to explain another physiological symptom attested in ALL. I refer here to descriptions of sleeplessness suffered by women who are yearning in vain for their lover. The deserted female lover curses her successful rival, saying: "May she, like me, [be afflicted] with sleeplessness! May she be dazed and [restless] all night long!"[107] and the envious woman continues: "My eyes are so tired, I am sleepless from gazing at him".[108] In the same vein, a woman is cursed in a love incantation: "Be awake at night-time! At day-time may you not sleep! At night-time may you not sit down!"[109] I suggest that sleeplessness or insomnia, together with loss of appetite, should be understood as different physiological symptoms of lovesickness caused by love, or more probably by unrequited love. (More on sleep and sleeplessness, cf. § 6.1).

---

104 Fox 1985, 21 (ref. Shalom Paul).

105 Arberry 1953, 38.

106 To the best of my knowledge, no form of voluntary abstention from food – in religious fasting or in grief – is attested in Akk. literary or liturgical texts. It is to be noted that the man in the description of lovesickness in *šumma ūm ištēn mariṣma* presented above, is eating and drinking but he is not gaining weight. Furthermore, various hemerological texts indicate foods to be avoided on certain days – but they never prescribe complete fasting (Livingstone 2013, 263–264). In fact, besides the medical expressions *balum patān* and *lā patān*, I know of only one verb, *šurrûm*, which means "to fast" (CAD Š/3, 360b). This rare verb is recorded in two sources: in the late Aluzinnu-text, where it is paralleled to *bubūtum*, "hunger", and in the Neo-Assyrian letter, written by Balasî and Nabû-aḫḫe-erība to the king Esarhaddon. In their epistle, the two scholars urge the king to start eating after three days of fasting (Parpola 1993, 33 = SAA 10, 43: 7–14). In his commentary to the letter, Parpola (1983, 57–58) stressed that "to understand this letter correctly it is essential to realize that its recipient (= the king) was seriously ill at the time the letter was written…" and that "there is no need whatever to assume that the king's three-day fast was a periodic necessity imposed on him by the official cult". This inference ties in well with another letter to Esarhaddon, where Adad-šumu-uṣur emphasizes that "eating of bread and drinking of wine will soon remove the illness of the king. Good advice is to be heeded: restlessness, not eating and not drinking disturbs the mind and adds to illness" (Parpola 1993, 159 = SAA 10, 196 rev. 10–18). These two letters make it clear that in Mesopotamia not-eating is directly related to being sick. More on fasting and voluntary not-eating in Mesopotamian sources, see Wasserman, 2016.

107 ZA 49, 168–169 ii 8–9 (№ 16): *kīma yâti lā ṣalālum* [*lū emissi*] *kali mūšim likūr* [*lidlip*].

108 ZA 49, 168–169 iii 20–21 (№ 16): *anḫā īnāya danniš dalpāku ina itaplusišu*.

109 ZA 75 (1554)b 38–40 (№ 28): *dilpī mūšītam urrī ē taṣlalī mūšī ē tušbī*.

## 4.4 Lovemaking and Copulating

Different verbs are used to describe the act of copulation.[110] The verb *reḫûm*, in the context of "to have sexual intercourse", appears once,[111] the verb *ṭeḫûm*, "to approach sexually" twice,[112] and the more explicit *niākum* thrice (note the incipit "let me have sex with your aunt!").[113] In the MB incantation from Hattuša the rare verb *garāḫum*, "to copulate (perhaps related to *garāšum*, "to advance sexually") is attested for the first time outside of lexical texts.[114] The more romantic *edērum*, "to embrace", is found six times,[115] and *našāqum*, "to kiss", is attested only twice.[116] The extreme paucity of references to kissing in the corpus of love-related texts, and other references of *našāqum* in literary texts,[117] show that kissing was considered first and foremost a social gesture designating honor and respect, or to a lesser extent familial closeness – but not an act fully belonging to the realms of sexual rapport and intimacy.[118]

---

110 See Wiggermann 2010, 411. I do not treat the different terms for sexual relationship used in daily-life and legal texts, such as *lamādum* or at times *aḫāzum*. These non-literary texts employ a different set of straightforward expressions that are unknown in literary texts, as, e.g., *ša zikarim*(NITA) *u sinništim*(MUNUS), "(a matter) of man and woman" (Anbar 1975, 120–122: 7–8 and Westbrook 1984, 754).

111 PRAK 1 B 472 ii 7' (№ 13).

112 CUSAS 10, 10: 36 (№ 4), KBo 36, 27: 21' (№ 21). (See Paul 2002, 492).

113 CUSAS 10, 12: 19 (№ 18): *aḫāt abīki lunīk*, see also KBo 36, 27: 20' (№ 21) and maybe MIO 12, 52–53: 12' (№ 10. A broken line). Heeßel (2000, 258) understands this verb as referring specifically to illicit sexual intercourse ("verbotenen Geschlechtsverkehrs"). This understanding of *niākum* is supported by some newly published omens concerning taboo sex: masturbation, bestiality, and sleeping with one's mother (George 2013, 299–300: 4, 8, 11, 15, 20, rev. 6', 8'). Also physiognomical omens about women tell the same: *nâkat*, "promiscuous", stands as the opposite of legitimate and fruitful sexual marital relations (Böck 2000, 154: 42, 156: 75–78, 159: 144, 167: 214, 223 and esp. 167: 231). And yet, in some OB literary texts, *niākum* does not carry a negative overtone, as proves the birth incantation YOS 11, 86: 1–2: *ina mê nâkim ibbani eṣemtum*..., "In the fluid of conception the substance was created...". Clearly, here *niākum* does not mean illicit intercourse or fornication, but intercourse in general. The same non-negative meaning may, perhaps, be found also in MIO 12, 52–53: 12' (№ 10), if correctly restored.

114 KBo 36, 27: 15'–16' (№ 21).

115 KAR 158 vi 19' (№ 19), Moussaieff Love Song obv. 1, obv. 14 (№ 11), ZA 49, 168–169 ii 23 (№ 16), YOS 11, 24 i 20 (№ 15).

116 ZA 49, 168–169 ii 23 (№ 16), and CUSAS 10, 13: 2 (№ 5) – partially restored (see commentary to this line).

117 As, e.g. Gilg. II i 11 and SB Gilg. XII 23 and 25 (= George 2003, 172 and 728 respectively), and Enūma eliš VI 87 (= Lambert 2013, 114).

118 But this is probably not the case in non-literary texts. In an OB letter (Anbar 1975, 120–121: 7–8) a woman, most likely a prostitute, takes an oath that she will not have any further sexual relations with a certain man. She vows that he *lā iturru ša zikarim u sinništim lā iqabbiamma šaptīya lā inaššiqu*, "He will not turn (to me), he will not propose having sexual relationship (lit. "that [matter] of man and woman), and he will not kiss my lips". (On this letter, see further Westbrook 1984, 754). The sexual aspect of (public) kissing is also made clear in a Sum. proverb which adds kissing (in public?) to a list of detestable and revolting actions: "To serve beer with unwashed hands, to spit without trampling upon it, to sneeze without covering it with dust, to kiss with the tongue (eme... ak) at midday without providing shade, are abominations to Utu" (SP 3.8 = Alster 1997: 80).

An interesting group of idioms which describe physical amorous activity – copulation in the strict sense or lovemaking in the wider sense – is found in the Moussaieff Love Song (№ 11): *dādī mašāḫum*, "to plunder the attractiveness (of the woman)",[119] *appi lalêm nasāḫum*, "to pull out the 'tip of (the woman's) desire'" (probably referring to the clitoris),[120] *rāmam šalālum*, "to take (the man's) love as captive",[121] *libbam dādī mullûm*, "to fill the (man's) heart with attractiveness,[122] and *šalûm*, "to plunge (into love)".[123]

Elliptical expressions for intercourse exist as well.[124] The verb *šakānum*, lit. "to place", is used a few times sexually: "He has taken by force... He placed (it) and (now) he is silent",[125] and "Do not place (me?) in the salt" (where "salt", or "salt in the field", refer to the female sex organ),[126] or the unequivocal call of Ištar to the city boys "Place (it) (*šuknā*), guys, *in* the pretty vulva!".[127] Consequently, *pašāḫum*, lit. "to relax", means to reach sexual climax.[128] Another metaphoric description of coitus is found in an incipit in a catalogue: "A *mare*(?) of a horse – she goes up and down".[129] A similar description of undulating movement to evoke sexual intercourse is found in the first mill. love ritual: "I have raised you(f.) up as (high as) a wall, I have brought you(f.) down as (low as) a ditch".[130] The expression *šipram epēšum*, "performing the work" is used to designate lovemaking.[131]

It is to be noted that all direct or indirect descriptions of sexual intercourse in the corpus refer to the main sexual organs, namely penis and vagina, and no mention is made to oral or anal sex,[132] though these sexual practices, especially the latter, are attested in non-literary texts.[133]

---

119 Moussaieff Love Song obv. 2 (№ 11).

120 Moussaieff Love Song obv. 2 (№ 11).

121 Moussaieff Love Song obv. 3 (№ 11).

122 Moussaieff Love Song obv. 7 (№ 11).

123 Moussaieff Love Song obv. 15 (№ 11), to which compare CUSAS 10, 8: 4–5 (№ 2): *kabtatī išalli libbam muḫattitam*, "My mood plunges into the infesting heart".

124 A still not fully understood idiom for sexual rapport is found in the seduction scene of Šamḫat and Enkidu. The epic uses *napīssu leqûm*, lit. "taking his scent". Does it mean only "getting very near" as George 2003, 796 (following Jacobsen) believes? I tend to follow CAD N/1, 305 with its "euphemism for virility".

125 CUSAS 10, 12: 13–14 (№ 18): *imtašuḫ... iškunma iqâl*.

126 CUSAS 10, 10: 38 (№ 4): *ina ṭābtim lā tašakkanī<nni?>*.

127 Or. 60, 340: 18 (№ 12): *šuknā eṭlūtum ana ḫurdati damiqtimma*.

128 Or. 60, 340: 16 (№ 12): *iptanaššaḫū ana ūriša*.

129 CUSAS 10, 12: 27–28 (№ 18): *perdi*! *sīsîm telli u turrad*. With clear association to the verb *rakābum*, "to ride, to mount", which is also used to denote sexual intercourse. For *ritkubum*, "to ride together = to copulate", cf. Groneberg 1986, 189.

130 Lambert 1975, 124: 9: *ušaqqēki kī dūri ušappilki kī ḫirīṣi*. (The entire passage describes sexual intercourse).

131 CUSAS 10, 12: 16 (№ 18): *lūpiš šipram*... (continuing with body parts).

132 I know of only one case in Akk. literature where the practice of fellatio is possibly hinted at: SB Gilg. VI 68 (= George 2003, 622–623), where Ištar says: Išullāniya *kiššūtaki*(sic) *ī nīkul*, "Oh my Išullānu, let us taste your power". (The *-ki* before the precative *ī* is a sandhi writing, namely, the "power" which is tasted is that of the male, cf. George 2003, 836f.). For "eating" used euphemistically for copulating, see Paul 1997, 106 n. 4 and 2002, 495–496. Cooper (2006–2008, 13) hesitantly suggests that fellatio might be meant in the Sum. myth Inanna and Enki (= Farber-Flügge 1973, 108): 37–38, where gìš dug₄-dug₄, "sexual intercourse" and ki sub "kissing" precede nam-kar-kid, "prostitution".

133 See CAD Q 255d. Another sexual activity which is not mentioned in the corpus of ALL, but known

## 4.5 Sexual Climax

Sexual climax is hinted at in a woman's speech where, at the peak of her sexual delight, she encourages her male partner: "Burn your craving upon me! My love is poured on you entirely. Take as much as you desire!".[134] It is notable that, contrary to what one might expect, the fluid aspect of sexual desire is attributed to the female, not to the male. Semen, *per se*, is not mentioned in the corpus.

Another idiom that may possibly refer to the male sexual orgasm is *ernittam kašādum*, lit. meaning "to reach victory". The term *ernittum* is well attested in literary texts where it designates a loud vocal expression of joy at military triumph.[135] In love incantations this idiom is found three times: "Why is your(m.) *ernittum* as bad as (that) of a little child?",[136] and "You, like a boar, [lay(?)] on the ground, until I gain my *ernittum* like a child!",[137] and in a broken context "I shall achieve my *ernittum* […] over [my slanderers], …, When our sleep […] We shall achieve [*ernittum*]".[138] The word *ernittum* continues, therefore, to denote a sonorous expression of joy when gaining control over a rival, but the explicitly sexual context raises the possibility that it carries a special nuance of a "love cry" when reaching sexual climax. Corroboration of this idea comes from the MB incantation from Hattuša: "I am mating you, – oh Nanāya! I am mating you, – oh Nanāya! Like a sheep! Ululation! Like (of) a pregnant woman, a battle cry!".[139] Schwemer (2004, 66) also understood the two terms *alālum*, and *tanūqātum* as referring to "Liebesgestöhn".

## 4.6 Direct and Indirect References to Sexual Organs

Semantically speaking, there are two kinds of reference to sexual organs in the corpus: direct and non-direct. The former are lexical-anatomical designations, the latter euphemistic or elliptical designations.[140] I will treat the two groups one after the other (all references can be found in Appendix 6).

---

from other genres, notably omens, is male masturbation. For these omens see Guinan 1997, 474: 12, and recently Stol 2014.

134 YOS 11, 24 i 24–i 25: *ina ṣēriya ṣurrup lalâka tabikkum râmī tapḫaram liqe mala ḫašḫāti* (the stative form ending with *-āti*, is an archaic 2 m. sg., and refers to the man).

135 See, e.g. CH xlviii 28–31: *irnitti* [d]*Marduk elîš u šapliš ikšud*, "He (the king) achieved victory for Marduk above and below", or CT 15, 3: 4 (hymn to Adad): *nišemme ernittašu waštat*, "we hear his (Adad's) cry is unyielding".

136 ZA 75, 198–204d 54 (№ 30): *ammīni kīma ṣeḫrim lā'im ernittaka lemnet* (see also YOS 11, 21b 13–14: *waštāti kīma* [*ṣeḫrim*?] *lemnet erni*[*ttaka*...], "You(m.) are harsh as [boy], your e. is bad".

137 ZA 75, 198–204i 109–110 (№ 34): *atta kīma šaḫîm qaqqaram* [x x x] *adi kīma ṣeḫrim elleqû erni*[*ittī*].

138 ZA 49, 168–169 ii 25–29 (№ 16): *akaššad ernittī* […] *eli da*[*bbibātiya*] *u damqiš ar-r*[*a-i-mi-ia* …] *inūma šittan*[*i* …] *nikašša*[*d ernittam*?].

139 KBo 36, 27: 15'–16' (№ 21): *agraḫki Nanāya agraḫki Nanāya kīma immeri alālama kīma arīti tanūqātumma*.

140 On euphemistic expressions in love literature in the ancient Near East, see Paul 2002. For the Hittiteterminology of sex organs and sexual activities, see Peled 2010a.

Direct appellations in the corpus to female sexual organs, more exactly to female pudenda, are *ūrum* and *ḫurdatum*; *utlum* and *sūnum* are found to designate "lap"; and *tulûm*, "breasts".[141] In two love incantations from Isin one finds the expressive designations *pûm ša šārātim* and *ūrum ša šīnātim*, "hairy mouth" and "urinating vulva", referring to the female sexual organ.[142] Interestingly, the common term *biṣṣūrum*, "vagina", is not attested in the treated corpus. This might be accidental, since *biṣṣūrum* is used extensively in the first mill. love ritual,[143] but it might also be due to the fact that *biṣṣūrum* is the term used for this organ in daily life,[144] and thus less appropriate for literary expression. Another term which is absent from the corpus but found in the late love ritual is *rēmum*, "womb" and with semantic expansion also "vulva".[145]

Non-direct references to the female sex organ use three different metaphorical terms: "gate", "field", and various animals. The euphemistic designation *bābum*, "gate", is found in the Isin love incantation: "I have opened for you – Oh Erra-bāni – my seven gates!"[146] The Moussaieff Love Song (№ 11) is even clearer: "That which you love, my vulva, is laid down for you: wide, spacious gate".[147] A "locked gate" is found in the first mill. love ritual: "Into your vulva (*biṣṣūrum*) which you guard (lit. on which you trust) I will cause my dog (= penis) enter and will shut the door (*bābum*).[148] I will cause a dog enter and will shut the door. I will cause a *ḫaḫḫuru*-bird (= penis) enter and it will nest there".[149] In a Sum. dialogue between two women, a "locked gate" is attested as well: ká-zu ká-na nu-dím

141 Breasts, *tulûm*, are not typically connected to the sexual domain in Akk. They are referred to in a straightforward manner, as a body part which is mostly connected to breast feeding. It is rather, *irtum*, "chest", which is used in ALL (see PRAK 1 B 472 i 10' = № 13 and CUSAS 10, 12: 26 = № 18). A similar situation is described by Chandezon et al. (2014, 301) regarding breasts in the interpretation of Greek erotic dreams.

142 As Jana Matuszak pointed out, the metaphorical equation vagina ≈ mouth is found also in Sum. literature. In a dialogue between two women, one woman insults the other, saying: ka-zu-gen₇ galla₄ˡᵃ-zu-gen₇ "Your mouth is like your vagina" (Matuszak 2012, 62: 4). The same association, but positively turned, is also found: ka-ka-a-ni-gen₇ galla₄ˡᵃ-ni zé-ba-àm, "Her vagina is as sweet as her [= the goddess Bau] mouth" (Šu-Sîn A 21 = ETCSL 2.4.4.1, and see similarly Dumuzi and Inanna Y 49–50 = ETCSL 4.08.25). On euphemistic renderings of mouth for vagina, prevalent in Rabbinic sources, see Paul 2002, 496f.

143 Cf. e.g. Lambert 1975 104: 7–11.

144 See, e.g. *lā anīkuši išarī ana biṣṣūriša lā īrubu*, "I did not have sexual intercourse with her, my penis did not penetrate her vagina" (PBS 5, 156: 3, cited in CAD N/1, 197b 1a), *lipištam lā kattam našêti u ašar abu u ummum pānīka ittaplasū u ištu biṣṣūrim tamqutamma…*, "You carry blood not of your own (family) and in the place where (your) father and mother behold you (for the first time) and where you have fallen from (your mother's) vagina…" (Marello 1992, 117: 36). See also Böck 2000, 164: 201–202 (physiognomical omens).

145 Cf. e.g. Lambert 1975 112: 6–14.

146 ZA 75, 198–204i 117 (№ 34): *uptettīkum sebet bābiya Erra-bāni.*

147 Moussaieff Love Song rev. 8 (№ 11): *ša tarammu ūrī nadīkum bābum rapšum šuddulum.*

148 And cf. the physiognomical omen *šumma sinništu ḫurdatam rapšat*, "If a woman has a wide vagina…" (Böck 2000, 160: 153).

149 Lambert 1975, 122: 11–12: *ana biṣṣūriki ša taklāti kalbī ušerreb bāba arakkas kalba ušerreb bāba arakkas ḫaḫḫuru ušerreb qinna iqannan* (see also Hecker 2005, 176 n. 63). On the meaning of this canine coitus, see commentary to ZA 75, 198–204a 21–22 (№ 27).

al-kéš-da lú gù dé-a nu-ĝál "Your gate is not made to be a gate; it is locked up. It does not call for a man!".[150]

The vagina is also a "field", or even "sown field". A man scolds his female ex-lover, accusing her of having too much sex with other men: "Do not place (me?) in the salt, your field is all too well known!".[151] Plowing a field, as a metaphor for copulation, is used lyrically, not scornfully, in the Moussaeiff Love Song (№ 11): "The field is plowed up for you. You know its dimensions; it is plowed early for you; (You know) its meadows".[152] A direct consequence of this metaphor, the "cultivator" (*errēšum*) defines the one who plows the field, namely the man who has intercourse with a woman: "(One) is going out(f.), (another) is open(f.) – two are their(f. pl.) plowmen. [...] to the second of her plowmen (she says): '(You are) not the shepherd!'". [153] Somewhat similarly, the female sex organ is also called "canal", again in a derogatory way: "To your canal – no one will come near it!".[154]

Finally, the female sex organ is referred to by the names of various animals. The clearest example in the corpus is found in the Kiš text PRAK 1 B 472 i 12' (№ 13), where *ḫudušsum*, perhaps some kind of frog, dark in color, refers to female pudenda. Again, the first mill. love ritual offers more examples of this semantic path and enumerates different animals which are metaphorically connected to the female vulva (here euphemistically called *rēmum*): "the lizard (*ṣurārû*) of [your] vulva... the gecko (*pizalluru*) of [your] vulva...the wild cat (*muraššû*) of [your] vulva... The mouse (*ḫumṣīru*) of your vulva...".[155] It must be admitted, however, that it is not clear whether the wild animals stand for the male or the female sex organ.[156] If the latter possibility is correct, Akk. is not unique in semantically attaching animals to the female sex organ. [157] Animals serve as indirect designations for this part of the body in colloquial (and often vulgar) speech in other

150 Matuszak 2012, 62: 15.

151 CUSAS 10, 10: 38–39 (№ 4): *ina ṭābtim lā tašakkanī<ni?> eqelki ḫukkum*. It is not impossible that the obscure phrase in CUSAS 10, 13: 8 (№ 5): *mu-di-*{UD}*-ši*! *eq-li-im*, "The ... of the field ...", goes in this direction.

152 Moussaieff Love Song rev. 9 (№ 11): *ugārum eriški tīdî maniātišu ḫarpiš eriški tawwerātišu*. On this metaphor, see Livingstone 1991.

153 CUSAS 10, 12: 20–21 (№ 18): [*wā*]*ṣiat pētât šinā errēšāšina* [...] *ana šanîm errēšiša ul rē'ûm*. George (2009, 75, ad 20) raises the possibility of a word-play between *errēšum*, "cultivator" and *ērišum*, "bridegroom" was intended here.

154 CUSAS 10, 10: 36 (№ 4): *ana pattiki mamman ul iṭeḫḫēši*.

155 Lambert 1975, 112: 10–14.

156 In a first mill. incantation with a ritual destined to make a bordello prosper one finds a "snake" as clearly referring to a penis (Panayatov 2013, 293: 30). The possibility that at least some of these wild animals could be metaphors for penis gains support from a Sum. short wisdom literature composition (a "proverb" in the common, but inaccurate, nomenclature) which describes a man of old age: "I, a youth, my god, the strength of my personal god, and my youthful vigor have left my loins like a runaway donkey. My black mountain has produced white gypsum. My mother [var: turned a man] from the forest toward me, he gave me paralyzed hands. My mongoose, which used to eat strong-smelling food, can no longer stretch its neck toward a jar of fine oil" (SP 17 Sec. B3 = Alster 1997, 238. Cf. also 19 Sec. A1 = Alster 1997, 243). In his commentary Alster (1997, 436) suggests that "The mongoose is a metaphor for the old man's nose, which has lost its sense of smell". But this, clearly, is not the case: the mongoose refers metaphorically to an organ whose function has deteriorated with age, certainly not the nose. (For "eating" used euphemistically for copulating, cf. Paul 2002, 495f.).

157 Note also *laqlaqqu*, "stork", which designates the female genitals in lex. texts (CAD L 102, 2).

languages as well, as the ready English examples *pussy*, *kitty*, or *beaver*, and German *Muschi* show.

And what about the references to the male genital organs? Even more than female intimate parts, they are mostly veiled in euphemism. One such case is found in a love incantation from Isin, where *palûm*, "staff" is used.[158] It reads: "Truly, even the garlic plant carries its own staff! Truly, even the bull carries its own staff!"[159] Another euphemistic term for penis is *sukannīnum*, "dove".[160] A passage from an *irtum*-song goes: "I have thrown my coop on the young man, so that I may catch the 'dove'; (The coop) of my delights Nanāya will fill for me"![161] A "bird", and more specifically a "dove", denoting euphemistically the male sex organ, are known from other languages, as e.g. *uccello*, "bird", in Italian or *ḥamāma*, "dove", in colloquial Arabic.[162]

Metonymic epithets are also found, referring indirectly to male genital organs. In an incipit listed in the catalogue KAR 158 (№ 19) *ṣurrum*, "obsidian", a particularly hard stone, designates the male erection: "Your love is an obsidian-blade, your lovemaking is golden".[163] Even less direct are elliptical expressions for the masculine member. One of the Isin love incantations uses the non-explicit term "that of..." or "that which..." for penis: "You, lay with me so that I may pluck your bristle! Take for me 'that which is in your hand' and place (it) in my hand!",[164] and a hymnal text from Larsa reads: "reach 'mine' and 'that of my *love*'".[165] Two unmistakable and rather vulgar elliptic references to the male erection are found in a catalogue of love lyric incipits published by George: "big one, big one, do not arise!"[166] And "it is so enlarged! That of an elephant is smaller than yours!"[167]

But direct anatomic references to the male sexual organ, however rare, do exist in the corpus. A clear-cut anatomic designation in KAR 158 (№ 19) – *rebītum*, "genitals, groins,

158 A similar vegetal metaphor for penis is found in the Sum. composition Gilgameš, Enkidu and the Netherworld where g i š, "penis" is compared to g i š - ù r s u m u n, "rotten beam" (see, Gadotti 2014, 287: 251). Modern English slang also uses "wood" for "erect penis".

159 ZA 75, 198–204i 112–113 (№ 34): *u šūmum inašši palâ ramānišu u alpum inašši palâ ramānišu*. The continuation makes it clear that the prominent pinkish flower of the garlic and the "staff" of the bull refer to the masculine member: "Just like the river had flowed over its bank, so I will engender myself! (so) I will engender my body!". On the motif of self-insemination see Cooper 1996.

160 It is possible that the woman addressing the man as *summatī*, "my dove" in Moussaieff Love Song obv. 14 (№ 11) is also hinting at that direction.

161 Fs. Renger 192–193 i 16–20 (№ 6): *quppī addi eṭlamma u sukannīna luṣbatma ša ṣīḫātiya* *ᵈNanāya tumallâm.*

162 Other clear cases of a "bird" standing metaphorically for the phallus are found in the late first mill. love ritual. Lambert 1975, 110: 35: *baqān iṣṣū[r]umma lubqunki*, "Plucking of a bird let me pluck you(f.), and Lambert 1975, 122: 12: *ḫaḫḫūru ušerreb qinna iqannan*, "I will make a *ḫ*.-bird enter (your genitals, f.) and it will build there a nest". More on this, see commentary to Fs. Renger, 192–193 i 8 (№ 6).

163 KAR 158 vii 43'–44' (№ 19): *râmka lū ṣurru ṣīḫātuka lū ḫurāṣu*. The Obsidian in this metaphor should not be confused with the *aban râmi*, "the stone of love", mentioned in Abnu šikinšu as a red stone (Schuster-Brandis 2008, 423).

164 ZA 75, 198–204d 59–60 (№ 30): *atta itīlamma lunassiḫam zappīka ša qātika liqeamma ana qātiya šukun.*

165 YOS 11, 24 i 26 (№ 15): *yâtam u ša râmiya kušdīm.*

166 CUSAS 10, 12: 5 (№ 18): *rabûm rabûm lā tetebbēma.*

167 CUSAS 10, 12: 9 (№ 18): *arrak ša? pīrim iṣṣeḫḫerak*[*a*], and cf. also l. 8: *abbunti luštuḫm*[*a*] "Let me grow long for the girl!".

or even testicles" – was missed by previous scholars because the sign *-it* was erroneously left unwritten: "Your genitals are lapis-lazuli of the mountain".[168] The straightforward term for penis, *išarum*, may be found in the love incantation from Hattuša, if the proposed reading of the Sumerograms is correct: "Penis! Approach! Penis! Approach her bedroom!".[169] Another difficult passage may perhaps refer to the male erection: "I encircle (you) like a wife, so that (you?) will *not become "stiff"*.[170]

One should be careful in interpreting every difficult term or opaque line in the corpus as a concealed reference to sexual organs, but there are more references to this semantic field than was previously recognized.

## 4.7 Love, Desire and Anger

The association of desire and anger, even rage, is not unknown in ancient literatures. Medea in ancient Greek literature offers the best embodiment of the explosive relation between desire and rage.[171] Also in some cases in our corpus desire is pictured as an eruption of strong and uncontrolled emotion, not dissimilar to anger or madness.[172] Fire and burning are the key-metaphors here. The love incantation VS 17, 23 (№ 24) ends with the colophon "Incantation (to calm) the fire of the heart",[173] and a woman in the love dialogue evoking the king Rīm-Sîn of Larsa says in ecstasy: "Burn your craving upon me!".[174] A frenzy of delight is found towards the end of the OAkk love incantation, where the love-charm (*ir'emum*/*irimmum*) is said to bring the resisting woman to rapture: "The love-charms have persuaded her, driven her to ecstasy".[175]

The clearest example of a link between desire and rage is found in one of the love incantations from Isin, ZA 75, 198–204g (№ 32), which focuses on "the anger of Nanāya" (*uzzum ša Nanāya*). Its opening proves that the divine anger of desire is fire-like, as it can be extinguished by cold water: "[Anger!], anger! Keeps s[tand]ing in his heart! Let me give you(m.) cold water to drink! Let me give you(m.) ice and cool drinks to drink!"[176] The qualities of this raging desire are that of wild beasts, leaping and devouring like a lion or a

168 KAR 158 vii 49' (№ 19): *re-bi-<it>-ka ša uqni šadî*. More on that, see in the commentary to this line.

169 KBo 36, 27: 21' (№ 21): *išaru*(GÌŠ) *ṭeḫi*(TE) *išaru*(GÌŠ) *ṭeḫi*(⌈TE) DA⌉.GA.AN.NI.

170 CUSAS 10, 9: 13 (№ 3): *asaḫḫur kīma aštim ana* [*lā*] *ma-ka-*⌈*ki*?⌉, and see commentary to this line.

171 On this, see Sissa 2008, 15–19.

172 Indirect support of the relation which Mesopotamians knew to exist between sexual desire and anger can be found in the series Šumma ālu. After four consecutive omens which deal with sex ("If someone has sexual relations with a woman in a river…; If someone has sexual relations with a woman in captivity…; If someone has sexual relations with a woman and steals any of her property…; If someone marries a prostitute…") comes an omen which concerns anger: "If an angry person reconciles with someone – the angry gods will return [to him]" (Moren 1977, 67: 1–5).

173 VS 17, 23: 8 (№ 24): KA-inim-ma *išāt libbim*(IZI.ŠÀ.GA), and see commentary to this line.

174 YOS 11, 24 i 24 (№ 15): *ina ṣēriya ṣurup lalâka*.

175 MAD 5, 8: 30–31 (№ 22): *ir'emū udabbibūšima u iškunūši ana muḫḫûtim*.

176 ZA 75, 198–204g 78–81 (№ 32): [*uzzum*] *uzzum it*[*anazza*]*z ina libbišu lušqīka* [*m*]*ê kaṣûtim lušqīka šurīpam takṣiātim*.

wolf: "Anger! anger! Co[mes to me] like a wild bull, ke[eps jumpin]g on me like a dog. Like a lion, (anger) is fierce-ranging, like a wolf, (anger) breaks into a run".[177]

Having described the main ways in which the corpus treats the different emotional and corporal aspects of love and attraction, I now present other semantic fields which characterize the corpus of ALL.

# 5. Semantic Fields (Other than Love) Typical of the Corpus

## 5.1 Flora

Flora is one of the most typical semantic features of ALL (see Appendix 2).[178] Although semantically central,[179] quantitively its attestations are not significantly greater than in other sections of the Akk. literary system.[180] The importance of this semantic field lies in the essential analogy between vegetal abundance and human or divine sensuality – an analogy which is omnipresent in the literatures of the ancient Near East.[181]

The key terms in this semantic field are *inbum*, "fruit, flower, sexual appeal", which is attested no less than 14 times,[182] and *kirûm*, "garden, orchard", which is attested 8 times (mainly in KAR 158 = № 19).[183]

## 5.2 Fauna

Fauna – domestic and wild – is also present in ALL – less important than flora but still significant (see Appendices 3 and 4). Unlike flora, this semantic field focuses not on sensuality or amorous relations between the protagonists, but rather on the *force* of sexuality *per se*. It is not accidental that fauna is found especially in love incantations, where the sexual vitality of animals is compared with human sexual activity. The two

177 ZA 75, 198–204g 85–89: *uzzum uzzum i*[*llakam*] *rīmāniš išt*[*anaḫḫiṭam*] *kalbā*[*n*]*i*[*š*] *k*[*īma nēšim ēz*] *al*[*ākam*] *k*[*īma barbarim lak*]*ātam* [*ú*?]-*ša*-[*ar*?].

178 See Lambert 1987, 27 nn. 16, 17, Goodnick Westenholz 1992, Stadhouders 2013, 311 n. 21, Groneberg 1999, 182–185.

179 Just a few examples: KAL 3, 75: 4' (№ 8): *asmat kī illūr ṣēri*, "She is luscious like an *illūru*-flower of the field", or PRAK 1 B 472 i 7' (№ 13): *muḫtanbū inbūka*, "Your(m.) fruits are profuse!".

180 Note that when nouns belonging to Flora are part of ritual instructions, they were not counted (e.g. *maštakal* in ZA 75, 198–204h 108 = № 33), since these cases are not part of the literary text *stricto sensu*.

181 See Paul 1997, 100 and passim.

182 CUSAS 10, 8: 10 (№ 2), CUSAS 10, 9: 23 (№ 3), CUSAS 10, 10: 30 (№ 4), Fs. Renger 192–193 i 2 (№ 6), MIO 12, 52–53: 8' (№ 10), PRAK 1 B 472 i 7' (№ 13), VS 17, 23: 3 (№ 24), YOS 11, 24 i 23, i 31 (№ 15), ZA 49, 168–169 iii 10, iii 11 (№ 16). See also Groneberg 1999, 182–184.

183 For the symbolism of the garden in love literature, see Paul 2002, 492.

important animals in the domestic sphere are the dog (*kalbum/kalbatum*) and the pig (*šaḫûm*).

Avian imagery is different. It is important to note that no less than 7 different terms for bird are found in the corpus (*allallum*, *iṣṣūrum*, *sukannīnum*, *summatum*,[184] *paspasum*, *šinūnūtum*, and *titkurrum*) making it the most important group in this semantic field. Birds are connected to human love in different ways: as argued by Groneberg (1986), their twittering is compared to human lovemaking. In addition, some birdcall reminds the protagonist of his, or her, lover.[185] And finally – as will be discussed later – birds bring good news from lovers who are apart.

## 5.3 Fabricated Objects

A careful lexical and semantic analysis of the corpus shows that more than flora and fauna, ALL tends to incorporate terms pertaining to fabricated objects (see Appendix 5): beds, kitchen vessels and utensils, articles of clothing, tools, boxes, boats, ropes and nets.[186] It would be correct to say that Akk. love-related literature reflects domestic – perhaps even manorial – rather than pastoral or bucolic, settings.

## 5.4 Human Body and Body Parts

The predominant semantic field in ALL is the human body and body parts (see Appendix 6). More than in any other group of Akk. literary texts, ALL focuses on the body and the self: c. 70 different body parts are attested in our corpus. The commonest body parts are *libbum*, "heart and mind", then *īnum* and *pûm*, "eye" and "mouth" respectively. Love in Akk. literature is therefore not conceptual or abstract, nor even sensory or perceptual, but somatic.[187]

In what follows I present some of the literary means which Akk. uses to define love, affection and sexual attraction. I delineate these means – mainly metaphor and pictorial representations – starting with two hitherto overlooked sets of polar-metaphors: sleep vs. being awake, and light vs. darkness.

---

184 For the dove in love-related compositions, see Groneberg 1999, 187–188.

185 The clearest example is Moussaieff Love Song obv. 9 and rev. 5 (№ 11), where the ducks' quacking evokes the image of the lover in the partner's mind. Note also the twittering of birds in the ritual for a prosperous borderllo (Panayatov 2013, 293: 30).

186 Musical instruments, as *ebbūbum* or *tigûm*, mentioned in the summary sections of the catalogue KAR 158 (№ 19) are not included.

187 This is true not only for love, but for other emotions in Akk. literature as well, see Streck 1999, 204: "Emotionen werden nie abstrakt gezeichnet, sondern immer als körperliche Reaktionen". (The topic of the "ancient Mesopotamian body" as historical construct and its different literary, medical, magical and legal representations, deserves special study, and cannot be treated here. For an excellent introduction to the field of the history of the body in Western (i.e. Christian and Jewish) culture, see Weinstein 2009 (esp. 15–20).

# 6. Key Metaphors and Motifs

## 6.1 Sleep, Dreams and Awakening

Sleep in ALL designates the particular state of mind of falling or being in love, and to fall out of love is "to wake up, to be awakened".[188] The words *šittum*, "sleep" and *ṣalālum*, "to lie down, to sleep", are attested 15 times in the corpus of ALL[189] – which is more than half the total number of attestations of these lemmas in the entire Akk. literary corpus.

A comparison found in an MB text explains the meaning of "sleep" in ALL in a straightforward way: "Your(f.) love is like sleep....".[190] Another example, regrettably in a broken context, reads: "When our sleep will [...] – we shall achieve [*our victory*(?)]".[191] Alongside *šittum* one may find the rare synonym *munattum* (pl. *munāmātum*), "morning slumber". One of the texts from Kiš reads: "In your soft lap, in the time of the morning slumber, your lovemaking is sweet".[192] The same image is found in an opening line from the Assur catalogue KAR 158 (№ 19): "Since I was sleeping in (my) darling's lap".[193] Consequently, the brutal end of love is referred to metaphorically as "to wake up". The male lover whose heart was turned to another woman tells his previous lover who still loves him: "Give up! Go away! Report to your counselor (= the goddess Nanāya) that we are (now) awake!",[194] namely the magic of our love is over. Being awake is also a sign of restlessness and agitation caused by separation from the lover. This idea is most beautifully expressed in a line from the Moussaieff Love Song (№ 11), whose Biblical reverberations cannot be missed: "...My eyes are drawn, my heart is awake (though) I am sleeping".[195]

But the semantics of sleep in the corpus is more complex than that, as it can also be used negatively.[196] Being deprived of sleep commonly describes an unfavorable situation.[197] In the context of love-related literature, sleeplessness befalls those who are yearning for love. It is a sign of unrequited love, and – as discussed above (see § 4.3) – a symptom of lovesickness. Sleeplessness is also seen as a punishment, a powerful weapon to be used between opponents. The deserted lover curses her successful rival, saying: "May she, like me, [be afflicted] with sleeplessness! May she be dazed and [restless] all night

188 On sleep in Mesopotamian sources see Steinert 2010. Sleep in the context of amatory texts is not discussed there.

189 *ṣalālum*: CUSAS 10, 10: 49 (№ 4), CUSAS 10, 12: 2 (№ 18), KAR 158 vii 48' (№ 19), Moussaieff Love Song obv. 6 (№ 11), YOS 11, 24 i 21 (№ 15), ZA 49, 168–169 ii 8 (№ 16), ZA 75, 198–204b 39 (№ 28). *šittum*: KAR 158 vi 19', vii 42' (№ 19), MIO 12, 52–53: 22' (№ 10), Moussaieff Love Song obv. 4, obv. 8(x2) (№ 11), PRAK 1 B 472 ii 7' (№ 13), ZA 49, 168–169 ii 28 (№ 16).

190 MIO 12, 52–53: 22' (№ 10): *râmki kīma šitti.*

191 ZA 49, 168–169 ii 28–29 (№ 16): *inūma ši-it-ta-n*[*i* x x x x x] *nikašša*[*d ernittam*?], and see above § 4.5.

192 PRAK 1 B 472 i 4'–6' (№ 13): *inutlika rabbi šī munāmāti dādūka ṭābū*, and in the same text, see also l. ii 7': *anna šittum ta-ri* [...], "Indeed, sleep will po[ur...]".

193 KAR 158 vii 48' (№ 19): *ištu ṣallāku ina sūn māri.*

194 ZA 49, 168–169 i 19–21 (№ 16): *mugrī atalkī ana māliktiki šunnî kīma ērēnu.*

195 Moussaieff Love Song obv. 6 (№ 11): *katmā īnāya libbī ēr ṣallāku*, and see also obv. 4 and obv. 8.

196 See in general Steinert 2010, 249–256.

197 Cf. CAD Ṣ 69, 2'.

long!"[198] and the envious woman continues with the verb *dalāpum*: "My eyes are so tired, I am sleepless from gazing at him".[199] Sleeplessness, perceived by the threatened party, is described in a bilingual diatribe between two women. In Dialogue 5, a woman accuses her rival of wanton behavior, of acting frivolously and intimidating decent neighbors: "(You are) perpetually standing about in the city squares, and constantly prowling around in the streets, constantly sitting on the threshold of all people… the wife of a man and the child of a man, who live in the city quarter, cannot sleep because of you (Sum. her)."[200] The decent ladies cannot sleep because of the bad woman, the subject of this diatribe, who keeps walking in the streets, seducing the (married) men in her neighborhood.

Interestingly, though sleep can mean being in love, its absence is at the same time a sign of amorous activity, for sleep, after all, is a waste of time for busy lovers. The man orders his female lover in an incipit from a Babylonian catalogue: "If I fall asleep – you, wake me up!",[201] and in a text which hails the lovemaking of King Rīm-Sîn of Larsa one reads: "Let us practice the work of lovers all night long, let us not sleep!"[202] Similarly, an incipit in KAR 158 (№ 19) reads: "Go away sleep, let me embrace my darling!"[203] The ambiguous character of sleep in love-related texts is wonderfully demonstrated in a line from the Moussaieff Love Song (№ 11): "I repeat: 'Oh sleep, come to me like to a baby! Go out from me, Oh sleep!'"[204]

Finally, the flimsiness of love which causes lovers to alternate between sleep and wakefulness, is compared in ALL to a dream, *šuttum*. The young man who falls in love with a far away girl says: "[One who has] a loved-one chases (lit. sees) a dream",[205] and a woman in another text describes her agony after being rejected by her lover using the same term: "I kept forgetting my words, I cannot make my mind which is like a dream".[206]

Sleep in ALL thus carries a variety of meanings: it designates the lovers' emotive existence in a parallel reality, and consequently its absence means a falling out of love or unrequited love. At the same time sleep is seen to hinder lovers, stopping them from

---

198 ZA 49, 168–169 ii 8–9 (№ 16): *kīma yâti lā ṣalālum* [*lū emissi*] *kali mūšim likūr* [*lidlip*]. And the same curse reappears in the love incantation ZA 75, 198–204b 38–40 (№ 28): *dilpī mūšītam urrī ē taṣlalī mūšī ē tušbī*, "Be(f.) awake at night-time! At day-time may you(f.) not sleep! At night-time may you(f.) not sit down!".

199 ZA 49, 168–169 iii 20–21 (№ 16).

200 Dialogue 5: 110–113: sila-a gub-gub e-sír-ra ni ni$_{10}$-ni$_{10}$ kun$_{4}$ mu-lu{//lú}-e-ne-ka tuš-tuš-ù /…/ dam mu-lu du$_{5}$-mu mu-lu{//lú} dag-ge$_{4}$-a tìl-la ù nu-mu-un-na-ku-ku-ù-ne // *muttazzizat rebiātim sāḫirat sūqātim muttaššibat askuppāt awīlē* /…/ [*aš*]*šat awīli mārat awīli ša ina bābtim wašbā ula iṣallalāki*. Cf. also ll. 128–129 in the same Dialogue 5 (quoted from N28 = CBS 6999, unpublished): bún du$_{11}$-du$_{11}$ guruš iri-ka lul sè-sè-ke / ki-sikil tur dag-ge$_{4}$-a tìl-la ù nu-mu-un-na-ku-ku, "(She is) constantly backbiting, slandering the the young men of the city. The young girls who live in the city quarter cannot sleep because of her". The passages quoted from Dialogue 5 and their translations come from Jana Matuszak's forthcoming PhD thesis. I am grateful to her for kindly agreeing to share her work in progress.

201 CUSAS 10, 12: 2 (№ 18): *šumma aṣṣallal dikênni atti.*

202 YOS 11, 24 i 20–21 (№ 15): *i nīpuš šipram ša murtâmī kal mūšim ē niṣlal.*

203 KAR 158 vi 19' (№ 19): *šittu atlakī māra lūdir* (see also vii 42': *barmātu īnāya imdalâ šitta*).

204 Moussaieff Love Song obv. 8 (№ 11): *uterram alkīmmi šittum* ⌈*la-ḫi?-iš*⌉ *ṣîam šittum.*

205 CUSAS 10, 8: 14 (№ 2): [*rāš*]*i raʾīmtim nāṭil šunātim.*

206 CUSAS 10, 9: 9–10 (№ 3): *umtašši awātiya ṭēmī ul ṣabtāk kīma* [*šu*]*tti*. A dream is mentioned also, in a heavily broken context, in A 7478 iii 4 and iii 12 (№ 1).

lovemaking. The concept of dream is used to characterize the emotional uncertainty and existential fragility of the person in love.

## 6.2 Light and Darkness

The second pair which metaphorically denotes love is "light" vs. "darkness". A good example of this is found in an incipit from KAR 158 (№ 19): "My love is the light that illuminates the eclipse".[207] It is not clear whether the speaker is male or female, but the metaphor is clear: light here equals love and darkness – in this case an eclipse – equals the absence of love.[208] This metaphorical equation explains a difficult line in a text published by George, where the obnoxious man, angry at the non-compliance of his lover, asks rhetorically: "Shall I give my love where the heart of darkness is?"[209] The expression *libbi ekletim*, "heart of darkness" (which could be a good Akk. translation of the title of Conrad's 1899 novel) is a metaphorical description of the unyielding woman. To the man who speaks, the woman's rebelliousness means that she does not love him properly, and he will thus not give his light, namely his love, to her dark, unloving heart.[210]

Grasping the metaphorical meaning of light in ALL paves the way to a better understanding of other passages as well. Mark the following lines, from the Isin tablet of love incantations. The woman turns to the man, saying: "Look at me and be rejoiced like a harp! Like (through) Seraš (beer) may your heart be bright! Shine on me regularly like Šamaš! Renew (yourself) on me like Sîn! ... and may your love be new!"[211] The woman is appealing to the man, asking him to shine on her regularly, expressing her desire for the unfailing attention of her beloved. A similar wish is found in a few incipits in KAR 158 (№ 19): "Shine to me like the star of da[wn]",[212] "*Hooray*! (My) darling is shining – come in!",[213] "Hail our goddess, oh the dawn-watch!"[214] and "I have competed with the sun, Oh our lord!"[215]

The metaphor of light cannot be made clearer than in the opening of this love incantation: "The daughters of Anu, the lights of heaven, [*in day-ti*]*me*(?) purified the sky

207 KAR 158 vii 45' (№ 19): *râmī nīru mušnammeru atallî*. And note the summary in viii 30': "2 Akk. *nūru*-songs", lit. "Light-songs".

208 This metaphorical dichotomy stands, I believe, behind some physiognomical omens relating to women: "[If (the woman is….], she will go in the dark (*ekliš illak*), [If (the woman is….], she will go in the light (*namriš illak*)" (Böck 2000, 156: 79–80, see also 158: 114–115).

209 CUSAS 10, 10: 7 (№ 4): *ašar libbi ekle*[*tim ana*]*ndin râmī*, and see the parallel line in ZA 49, 168–169 ii 17 (№ 16).

210 And see also the broken line *ša-am-ḫu mu-ù*ʾ*-a-ti-ni* $u_4$*-ma-am ek-le-e-t*[*a*?*-am*?] *ta*-[x x] x [....], "The exuberant, our Muʾati, in daylight and darkness […]" in MIO 12, 52–53: 15 (№ 10).

211 ZA 75, 198–204a 24–28 (№ 27): *amrannima kīma pitnim ḫuddu kīma Seraš libbaka liwwir kīma* ᵈ*Šamšim ittanpuḫam k*[*īm*]*a* ᵈ*Sîn idišam* [x x I]G *u râ*[*mk*]*a līdiš*.

212 KAR 158 vii 2' (№ 19): *upḫa kī kakkab šē*[*ri*].

213 KAR 158 vii 16' (№19): *e-la-ia māru lū namer erba*.

214 KAR 158 ii 21' (№ 19): *tišmarī ilatni namārītu*.

215 KAR 158 vii' (№ 19): *šamša ašni bēlani*. Note that light and dawn are mentioned in the very broken fragment PRAK 2 C 125: 1, 3, 4 (№ 14d).

of Anu. Love came about, twittering over the people; May Love twitter over me!"[216] The opening *historiola* is not used merely as literary ornament. Light is physical love, and the rosy-fingered Daughters of Anu coloring the sky before sunrise are its cosmic manifestation.

Light has also corporal manifestation, as seen in the first line of the Moussaieff Love Song (№ 11). The male lover is described as one who brings a smile, lit. brightness, lightness: "[In] his *coming* brightness is brought about".[217]

A special case of the light metaphor is found in A 7478 (№ 1), where a flash of lightning is used to describe the sudden appearance of the lover. The lightning, which the Chicago text specifies as "the lightning of Adad", ties in well with the equation of light = love and darkness = absence of love: "The lightnings of Adad in his presence, indeed, the lightning of lovemaking stroke upon me like an ear of barley before the appropriate time".[218] Unlike other terms for light *nūrum*, or *nīrum*, the verb *nawārum*, "to shine", and the heavenly bodies (the sun, the moon and the stars), lightning, *birqum*, is not a stable source of light. When lightning strikes, it does so for an instant, before total darkness returns. This image accurately reflects the woman's fragility: her lover arrives suddenly, captures her heart, shakes up her entire existence and disappears, leaving her in emotional darkness. A true *coup de foudre*. The continuation of the text makes it clear that the lightning, though powerful and exciting, is not what the woman desires. She hopes to look at the man's stable light, his *nannārum*: "I am looking at your luminosity … Let me see your radiance!"[219]

## 6.3 Birds and the Separated Lovers

The 10 occurrences of bird references in ALL amounts to half of all such occurrences in the corpus of Akk. literature of the third and second mill. One may therefore conclude that avian imagery is a typical semantic feature of love-related literature in Akk. Birds denote the fragility and delicacy of the love relationship, often expressing the separation of lovers.[220] But birds are also bearers of good tidings. The woman says: "May your(m.) message come to me.., may your(m.) message come to me, so that I, oh I, will hear your(m.) well-being. The bird will *make known*(?) the *n*[*ews*(?)]…".[221] The quacking of the ducks in morning time reminds the lovers of each other and reminds them of their nocturnal

---

216 CUSAS 10, 11: 2–6 (№ 20): [*mār*]*āt Anim nipiḫ šamê* [*u₄*?-*ma*?]-*am ullilāma* [*š*]*amê ša Anim ibbašši râmum eli nišī iḫappup râmum liḫpupam ina ṣeriyia.*

217 Moussaieff Love Song obv. 1 (№ 11): *i*[*na a*]*lākišu iššakkan nawartum*. See also rev. 3: *libbī liwwir*, "May my [he]art be bright!" and rev. 7: *anāku ina bītim lumaḫḫirka nawār kabattim kuzbam tartāmam*, "I, in the house, let me make you accept happy (lit. bright) mood, attractiveness, mutual love". Finally, note obv 13: *šarūrū libbini*, "gleaming of our heart", referring no doubt to the male lover.

218 A 7478 i 11–14 (№ 1): *birqū ša* ᵈ*Adad ina ṣērišu mā ibta*<*riq*> *birqum ša ṣīḫātim elīya kīma šubultim ša lā simānim.*

219 A 7478 iii 30–31 (№ 1): *nannārika amma*[*r*] … *zīmīka lūmur.*

220 The male lover is compared to the bird in a broken passage in A 7478 ii 4, and iv 26 (№ 1).

221 PRAK 1 B 472 ii 9'–11' (№ 13): *šipruk līlika* [...] *šipruk līlikamm*[*a* ...] *lušme šulmaka anā*[*ku* ...] *iṣṣūrum tušūdi li*-[*ša*?-*na*?-*am*?].

delights: "By day-light – there are joyful calls of the duck. When the night has gone I have pursued her".[222] The combination of twittering sounds and flapping wings, characteristic of small birds, offers a powerful metaphor for the agitation of the impatiently loving heart: "I (Text: he) awoke to the noise of swallows, writhed in (my) bedroom on the bed. The lov[e-charm] returned into m[y hear]t!",[223] and similarly: "My bedroom (is) like twittering (birds); my mind went crazy."[224] The sound of a bird may, however, be that of sorrow and despair, as seen in an incipit from KAR 158 (№ 19): "Oh bird, my mourning dove(?), your(f.) voice is (like that of) a wailer".[225]

The literary motif that birds may be carriers of meaningful messages[226] rests on the Mesopotamian notion that it is possible to identify human words in the calls of certain birds. The famous birdcall text from Sultantepe (Lambert 1970b) and the Sum. myth Nanše and the Birds (Veldhuis 2004) demonstrate this notion well.[227]

## 6.4 Looking at the Object of Desire: Another Motif of Separation

More than ten years ago Goldhill (2002, 374) announced that "The erotics of the gaze is a hot subject. 'The look' has become a privileged site for articulating the tensions and ambiguities of how 'erotic experience' is conceptualized in contemporary society".

In ALL too the intricate semantics of the act of seeing warrants separate discussion. My starting point is the observation that the three main verbs of seeing in the corpus, *amārum*, *naṭālum* and *naplusum*, are always connected to the relationship between the lover and the beloved. Put differently, the lovers in ALL seem to be looking only at their objects of desire, and at nothing else.[228]

---

222 Moussaieff Love Song obv. 9 (№ 11): *alālū paspasim urriš mūšītum illikma anāku erdēši* (and see also rev. 5).

223 CUSAS 10, 8: 20–23 (№ 2): [*arrig*]*im šinūnūtim eggeltâm* [*in*]*a uršima agrur ina mayyālim ittūram iri*[*mmum*] *ṣēriš kab*[*tātiya*]. See also A 7478 iii 19 (№ 1) (broken context).

224 Moussaieff Love Song obv. 10 (№ 11): *uršī kīma ṣabrātim kabattī imḫi*. See also Panayatov 2013, 293: 30.

225 KAR 158 vii 34' (№ 19): *iṣṣurtu titkurrī lallaru rigimki*. The bird name *titkurru* (CAD T 435) is a hapax. The abrupt context of the incipit does not permit any identification. Translation is therefore provisional.

226 An interesting twist on this motif is found in the myth of Anzu. In Anzu II 18, 135, III 113 we read: "Let the winds carry his wings as good tidings (*bussurtu*)". In this case the bird, i.e. Anzu, the "bad guy" in the plot, cannot function as the messenger of good news. Hence, the winds take on the role of bearers of good news, in the form of the dead wings of the flying monster (cf. Enūma eliš IV 132 = Lambert 2013, 92–93).

227 A later parallel to this ancient Mesopotamian notion comes from the Renaissance, where parrots in art works were seen as announcing the arrival of the Virgin Mary by pronouncing "kaire", translated to Latin as "ave" (S. Cohen 2008, 49–50). Already Pliny, in his Natural History (Book X, Chap. XLII) describes the parrot as the bird which "salutes emperors", by uttering "ave!". A similar tradition shows up in a Hebrew text known as "Chapter of Song" (Pereq Shirah) which lists the names of different animals, each of which praises god with a different verse from the Bible (see the Jewish Encyclopedia online, s.v. Shirah, Pereḳ (Pirḳe): http://www.jewishencyclopedia.com/articles/13588-shirah-perek-pirke, retrieved 4.3.2014).

228 Only once a goddess looks at the city of Babylon: MIO 12, 52–53: 3' (№ 10): *tappal*[*is B*]*ābili ina*

This situation recalls the erotic gaze in Greek romantic novels, where "penetrating and longing gaze... [are] a kind of copulation" (Goldhill 2002, 378), with one significant difference: the protagonists in the corpus of ALL look at the beloved *solitarily*, never reciprocally. In other words, seeing and looking in the corpus of ALL is an expression of unrequited desire. If in Achilles Tatius' *Leukippe and Cleitophon* (2nd cent. AD), a tale in the Greek romance genre in the Roman era, "the eye was 'ambassador of love'", in the corpus of Akk. love-related compositions the eye is a 'beggar of love'.

A woman who is in love with a disdainful man complains: "I talk about you constantly, I am consumed, I am troubled, I am distorted(?), I craved you again – (and) became distressed. I saw your face: you are a god!"[229] Another case describes a series of actions, the climax of which is the moment at which the woman looks at the neglectful male lover: "I shall embrace him, I shall kiss him, I shall gaze at [him], I shall achieve my victory over [my] sl[anderers]".[230] The same text continues with the despairing woman's complaint: "My eyes are very tired, I am sleepless from gazing at him...".[231] A woman in another text implores her capricious lover: "I am looking at your luminosity... Let me see your radiance!"[232] One of the lovers, perhaps the man, in the Moussaieff Love Song, expresses the will to see the beloved in metaphorical terms: "Let me see the orchard of the *almond* trees!",[233] and a love incantation describes the agony of the woman who is unable to catch hold of her lover's gaze: "Where goes your(m.) heart? Whereto l[oo]k your(m.) eyes? To me [may your(m.?) heart go!] At me [may your eyes look!] Look at me as [...] See me ... [...]".[234] A girl, in another love incantation, is determined to end her misery and finally gain her beloved. Her words end not with a wish for an anticipated physical encounter, but for eye contact with him: "I have torn the thorn, I will be sowing a vine! I have poured water onto the fierce fire. Love me as your lamb, encircle me as your small cattle. Look at me!"[235]

Seeing the spurning beloved is the highpoint of yearning; even Ištar's amatory pursuit of Dumuzi reaches the point at which she sees him (before losing him again): "Ištar saw the beloved which she was seeking *in*(!) the hut of the 'Lord of Oath' and said to him...".[236] An incipit from the Assur catalogue recounts the first glance of a beloved, the moment at which a burning emotional and sensual attraction is triggered: "Lad, since I have seen [you]".[237] Another incipit, from Babylon, depicts a similar scene: "Let me look at you(m.)

---

*īnīša dam*[*qātim*], "She looked on Babylon with her kind eyes ...".

229 CUSAS 10, 9: 14–17 (№ 3): *adabbubkama kayyamān aklāk dūwāku ewêku šanîš uzammīka ātašuš pānīka āmur ilāt*(*a*).

230 ZA 49, 168–169 ii 23–ii 26 (№ 16): *eddiršu anaššiq*[*šu*] *attanaplas el*[*šu*] *akaššad irnittī ... eli dā*[*bibātiya*].

231 ZA 49, 168–169 iii 20–21 (№ 16): *anḫā īnāya danniš dalpāku ina ittaplusišu.*

232 A 7478 iii 30–31 (№ 1): *nannārika amma*[*r*]... *zīmīka lūmur.*

233 Moussaieff Love Song rev. 2 (№ 11): *lūmur kirî lammī.*

234 ZA 75, 198–204e 62–67 (№ 31): *ayyiš libb*[*ak*]*a* [(x x)] *illak ayyiš ina*[*ṭṭalā*] *īnāka yâšim l*[*i*...] *yâti l*[*iplu*]*s* x x [...] x [*amr*]*anni k*[*īm*]*a*? x x [...] *ittaplasanni...*

235 MS 3062: 7–16 (№ 23): *assuḫ bāštam azarru karānam ana išātim ezzetim mê ašpuk kīma puḫādika rāmanni kīma ṣēnim nasḫiramma amranni.*

236 LKA 15 obv. 5 (№ 9): *īmurma Ištar narāma iše*ʾʾ*u ana gupri bēl tamātima issaqqaršu.*

237 KAR 158 vi 26' (№ 19): *eṭlu ištu āmuru*[*ka*].

by the light of the windows!".[238] And finally, a group of women, a chorus perhaps, express in unison their urge to see the beloved – in this case the king Rīm-Sîn of Larsa: "…we are praising his appearance (lit. seeing him), (as) in ancient times…",[239] and still in the same composition a woman is described as glancing at the unattainable king: "She looked on your features…".[240]

Two things should be noted. First, in each of the above examples it is the woman who is looking at the man,[241] and secondly the man, the object of the longing gaze, is not returning the gaze: he is either unaware of it, or deliberately ignoring it. There is no mutuality in the process of seeing; the gaze is not an intimate act which binds the lovers, rather it reinforces a sense of separation, even the isolation of the gazer. This point is made perfectly clear in a dialogue where a desirous woman is looking at the man she loves, and concludes sadly: "The boy is not aware of the (girl) watching him".[242]

Where men are the subjects of seeing, their gaze is different: it is not so much focused on the woman they crave, but rather it is turned inward, focused on their own despair and longing. A man separated from his girl complains: "[One who has] a loved-one chases (lit. sees) a dream",[243] meaning that love is not looking at a real person, but at a phantom. And he continues with a hypothetical question, claiming that if this situation of painful separation was intended by the gods, then lovers could not exist (lit. "be seen"): "[Had] Ištar schemed this affair lovers could not [ever] be seen!".[244] The gender-power paradigm, expressed through the dynamics of seeing, is rarely inversed. In the following lines the woman ignores, even rejects, the man who is looking at her: "I raised my voice to her, but she did not turn to me, I gazed (at her) but she did not look at me".[245] It is not accidental that this line comes from one of the love incantations, a group of texts in which women seem to embody a less submissive social role, different to other texts found in the core group in ALL. The active role of the female lover in love incantations is thrown into relief in two cases from the Isin tablet of love incantations, where the man is manipulated to look at the woman and thus submit to her sexually: "Look(m.) at me and be rejoiced like a harp!…",[246] and "When you see me be soothed(m.) like (one who drinks) beer…".[247]

Here a comparison of our corpus with the sex omens studied by Guinan is illuminating. Two consecutive omens in Šumma ālu read: "If a man keeps looking at the vagina of his woman, his health will be good and his hand will obtain things that are not his", and "If a man, while being with a woman, she keeps looking at his penis facing

---

238  CUSAS 10, 12: 6 (№ 18): *luppalsakka innūr apātim*.

239  YOS 11, 24 i 15 (№ 15): *ana amārišu nizammeru ištu ullam*.

240  YOS 11, 24 ii 8 (№ 15): *zīmīka iṭṭul*.

241  But note the doubts regarding the sex of the gazer in Moussaieff Love Song rev. 2 (№ 11).

242  CUSAS 10, 9: 4 (№ 3): *ul īde mārum nāṭilassu*. Interestingly, this motif is found also in archaic Greek poetry, and our line has a counterpart in Anakreon 360, where the beloved is similarly not aware of the desperate eyes focused on him: "Boy with girlish eyes, / you hardly seem to notice / my efforts to catch you, oblivious / charioteer of my soul" (trans. Mulroy 2002, 131).

243  CUSAS 10, 8: 14 (№ 2): *[rāš]i rāʾimtim nāṭil šunātim*.

244  CUSAS 10, 8: 16 (№ 2): *[šumm]an iškun dIštar šipram anniam [immat]īm ay in<na>amrū rāʾimū*.

245  YOS 11, 87: 4–5 (№ 26): *assīšimma ul itūram āmuršima ul ippalsam*.

246  ZA 75, 198–204a 24–28 (№ 27): *amrannima kīma pitnim ḫuddu*.

247  YOS 11, 21c 28 (№ 25): *ina amāriya kīma Seraš napšera* (and cf. ZA 75, 198–204e 66–69).

him,[248] whatever he finds will not remain in his home". Guinan (1997, 466) summarizes these two omens, saying:

> Omens 4 and 5 turn on the understanding that "seeing" is an act of taking. Power is wielded by the subject who looks at another. To be the object of look makes one vulnerable and exposed… the man's looking is an obtrusive act. It is based on the proper relationship between male subject and female object and is auspicious… (The) bold looking designates a man who reaches out and takes.

The same attitude towards the female gaze is found in a physiognomic omen which reads "If (a woman) is constantly looking at her husband, her husband will regularly fornicate with another man's wife".[249]

It turns out that a woman enticing the man to look at her, as depicted in the two love incantations cited above, "follows the notion of the canonical series which sees only the masculine gaze as auspicious". The dominant power paradigm, as expressed in the act of seeing, is made clear in a passage from the OAkk love incantation MAD 5, 8 (№ 22), where the excited male suitor uses magic in order to catch, to physically control, the eyes of the resisting woman: "I have seized now your drooling mouth (lit. "mouth of sap"), I have seized your shining eyes, I have seized your urinating vulva (lit. "vulva of urine")".[250] The scene, in fact, is not far from rape.

On the background of these comments we can appreciate how unusual YOS 11, 87 (№ 26) is. In this love incantation the man is looking at the woman – seemingly following the power paradigm found in Šumma ālu – but his gaze, like his desire, falls short, and he does not obtain what he wants. Looking in this case is a sign of weakness, not of superiority, and the party that ignores the loving look is the dominant one.

Table (4): *Appendix 1: Semantic Field of Love and Lovemaking*

| **Word** | **Translation** | **Texts** |
|---|---|---|
| *bēlum* | lord, master | ASJ 10, 18: 13; CUSAS 10, 10: 37; PRAK 2 C 125: 2, 4; YOS 11, 24 i 11, ii 2; KAL 3, 75 iii 8'; KAR 158 i 22', v 5'(?); ZA 49, 168–169 [iii 23], iv 16 |
| *dādum*, pl. *dādū* | darling, favorite (in pl. sexual attractiveness) | A 7478 i 2; ASJ 10, 18: 13; CUSAS 10, 8: 6; CUSAS 10, 9: 24; KAR 158 vii 11'; MAD 5, 8: 32; MIO 12, 52–53: 1, 9, 10; Moussaieff Love Song obv. 2, obv. 7; PRAK 1 B 472 i 6'; YOS 11, 24 i 23, i 31; YOS 11, 87: 8 |
| *ḫabābum*/ *ḫapāpum* | to murmur, chirp, twitter, to be amicable | CUSAS 10, 9: 32 |

248 For *šutātû*, see CAD Š/3, 399.

249 Böck 2000, 167: 231: *šumma ittanaplas mussa* (var. DAM-*su*, probably intending *aššassu*) *aššat amēli ittanayyak*.

250 MAD 5, 8: 12–16 (№ 22): *āḫuz pâki ša rūqātim āḫuz burramāti ēnīki āḫuz ūrki ša šīnātim*.

| Word | Translation | Texts |
|---|---|---|
| *ḫarmum* | lover, consort | JAOS 103, 26–27: 1, 2; KAR 158 i 6', ii 4' |
| *ḫāwirum* | husband | PRAK 2 C 41: 4' |
| *ḫībum* | beloved | ZA 49, 168–169 iii 17 |
| *inbum* (also in App. 2: Flora) | fruit, flower, sexual appeal | CUSAS 10, 10: 30; CUSAS 10, 8: 10; CUSAS 10, 9: 23; Fs. Renger 192–193 i 2; MIO 12, 52–53: 8'; PRAK 1 B 472 i 7'; VS 17, 23: 3; YOS 11, 24 i 23, i 31; ZA 49, 168–169 iii 10, iii 11 |
| *irʾemum*/ *irimmum* | charm, love-charm | CUSAS 10, 10: 3; CUSAS 10, 8: 22; KAR 158 v 4'; MAD 5, 8: 1, 3, 30; MIO 12, 52–53: 11'; YOS 11, 24 i 2; YOS 11, 87: 1; ZA 49, 168–169 [ii 12] |
| *kuzbum* | attractiveness, sexual appeal | MIO 12, 52–53: 9; 14'; Moussaieff Love Song rev. 7 |
| *lalûm* | exuberance, sexual charm | KAR 158 ii 50', vii 52'; MIO 12, 52–53: 1, 15'; Moussaieff Love Song obv. 2 (in *appi lalêm*), rev. 6, rev. 12; PRAK 1 B472 i 10'; YOS 11, 24 i 24 |
| *mārum* | son, boy, darling | KAR 158 i 37' |
| *menûm* | to love | KAR 158 viii 4'; YOS 11, 24 i 21 |
| *murtâmum* | lover | KAR 158 ii 7', vii 7'; PRAK 1 B 472 ii 16' |
| *narāmum* | loved one | CUSAS 10, 9: 27; Fs. Renger 192–193 i 21, iii 27'; JAOS 103, 26–27: 10; MIO 12, 52–53: 3, 13', 14 Renger 192–193 iv 10'; MIO 12, 52–53: 7, 8; YOS 11, 24 i 7, i 26, i 30; ZA 49, 168–169 ii 6, [i 27], iv 10' |
| *rāmum* | loved, beloved | Fs. Renger 192-193 i 1, i 6, i 11, [i 25], iv 14''?, iv 17' |
| *râmum* | to love, to make love | A 7478 iv 35; ASJ 10, 18: 12; CUSAS 10, 9: 27; CUSAS 10, 10: 7; CUSAS 10, 11: 5, 6; CUSAS 10, 12: 7; CUSAS 10, 8: 6; Fs. Renger 192–193 i 21, iii 27'; Fs. Renger 192–193 iv 14''?; JAOS 103, 26–27: 10; KAR 158 i 5', ii 9', ii 41', vii 29', vii 43; KBo 36, 27: 20'; MIO 12, 52–53: 3, 13', 14', 9, 10, 18', 22'; YOS 11, 24 i 5, i 25; YOS 11, 87: 23; ZA 49, 168–169 i 11, i 23, [ii 5], ii 18, iii 8, iii 12, iii 19, iv 8; ZA 75, 198–204a 29; ZA 75, 198–204c 50, 51 |

| Word | Translation | Text |
|---|---|---|
| *ra'īmum*, f. *ra'īmtum* | loved, beloved | A 7478 ii 25, ii 28; ASJ 10, 18: 7; CUSAS 10, 10: 7, 34; CUSAS 10, 8: 14, 17; CUSAS 10, 9: 20, 27; Fs. Renger 192–193 iv 10'; MIO 12, 52–53: 7, 8; YOS 11, 24 i 7, i 26, i 30; ZA 49, 168–169 ii 6, [i 27], 10 iv |
| *ra'ūmtum* | beloved | KAR 158 vi 22' |
| *ritūmum* | lovemaking | Fs. Renger 192–193 iv 5'; MIO 12, 52–53: [3] |
| *ru'āmum* | lovemaking, seductiveness | A 7478 iii 32; KAR 158 ii 8'; ZA 49, 168–169 i 30 |
| *ṣiāḫum* | to laugh, to be alluring | CUSAS 10, 8: 2; KAR 158 ii 7', vii 7', vii 41' |
| *ṣīḫtum*, pl. *ṣīḫātum* | laughter, flirtations, amusements, delights | A 7478 i 13, ii 12, ii 15, iii 9, iii 13, iii 18, iii 26, iv 36; CUSAS 10, 8: 3, 13; Fs. Renger 192–193 i 8, i 13, i 19; KAR 158 vii 3', vii 35', vii 37', vii 44'; Moussaieff Love Song obv. 11; YOS 11, 24 i 4; YOS 11, 87: [27]; ZA 49, 168–169 iii 13 |
| *ṣūḫum*, *ṣuḫḫum* | laugh, laughter, love play | YOS 11, 24 i 4 |
| *šudātum* | lover | JAOS 103, 26–27: 20 |
| *tarāmum* | beloved one | KAR 158 vii 38' |
| *tartāmum* | mutual love | Moussaieff Love Song rev. 7 |

Table (5): *Appendix 2: Semantic Field of Flora*

| Word | Translation | Texts |
|---|---|---|
| [*armannum*] | apricot? (a tree) | Fs. Renger 192–193 i 4 |
| *amurdinnm* | bramble? | ZA 75, 198–204d 53 |
| *ašūḫum* | pine-tree (kind of) | KAL 3, 75 ii 8 |
| *ballukkum* | tree;<br>an aromatic substance | PRAK 1 B 472 i 8' |
| *baštum* | a spiny plant | MS 3062: 7 |
| *burāšum* | juniper | LKA 15 obv. 7 |
| *eqlum* | field, terrain | CUSAS 10, 10: 28, 39; Moussaieff Love Song rev. 5 |
| *erēnum* | cedar (a tree) | CUSAS 10, 12: 33, 34; KAR 158 vii 28'; MAD 5, 8: 29 |
| *girimmum* | fruit (a kind of) | A 7478 iii 16; VS 17, 23: 2 |

| **Word** | **Translation** | **Texts** |
|---|---|---|
| *gišimmarum* | date-palm | KAL 3, 75 ii 4 |
| *ḫašḫūrum* | apple (a tree) | A 7478 i 8; Fs. Renger 192–193 i 4 |
| *illūrum* | flower (red?) | KAL 3, 75 iii 4'; LKA 15 obv. 3; Moussaieff Love Song obv. 13 |
| *inbum* (also in App. 1: Love) | fruit, flower | A 7478 i 10; CUSAS 10, 10: 30; CUSAS 10, 8: 10; CUSAS 10, 9: 23; Fs. Renger 192–193 i 2; MIO 12, 52–53: 8'; Moussaieff Love Song obv. 12, obv. 13; rev. 5; PRAK 1 B 472 i 7'; VS 17, 23: 3; YOS 11, 24 i 23, i 31; ZA 49, 168–169 iii 10, iii 11 |
| *iṣum* | tree, wood | JAOS 103, 26–27: 8; LKA 15 obv. 3 |
| *kanaktum* | tree (incense-bearing) | MAD 5, 8: 5, 10; PRAK 1 B 472 i 8' |
| *karānum* | vine, wine | CUSAS 10, 8: 9; MS 3062: 8; YOS 11, 24 i 18 |
| *kirûm* | plantation, orchard | KAR 158: vii 26'; vii 28'; vii 35'; vii 38'; MAD 5, 8: 9, 17; Moussaieff Love Song rev. 2, rev. 5 |
| [*nurmûm*] | pomegranate | LKA 15 obv. 2 |
| *qištum* | forest, wood | LKA 15 obv. 4; ZA 75, 198–204d 53 |
| *sissinnum* | spadix (of a date-palm) | PRAK 1 B 472 i 11' |
| *ṣarbatum* | poplar (a tree) | MAD 5, 8: 19 |
| *ṣippātum* | orchards, plantations | Moussaieff Love Song rev. 12 |
| *še'um* | barley | Moussaieff Love Song rev. 5 |
| *šubultum* | ear of barley | A 7478 i 14 |
| *šūmum* | garlic | ZA 75, 198–204i 112 |
| *taltallûm* | pollen, stamen (of date-palm) | KAL 3, 75 ii 6 |
| *taskarinnum* | boxwood (a tree) | MAD 5, 8: 21 |
| *tibnum* | straw, chalf | A 7478 ii 6 |
| *uḫinnum* | fresh dates | KAL 3, 75 ii 4 |
| *zassarum* | vegetable (a kind of) | ZA 75, 198–204h 102 |

Table (6): *Appendix 3: Semantic Field of Domestic Fauna*

| Word | Translation | Texts |
|---|---|---|
| *alpum* | bull, ox | CUSAS 10, 12: 17; ZA 75, 198–204i 113 |
| *atānum* | she-ass | MAD 5, 8: 24 |
| *būrum* | calf | A 7478 iii 22; YOS 11, 87: 22 |
| *enzum* | goat, she-goat | MAD 5, 8: 23 |
| *immerum* | sheep (mostly m.) | KBo 36, 27: 16' |
| *kalbatum* | bitch | CUSAS 10, 10: 43 |
| *kalbum* | dog | JAOS 103, 26–27: 11, 15; ZA 75,198–204a 10, 21, 35; ZA 75, 198–204d 57; ZA 75, 198–204h 107 |
| *kalumtum* | lamb (f.) | MAD 5, 8: 23 |
| *kalūmum* | lamb | JAOS 103, 26–27: 30 |
| *laḫrum* | sheep, (mostly f.), ewe | MAD 5, 8: 23 |
| *mīrānum* | puppy, young dog | ZA 75, 198–204h 106 |
| *mūrum* | bull (young), foal (of donkey or horse) | MAD 5, 8: 24 |
| *paspasum* | duck | Moussaieff Love Song obv. 9, rev. 5 |
| *puḫādum* | lamb | MAD 5, 8: 23; MS 3062: 12 |
| *ṣēnum* | flock (goats and sheep) | JAOS 103, 26–27: 29, 31; MAD 5, 8: 22; MS 3062: 14 |
| *šaḫûm* | pig | ZA 75, 198–204a 21; ZA 75, 198–204d 58; ZA 75, 198–204i 110 |

Table (7): *Appendix 4: Semantic Field of Wild Fauna*

| Word | Translation | Texts |
|---|---|---|
| *allallum* | bird (a kind of) | CUSAS 10, 12: 4 |
| *arwûm/armûm* | gazelle (m.) | CUSAS 10, 12: 12; ZA 49, 168–169 iii 3 |
| *ašnugallum* | snake (a kind of) | CUSAS 10, 11: 8 |
| *būlum* | animals, livestock | LKA 15 obv. 2, 6 |
| *ḫuduššum* | frog | PRAK 1 B 472 i 12' |
| *iṣṣūrum* | bird | A 7478 ii 2; KAR 158 vii 33'; PRAK 1 B 472 ii 11' |
| *iṣṣūr ḫurri* | rock partridge | A 7478 iv 26 (perhaps also ii 2) |
| KIN$^{ku6}$ | fish (a kind of) | ZA 75, 198–204h 101 |
| *lābatum* | lioness | KAR 158 i 13' |

| **Word** | **Translation** | **Texts** |
|---|---|---|
| *nūnum* | fish | ZA 75, 198–204a 23 |
| *pīrum* | elephant | CUSAS 10, 12: 9 |
| *rīmtum* | cow (wild) | CUSAS 10, 11: 9 |
| *rīmum* | bull (wild) | CUSAS 10, 12: 12 |
| *samānum/ šamānum* | weevil | CUSAS 10, 10: 14; ZA 49, 168–169 i 7 |
| *sisûm* | horse | CUSAS 10, 12: 28 |
| *sukannīnum* | dove, pigeon | Fs. Renger 192–193 i 9, i 17 |
| *summatum* | dove, pigeon | Moussaieff Love Song obv. 14(?) |
| *šinūnūtum* | swallow (a kind of) | A 7478 iii 19; CUSAS 10, 8: 20 |
| *titkurrum* | bird (a kind of) | KAR 158 vii 34' |

Table (8): *Appendix 5: Semantic Field of Fabricated Objects*

| **Word** | **Translation** | **Texts** |
|---|---|---|
| *anṣabtum* | ring, earring | PRAK 1 B 472 i 9' |
| *aptum* | window | CUSAS 10, 12: 1, 6; ZA 49, 168–169 iii 18 |
| *assammum* | goblet, drinking vessel | MAD 5, 8: 28, 29 |
| *bābum* | gate, entrance | ZA 75, 198–204i 117 |
| *daltum* | door | JAOS 103, 26–27: 7 |
| *dūrum* | wall, city wall, rampart | CUSAS 10, 10: 14; Or. 60, 340: 14; ZA 49, 168–169 i 7 |
| *eleppum* | boat | KAR 158 vi 17' |
| *eršum* | bed | CUSAS 10, 12: 36 |
| *ḫaṭṭum* | scepter | KAR 158 vii 33' |
| *ḫuršum* | storehouse (kitchen) | A 7478 i 3 |
| *indūrum* | water skin | KAR 158 ii 53' |
| *išḫilṣum* | shred (pot) | CUSAS 10, 10: 42 |
| *kakkum* | stick; weapon | KAL 3, 75 iii 8' |
| *makūrum* | processional boat | KAR 158 vi 17' |
| *mallatum* | bowl, dish | JAOS 103, 26–27: 5, 14 |
| *maturrum* | boat (kind of) | KAR 158 i 41' |
| *mayyālum* | bed, resting place | CUSAS 10, 8: 21; KAR 158 ii 51'; KBo 36, 27: 19'; YOS 11, 24 i 22 |
| *mešēltum* | whetstone | CUSAS 10, 12: 18 |

| Word | Translation | Texts |
|---|---|---|
| *munûm* | bed, resting place | Fs. Renger 192–193 [i 5]; PRAK 1 B 472 i 8' |
| *murammiktum* | washbasin | A 7478 i 5 |
| *namḫārum* | vessel (kind of) | LKA 15 rev. 3 |
| *našappum* | basket | Moussaieff Love Song rev. 4 |
| *nēbeḫum* | band, belt, sash | YOS 11, 87: 25 |
| *nīrum* (*imittum*/*šumēlum*) | yoke | Moussaeiff Love Song rev. 13 |
| *palûm* | staff (kind of) | ZA 75, 198–204i 112, 113 |
| *parakkum* | cult dais, sanctuary, chapel | KAR 158 i 12' |
| *paršīgum* | headdress, turban, keffieh | YOS 11, 87: 23 |
| *paruššum* | sharp stick, goad | Moussaieff Love Song obv. 8 |
| *pasuttum* (pl. *pasumātum*) | net | JAOS 103, 26–27: 22 |
| *patrum* | sword, dagger | CUSAS 10, 12: 18 |
| *pitnum* | musical instrument | ZA 75, 198–204a 24 |
| *quppum* | box, chest, cage | Fs. Renger 192–193 i 16 |
| *riksum* | knot, bond, contract | YOS 11, 87: 19 |
| *sangûm* | object/material (see Wassermann 2015) | VS 17, 23: 6, 7 |
| *sikkatum* | peg, nail, part of a lock | Fs. Renger 192–193 [i 23] |
| *sikkūrum* | bar, bolt | JAOS 103, 26–27: 6, 8 |
| *ṣulūlum* | roof, canopy, shelter | LKA 15 rev. 5 |
| *šēnum* | sandals, shoes | JAOS 103, 26–27: 21 |
| *šummannum*/*šummunnum* | halter, tether | YOS 11, 87: 21; ZA 75, 198–204a 36 |
| *tibbuttum* | musical instrument | MAD 5, 8: 26 |
| *ullum*/*ḫullum* (*imittum*/*šumēlum*) | neck ring, collar | Moussaeieff Love Song rev. 14 |
| *uppum* | tube, socket | ZA 49, 168–169 iii 18 |
| *uršum* | bedroom | Moussaieff Love Song obv. 10 |

Table (9): *Appendix 6: Semantic Field of Human Body and Body Parts*

| Word | Translation | Texts |
|---|---|---|
| *aḫum* | arm, side | YOS 11, 87:17 |
| *appum* | nose | CUSAS 10,8: 8; LKA 15 obv. 3; ZA 75, 198–204c 48, 49 |
| *appi lalêm* | 'tip of desire' (clitoris?) | Moussaieff Love Song obv. 2 |
| *bāmtum* | chest, thorax | Or. 60, 340:15 |
| *birkum* | knee | ZA 49, 168–169 [iv 4] |
| *būdum/pūdum* | shoulder | MAD 5, 8: 29; PRAK 1 B 472 i 10'; ZA 49, 168–169 [iv 20] |
| *būnum* | goodness, pl. face | KAL 3, 75 iii 5' |
| *eqbum* | heel | ZA 75, 198–204h 103 |
| *ḫallum* | thigh (upper) | PRAK 1 B 472 i 15'; ZA 75, 198–204a 22 |
| *ḫubbušum* | swollen up (human body part?) | ZA 75, 198–204a 36 |
| *ḫurdatum* | female pudenda | Or. 60, 340:11, 18; PRAK 1 B 472 i 13' |
| *idum* | arm, side | MAD 5, 8: 25 |
| *illātum/elliātum* | saliva | ZA 75, 198– 204a 9 |
| *imnum* | right (side); hand | KAR 158 vii 8'; YOS 11, 24 i 19 |
| *irtum* | breast, chest | PRAK 1 B 472 i 10' |
| *išarum* | penis | KBo 36, 27: 21' |
| *īnum* | eye | CUSAS 10, 12: 26; KAR 158 vii 42', vii 8'; LKA 15 obv. 4, rev. 4 ; MAD 5, 8: 14; MIO 12, 52–53: 3'; Moussaieff Love Song obv. 6, obv. 7; VS 17, 23: 7; YOS 11, 24 i 13; ZA 49, 168–169 iii 20; ZA 75, 198–204a 10; ZA 75, 198–204e 63 |
| *kabattum/kabtatum* | liver, mood, mind, intention | A 7478 ii 7; CUSAS 10, 8: 4, 10, 15, 23; KAR 158 vii 4'; Moussaieff Love Song obv. 10, rev. 7; ZA 75, 198–204a 34 |
| *kiṣallum* | ankle | CUSAS 10, 12: 10 |
| *lānum* | form, stature | MIO 12, 52–53: 12 |

| Word | Translation | Text |
|---|---|---|
| *libbum* | heart; inner body | A 7478 ii 26; CUSAS 10, 10: 7, 22; CUSAS 10, 8: 2, 5, 15, 18; CUSAS 10, 9: 8, 18, 32, 33; Fs. Renger 192–193 iv 10'; CUSAS 10, 13: 3, 7; KAL 3, 75 iii 11'; KAR 158 ii 22', ii 44', vii 39'; MIO 12, 52–53: 7, 8, [16']; Moussaieff Love Song obv. 6 (x2), obv. 7, rev. 3, rev. 4, rev. 10; PRAK 1 B 472 i 2'; VS 17, 23: 8; YOS 11, 21c 27; YOS 11, 24 i 8, i 17, i 20, ii 7; YOS 11, 87: 4; ZA 49, 168–169 [ii 17]; ZA 75, 198–204d 57; ZA 75, 198–204e 62; ZA 75, 198–204h 102, 104; ZA 75, 198–204i 120 |
| *liptum, lipittum* | mole | CUSAS 10, 10:19 |
| *muḫḫum* | head, skull | ZA 75, 198–204a 11, 23; ZA 75, 198–204i 109 |
| *pagrum* | body, self | ZA 75, 198–204i 116 |
| *pānū* | front, face | CUSAS 10, 11: 9; CUSAS 10, 9: 17; KAL 3, 75 ii 10; LKA 15 rev. 4; MIO 12, 52–53: 8'; ZA 75, 198–204a 10; ZA 75, 198–204d 55 |
| *pappum* | lock, strand of hair | Moussaieff Love Song rev. 8 |
| *pītum* | opening | KBo 36, 27: 18' |
| *purīdum* | leg | ZA 75, 198–204a 30; ZA 75, 198–204h 105 |
| *pûm* | mouth | CUSAS 10, 10: 33; CUSAS 10, 9: 29; JAOS 103, 26–27: 37; KAR 158 vii 47'; MAD 5, 8: 12, 32; Moussaieff Love Song obv. 6, rev. 5; PRAK 2 C 134 ii 6'; ZA 49, 168–169 iv 16; 75; 198-204e 71; ZA 75, 198–204h 100, 101 |
| *pî napšarim* | opening of the uvula | CUSAS 10, 12: 16 |
| *pûm ša šārātim* | 'mouth of hair' – female genitalia | ZA 75, 198–204a 16 |
| *pūtum* | forehead | CUSAS 10, 10: 19 |
| *qablum* | hips, middle | Or. 60, 340: 15; PRAK 1 B 472 i 12'; YOS 11, 87: 26; ZA 75, 198–204a 31 |
| *qerbītum* | center part of the body, loins | A 7478 iii 33 |

| Word | Translation | Texts |
|---|---|---|
| *qaqqadum* | head | YOS 11, 24 i 11 |
| *qarnum* | horn | YOS 11, 87: 2 |
| *qātum* | hand | LKA 15 rev. 6; MAD 5, 8: 28; PRAK 1 B 472 i 11', ii 12'; YOS 11, 87: 15; ZA 75, 198–204d 60 |
| *rebītum* | abdomen, groin, male genitalia | KAR 158 vii 49' |
| *rēšum* | head | PRAK 1 B 472 i 9'; YOS 11, 87: 24 |
| *ru'tum, ruḫtum* | spittle, saliva, sap | MAD 5, 8: 5, 10, 12; ZA 75, 198–204a 18 |
| *sāqum* | thigh | MAD 5, 8: 4 |
| *sūnum* | loin, lap | KAR 158 vii 48'; Moussaieff Love Song obv. 11; PRAK 2 C 30: 3' |
| *ṣalmum* | effigy, image, figure, statue | MIO 12, 52–53: 11 |
| *ṣawārum* | neck | MAD 5, 8: 35, 36 |
| *ṣurrum* | interior, heart | Moussaieff Love Song rev. 3 |
| *šaptum* | lip, rim | A 7478 iv 3; MAD 5, 8: 27; MIO 12, 52–53: 1; YOS 11, 24 ii 7; ZA 49, 168–169 ii 21 |
| *šassūrum/sassūrum* | womb | CUSAS 10, 10: 40 |
| *šārtum,* pl. *šārātum* | hair | A 7478 iv 2; ZA 75, 198–204a 16 |
| *šer'ānum/šir'ānum* | vein, artery, ligament, tendon, nerve, sinew | CUSAS 10, 12: 17; ZA 75, 198–204a 32 |
| *šēpum* | foot | ZA 75, 198–204c 49 |
| *šiknum* | form, appearance | KAL 3, 75 ii 10 |
| *šīnātum* | urine | MAD 5, 8: 16; ZA 75, 198–204a 17, 19 |
| *šīrum* | flesh, body | CUSAS 10, 10: 41 |
| *šumēlum* | left-hand | PRAK 1 B 472 i 13' |
| *šur'um/šūrum* (*šu-ri-ni*) | eyebrow | PRAK 1 B 472 ii 13' |
| *tulûm* | breast | PRAK 1 B 472 i 14'; YOS 11, 24 ii 5 |
| *ṭulīmum* | spleen | CUSAS 10, 12: 16 |
| *ubānum* | finger, toe | CUSAS 10, 12: 27 |
| *utlum* | lap | PRAK 1 B 472 i 4' |

| Word | Translation | Texts |
|---|---|---|
| *ūrum* | pudenda, nakedness | CUSAS 10, 12: 10; MAD 5, 8: 15; Or. 60, 340: 16; Moussaieff Love Song rev. 8; ZA 75, 198–204a 17, 19 |
| *ūrum ša šīnātim* | pudenda of urine, urinating vulva | MAD 5, 8: 15–16; ZA 75, 198–204a 17 |
| *uznum* | ear, wisdom | PRAK 1 B 472 i 9'; ZA 75, 198–204h 100 |
| *zappum* | bristle | ZA 75, 198–204d 59 |
| *zibbatum* | tail | YOS 11, 24 i 2; YOS 11, 87: 3 |
| *zīmum* | face, appearance | A 7478 iii 31; YOS 11, 24 ii 8 |
| *zumrum* | body; person | ZA 49, 168–169 iii 9 |

# The Corpus

## I. The Core Group of Akkadian Love Literature: Dialogues, Monologues, Descriptive Compositions

## № 1 The Lightning of Lovemaking Passed upon Me (A 7478)

Copy: below
Tablet Siglum: A 7478
Photo: below (all by Andrew Dix, Courtesy the Oriental Institute)
Edition: below (Figs. 1–10)
Collection: The Oriental Institute, Chicago
Provenance: Nippur? Sippar?
Measurements: 8.7x14.5x1.1 cm
Period: OB

**Introduction**

A 7478 is a two-columned whitish-yellow tablet. The accession files of the Oriental Institute inform that the tablet was purchased from a dealer who claims it comes from Nippur. This should be regarded with caution, as other tablets from the same lot are known to come from Sippar. In addition, the physical features of the Chicago tablet – its size, and its two columns arrangement – remind one of the famous love dialogue ZA 49, 168–169 (№ 16) which is documented as being unearthed in Sippar. And so, although the finding spot of the tablet remains unknown, Sippar seems a good candidate for its original provenance.

Despite its having been catalogued many years ago, A 7478 remained largely unknown to the academic community (two passages from it were, however, cited in the CAD, see in the commentary below).

It was Marten Stol who initially drew my attention to this unique text. Stol came across the tablet while working on administrative records in Chicago in the 1970s, and correctly identified it as a literary text. In February 2014, with typical generosity, he sent me his partial preliminary transliteration of the obverse. At my request, Walter Farber, curator of cuneiform tablets at the Oriental Institute, later granted me permission to copy and publish the tablet. I am grateful to these two colleagues.

The tablet is written in a cursive, but not inexperienced hand. It contains some cases of wrongly written signs, dropped signs, and dittography,[251] but the tablet is certainly not the work of a beginner-scribe. Epigraphically, A 7478 resembles other literary compositions of the early, or central OB period. Grammatically, however, it shows distinctive archaic features: mimation is found throughout and loc. adv. is attested.[252] More important is the writer's preference to attach prepositions to following nouns.[253] Epigraphically too, the tablet exhibits traits of early OB script. Note especially the archaic

251 See *ša sí-ma*!(Text: ZA)/*a-ni-im* (i 8), *na-na-ri-ka*?!(Text: RA) (iii 30), *ša-ar-ti-ka* {TI-KA} (iv 1).

252 *aṭṭulma ṣí-ḫa-tu-ka* (iii 9) and perhaps also *i-ta-na-ap-*<*ra*>*-š*[*u*] (ii 4).

253 E.g. *iḫḫuršim* (< *ina ḫuršim*, i 3), *ippan šattim* (< *ina pan šattim*, i 9), or *ikkala šubtī* (< *ina kala šubtī*, i 29). See also i 4, i 7, ii 10, ii 34, iii 4, iv 1, iv 36 but cf. ii 13 (*ana mīnim*).

*ud* sign[254] and the *la* sign.[255] Hence, I would cautiously suggest that the text is, at the latest, a product of the Hammurāpi era, perhaps based on an older original.

The tablet is in bad condition. The reverse is especially worn out and flakes are falling off. My copy and edition of the tablet which follow reflect the sad state of the text.

Two alternating voices appear in the text: a woman who is in love with a man, and a descriptive, third person voice, which – for the sake of simplicity – will be referred to as 'chorus'. Sometimes, as in the opening passage, a utensil and the woman talk to each other, exchanging questions and answers.

The poor condition of the tablet, especially its reverse, makes the flow of the text very difficult to grasp. It is nevertheless clear that the woman, the text's main protagonist, suffers emotional turmoil, probably because of the unpredictable attitude of her lover. Anger replaces passion, and reconciliation replaces anger. The most interesting part is the beginning, where the text describes the flurry of emotions, to which the infatuated woman is subject.

Obv.
col. i

| | |
|---|---|
| i 1 | [*u*]*z?-zu?-uk-tam li-di-na-*[*am?*⌉ |
| i 2 | *ù ḫi-me-tim da-d*[*i*]*-ka* |
| i 3 | *e-ru-ub i-ḫu-ur-ši-im* |
| i 4 | *i-ba-lum a-ka-lim ṣa-la-a-ku* |
| i 5 | [*m*]*u-ra-mi-ik-ti i-di-ni di-a-ni* |
| i 6 | *mi-nam ep-še*$_{20}$*-e-ti-i-ma* |
| i 7 | *i-ba-lum a-ka-lim ṣa-*⌈*la-at*⌉ |
| i 8 | *ki-ma ḫa-aš-ḫu-ri-im ša sí-ma*!(Text: ZA)-/*a-ni-im* |
| i 9 | *ša i-pa-an ša-tim it-bu-*⌈*ku*⌉ |
| i 10 | *i-ni-ib-šu i-ba-a-ú-m*[*a*] |
| i 11 | *bi-ir-qú ša* ^d^*Adad*(IM) *i-na ṣé-ri-/šu* |
| i 12 | *ma ib-ta bi-ir-qum* |
| i 13 | *ša ṣí-ḫa-tim e-li-ia* |
| i 14 | *ki-ma šu-bu-ul-tim ša la sí-/ma-ni-im*! |
| i 15 | *šu-pu-uk-tam it-tal-ku* |
| i 16 | *ù ki-ma e-re-eb* ⌈*ša-tim*⌉ |
| i 17 | *i-su-ú-ḫu lu/šu-*[x x] ⌈x⌉ x |
| i 18 | *im-ta-al-ku-ma* ⌈*it-ti*⌉ [x]-⌈x⌉-/*šu* |
| i 19 | *i-li-ku ḫa-ra-na-am* |
| i 20 | ⌈*a*⌉*-na-ku a-na ma-ri-im l*[*i-*x-x] |
| i 21 | x-⌈*ku?*⌉*-tam a-si* x (x) ⌈*i*⌉*-ni-i*[*m?*] |
| i 22 | ⌈*ú-la*⌉ *i-še-a-am* ⌈*a*⌉*-mi-*⌈*ni*⌉-x (x)] |
| i 23 | ⌈*ù? i-ta/ša*⌉*-a-* (vacant) [x] |
| i 24 | *it?-ta-*[0]*-bi-i-ma* [x (x)]-*uš* |

254 i 1, i 15, i 21 and passim.

255 i 22, i 29 and more.

| | |
|---|---|
| i 25 | *li-im-*⸢*ta-al?*⸣-[*ku?* x x] ⸢*i-na* x x⸣-*šu* |
| i 26 | *li-*⸢*li?*⸣-[0]-*ku-ma ḫ*[*a-ra-na-am*] |
| i 27 | ⸢*e?*⸣-⸢*le?*⸣-*qé* ⸢x x⸣ [x x x] |
| i 28 | *a* x x [x] ⸢*ki-tam*⸣ *lum-*[*nam?*] |
| i 29 | x x-*am i-ka-la šu-ub-ti* |
| i 30 | *li-*x-x *a-na i-lim da-a-a-nu* |
| i 31 | *ma-a-*⸢x⸣ x ki *le e? šu?-ma* |
| i 32 | *a za-*[x] x-*ši-i* |
| Lo. Ed. | |
| i 33 | [x? x?] ⸢*il?*⸣-*li-am* |
| i 34 | [x? x?] *ma-*x ⸢*bu?*⸣-*bu-tim* |
| col. ii | |
| ii 1 | [x (x)] *ta ti kum* ⸢*e*⸣-[*li-ia/šu*] |
| ii 2 | *ki-ma i-ṣú-ri-i*[*m* x x (x)] |
| ii 3 | *ša aš-*[*š*]*um ú-*⸢*um?*⸣ [x x x (x)] |
| ii 4 | *i-ta-na-ap-*<*ra*>*-š*[*u*] ⸢x⸣ [x x] x |
| ii 5 | *ki-ma za-bi-il ša-ḫa-ar-*[*ri*] |
| ii 6 | *ša ti-ib-ni-im lu-qú-ta-at* |
| ii 7 | *ka-ba-at-ti i-zi-za-*⸢*am?!*⸣ |
| ii 8 | *u*$_4$*-mu-um a-na pa-ša-ri-im* |
| ii 9 | *ki-ma wu-lu-*⸢*di!?*⸣*-im i-na-*⸢*ak?-ki*⸣*-ir* |
| ii 10 | *i-qí-im tu-še*$_{20}$*-ši-ba-an-ni* |
| ii 11 | *a-na-ṭá-al ša-pa-ra-a*[*m*] |
| ii 12 | *ša ṣi-ḫa-ti-ia i-ka-la-an-*⸢*ni*⸣ |
| ii 13 | *ù a-na mi-ni-im ki-ma kasap*(KÙ.BABBAR) |
| ii 14 | *ḫu-bu-ul-li-im* ⸢*tu?!*⸣*-s*[*a?/ga?*-x-x] |
| ii 15 | *ṣi-ḫa-a-ti a-na ṣa-ma-r*[*i*]-[*im?*] |
| ii 16 | *ù at-ta i-ṣa/za-*⸢x x⸣-⸢*ru?*⸣ |
| ii 17 | *i-ri-*⸢*iš?-tu?*⸣*-ka* |
| ii 18 | ⸢*i*⸣*-ta-la-ak-ma i-š*[*e-e*]*r* |
| ii 19 | $^{id}$Idigna *im-ma-tim-*⸢*ma?*⸣ |
| ii 20 | *i-ša-at-ti el-lu-tim me-*⸢*e*⸣ |
| ii 21 | ⸢*il?*⸣*-la-ak-ma i-*⸢*mu?*⸣*-tam* |
| ii 22 | $^{i[d]}$Idigna *im-ma-tim i-ša-a*[*t?-ti?*]*-am?* L[I] |
| ii 23 | *a-ḫu-la-ap-*⸢*ma?*⸣[*i*]*q?-bi?* [x x x] |
| ii 24 | ⸢x-x-*im*⸣ *ša i-li-k*[*u*] x x [x (x) (x)] |
| ii 25 | [x]-⸢*ub?*⸣ *rē'û*(SIPA)*-ma a-na ra-i-im-tim* |
| ii 26 | *u*$_4$?-x x ⸢*a-na*⸣ *li-bi te-er-ti-im* |
| ii 27 | *ba* ⸢x x x x⸣ *te* ⸢x x⸣ |
| ii 28 | ⸢*la? i?*⸣*-ha-*x x *ra-*[*i*]*-im-tim* ⸢(x)⸣ |
| ii 29 | *ma-ru?-ma a-*x-x (x) *le-qí* |
| ii 30 | [x x x] ⸢*za? zi?*⸣ x x *ši* x x |

| | |
|---|---|
| ii 31 | *ki-ša* x x x x x x x x (x) |
| ii 32 | ⌈*a?-ša?*⌉-*am?* ⌈*da?*⌉ x x x x x (x) |
| ii 33 | x x x x [x x x x x x] |
| ii 34 | *i-li-li-a-tim* [(x x x)] |
| ii 35 | x x x x [(x x x x x)] |

Rev.
col. iii

| | |
|---|---|
| iii 1 | (broken) |
| iii 2 | x [x x x x x x x x x] |
| iii 3 | *ki-ma?! a*-⌈*ar*⌉ [x x x x x x] |
| iii 4 | *i*-⌈*šu*⌉-*ti*(-)*ma* x [x x x]-*a-ši* |
| iii 5 | *it-ta-am* ⌈*da?-am?-qa?*⌉-*am* |
| iii 6 | *i*-x x x x x x |
| iii 7 | [x] *ša*-AK-*ti*-x [x x]-*bi-ka* |
| iii 8 | [x] *la? ú ta i-ši* [x (x)] x |
| iii 9 | ⌈*aṭ*⌉-*ṭú-ul-ma ṣí-ḫa-tu-ka* |
| iii 10 | *i?-ta* x x *i* x *am bi? il?*-x |
| iii 11 | *ar-ḫa-at?* x *ši im be*-x |
| iii 12 | *ú? šu-ti-šu it-ba?* x *šar?-ru?* |
| iii 13 | *be-lum e-ḫi-id-ma ṣi-ḫa-t*[*im*] / x ⌈*ri?*⌉ x |
| iii 14 | x x x x [ x x x x] |
| iii 15 | *k*[*i*] ⌈x x x x⌉-*am* [x x] ⌈x⌉ |
| iii 16 | *a-na ki* ⌈*gi?-ri-im*⌉ x [x x] x x |
| iii 17 | [x x x x] x *ša me-eḫ-r*[*u* x] x x |
| iii 18 | [x x x x] *ṣi-ḫa-tim i*-x [x x] |
| iii 19 | [x x x x] ⌈*ù*⌉ *ši-nu-nu?-tum?* [x x x] |
| iii 20 | [x x x x x] x x [x x] |
| iii 21 | [x x] *ṣi* [x x] x *a* [x x x] |
| iii 22 | ⌈*ki-ma*⌉ ⌈*bu?*⌉-*ri-im* x [x x x] |
| iii 23 | [x x] x x ⌈*ṣa*⌉-*aḫ*-⌈*ḫa*⌉ [x x x x] |
| iii 24 | *ki-ma?* x x ⌈*ṭì?-id*⌉-*di-im i*-[x x x x] |
| iii 25 | x x x x *a?* [x x x] |
| iii 26 | *ú-ṣa-am-ma a-na ṣi*-⌈*ḫa*⌉-*t*[*i-šu*] |
| iii 27 | *la i-na-di-na ka-ia-n*[*a?* x x] |
| iii 28 | *lu-uš-pu-ur a-ka-pa?*-⌈x-*ka*⌉ |
| iii 29 | *li-il-ka sú?*-⌈*ri?*⌉-⌈*iš*⌉ |
| iii 30 | *na-na-ri-ka*!?(Text: RA) *am-ma-a*[*r*] *im*-⌈*ri*⌉ |
| iii 31 | *zi-mi-ka lu-mu-ur* |
| iii 32 | *ù* ⌈*a-na*⌉-*ṭá-al ru-a-am* [x]-*ti? lu-pu-/uš* |
| iii 33 | *ba-ni qé-er-bi-i-tim* |
| iii 34 | x *re-ši* x-*eš-tum* |
| iii 35 | [x x] x x [x x] x x x |

Up. Ed.
iii 36 *i-na* x x ⸢*a*⸣*-bu-u*[*k*]
iii 37 *tu*!-⸢*uš*⸣*-ta-am-ri-iṣ*

col. iv
iv 1 ⸢*ša*⸣ *bi šu* (x) *i?-zi-iq-ni-ka*
iv 2 *ša-ar-ti-ka* {TI KA}
iv 3 *ša-ak-n*[*a*] *ša-ap-ta-a-a*
iv 4 ⸢*um?*⸣*-ma ša*!(Text: TA) *du-ri-im lu-pu-*⸢*uš*⸣ / AL
iv 5 *ù ma?-*⸢*ri* ⸣ <*i?*>*-qá-ba-an-ni*
iv 6 *ù ú-še-e*[*š-m*]*i-an-ni*
iv 7 *a-na um-mi-im ša* [x x]-⸢*ú*⸣
iv 8 *ù a-na* [x x x x x x]*-šu*
iv 9 *ša* ⸢*ak*⸣?-⸢*lu?* x⸣ [x x x-*t*]*im?*
iv 10 ⸢*ù*⸣ x x x x x x] x-*nam?*
iv 11 ⸢*ù?*⸣ [x x x x x x x]*-tim*
iv 12 ⸢x x x x x x x⸣ ⸢*ta?*⸣*-am*
iv 13 x x [x x x] a-x-⸢*ka? ra?-bi?-im?*⸣
iv 14 *tu?-*⸢*úr?*⸣ *te-*x x*-am ra?-*⸢*bi?*⸣-⸢*ka*⸣
iv 15 *ti-i-ba it-tu-*⸢*úr?*⸣-[(x)]
iv 16 *i-na šu* x *ma ta-*x-[x]-⸢*ni?*⸣
iv 17 *ù* x [x x x]-⸢*a?-ni?*⸣
iv 18 *ki-ma ši?* x-[x x x x]
iv 19 *ṣi-i-tam*!? *t*[*a-*x x x]
iv 20 [x x] *i-na* [x x x x]
iv 21 [x] *ti a wi* [x x x x x]
iv 22 *e ti-di-im* [x x x x x] / x-*ir*
iv 23 *ta* [x] x [x x x x]-ni
iv 24 *ki-i* x x [x x x] x x
iv 25 *ab* [x] *ma is* x *ti* x*-ri-*[*i*]*m*
iv 26 *ki-ma? i-*[*ṣu-ur ḫu-ri-im*]
iv 27 ⸢*il?*⸣*-li-*⸢*ik?*⸣ x *am?-ša*
iv 28 x x (x) *a-*⸢*na?*⸣ *mi-ma-šu*
iv 29 [x x] *ṣa-am* [x x] ⸢*ša?*⸣ x x / x x
iv 30 [x x] x x *is? úr?* x
iv 31 [x x x x] *ṣi-i-ru-*⸢*tim*⸣
iv 32 *i-ša-*x [x x x] *pa?-*⸢*am?*⸣
iv 33 ⸢*i-ta-na-bi-ra-ma*⸣

Up. Ed.
iv 34 *ù a-na-ku i-qá-*⸢*at*⸣
iv 35 [*r*]*a-mi-ka*

Left Ed.

iv 36 *i-qá-at <ṣi>-ḫa-ti-ka da-am-qá-tim a-ta-na-ḫa-az pu-uz-ra-*[*am*]

**Translation**

Obv.

col. i

i 1 (She:) *May he give me the …*
i 2 of ghee, your(m.) passion!
i 3 I entered into the pantry,
i 4 lying to sleep without eating.
i 5 My washbasin, when judging the judgment (said):
i 6 "Why are you doing so that
i 7 you are lying down to sleep without eating?"
i 8 (She:) Like a ripe apple,
i 9 which in the beginning of the year heaped up
i 10–11 its fruit, and the lightnings of Adad passed over it,
i 12–13 so, indeed, the lightning of lovemaking passed upon me –
i 14 like an ear of barley, which before its appropriate time
i 15 turned into a *heap* of grain,
i 16–17 and which (one) deducted as an *income of the year.*
i 18 (Chorus:) They took consult with each other
i 19 (and) took the road.
i 20 (She:) I … *my heart*(?) to the darling
i 21 … I have… *ey*[e]?
i 22 He is not seeking why …
i 23 And he…
i 24 he stood up(?)… in(?) him
i 25 (Chorus:) May they *confer*(?)… in…
i 26 May they take the r[oad].
i 27 (She:) I will *take*(?) …
i 28 … Justice, ev[il?]
i 29 … in all the dwelling places(?) …
i 30 May the judges ... to the god
i 31 …
i 32 …

Lo. Ed.

i 33 … *is going up*(?)
i 34 … hunger

col. ii

ii 1 (She?:)…
ii 2 like a bird [of …]

| | |
|---|---|
| ii 3 | which because of … […] |
| ii 4 | is constantly *flying* around... |
| ii 5 | Like a worker carrying a net |
| ii 6 | for straw you(m.) keep plundering little by little |
| ii 7 | my mood. *Stand by me*! |
| ii 8 | The day for reconciliation |
| ii 9 | is *difficult* (lit. hostile) like giving birth. |
| ii 10 | You have made me sit (tied) in string(s): |
| ii 11 | I am looking for a message |
| ii 12 | of my lovemaking, (but) he withholds (it) from me. |
| ii 13–14 | And why, as if it is money of debt, you… |
| ii 15 | (*Instead of*) *striving* for (my?) lovemaking? |
| ii 16 | And you(m.), they/he will…. |
| ii 17 | Your *desire*. |
| ii 18 | (Chorus:) He departed and went straight away. |
| ii 19 | Oh the Tigris-river, when |
| ii 20 | will he drink pure water? |
| ii 21 | He is walking *in the heat*(?) |
| ii 22 | The Tigris-river, when will he dri[nk]? |
| ii 23 | 'Mercy!' he said … |
| ii 24 | The… which went … |
| ii 25 | … the shepherd to the beloved-one(f.)! |
| ii 26 | ….. to the message |
| ii 27 | … … |
| ii 28 | He(?) should not … the beloved-one(f.) |
| ii 29 | The *darling*… |
| ii 30 | … … |
| ii 31 | … … |
| ii 32 | … … |
| ii 33 | … … |
| ii 34 | In the evening … |
| ii 35 | … … |

Rev.
col. iii

| | |
|---|---|
| iii 1 | [… …] |
| iii 2 | … … |
| iii 3 | (Chorus?:) Like … … |
| iii 4 | In a *dream*… … her |
| iii 5 | the sign, the good fortune … |
| iii 6 | he/she … … |
| iii 7 | (She?:)… … your(m.) |
| iii 8 | … … |
| iii 9 | When I gazed at your lovemaking |

| | |
|---|---|
| iii 10 | … … |
| iii 11 | (Chorus?:) She is quick … |
| iii 12 | *in*(!) his dream he *rose* … |
| iii 13 | Oh lord, pay attention and … the lovemaking. |
| iii 14 | … … |
| iii 15 | … … |
| iii 16 | … like a *fruit* … |
| iii 17 | … whose equal… |
| iii 18 | … lovemaking … |
| iii 19 | … and *swallows* … |
| iii 20 | … … |
| iii 21 | … … |
| iii 22 | Like a calf… |
| iii 23 | …*small*… |
| iii 24 | Like… of clay he… |
| iii 25 | …… |
| iii 26 | I am going out towards [his] lov[e-making] |
| iii 27 | (but) he does not give (it) to me regularly. |
| iii 28 | May I send to… *your*(?) … |
| iii 29 | May he come *soon*. |
| iii 30 | I am looking at your(! Text: my) luminosity … |
| iii 31 | Let me see your radiant face! |
| iii 32 | Indeed, I will observe – let me make love (to you), |
| iii 33 | Oh beautiful *of loins*! |
| iii 34 | … … |
| iii 35 | … … |
| iii 36 | In … … |
| iii 37 | you became troubled. |

col. iv

| | |
|---|---|
| iv 1 | (She:) … in your beard |
| iv 2 | (and) in your hair |
| iv 3 | my two lips are set, |
| iv 4 | saying: "let me build *that of a wall* …!" |
| iv 5 | Indeed, my darling *is proclaiming* me |
| iv 6 | and made me hear (it). |
| iv 7 | To (my) mother who … |
| iv 8 | and to his … |
| iv 9 | which … … |
| iv 10 | … … |
| iv 11 | … … |
| iv 12 | … … |
| iv 13 | … your *big*… |
| iv 14 | *Return the* … of your *big*… |

| | |
|---|---|
| iv 15 | Raise towards me! *He turned.* |
| iv 16 | In … … |
| iv 17 | And … … me |
| iv 18 | Like … … |
| iv 19 | *In the sunrise …* |
| iv 20 | … in … |
| iv 21 | … … |
| iv 22 | *You(f.) should not know…* |
| iv 23 | *You…* … |
| iv 24 | Like … … |
| iv 25 | … … |
| iv 26 | Like a rock-partridge |
| iv 27 | He went… her… |
| iv 28 | … *to(?) anything of his.* |
| iv 29 | … … |
| iv 30 | … … |
| iv 31 | … the exalted ones. |
| iv 32 | … … |
| iv 33 | They keep crossing over. |

Up. Ed. + Left Ed.

| | |
|---|---|
| iv 34–36 | And I, through your love and your good lovemaking I find refuge again and again. |

**Commentary**

i 1: One expects "may you give me…", but *liddina*(*m*), 3 sg. m., is clear. The last sign, read as -[*am*], could perhaps be -[*ki*-(*im*)], or less likely -[*ka*] (so Stol in his preliminary edition). – I cannot figure out what [*u*]*Z-Zu-uk-tam* is.[256] The following lines, which include *ḫimētum*, *dādū* and *ḫuršum*, hint that *uZZuktu* (if correctly read) is likely to be a desired edible substance or some positive abstract notion.

i 3–7: For the symptom of loss of appetite as a sign of lovesickness see § 4.3 above.[257] – For the topos of going to sleep on an empty belly, cf. The Poor Man of Nippur 42: "Daily I am lying to sleep without a meal".[258]

i 5: *murammiktum*, "washbasin", is attested so far only once in an OB dowry list. The text, I suggest, describes the infatuated woman in the kitchen, talking to the utensils around. One

256 If the reading is correct, two lemmas are possible: NA *ussuktu* (CAD U/W 281a), designating a negative concept whose meaning is unclear, and the lexically attested plant *ussuḫtum* (CAD U/W 280b). Neither seem to fit the context.

257 Another case of hunger in ALL is found in Moussaieff Love Song: obv. 4 (№ 11): *akūd arurtu'a*, "I got worried in my hunger".

258 Gurney 1956, 152–153: 42: [*ūmiš*]*amma ina lā mākālē bīriš ṣal<lā>ku.*

can imagine her looking at her own face reflected in the water of the washbasin. – *i-di-ni di-a-ni* is parsed *i*(*n*) *dīnī diāni*(*m*), "when judging the judgement (of love)", an infinitive construction with case attraction. The woman asked the washbasin to serve as an honest judge in the relationship with her lover, and the utensil expresses its amazement at the woman's behavior, viz. going to sleep without eating.

i 8: *kīma ḫašḫūrim ša sí-ma*!*-a-ni-im*:[259] Ripe apples are a known image in ALL,[260] but what about *sí-ma*!*-a-ni-im*? Are we to understand here *simanum* "season, proper time" (CAD S 268–271) or *simānum*, "name of the third month of the Babylonian calendar" (CAD S 271)? Charpin (1993–1994, 18b) suggested persuasively that the two lemmas, separated by the dictionaries,[261] are closely related, if not identical; the former carrying a general and abstract meaning, the latter semantically narrowed to a specific noun. Based on the material at hand,[262] one can say that *simānum* carries the abstract meaning of "proper, appropriate time", and only in those cases where the determinative ITI precedes it, the month name *Simānum* is intended. Hence, since no determinative is found in our line, the simpler choice would be to understand here "like an apple of the appropriate time".[263]

i 9: *pān šattim*: Spring is known to be the time of lovemaking,[264] but the first fruits were not necessarily considered good, as the following proverb proves: "early fruiting (brings) miserable crop".[265] It is to be noted in addition that in the beginning of the year – Nisan, i.e. March/April – apples are not ripe yet, as they have only finished their blooming. The text insinuates that the man is not really good for the woman; he seems sweet and ripe – but in fact not fully sweet or ripe. Loving this man – so the woman tells us – is not an easy task.

---

259 *sí-ma*!(Text: ZA)*-a-ni-im* is clearly a mistake. Rading *sisānum*, "locust", makes no sense, and *tazzizzānim*, "you (pl.) have stood in front of me…" (with *ta* instead of *ša*, which are clearly distinguished in this text) is also not good.

260 Fs. Renger 192–193 i 4 (№ 6) and KAL 3, 75 iii 5' (№ 8). Apples in Biblical love lyrics were treated by Paul 1997, 100. For apples in ancient Greek erotic spells, see Edmonds 2014, 288.

261 AHw 1044a also separates the two lemmas: *simānu*(*m*) I, "(richtiger) Zeitpunkt, Zeit" and *simānu*(*m*) II, "der 3. bab. Monat".

262 To what is collected in the dictionaries, see also the following OB sources (refs. Marten Stol): ARM 27, 2: 8, 41, 102: 23, 170: 29, FM II, 160 (no. 86): 14, FM 4, 30 n. 174 (A. 227), FM 7, 28 (no. 9): 19, FM 8, 55 (no. 11): 11–12, 84 (no. 25): 7, and Atraḫsis I 305 (Lambert/Millard 1969: 64–65). These references, and others, show that *simānum*, at least in OB, refers to the successful completion of regular cycles, be it in agricultural works, in the growth of barley, trees or plants, or in the preparation of meals.

263 Yet, late sources may perhaps indicate that our *kīma ḫašḫūrim ša simānim* could still be translated more concretely as "like the apple of the month of Simān". First, in the NA love dialogue of Nabû and Tašmetu, the month name of Simān is found in connection to the apple (see Livingstone 1989 [= SAA 3], 36 rev. 6: $^{giš}$ḪAŠḪUR $^{iti}$SI[G$_4$...]). Second, in a Selucid astro-magical text it is clearly stated that the 10$^{th}$ day of the month of Simān is the appropriate time to perform KI.ÁG.GÁ NÍTA *ana* MUNUS, "(the ritual to enhance) love of a man to a woman" (BRM 4, 20: 5–6 // BRM 4, 19: e–f (see Scurlock 2005–2006, 131 and now Geller 2014, 28 and 33). There was therefore a solid – albeit perhaps late – tradition according to which the month of Simān in particular is favorable for love between man and woman. This tradition may be present already in our OB text.

264 See YOS 11, 24 i 14 and i 18–19 (№ 15).

265 Lambert 1960, 279: 7: *inbu pān šatti mutḫummu nissāti*.

i 9–10 *ša …itbuku inibšu*: As *tabākum* is never intransitive, the acc. relating to this verbal form must be *inibšu*, in the next line (MPS).

i 10: *i-ba-a-ú-ma*: The use of *bâʾum* with light can be compared to its usage with fire (see AHw 117, 3e).

i 12: *mā ibtāʾ birqum*: Lightning is mentioned frequently in weather omens (see the index in Gehlken 2012 sub *birqu*). Most of the omens mentioning lightning are negative and portend bad. One of them is especially interesting, as it indicates that lightning is infelicitous for lovers: "If Adad thunders, and if the day clouds over and it rains, (and if) a rainbow arches and lightning flashes like fire from the south towards the north, Adad will make multicolored stones pour down, companions will part company, brothers will leave each other, wife and husband will be divorced".[266]

i 14: *kīma šubultim ša lā simānim*: The collocation with *lā simānim* makes it clear that the writer meant *šubultum*, "an ear of barley", not *šūbultum*, "gift, consignment". The same expression, only positively, is found in a love-related composition from Assur: "She is luscious like an *illūru*-flower of the field, like an ea[r of barley of] Ištar of appropriate shape".[267] The appearance of a premature ear of barley is mentioned as a negative sign in Šumma ālu: "If an ear of barley is seen before its appropriate time, the land will change its governor… the furrow will diminish its yield".[268] Finally, lightning and ears of barley (associated probably through their zigzag shape) are connected in some weather omens: e.g., "[If lightning] flashes and turns greenish, Adad [will…] the early barley".[269] Here too, lightning augurs bad luck.

i 15: *šupuktum*: The meaning of this lemma, unknown elsewhere, must be similar to *šipkum*, "accumulation, heap" (CAD Š/3, 70). – *ittalku*: The verb *alākum* is used here idiomatically with the meaning "to turn into…", similarly to *karmūtam alākum*, "to fall into ruins", *labīrūtam alākum*, "to grow old", or *muškēnūtam alākum*, "to become poor", etc. (CAD A/1, 315–316).

i 16: *erēb ša-tim*: Following M. Stol, I read here *erēb šattim*, connected to the adjecitival construction *šattum ēribtum*, "the coming year, the next year" (see Stol 2012b, 575).

i 17: *i-su-ú-ḫu*: Regardless of the unusual spelling, this verbal form must be derived from *nasāḫum*, either meaning "to deduct" (CAD N/2, 9, 5), or referring to the passing of time (Sum. ba-zal, CAD N/2, 10, 8).

266 Gehlken 2012, 73: 16–17.

267 KAL 3, 75 iii 11'–12' (№ 8): *asmat kī illūr ṣēri kī šubi[lte ša]* $^{d}$*Ištar ša simāni būni*.

268 CT 39, 5: 51: *šumma šubultum*(ŠE.DURU$_5$) *ina lā simāniša innamir*(IGI.DU$_8$) *mātu*(KUR) *šakinša išanni*(MAN-*ni*) … *šerʾu*(AB.SÍN) *billassa*(GUN-*sa*) *iḫarraṣ*.

269 Gehlken 2012, 131: 17.

ii 4: *i-ta-na-*AB*-š*[*u*]: As it appears, this is a *bašûm*-Ntn form (*ittanabšû*), but this rare form is unlikely here. Instead, the bird mentioned in ii 2 raises the tempting possibility to emend the text to *i-ta-na-ap-<ra>-šu*, "flying around, flying repeatedly". Yet another possibility is to read *ittanapšu*, a form of *epēšum*-Gtn (without umlaut, as *ittabīma* in i 24). Taking this option, the bird is not described as flying but as busy building its nest. (MPS).

ii 5–6: *kīma zābil šaḫar*[*ri*]: The phrase is cited in CAD Š/1, 81a. As I understand it, the woman complains (ii 7) that the man is not eager enough, or at least too slow, in his amorous advances. His reluctance is compared to collecting straw, a slow and tedious task.

ii 6: Plucking and collecting fruits and other vegetal items is metaphorically used in love literature through the ancient Near East, see Paul 1997, 107. (*luqqutat*: 2 sg. m. stative, standing for *luqqutāta*).

ii 7: *i-zi-za-am*?!: For this form of *izuzzum*-imp., one expects *izizam* (but by the end of the line I see *an-ni*). Alternatively, one could consider *ezēzum*, "to be angry", which would go well with *kabattum*, but this verb is inflected in the (u) class in OB, and only in the first mill. it joins the (i) class.

ii 8–9: *ūmum ana pašārim kīma wulludim inakkir*: This simile describes the difficulty in reaching reconciliation (ii 6–7). The metaphor of giving birth is found also in the Dialogue of Pessimism: "Giving (money) is (as nice) as making love to a woman, but getting (it) back is (as difficult) as having children".[270]

iii 4: The second sign looks different to the fourth one which is clearly *-ma*, hence *i-*[*ma*]*-ti-ma* (M. Stol) is less likely.

iii 12: The first worn sign looks more like *ú*, but *i* is not impossible. The latter would make better sense: *iššuttišu* (< *in šuttišu*), "in his dream".

iii 13: *bēlum e-ḫi-id-ma*: Reading by M. Stol. For other occurrences of the imp. *eḫid* (*naḫ*/*ʾādum*) see CAD N/1, 3b. The verb *naḫ*/*ʾādum* tends to appear in hendiadic constructions, and I assume that the main verb, whose acc. is *ṣīḫātim*, stood at the end of the line.

iii 19: *ši-nu-nu?-tum*?: Reading by M. Stol. Swallows are found also in CUSAS 10, 8: 20 (№ 2).

iii 22: *kīma būrim:* The same simile, "like a calf", is found in YOS 11, 87: 22 (№ 26).

270 Lambert 1960, 148: 67: *nadānu kīma râm*[*e sinniš*]*ti u turru kīma alādi mārū.*

iii 26: "Going out" in ALL carries the meaning of "promiscuous, being ready sexually", see commentary ad VS 17, 23: 3 (№ 24).
iii 29: *līlka sú?-[ri?]-[iš]*: If not *surriš*, "quickly, soon", one could derive this lemma from *ṣurrum*, "heart", as in Moussaieff Love Song rev. 3 (№ 11).

iii 33: *bani qerbītim*: When referring to the body parts, *qerbītum* (lit. "middle, interior") designates a part of the sheep's lungs or the womb (CAD Q 214). Here *qerbītim* refers to the man, rendering the central part of the male body.

iv 4: *ša dūrim lūpuš*: The (woman's?) intention to build a wall is not clear, but it may be compared to other cases where lovers express their will to lay siege to, or to encircle, their mate: "I shall lay siege to you",[271] and "I encircle (you) like a wife".[272] – The last sign of the line, appended at the end of the line below, is a clear AL, the meaning of which eludes me.

iv 5: From this point onwards the lines start to be slanted upwards.

iv 34–36 (Up. Ed. + Left Ed.): This sentence is translated in CAD P 557a: "do I not always seek refuge at the gracious hand of your beloved, man or woman?", but [*ra-im*]-*ti-ka*, suggested by the CAD, should be corrected to *<ṣi>-ḫa-ti-ka* (the signs are clear). The prepositional phrase *iqqāt* must be understood idiomatically as an *instrumentalis*, "through (the agency of)…, because of…", etc. A fine parallel to these ending lines comes from a love dialogue, where the woman useses the same sequence of *râmum* and *ṣīḫātum* preceded by *iqqāt*: "I seek [your] pleasures, my lord, I yearn for [your] love (*râmum*). Because *of* (*iqqāt*) your delights (*ṣīḫātum*)...".[273]

271 ZA 49, 168–169 i 27 (№ 16): *alawwīki nītam ina ṣēriki.*

272 CUSAS 10, 9: 13 (№ 5): *asaḫḫur kīma aštim.*

273 ZA 49, 168–169 iii 11–15 (№ 16): *asaḫḫur inbi[ka] bēlī zummāku râm[ka] iqqāt ṣīḫātuka….*

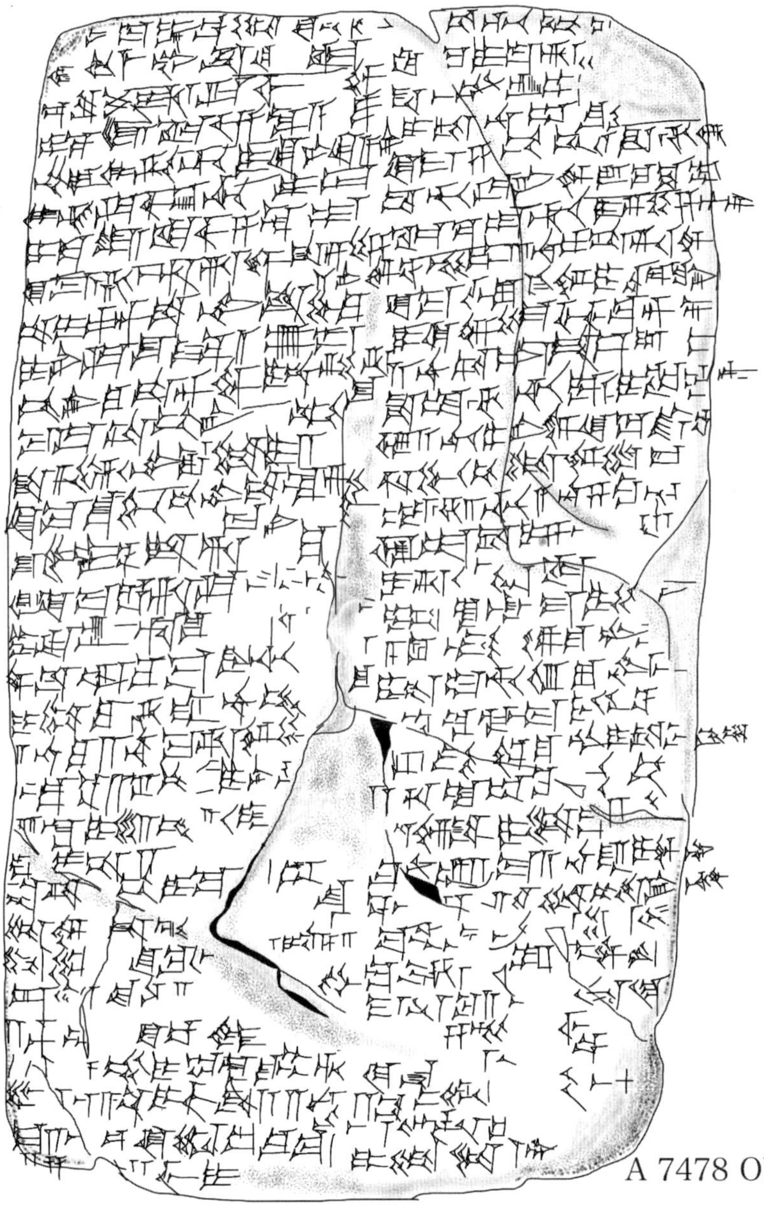

A 7478 Obv.

Fig. 1: A 7478 Obv.

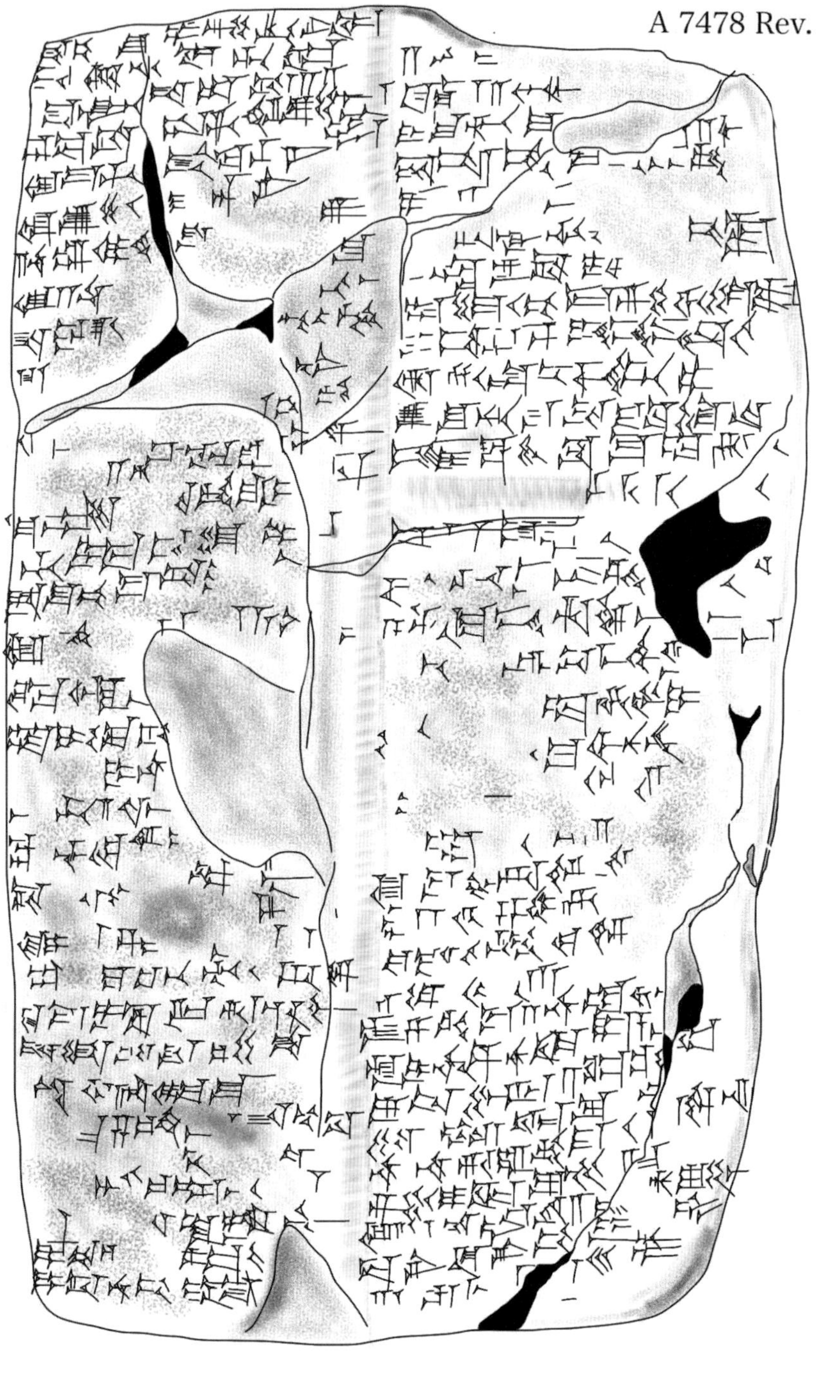


Fig. 2: A 7478 Rev.

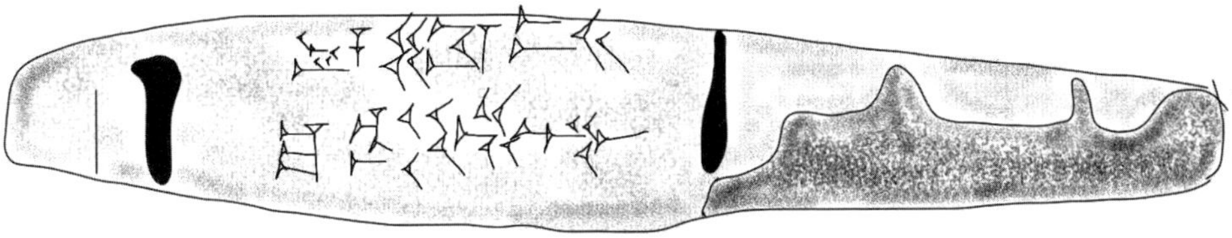

A 7478 Lo. Ed.

Fig. 3: A 7478 Lower Edge

A 7478 Up. Ed.

Fig 4: A7478 Upper Edge

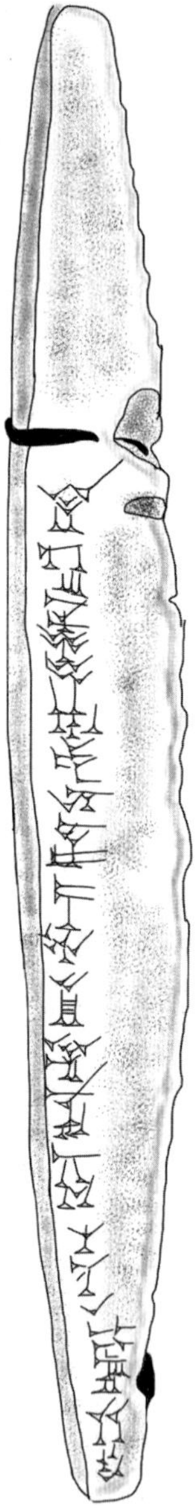

A 7478 Le. Ed.

Fig. 5: A7478 Left Edge

Fig. 6: A7478 Obv.

Fig. 7: A7478 Rev.

Fig. 8: A7478 Lower Edge

Fig. 9: A7478 Upper Edge

Fig. 10: A7478 Left Edge

# № 2 My Mood Plunged into the Infesting Heart (CUSAS 10, 8)

Copy: George 2009, Pl. XXII
Tablet Siglum: MS 2866
Photo: George 2009, Pl. XXIII, CDLI no. P251898
Edition: George 2009, 50–53
Collection: Schøyen Collection, Oslo
Provenance: Sippar?
Measurements: 11.5x5.8x2.7 cm
Period: OB

**Introduction**

This text, justifiably called 'lyric', concerns a male suitor who falls in love with a daughter of a person living far away (she is referred to as *rēqet*, "distant", l. 13). The text describes his despair and emotional ups-and-downs.

The following reasons suggest that this text, as CUSAS 10, 9 (№ 3), is an advanced draft composed by a consummate scribe: The hand is very cursive (e.g. *ka-ab-ta-ti*, l. 4, where *ab* and *ta* look very similar); the spelling is inconsistent (*li-bi*/*li-ba-am*, ll. 2, 5, 15, vs. *li-ib-bi*!, l. 18, which can be paralleled by the plene writing in *ap-pi*!*-im*, l. 8); the distribution of text to lines is not well calculated (ll. 1–4, 8–9), and the reverse is left almost entirely blank. If my suggestion that the text is a draft is accepted, it may explain two difficult lines – 10 and 19 – as failed compositional attempts which should be skipped over.

Obv.

| | |
|---|---|
| 1 | *ma-ar-ti a-la-ni* |
| 2 | *li-bi i-ṣí-ik* |
| 3 | *ṣí-ḫa-at a-li-tim it-ba-al* |
| 4 | *ka-ab-ta-ti* |
| 5 | *i-ša-al-li li-ba-am mu-ḫa-ti-tam* |
| 6 | *da-du-ša ra-mu mu-ḫa-ti-tu* |
| 7 | *ki-ma di-iš-pi-im ṭa-ba-at* |
| 8 | *a-na ap*!*-pi-í-im* |
| 9 | *ki-ma ka-ra-nim eš-še*$_{20}$*-et* |
| 10 | *in-bi-*<*ša*?> *ka-ab-ta-tu* |
| 11 | *ki-ma ba-la-ṭì-im sí-qí-ir šu-mi-ša* |
| 12 | *la še*$_{20}$*-bu* |
| 13 | [*r*]*e*?*-qé-et-ma ṣí-ḫa-as-sà mu-na-mi-ša-at* |
| 14 | [*ra-š*]*i ra-i-im-tim na-ṭi-il šu-*⌈*na*⌉*-tim* |
| 15 | [*ḫe-pí*?]*-ma li-bi sà-ab-sà-at ka-ab-ta-tum* |
| 16 | [*šum-ma*?]*-an iš-ku-un* $^{d}$*Iš*$_8$*-tár ši-ip-ra-am* ⌈*an-ni*⌉*-a-am* |
| 17 | [*i-ma-t*]*im*? *a-a in-*<*na*>*-am-ru ra-i-mu* |
| 18 | [*li-i*]*b-bi*!(Text: ŠE)*-ma i-li-iṣ i-wi-ir ka-ab-ta-ti* |
| 19 | [x x]*-ma ki-na-tum ḫar-du ù a-ri-ru* |

20 *[a-ri-g]i-im ši-nu-nu-tim i-ge-el-ta-am*
21 *[i-n]a ur-ši-ma-ag-ru-ur i-na ma-a-a-/li-im*

Rev.
22 *it-tu-ra-am i-ri-[mu-um]*
23 *ṣe-ri-iš ka-ab-[ta-ti-ia]*

**Translation**
Obv.
1–3 Daughter of an *exile* – my heart rejoiced; (she) took away the laugh of (my) mother.
4–5 My mood plunged into the infesting heart –
6 her lovemaking is an infesting love.
7 She is sweet as honey,
8–9 She is fresh like wine to the nose.
10 (My) mood is (*fixed on her*) fruits.
11–12 As life, mentioning her name is insatiable,
13 Though she is distant, her merriment sets in motion.
14 [One who has] a loved-one chases (lit. sees) a dream:
15 my heart [is broken], my mood is agitated!
16–17 [Had] Ištar schemed this affair, lovers could not [*ever*] be seen!
18 My he[art] rejoiced! My mood became cheerful!
19 ... is the truth. Restless and constantly trembling:
20–21 I (Text: he) awoke to the noise of swallows, writhed in (my) bedroom on the bed:

Rev.

22–23 The lov[e-charm] returned into m[y hear]t!

**Commentary**
1: Reading *a-la-ni*, from *ālānûm*, "an exile, person living abroad" (CAD A/1, 334b) seems preferable to *a-la-lí* suggested by George. This reading is orthographically simpler (*lí* is hardly used syllabically in literary texts) and it makes better sense than "Oh girl whoopee!". Reading *ālānûm* fits well the appellation *rēqet*, "distant", for the daughter (l. 13) and offers a good parallel to YOS 11, 87: 11 (№ 26), where the beloved woman is referred to as *mārtu awīlim*, "a daughter of a gentleman", and to CUSAS 10, 10: 17 (№ 4), where the woman is called *marāt pūḫi*, "a daughter of a substitute". A term designating a social status – *ālānûm*, "an exile" – is therefore expected here.

2: *i-ṣí-ik*: This form of *ṣâḫum* can be added to the list of cases of spirantized *k* in Streck/Wasserman 2008, 351–352.

4–6: With George (2009, 52) *mu-ḫa-ti-tam* and *mu-ḫa-ti-tu* are active participles forms of **ḫatātum*-D, denominative of *ḫuttutum*, "louse ridden (person)". Though "hardly an attractive image", as put by George, strong love is known to be considered an infectious disease in the literature of the ancient Near East. Note further that Heb. root √dbq denotes attraction by love and by leprosy (Gen. 2: 24, 34: 3; 2 Kings 5: 27). – The verb *šalûm*, "to submerge, to immerse in water", referring to being immersed in love, is found also in Moussaeiff Love Song (№ 11).[274]

7, 8–9: George parsed this passage to ll. 7–8 and 9. But honey, the sweet substance *par excellence*, is consumed orally. Wine, on the other hand, is odorous.[275] I prefer therefore to divide this passage differently: ll. 7, and 8–9. This division, with *…ṭābat …eššet*, 3 sg. f. stative, at the end of each sentence, results in a chiastic construction: *kīma* $X_1$ $stative_1$ … *kīma* $X_2$ $stative_2$. – It is to be noted that the male lover describes his beloved by referring to the faculties of taste and smell, not to sight. This, I believe, is another hint that she is far away, forcing the speaker to describe her using the two senses which keep her memory in his mind. – The collocation *inbum* and *eššum* is found in Moussaeiff Love Song obv. 12 (№ 11).[276]

10: *inbī<ša> kabatatu*: This elliptic sentence resists intepretation, hence my provisional emendation and translation. The line may in fact be a scribal mistake: once it is skipped over, the text runs smoothly with three parallel phrases, each of which is based on a comparison: [7]*kīma dišpim ṭābat* [8]*ana appim* [9]*kīma karānim eššet* [11]*kīma balāṭim siqir šumiša* [12]*lā šebû*, "She is sweet as honey, she is fresh like wine to the nose. As life, mentioning her name is insatiable".

12: *la še₂₀-bu*: "insatiable", referring to the sweet sensation caused by uttering the name of the beloved-one. For words tasting sweet in Akkadian literary texts, see Wasserman 1999.

13: *[r]e?-qé-et-ma*: George (2009, 52) derives this form from *raqûm*, "to hide" and translates "her smile is hidden(?) yet stirring to motion". I derive this verb from *rêqum*, "to withdraw, to go away, to depart", stressing the distance between the speaker and his beloved-one.

14: *[rāš]i rāʾimtim nāṭil šunātim*: The emotional see-saw that befall the one who is in love is compared to a dream. For this metaphor, see Overview § 6.1.

15: *[ḫe-pi?]-ma libbī*: I follow George's restoration. A broken heart, also in connection to anger, is found in an OB anger incantation: "It (anger) broke the bowl(?) of his heart".[277]

---

274 Moussaieff Love Song obv. 15 (№ 11): *gana lušalliam ludbu[b* x x x (x)]*-nu*?, "Come on! I want to plunge (into your love)! Let me tal[k (sweet words to you!)]".

275 For fresh, i.e. new wine, see Chambon 2009, 8–9.

276 Moussaieff Love Song obv. 12 (№ 11): *[u]rabbâkkum inbam ešša[m]*, "I will grow for you(m.) a new fruit!"

277 UET 6/2, 399: 10–11: *iḫpi qú-li-a-am ša libbišu*.

16: Ištar creating (*šakānum*) beloved creatures or love-affairs is also mentioned in YOS 11, 87: 4 (№ 26) and ZA 75, 198–204c 42–43 (№ 29).

16–17: George takes the these two lines together, translating: "[Supposing(?)] Ištar has set (me) this task, may no (other) lovers [ever(?)] appear!". There is no case in OB literature of a bi-partite irrealis conditional sentence with *ay* (only the negations *lā* and *ul* are found, see Wasserman 2012, 209). But since sentences with the enclitic particle *-man* do appear with precative forms (Wasserman 2012, 125f.), it is not surprising that the negation *ay* is also attested.

19: In spite of George's (2009, 53) hesitations, I suggest that *ḫardu*, "wakeful" and *āriru*, "trembling" (with AHw 65 "zittern"), describe the agitated lover in his bed.

20: The alliteration *nāṭil šunātim* (14) and *rigim šinūnūtim* (20) tell us that the man interprets the birds' sound as the woman's words of consent. For more on the motif of birds bringing a message of hope to desperate lovers, see Overview § 6.3. – *šinūnūtum*/*sinuntum*, "swallows" (Sum. sim$^{\text{mušen}}$, cf. Veldhuis 2004, 279f.) appear also in a broken line in A 7478 iii 19 (№ 1). – *i-ge-el-ta-am*: Another case of the prefix *i-* written instead of *e-*, within an *e*-voweled verb, is ARM 28, 106: 19: *u anāku i-še-eb-bi-ma* (MPS).

## № 3 My Fruits Are Unforgettable (CUSAS 10, 9)

Copy: George 2009, Pls. XXV–XXVI
Tablet Siglum: MS 5111
Photo: George 2009, Pl. XXIV, CDLI no. P254179
Edition: George 2009, 50–53
Collection: Schøyen Collection, Oslo
Provenance: ?
Measurements: 9.5x5.5x2.5 cm
Period: OB

**Introduction**
An emotional monologue of a woman in love, combined with a descriptive voice. Mimation is often omitted (George 2009, 54–55), but the use of epenthetic vowels (George 2009, 54), and the form of the signs *ma* (ll. 10, 13) and *la* (l. 15) seem to indicate an earlier date (note also the 3 sg. f. form *tūqâku,* l. 20). The text contains a number of scribal errors: signs are omitted (ll. 4, 10, 30, 32) and a word is wrongly written *ka-*$_{ma}$*-a-a-an* (l. 14). Note also the ungrammatical form WA-*ri-is* (l. 29). Taken together, these features indicate that the text, as CUSAS 10, 8 (№ 2), is a compositional draft.

Obv.
1 ⌈*a-na-ku*?⌉ [...]
2 *a-ša-ka-an?-ma* x x [x x]
3 *a-ta-i-da a-ta-*⌈*ṣa*⌉*-*[*a*]*r* [x] x / x x [x]
----
4 *ú-ul i-de* [*m*]*a-rum* ⌈*na*⌉*-ṭí-*<*la*>*-*⌈*sú*⌉
5 *a-ka-*⌈*ši-im*⌉ *ma-di-iš* ⌈*le*?⌉*-qá-*⌈*ku*!⌉
6 *ú-ul uš-t*[*a?-me*]*-eq a-na m*[*a-ma-a*]*n*
7 ⌈*ri*⌉*-š*[*a-ni*? *ḫu-u*]*m?-ṭám-ma* ⌈*na*⌉*-ra-mu-um*
8 [*li*?]*-bi* ⌈*i*⌉*-te-*⌈*eg*⌉*-ra-am du-*⌈*šu-up-ta*⌉*-ka*
----
9 *ú-um-ta-aš-ši a-wa-ti-ia*
10 *ṭe*$_4$*-mi* <*ú*>*-ul ṣa-ab-ta-*⌈*ak*⌉ *ki-ma* ⌈*šu*?⌉*-ti*
11 *pa-ni-ti-ia aḫ-sú-us*$_4$*-ma*
12 *ša šu-mu-ḫa-ak i-li it-ti-ka*
13 *a-sá-ḫu-ur ki-ma aš-ti-im a-*⌈*na*⌉ ⌈*la*?⌉*-a / ma-ka-*⌈*ki*?⌉
----
14 *a-da-bu-ub-ka-ma ka-*$_{ma}$*-a-a-*⌈*an*⌉
15 *ak-la-ak du-wa-ku e-wa-*⌈*ku*?⌉
16 *ša-ni-iš ú-za-mi-ka*
17 *a-ta-šu-uš* [*p*]*a-ni-ka*(-)*mu-ur*
18 *i-la-at* ⌈*ú-sé*⌉*-le-ka li-i*[*b*]*-/ba-ka li-ri-*⌈*ša*!*-ni*⌉

Rev.
19 *at-ta-a-ma mu-di-ti-i-ma*
20 *ù ra-i-ma-tu lu tu-qá-ku*
21 *na-as-qá-ku wa-aš-ra-tu ù a-ma-*[*tu*] / *e-li-k*[*a*]
22 *ki-tu-um ši(-)ia-ti it-ta-ka* ⸢*da*⸣-⸢*mi*⸣-*iq-ta*!
----
23 *in-bu-ú-a ú-ul ša mi-ši*
24 *da-du-ú-a ú-ul ša ka-ša-di*
25 *e-re-du-ku wa-aš-ra-ak*
26 *ù ši-ri-ik-ta-ka ra-mi-i-ma*
27 *ra-i-im-tu a-na al*?-[x-(x)]-*mu* / *i-la-am* [*t*]*u*-⸢*ši*?⸣-⸢*r*⸣*e*?-⸢*ma*⸣
----
28 *ia-ti im-ma ir-ti-qá-ni*
29 *i-na pi-ši-na ú-ul* WA-*ri-is ḫa*?!-*bi-bi*
30 *a-ki-la-at ka-ar-*<*ṣi*>*-i-a*
31 *ú-ul i-a-da-ra m*[*u-ši*] ⸢*ù ur*⸣-*ri*
32 *li-*<*iḫ*?>*-bu-ub a-a il-qé li-ba-*⸢*ka*⸣ / *sá-r*[*a-t*]*i*
----
33 *a-na li-bi-*[x (x)] x x x-⸢*tim*?⸣
34 *ma-da mi-*⸢*ma*⸣ [x] x-i *ma-l*[*i*?]
35 *ša* [x] x ⸢*ia-ti*⸣ *d*[*i*?-(x) x]

Up. Ed.
36 [x (x)] x-*ar ú-u*[*l* x x x] / x x [x x x]

**Translation**

Obv.
1 I am […]
2 I shall place […]
3 I shall be attentive, I shall watch out [...]
----
4 The boy is not aware of the (girl) watching him.
5 To you I am very much attracted(?),
6 I have not devoted myself to anyone:
7 Rejo[ice in me, co]me quickly, Oh beloved!
8 Your sweetness coiled around my [he]art(?).
----
9 I kept forgetting my words,
10 I cannot make my mind which is like a dream.
11 I think of the (girl) before me.
12 I who am blooming, my fate (lit.: god) is with you!
13 I encircle (you) like a wife, so that (you?) will *not become “stiff”*.
----
14 I talk about you constantly,

| | |
|---|---|
| 15 | I am consumed, I am troubled, I am distorted(?), |
| 16–17 | I craved you again – (and) became distressed. |
| 17–18 | I saw your face: you are a god! |
| 18 | I implore you: let your heart rejoice in me! |
| ---- | |
| | |
| Rev. | |
| 19 | It is you who *makes me flourish*, |
| 20 | Verily! a lover awaits for you! |
| 21 | I am chosen – submissive, indeed a slave for you! |
| 22 | Truthful she is: me – your favorite sign! |
| ---- | |
| 23 | My fruits are unforgettable, |
| 24 | My attractiveness is unattainable. |
| 25 | I will be suitable for you, I will be submissive to you, |
| 26 | Verily! My love is your gift! |
| 27 | A loving (girl) brings luck to .... |
| ---- | |
| 28 | At daytime (when) he went away from me – |
| 29 | Gossiping concerning me was not cut off from their (the other women's) mouth. |
| 30–31 | Those who slander me are not gloomy, day and night. |
| 32 | Let your heart be (*amicably*) thrumming, may it not accept the lies! |
| ---- | |
| 33 | To the heart ... |
| 34 | Many things my ... is full. |
| 35 | ... me ... |
| 36 | ... not ... |

**Commentary**

4: In an SB fable the fox is also "not aware" of the fact that he is being watched: "The hunter c[atch]es him who does not know who watches him".[278] On the meaning of seeing the beloved, see in the Overview § 6.4.

6: *emēqum*-Št, "to pray devoutly", fits here well. (Restoring a form of *niākum*-Š is not impossible, but this verb must be excluded due to its meaning).[279]

8: For *egērum* with acc. see, e.g., [*šumma*] *ṣerru amēla īgir*, "if a snake coils around a man" (KAR 385 rev 30, cited in CAD E 41b 1a).

278 BWL 216: 25: *ša lā īdû āmiršu bēl birkī i-ṣ*[*a*]-[*ba*?]-[t]a-[šú]. See Streck 2012a 791.

279 Rarely is the verb "to have illicit intercourse" found in love-related literature, cf. CUSAS 10, 12: 19 (№ 18) and MIO 12, 52–53: 12' (№ 10), but see the birth incantation YOS 11, 86: 1 and the discussion in Overview § 4.4.

10: Copy shows very little space for [*šu*?]-*ti*, but more space is seen in the photo.

11: The previous girl (*pānîtum*) is mentioned also in CUSAS 10, 10: 27 (№ 4).

13: George (2009, 57) translates: "I appeal (to you) like a wife, so as not to beg(?)". A possible clue to this difficult line may be found in ZA 75, 198–204c 46–47 (№ 29): "I will encircle you!... The wives hate their husbands".[280] It seems that the female lovers in both texts encircle (*law/mûm*, or *saḫārum*) their man in order to prevent his lawful wife from reaching him sexually. Note that *mag/kāg/kum* carries a meaning of getting stiff, referring to male erection (CAD M/1, 28a, 1b). Another instance of "encircling" in amorous context (this time using the rare verb *duārum*) is found in MAD 5, 8: 21–24 (№ 22): "Encircle(f.) me between the boxwood trees, as the shepherd encircles the flock, as the goat (encircles) its kid, the sheep its lamb, the mare its foal!". – The short form *aštim* (instead of *aššatim*) is found occasionally in OB, see CAD A/2, 462b lex. sec.

15: *e-wa-ku*: The cognate Heb. root √ʿwy, meaning "to twist, to be distorted (regarding sinning against god)" strengthens George's (2009, 58) understanding of this form as "tortured(?)".

18: *ilāt* (< *ilāta*): For the female-lover the man is a god (see also ll. 12 and 27). The same comparison is found in the harlot's words to Enkidu: "I am looking at you; you are like a god!".[281]

19: *mu-di-ti-i-ma*: This participle can be derived from *edēšum* (for the constant renewal of love, see Overview § 6.2), or from *dešûm*-D "to let flourish, prosper".[282] The floral image is preferred here.[283]

20: George (2009, 58) noticed that the particle *lū* opens an oath. The swearing formula, however, is introduced already by the particle *u*, which is not a conjunction but an exclamation, similar to the use of *waw al-qassam* in Arab., "*waw* of oath" (cf. also l. 26).

22: I take *ši*(-)*ia-ti* as a crasis of *šî* and *yâti* (George differently).

28–32: These lines refer to the slandering women (the *dābibātum*), prevalent in the love dialogue ZA 49, 168–169 (№ 16).

28: George understands this line as referring to the girls who accompany the female-lover. I prefer to see it as referring to the male lover who is leaving in the morning after a long

280 ZA 75, 198–204c 46–47 (№ 29): *alammika ... aššātum mutēšina izirrā*.

281 Gilg. II ii 53 (= George 2003 174–175): *anaṭṭalka Enkidu kīma ilim tabašši*.

282 The phenomenon of writing *š* with *t*, is mentioned in GAG § 29 b. This so-called spirantization of *t* is only sporadic, perhaps reflecting actual pronouncement, but certainly not regular. Groneberg 1971, 150–151 listed more such forms (some of them are, to my mind, simple scribal mistakes of *ta* written as *ša*).

283 A similar form is probably found in CUSAS 10, 13: 8 (№ 5).

night of lovemaking, causing the gossiping women to mock the woman (and therefore, *irtīqanni* not *irtīqāni*, as George suggested).

29: WA-*ri-is*: Perhaps WA is to be read with the rare OB syllabic value *pa*₁₂, as *paris*. – For *ḫa*?!-*bi-bi* cf. commentary to l. 32.

32: The precative form *li-*<*iḫ*?>*-b/pu-ub/p* in this line and *ḫa*?!-*bi/pí-bi/pí* (l. 29) are derived from *ḫabābum*, with its variant *ḫapāpum*, "to murmur, chirp, twitter, and also "to croon at". This clearly onomatopoetic verb designates differnet hissing, buzzing, or humming sounds. Here it designates the warm thrumming of the loving heart, while in l. 29 it refers to the murmuring of the gossiping women. George 2009, 70 (cf. also CUSAS 10, 11: 5, 6 (№ 20)) suggests to widen the semantic scope of this verb to mean also "to make love", but this, as far as the corpus here goes, is unnecessary. Whether *ḫabābum* is related to the verb *ḫâbum*, "to love" (AHw 306a, and *ḫībum*, "beloved", AHw 344b) is questionable, esp. as Arab. shows that the first consonant of the two verbs is different (so already George 2009, 59).[284]

284 On the irregular correspondence between Arab. *ḥ* vs. Akk. *ḫ*, see Kogan 2011, 84–85.

# № 4 I Scorn the Girl Who Does Not Adore Me (CUSAS 10, 10)

Copy: George 2009, Pl. XXVIII
Tablet Siglum: MS 3285
Photo: George 2009, Pl. XXVII, CDLI no. P252226
Edition: George 2009, 60–66
Collection: Schøyen Collection, Oslo
Provenance: ?
Measurements: 13.0x6.5x2.5 cm
Period: OB

**Introduction**

A monologue of a man talking scornfully to his former lover. She still loves him, but he left her for another woman, accusing her of disrespect and not being able to bear children. As recognized by George (2009, 60) a passage in the text (ll. 9–16) stands as a close-to-verbatim parallel to ZA 49, 168–169 (№ 16). The monologue is discourteous, even insolent, making use of colloquial idioms, some of which are difficult to construe (ll. 38, 39, 40–42, 43, 44). Based on grammatical features the text can be dated to the OB period. The close parallel to ZA 49, 168–169 (№ 16), a text which mentions Hammurāpi, strengthens this observation.

Obv.

1 *[e-ze]-⌈e⌉-er la ⌈mu⌉-sé-⌈ep⌉-[pi-tam]*
2 *⌈ú-ul⌉ a-ḫa-aš-ši-iḫ la mu-ka-⌈zi⌉-ib-tam*
3 *ú-ul a-na-ad-di-iš-ši-im i-ri-mi*
4 *a-ša-aq-qú el-ša*
5 *da-ba-bu-um a-na la ma-ga-r[i-i]m*
6 *mi-nam i-ba-aš-[š]i?*
7 *a-šar li-ib-bi ek-le-[tim a-na-a]n-di-in ra-mi*
8 *ú-ul ú-sà-an-na-qá-a[š/an-šu/ni ma-am]-ma-an*

----

9 *ḫu-uṣ-bi ez-bi ta-aš-t[a-ak-ni? q]ú-li*
10 *la ma-gal da-[ba-bu-um]*
11 *qá-bé-e qá-bu-um-m[a* x x x x]
12 *ú-ul e-n[i-a-ak-ki-i]m*
13 *ša a-na sí-in-ni-iš-t[im ip-pa-ra-qá-du]*
14 *sà-ma-an du-ri-im [šu-ú]*
15 *šum-ma la it-*[KU-*ud*]
16 *⌈ú-ul⌉ a-wi-lum m[i-ḫi-ir-šu]*

----

17 *ma-⌈ra?⌉-[a]t pu-ḫi wa-a[l-da-ti]*
18 *i-na [la] ši-ri-[ik-tim]*
19 *ti-ši-i li-⌈pi⌉-it-tam [i-na p]u?-⌈tim⌉*

20 *a-di* [*tu*]*-qal-la-l*[*i*] *ta-*[*ab-t*]*a?-aš-ši*
21 *lu-uq-bi-ki-im ša aš-*[*ri*]*-*[*ki*]
22 *ú-ul te-še*$_{20}$*-em-me-en-ni at-*[*ti*]
23 *wa-ar-ku li-ib-bi-i-ki*
24 *ú-*[*pe-e*] *ra-ak-ba-ti-i-ma*
25 *ru-ú-ʾa*$_{4}$*-am tu-uk-ta-na-aš-ša-di*
----
26 *e*[*t?*]*-qé-et a-li bu-ur sí-ḫi-i-ki*
27 *uṣ-ṣi-i-ṣi pa-ni-a-tim*
28 *ki-ma eqel*(A.ŠÀ*-el*) *id-ra-ni-im*
29 [*a*]*-ḫa-ad-du-ú ka-la-a-ma*
30 [*a*]*ḫ*!*-du-ú in-ba-am*
31 [*a-ḫ*]*a-*[*du-ú*] *ka-la-*[*a-ma*]

Rev.
32 *ù?* [...]
33 *pi-a-*[*am*] [...]
34 *ra-i-mu-u*[*m* ...]
----
35 [*la*] *ta*!(Text: ŠA)*-aš-ta-a*[*k-ka-ni* x x] x*-nu-um*
36 *a-na pa-ti-i-*[*ki ma-ma-an*] [*ú*]*-ul i-ṭe*$_{4}$*-eḫ-*<*ḫe*>*-ši*
37 *be-*[*la?*]*-ki e-ep-ši-e-et-ki*
38 *i-na* [*ṭa*]*-ab-tim la ta-ša-ak-ka-ni-*<*ni?*>
39 *eqel*(A.ŠÀ)*-ki*! *ḫu-uk-ku-um*
----
40 *ša la tu-ub*!*-lim i-na sà-as-sú-ri-i-ki*
41 *ki-ma še*$_{20}$*-er ni-ši ṭe*$_{4}$*-e-ma-am*
42 *a-na-ku iš-ḫi-il-ṣa-am a-la-a-at*
43 *ka-al-ba-tam ú-uš-ša-ar*
44 *la-i-im ab-nim a-na wa-ša-ri-i-ki*
45 *ma-ti qá-ba-a-*[*šu*] *li-iš-ku-un*
----
46 *šu-ur-ru-um-ma at-ti i-nu-ma iq-ri-ba-a*[*k-ki-im*]
47 *ki-ma* [d]*Bi-li-li ta-*[*du*]*-um-mi*
48 *ta-su-úr-ri* [*š*]*a-at-tu-ú-ri*
49 *a-na ṣa-la-li-im*
50 *te-em-mi-di ni-zi-iq-tam ra-ma-a*[*n-ki*]

**Translation**

Obv.
1 I scorn the girl who does not adore (me),
2 I have no desire for the girl who does not play up to (me),
3 I shall not give her (my) allures!
4 I shall stand over her!
5–6 Talking in order to disagree - why does it exist?

7 Shall I give my love where the heart of darkness is?
8 No one can control [me/it]!
----
9 Break off, leave! You ma[ke me speech]less,
10 (there is) not much to talk (about)!
11 What I said is said and [...]
12 I will not ch[ange it for y]ou!
13 The one who [lies down] for a woman,
14 is (nothing but) a weevil of the wall!
15 If he does not *th*[*rive*],
16 he is no match for a man.
----
17 You(f.) were born the daughter of a substitute,
18 with no dowry!
19 You have a mole on (your) forehead!
20 As long as you show no respect, pu[tting yourself] to shame,
21 I shall tell you where your (right) place is!
22 You do not listen to me, you.
23–24 (By) following your heart, mounting the clouds,
25 you keep chasing lovers away!
----
26 This goes over *(the limit)*! Where is the source of your rebellion?
27 Ask the previous women!
28 (You are) like a field of salt,
29 (can I) be happy with all (this)?
30 I was happy with the fruit,
31 (can I) be happy with all (this)?

Rev.
32 And [...]
33 mouth [...]
34 The loved one [...]
----
35 You should not put [...]
36 To your canal – no one will come near it!
37 Your lord, your task –
38 do not place (them) in the salt!
39 your field is all too well known!
----
40–42 The (fact) that you did not bring for me (good) news from your womb, as a baby of men – should I swallow (that) potsherd?
43 I will release the bitch!
44 One who bolts down a stone in order to release you,

45 when would he have his word?

----

46 Verily, you, when (somebody) came near [you],
47 you were convulsing like the goddess Belili,
48–49 you were dancing at dawn (*instead of*) sleeping.
50 You are imposing grief on yourself!

**Commentary**

5–6: *dabābum ana lā magārim mīnam i-ba-aš-*[*š*]*i*?: George (2009, 63) translates "Speaking up in order to disagree, how can that be shameful [on] her(?) account". If indeed the last sign is *ši*, then deriving the verb from *bašûm*, not *bâšum*, seems preferable: "talking in order to disagree - why does it exist?" The man is upset by the long and useless talking of the woman; he wants her to be compliant.

7: For the metaphor of light in ALL, see Overview § 6.2.

8: George (2009, 62) restores *ú-ul ú-sà-an-na-qá-a*[*š-šu mam*]*man*, but the sign before the break can just as well be *a*[*n*], hence perhaps *ú-ul ú-sà-an-na-qá-a*[*n-ni mam*]*man*, "no one will control m[e]!". The partial parallel line from ZA 49, 168–169 ii 19 (№ 16) strengthens this possibility: *mi-nam tu-sa-an-na-qá-ni-i*[*n-ni*], "Why do you (pl. f.) keep bothering [me]?".

15: *šumma lā it-*[KU-*ud*]: see commentary to ZA 49, 168–169 i 8 (№ 16).

17: *mārat pūḫi*: As a daughter of a substitute (*pūḫum*) – a man temporarily retained until another person returns his debt or completes his legal obligation, as going to a military campaign (see CH §§ 26, 33) – the woman is disrespected and not considered an integral part of the family, and therefore receives no dowry.

18: For *širiktum*, "dowry", in a similar context, see CUSAS 10, 9: 26 (№ 3).

20–25: This passage which describes the woman as disrespectful, following her heart thus bringing her man to shame, recalls the loose woman in CH § 143 who is "not guarded" (*lā naṣārum*), who "goes out" (*waṣûm*), and who disparages and belittles her husband (*bītam sapāḫum* and *mutam šumṭûm*).[285] The same picture of the bad woman emanates from omen literature, where some apodoses predict that, given specific physiognomic attributes, a woman will bring shame and damage to her husband in similar terms.[286]

24: *upê rakbātima*: The metaphor of clouds, used negatively, is found also in the love dialogue ZA 49, 168–169 i 28 (№ 16). The man threatens the unloved woman: "I shall gather my clouds on you".[287]

285 My thanks to Sofie Demare-Lafont for discussing these lines with me.
286 Böck 2000, 59.
287 ZA 49, 168–169 i 28 (№ 16): *urpīya akaṣṣar*.

27: For the notion of "the previous woman", cf. CUSAS 10, 9: 11 (№ 3).

28: *eqel idrānim*: The image of salt spread on fields may draw on real-life experience in Mesopotamia, where over-irrigated fields were known to become salinized. But more than an echo to a geographic phenomenon, this visual image, common in literary texts, denotes devastation, barrenness and dire want.[288] Since *eqlum*, "field", is a euphemistic term for the female sex organ (see Overview § 4.6), the man insults the woman twice: first hinting that she is infertile (cf. further commentary to ll. 40–41), and more subtly, that she is sleeping with many men.

40–41: *ša lā tublīm ina sassūriki kīma še$_{20}$-er nišī ṭēmam*: Assuming a crasis (*ki-ma ši-ir ni-ši* = *kīma āšir nišī*) George restores a verbal form <*tašakkanī*?> and translates: "You, who have not brought forth from your womb, you [impose(?)] (your) will like someone instructing the people". This difficult sentence can, I believe, be settled as it is. Lines 40–41 form a single complex phrase, opening with a object-relative clause (GAG § 165i), recapitulated by *ṭēmam* at the end of l. 41, all depending on the verbal form *lā tublīm*, "you did not bring for me". – Preceded by *ina sassūriki* I prefer reading *še$_{20}$-er ni-ši*, from *šerrum*, "baby", resulting in "baby of mankind", "a human child" (instead of the unclear *šīr nišī*, "the flesh of the people"). – A parallel to the idiom *ṭēmam wabālum*, referring probably also to a birth of a baby, is found in YOS 11, 24 ii 7 (№ 15): "Indeed, her lips are relaxed; she carries (good) news".[289]

42: *anāku išḫilṣam alât*: George translates ll. 42–43 as one couplet: "Must I swallow a potsherd and let the bitch go?". But it seems to me that the speaker *is* interested in getting rid of the woman (l. 43), and so I understand l. 42 as a rhetorical question whose answer is negative. The potsherd refers to the fact that the woman cannot bear a child. The difficult idiom "to swallow a potsherd" is, I suggest, a counterpart of the modern expression "to swallow a frog", referring to an event, or a fact, that is hard to accept.

44–45: *lāʾim abnim*: "Bolting down a stone" continues the image of "swallowing a potsherd" (l. 42). If understood correctly, the man declares that he must send away the woman now, for later it will be more complicated.

49: *a-na ṣa-la-li-im*: George takes it as *ṣallalum*, "night-owl". However, parallel passages suggest that this prepositional phrase is an infinitive *ana ṣalālim*, "to sleep": "Be(f.) awake at night-time! At day-time may you(f.) not sleep! At night-time may you(f.) not sit down!"[290], or "May she, like me, [be afflicted] with sleeplessness! May she be dazed and [restless] all night long!"[291] This negative description of the woman implies that she is

288 See CAD I/J 9b and Streck 2006–2008, 599. Especially revealing are the references from Atraḫasis (Lambert/Millard 1969, 78: 8 and 108: 48). A field sown with salt symbolizing the non-continuation of life in a conquered city is found in Jud. 9: 45.

289 YOS 11, 24 ii 7 (№ 15): *wašrā šaptāša ublam ṭēma.*

290 ZA 75, 198–204b 38–40 (№ 28): *dilpī mušītam urrī ē taṣlalī mūšī ē tušbī.*

291 ZA 49, 168–169 ii 8–9 (№ 16): *kīma yâti lā ṣalālum* [*lū emissi*] *kali mūšim likūr* [*lidlip*].

considered promiscuous (cf. ll. 28, 39). – For sleep as a key concept in ALL, see Overview § 6.1.

50: *temmidī niziqtam ramā*[*nki*]: A similar expression ends another OB dialogue between two disputing protagonists, the famous client and the fuller: "and you will cause a rash(?) to appear on your body".[292]

292 UET 6/2, 414: 41–42 ('At the Cleaners'): *ū teršītam pagarka temmid.*

# № 5 May There Be No Hindrance for Them (CUSAS 10, 13)

Copy: George 2009, Pl. XXXVII
Tablet Siglum: MS 2698/3
Photo: George 2009, Pl. XXXVII, CDLI no. P251711
Edition: George 2009, 76–77
Collection: Schøyen Collection, Oslo
Provenance: ?
Measurements: 5.0x7.0x2.2 cm
Period: OB

**Introduction**

The focus of this unusually written text, whose long lines continue from obverse to reverse,[293] is the goddess Ištar. The goddess is presented in her capacity as the divine overseer of love and sex.[294] As I understand it, the three opening lines of the text contain the requests of an envious woman, praying for the disruption of the steady amorous relations of a couple – probably a husband and his wife.[295] The successful results of such a prayer are echoed, e.g., in STT 257, a first mill. incantation and ritual addressed to Ištar, whose colophon is KA-inim-ma *sinništi ša mussa elīša šabsu*, "an incantation for a woman whose husband is angry with her".[296] This purpose is further amplified in the text, where one reads: "because he does not talk to me, because he is angry and does not speak with me…".[297] Similarly, the present text focuses on breaking the harmony between the man and the woman, directing divine help to disturbing the mutual understanding of the couple. The rest of the text glorifies Ištar with common epithets: she is the daughter of the moon god, the holder of world ordinances and the chief female deity of the pantheon.

1 [$^{d}$*S*]*în*(EN.ZU)*-ni-iš-tu-um ši-i it-ti a*?!-[*ḫa*?-*mi*?-*iš*? *la*] *da-am-qi-iš a-a* [*i*]-[*t*]*a-wu-ú*
2 *i-ša-a-at mu-ši-ti-im a-a* [*it*?-*ta-á*]*š*?-*qú-ú*
3 *mi-im-ma e-la-am ša li-*[*ib-bi-šu*]*-nu a-a íp-ta-aš-ru-ú*
4 *ti-iz-qá-ar-tum ma-ra-at* $^{d}$*Sîn*(EN.ZU) *ra-bi-tum*
5 *be-el-tum ša e-ni-im šu-tu-ra-at ma-an-nu-um it-ti-ki i-na*!(Text: TA)*-ma-*[*a*]*r*!
6 *i-pa-ar-ṣí ki-nu-tim bēltum*(NIN) *ra-bi-at be-li* [*ki*] *be-le-ti*
7 [*iš*]*-tu li-ib-bi-im e-*[*li-im*] [x x x] x *e-li um-mi-im wa-li-ti-ki*

---

293 In light of the discussion of the long lines of the Moussaieff Love Song (№ 11), this horizontal arrangmenet may be a sign of a later copying.

294 George 2009, 76 stresses the astral aspect of the goddess in this text.

295 The question whether a married couple would love each other or not, concerned also the physiognomical omen series Alamdimmû. Two consecutive omens in the series tell us that a cetain arrangement of hair on the forehead was an indication of whether a couple would love each other (*irtammû*), whether they would grow old (together), and whether happiness would prevail between them (Böck 2000, 85: 120–121).

296 Cf. Farber 2010, 74–77 and Abusch/Schwmer 2011, 372–374 (refs. Avigail Wagschal).

297 Farber 2010, 75: 6–7: *aššu lā itamma yâši aššu šabsuma lā idabbubu ittiya.*

|  |  |
|---|---|
|  | *šu-tu-ra-at* |
| 8 | *mu-de-*{UD}*-ši*! *eq-li-im* x ...] |
| 9 | [x x x x] x x [...] [*e*]*-lu-tim li-za-a*[*m-me-ru*] |
| (Gap) |  |

Up. Ed.

|  |  |
|---|---|
| 1' | *el-tum ki-it-tum ša pa-ar-ṣi*! |
| 2' | *šu-tu-ra-at ra-bi-iš ḫa-ma-ta*! *ṣí-ru-*[*tim*] |

**Translation**

|  |  |
|---|---|
| 1 | A woman she is! May they not talk favorably with *e*[*ach other*(?)]! |
| 2 | May they not [kis]s(?) [each other] in the course of night! |
| 3 | May they not tell each other whatever is pure in their hearts! |
| 4 | Oh exalted one, great daughter of Sîn! |
| 5 | The mistress of the *en*, you are superior: who can be seen next to you? |
| 6 | A lady through true ordinances, the great one of the lord, how majestic you are! |
| 7 | [*Conceived*(?)] from a pure *womb*, you surpass your bearing mother! |
| 8 | The *one(m.) that makes* the field *flourish*… |
| 9 | the pure … they will s[ing(?)]. |

Up. Ed.

|  |  |
|---|---|
| 1'–2' | The true goddess of ordinances, greatly superior, the head of the noble ones. |

**Commentary**

1: I follow George (2009, 77) in translating the first two words of the text as a nominal sentence "a woman is she!", referring to Ištar. (See his commentary on the unique exegetical spelling $^{d}$*Sîn*(EN.ZU)*-ni-iš-tu-um* and the use of the divine epithet *sinništum*, "woman", to goddesses.) However, contrary to George, the verb at the end of the line, *i-ta-wu-ú*, is in pl. (as are the verbs in the end of ll. 2 and 3), and consequently the subject of this sentence is very likely the couple. A corollary of the above is that *itti m*[*u-ti-ša*], restored by George, is hard to maintain (although, admittedly, the sign before the break does look as the beginning of *mu*). I cautiously put forward, therefore, that the text reads *itti aḫāmeš vel sim.*

2: *a-a* [*it*?*-ta-á*]*š*?*-qú-ú*: George reads *a-a* [*íp-pa-a*]*r*?*-ku-ú* and translates: "May she not fail (to appear) in the course of the night!", thus understanding that Ištar is conjured as the planet Venus. Yet, as suggested above, the subject of these lines is not Ištar, but a couple (in pl.), whose harmonious relations the speaker tries to break. Reading *ay ittašqū*, "may they not kiss each other" is therefore preferable (MPS).

3: Nocturnal talk in the sexual context was briefly discussed by Reiner (1990) who suggested that the expression *sinništa šudbubu* in first mill. rituals means to make a woman talk in her sleep so that "she will tell ... whether she has a lover, and who her lover is" (Reiner 1990, 422).[298] However, the reciprocate denotation of *iptašrū* excludes this interpretation, and makes it clear that the nocturnal talk in this case is the sweet verbal intimacy which welds the couple together. Note that all the verbs in ll. 1–3 are t-forms and all of them relate to actions done by the mouth (talking and kissing). The importance of verbal intimacy is mirrored, from the angle of male-focused domination, in Šimâ milka. There the man is advised not to reveal his heart to his wife, preserving thus her submissiveness: "Do not open your heart to your beloved wife (var. maid). (For otherwise) she will tell you 'Submit!' Even if she is furious, may you retain (your) gift in your sealed store house. Your wife should not know what's inside your purse".[299]

5: *innammar*: Copy and photo show clear *i-ta-ma-*[*a*]*r* which is a G pf. form. Yet this makes no sense here. The scribe had either N pf. in mind *ittanmar* (*i-ta-*<*an*>*-ma-ar*), or, more likely, N pres. *i-na*!*-ma-ar*.

7: The collocation *libbum ellum* plays on *mimma ellam ša libbišunu* (l. 3), only here it means, I believe, the physical designation of a holy womb.[300]

8: *mu-de-*{UD}*-ši*! *eq-li-im* x ...]: George translates "Those that thresh(?) the field", presumably from *diāšum*-D. I suggest, with caution, to read *mudeššû*, part. of *dešûm*, "to sprout", which is attested lexically only (CAD M/2, 163a "life-giver").[301] "Field" in this context may refer euphemistically to the female sex organ (see Overview § 4.6).

298 And see Scurlock (2005–2006, 126 n. 7) comment on this magical practice. Cf. the Biblical expression in Songs 7: 10 "And your mouth like choicest wine. Let it flow to my beloved as new wine, gliding over the lips of sleepers", which could be interpreted in accordance to Reiner's suggestion.

299 Y. Cohen, 2014, 90–91: 65–74: *ana aššati* (var. *ana amti*) *ra'īmtika ē taptâšši libbaka kunuš* (*iqabbi*) *lū šabsat lū tīšu nāmušta ina bīt kunukkika qereb kīsika aššatka ay ilmad.*

300 Cf. *illibbi*(?) *šūquri ibbû ilū šumšu zikru Anim lītelil rīm mātišu*, "(Still) in the precious womb the god summoned him. May the pronouncement of An be purified, the wild bull of his land!" (Guichard 2014, 12–13: 12–13).

301 For a possible similar form, see CUSAS 10, 9: 19 (№ 3).

# № 6 Where Is My Loved One? (Fs. Renger 192–193)

Copy: Groneberg 1999, 192–193
Tablet Siglum: MAH 16056
Photo: Groneberg 1999, 194–195, CDLI no. P424004
Edition: Groneberg 1999, 177–181
Studies: Wasserman 2003, Cat. No. 161, Nissinen 2001, 119–120, Foster 2005, 165–166, II 19.a, II 19.b
Collection: Musée d'Art et d'Histoire, Geneva
Provenance: Kiš?[302]
Measurements: 13.5x5.8 cm
Period: Late OB (Ammī-ditāna)

**Introduction**
A cursive and gracelessly written text, which contains, as its colophon states, four *irtum*-songs of the series "Where is my loved one, he is so dear" (*êš rāmī šūqur*). Neither the title of this series, nor any of its lines, are found in the Assur catalogue KAR 158 (№ 19). Unlike CUSAS 10, 12 (№ 18), the language of the text is metaphorical and not sexually bold, although its imagery is clearly erotic. The late OB dating of the tablet is secured by the mention of the name Ammī-ditāna, king of Babylon. Judging by the sharp angle of edge of the tablet seen in the photo, the tablet might have comprised more than two columns on each side.[303]

Obv.
col. i
i 1 [*e*?]-⌈*eš*?⌉ *ra-a-mi-i*° *šu*°*-qú-úr*
i 2 ⌈*ù*!⌉ *na-ši i-ni*!*-ib-šu-ú*°
i 3 ⌈*šu*/*ku*?⌉-[x (ras.)]-⌈*ul*⌉ *ú*?-⌈*ma*/*du*?⌉
i 4 ⌈*ki*⌉*-ma ḫa-aš-ḫu-ri* ⌈*si*?°⌉-⌈*ma*?⌉*-ni*
i 5 *ma-li ri-ša-a-tim m*[*u*]*-un*?° *m*[*i*?-x?]
----
i 6 *ra-a-mi a-*[*ṣe*°]*-ri*
i 7 *uš-ta-ṣi-a ù a-bi-à-*⌈*at*⌉
i 8 *ṣi-ḫa-ti-ia a-la-am-mi*
i 9 *ù sú*!(Text: BA)*-ka-an-ni-nu*
i 10 *uš-te-*(ras.)*e-li*
----
i 11 *ra-a-mi ša ṣe-e-ri ḫa-bi-i-lu*
i 12 *li-te-er-ru-ni-im-ma*

302 For Kiš as the original location of this tablet, which arrived at the museum from the antiquity market, see Groneberg 1999, 172.
303 Cf. Groneberg 1999, 176 n. 33. The text was collated from the excellent photo on CDLI no. P424004, confirming most of Groneberg's readings (collated signs are marked with °).

i 13 *ṣi-ḫa-ti-ia* [*ta°*]*-la-am-mi*
i 14 *ù° nu-ka-ri-ib°-bu*
i 15 *li-ib-la-am*
----
i 16 *qú-pí ad-di eṭ-la-am-ma°*
i 17 *ù sú-ka-an-ni-na*
i 18 [*lu°*]*-uṣ-ba-at-ma*
i 19 *ša ṣi-ḫa-ti-ia*
i 20 $^{d}$*Na-na*!(Text: ŠI)-*ia*!(Text: IṢ) *tu-ú-ma-al-la-a*[*m*]
----
i 21 [*lu?*] *ir?-ra-*{ṢI}*-am-ma*
i 22 [*ù*] [*ib?*]*-ra-am ku-ra*(over ras.)*-am-ma?* [x x]
i 23 [*su?*]*-uk-ka-al-lu si-ik-k*[*a-tam*]
i 24 [x x]-x x *ḫa-sa-a-si* [*li*]?-[...]
i 25 *ra?*]-[*m*]*i-i-k*[*i?*
i 26 ] x *ra* [

col. ii
(Only traces of the first 14 lines)

Rev.
col. iii
(c. 11 lines missing)
iii 12' *ir* [… …]
iii 13' x [... …]
iii 14' *a-ta*-x
iii 15' *ša t*[*a?*... …]
iii 16' *uš*-x [… …]
iii 17' *ši*-[
(c. 4 lines missing)
iii 22' x-[... ...]
iii 23' *m*[*a?* ... ...]
iii 24' *a-na* x
iii 25' *a?-li-ik-ku* x [... ...]

Up. Ed.
iii 26' *li-ib-ba a* [... ...]
iii 27' *i-ra-i-ma?* [... ...]
iii 28' *ša i-di-a* [... ...]
iii 29' *an-na ku-ú*[*r?* ... ...]
iii 30' *šum-ma uš* [... ...]

col. iv
iv 1' […] x *im?- ma* [x x]
iv 2' […] *ap?-sa-a-ša/ta* [x x]

iv 3' [...] *ša ar ra* PI° x
iv 4' [...] x? *uš-šu-ú?*
iv 5' [...] *ri-tu!-mu-um-*[*ma*]
iv 6' [*e-gi*]*-ir-re-e šu-ul-mi-i-ka*
iv 7' [*ù*] *da-ar ba-la-ṭi-i-ka*
iv 8' [*l*]*i-iš-ru-uk-ku Ištár Am-mi-di-ta-na*
iv 9' *e-di-iš-ma*° *ba*°*-al-*[*ṭa*]*-a-*[*ša?*]
iv 10' *ra-im-tum* [*li*°]<*-ib*>*-ši i-li-ib-*[*bi*]*-ka*
iv 11' *i-da-mi-iq-ti šu-qí-ir*°*-ši*
iv 12' *li-im-da li-im-da ši-ta-a-la*
iv 13' *ma-a šu-ra-su in-ḫé ú-ia*
iv 14' *ù ṣe-ḫé-er ra-a-mi*

----

iv 15' giš-gi$_4$-gál-bi

----

iv 16' 4 *i-ra-a-tum*
iv 17' *iš-ka-ar e-eš ra-a-mi* {ŠU QÚ}
iv 18' *šu-qú-úr*

**Translation**

Obv.
col. i.
i 1 Where is my loved one? He is so dear!
i 2 And does he bear his fruit?
i 3 …
i 4 Like apples of *the ripening period (*or: *the month of Simān*(?))
i 5 Filled with joy is the bed of [*my lover*(?)]

----

i 6–7 My love had to go out to the steppe,
i 7 (while) I spend (here) the night.
i 8 I *embrace* my delight,
i 9–10 but the dove rose aloft.

----

i 11–12 My love of the steppe, may the trappers return (him) back to me!
i 13 You will *embrace* my delights.
i 14–15 May the gardener bring (him) to me!

----

i 16 I have thrown my coop on the young man,
i 17–18 so that I may catch the dove;
i 19–20 (The coop) of my delights *Nanāya*(?) will fill for me.

----

i 21 *Indeed, he is loved,*
i 22 and the *short friend*(?) […]
i 23–24 *The minister* [...] *the peg.*

| | |
|---|---|
| i 24 | ... to remember [...] |
| i 25 | [...] your(f.) [*lo*]*ved one* [...] |
| i 26 | ... |
| | (col. ii – traces only) |

Rev.

col. iii

| | |
|---|---|
| iii 12'–23' | ... |
| iii 24' | To [... |
| iii 25' | I went to you [...] |

Up. Ed.

| | |
|---|---|
| iii 26' | *The heart I*(?)[...] |
| iii 27' | *He loved and* [...] |
| iii 28' | who *knows*... [...] |
| iii 29' | Indeed ...[...] |
| iii 30' | If ...[...] |

col. iv

| | |
|---|---|
| iv 1' | ... |
| iv 2' | ... |
| iv 3' | ... |
| iv 4' | ... |
| iv 5' | [...] lovemaking, |
| iv 6'–7' | An omen for your well-being and your everlasting life! |
| iv 8'–9' | May Ištar grant to you, Ammī-ditāna, her life anew! |
| iv 10'–11' | *May* the loved one *be* in your heart, (may) you cherish her favorably! |
| iv 12' | Learn(pl.), learn(pl.) and ask one another: |
| iv 13'-14' | "(*though*) its beginning is sighs of woe, *still* young is my love!". |
| ---- | |
| iv 15' | Its antiphon. |
| ---- | |
| iv 16' | 4 *irtum* songs |
| iv 17'–18' | (Of) the series "Where is my loved one, he is so dear". |

**Commentary**

i 4: *kīma ḫašḫūri* [*si*?]-[*ma*?]-*ni*: Groneberg suggests to read [*ar*?]-[*ma*?]-*ni*, "(apples of) Armānum". The photo shows that there is not enough space to accommodate the large sign *ar*. The NA love dialogue between Nabû and Tašmetu may offer a solution: $^{\text{giš}}$ḪAŠḪUR $^{\text{iti}}$SI[$G_4$...], "the apples of Siman" (SAA 3, 36: 6). See also KAL 3, 75: 5' (№ 8): iii 11'–12': "like an ea[r of barley of] Ištar of appropriate shape".[304] Whether *simānum* refers to the

304 KAL 3, 75: 5' (№ 8): iii 11'–12': *kī šubi*[*lte ša*] *Ištar ša si-ma-a-ni būni.*

third month of the Babylonian year, Simān (as is the case in the NA text), or more generally to the time of ripening fruits cannot be decided. For apples in the context of ancient Near Eastern love literature, see Paul 2002, 490.

i 5: *mali rīšātim m*[*u*]-*un*? *m*[*i*?-x?]. I take *m*[*u*]-*un* as a construct form of *munû* (CAD M/2, 207f.), although one would expect probably the form *munî*. This literary synonym for *eršum*, "bed" is found in PRAK 1 B 472 i 8' (№ 13): "Of incense is my bed, (smelling of) *ballukku*-plant".[305] A description of the lover's bed is common in Sum. love lyrics and is found in Songs 3: 7–9.

i 7 *uš-ta-ṣi-a*: Theoretically the form may be 1 or 3 sg., but it is unlikely that the woman would go out to the field and pass the night (*abīat*) there. I take therefore *uštāṣi* as an Št-form with passive meaning, "was made to go out", referring to the male protagonist. A similar situation, where the woman awaits her lover coming back from the field, is depicted in JAOS 103, 26–27 (№ 7). – Reading *a-bi wa-*[*ṣi*], "my father is out", instead of *a-bi-à-*[*at*], is not excluded.

i 8, i 13: The idiomatic meaning of *law/mûm* in ALL varies and is not always clear.[306] As I understand it, l. i 8 describes the woman who passes the night alone at home, while her lover is in the field. She is forced to embrace only the memory of delight, since her lover is far away. Similarly, in l. i 13 the lover is expected to embrace her in person.

i 9: *sú*!(Text: BA)-*ka-an-ni-nu*: In the end of the line Groneberg saw one more sign, {ḪI}, which to me is only a scratch. – The *sukannīnum* (Sum. tum$_{12}$-gur$_4$$^{mušen}$) is identified by Veldhuis (2004, 292) as "domesticated dove". In this text, however, it shows no sign of domestication. A dove is a common metaphor for the lover,[307] but here I believe it is used specifically as a euphemism for the male genitals, as *ḥamāma*, "dove", in modern colloquial Arab., Ital. *uccello*, "bird", Eng. *cock*, and modern colloquial Heb. *bulbul* (< a nightingale in Arab.) – all meaning penis (see Overview § 4.6).

i 11–12: The motif of the woman who encounters guardians, while searching for her lost lover – an encounter which is not free of sexual tension – is found also in Songs 3: 1–4 and 5: 6.

i 20: $^{d}$*Na-na*!(Text: ŠI)-*ia*!(Text: IṢ) *tu-ú-ma-al-la-a*[*m*]: My reading suggestion concerning the beginning of this line is conjectural. (Groneberg 1999, 179 read *an-na ù-tu*! *ú-ma*?-*al-la-a*[*m*], "die Zustimmung, die ich finde, füllt mich an(?)".) Some support for this reading is a similarly badly written Nanāya in MIO 12, 52–53: 9' (№ 10).

i 21–26: This passage eludes my understanding. The partial translation is only tentative.

305 PRAK 1 B 472: i 8' (№ 13): *ša kanakāti mūni balukkū*.

306 Cf. ZA 49, 168–169: i 27 (№ 16): *alawwīki nītam ina ṣēriki*, "I shall lay siege upon you".

307 See Lambert 1975, 118: 7–8 and Songs 2: 14, 4: 1, 5: 2, 6: 9.

iv 8'–11': A similar blessing to Ammī-ditāna stressing Ištar's love is found in the famous Ištar hymn dedicated to this king (Thureau-Dangin 1925, 171: 57–59).

iv 12': *limdā limdā šitālā*: This address (to the public? to a chorus?) has a neat parallel in the NA love lyric text about Nabû and Tašmetu, where one reads: "Thither, ask, ask, question question!".[308]

308 Livingstone 1989 (= SAA 3), 36 rev. 14: *ammîša šāl šāl sanniqā sanniqā*.

# № 7 Come In, Shepherd, Ištar's Lover (JAOS 103, 26–27)

Copy: Black 1983, 26–27
Tablet Siglum: BM 47507
Photo: Black 1983, 28
Edition: Black 1983, 30–31
Studies: Lambert 1983, Wasserman/Or 1998, 88, Wasserman 2003, Cat. No.75
Collection: The British Museum, London
Provenance: ?
Measurements: 8.4x5.5 cm
Period: Late OB

**Introduction**

This is the sole composition which is mentioned by its incipit in the Assur catalogue (KAR 158 i 6 = № 19). It is further significant that the text terminates with a catch-line to another composition, whose first line is the next incipit in the catalogue (KAR 158 i 7). This sequence proves unequivocally the actual existence of a series of love-related compositions in Babylonia, a cycle mirrored by the Assur catalogue. Although its exact provenance is unknown, there is no doubt that BM 47507 was unearthed in southern Babylonia (note the reading *sa* in ll. 13, 14). This fact strengthens the notion that the bulk of texts catalogued by KAR 158 stem from Babylonia. The text shows a mixture of OB and MB characteristics: On the one hand we find 3 sg. f. verbs prefixed with *t-* (ll. 4, 5, 36, 37), the archaic construct form in *-u* (l. 20), the attached preposition *in*(*a*) (l. 14), the terminative adv. *-iš* (ll. 12, 13), and the archaic form *māmū* (ll. 38, 39). On the other hand the consonant shift *lt* < *št* (l. 4) which points at a post OB, or MB period is already present, as also the vowel contraction of *i-a*, (*ma-ša-am-ma* in l. 2, *li-ip-pi-ta-*[*kum*]*-ma* in l. 7, and *mu-un-na-ni* in ll. 33, 35).

Black (1983) has accurately called this composition a 'ballad': it alternates between descriptive passages and direct speeches, its imagery is pastoral, and its tone peaceful, not erotically charged as other texts in the corpus.

Obv.

1 [*er*]*-ba-am-ma re-e-ú ḫ*[*a-ra-am* $^{d}$*Ištar-ma*]
2 *ma-ša-am-ma re-e-ú ḫa-r*[*a-am* $^{d}$*Ištar*]
3 *e-re-bu-uk-ka a-bi ḫa-di ka-šum-ma*
4 *um-mi* $^{d}$*Nin-gal tu-ul-ti-ia-al-*[*kum*]
5 *ša-am-na i-na ma-al-la-tim tu-maḫ-ḫi-ir-ka-ma*
6 *e-re-bu-uk-ka sik-ku-ru li-ri-šu-kum-ma*
7 *dal-tum ra-ma-ni-ši-ma li-ip-pi-ta-*[*kum*]*-ma*
8 *at-ta sik-ku-ru i-ṣu mi-in ti-*[*de?*]
9 *mi-nam ti-de e-re-eb ma-*[*ri?*]
10 *an-nu-ú a-ra-am a-ra-am na-aḫ-š*[*um*]
11 *kal-bi-šu ú-maš-ši-ra* *mi-in* [...]

12 *maḫ-ri-iš* $^{d}$*Nin-gal šu-ri-ba-*⌈*ni-in-ni-ma*⌉
13 *iš-tu maḫ-ri-iš* $^{d}$*Nin-gal i-ru-ba kal-la-sa*
14 *mi-ir-sa im-ma-al-la-tim i-zu-za-nim-ma*
15 *a-na kal-bi ù re-i ma-ri-iṣ šu-nun-dum*
16 *mi-na iz-zu-rù ú-bíl ub-lam-ma*
17 *il-lik ù il-li-ka ú-bíl ù ub-lam*
18 *šu-ul-ma-nu re-e-i ma-ri-iṣ-ma šu-nun-dum*
19 *ša-al-mat um-ma-tum ša-lim šar-rum-ma*
20 *ša-lim* $^{d}$*Dumu-zi šu-da-tu* $^{d}$*Ištar*
21 ⌈x x *pu-ṭur*⌉ *pu-ṭur še-ni-ka*
22 [...] ⌈*pu-ṭur*⌉ *pa-sú-ma-ti-ka-ma*
23 [...] *ṣu ni-ik-kal na-aḫ-šum*
24 [...] x *ka na-aḫ-šum-ma*
25 [...]*na-kar a-a ub-lam*
26 [...] *ni-ik-kal na-aḫ-šum*
27 [...]*ni-za-ar-riq*!*-ma*
28 [...] ⌈x⌉ *ni na-aḫ-šum-ma*
29 [...] *ri-gim ṣe-ni-ka*

Rev.
30 [...] ⌈x⌉ *ka-lu*!*-me-ka-ma*
31 [...] ⌈*ri*⌉*-gim-ma ṣe-ni-ka*
32 [...] ⌈*su*⌉*-pu-ra-ni ḫi-ṭi-ma*
33 [*ni-bi-šu*] ⌈*mu*⌉*-un-na-ni pu-ṭu-ra le-e-mi*
34 ⌈*mu na ra si*? *ka mi*⌉ *pá-ri-ir*!?(Text: NI)*-ma*
35 *ni-bi-šu mu-un-na-ni pu-ṭu-ra le-e-mi*
36 *ta-ku-uš Iš-tar a-na qé-reb su-pu-ri-šu-ma*

37 *pa-ša te*!*-pu-ša šu-a-tu ta-az-za-kar*
38 *ma-mu ki ṭa-bu ma-mu su-pu-ri-ka*
39 *mu-ka ḫa-li-lu ma-mi-ma tar-ba-ṣi*
----
40 *ur-ša-nam re-e-a a-za-am-mur-ma*
41 39 [MU].ŠID.BI.IM
42 *iškār*(⌈ÉŠ.GÀR⌉) *ma-ru-um-ma ra-im-ni*
43 *imgiddû*(IM.GÍD.DA) *Ta-qí-šum mār*(DUMU) *Me-me-*$^{d}$*En-líl-le šāpir*(UGULA) *bīt*(É) $^{d}$*Ištar*

**Translation**

Obv.
1 Come in, shepherd, Ištar's lover,
2 Spend the night here, shepherd, Ištar's lover,
3 At your entering, my father is happy for you,
4 my mother, Ningal, is rejoiced over you.
5 She served you oil in a bowl.

6 At your entering, the bolts rejoice over you,
7 the door itself shall be opened [for you]!
8 You, wooden bolt - what do you know?
9 What do you know? The entrance of my darling!
10 Indeed, I love, I love, oh, lusty one!
11 He freed his dogs ...
12 (saying:) “Let me come in front of Ningal!”
13 After her bride entered in front of Ningal,
14 they divided the sweet cake in the bowl.
15 The illustrious one is worried about the dogs and shepherds.
16 - Why are they insulting (him)? He brought and offered.
17 He went and came back, he brought and offered,
18 Yes, the illustrious one is worried about the shepherds’ affluence.
19 The company is well, the king is well,
20 Dumuzi is well, Ištar’s lover.
21 [... loosen,] loosen your sandals!
22 [...] unpack your nets!
23 [...] we shall eat, oh, lusty one!
24 [...] oh, lusty one!
25 [...] he refuses, he won’t bring.
26 [...] we shall eat, oh, lusty one!
27 [...] we shall sprinkle!
28 [...] oh, lusty one!
29 [...] the cry of your flock,

Rev.
30 [...] your lambs,
31 [...] the cry of your flock,
32 [...] *neglect*(?) our sheepfold!
33 *Recite for me* [*his name/number*], *he wouldn’t let (it) go*!
34 [...]
35 *Recite for me his name/number, he wouldn’t let (it) go*!
36 Ištar went into his sheepfold,
37 opened her mouth and said to him:
38 “How sweet are the water, the water of your sheepfold!
39 Your water murmur, it is the water of (your) animal stall!”
40 ‘I shall sing on the heroic shepherd.’
41 Total 39 lines.
42 Series: ‘Oh darling loving me.’
43 Library tablet of Taqšītum, son of Meme-Enlil, administrator of the temple of Ištar.

**Commentary**

4: *tu-ul-ti-ia-al-*[*kum*]: from *šiʾālum*-Dt, the sole attestation so far of this verb (see Lambert 1983 and CAD Š/1, 283). Another possible attestation of this verb is *šu-la-a-*[*ku*?], YOS 11, 24: i 32 (№ 15), in broken context.

5–7: The motif of doors that are glad to see a person can be found in later texts.[309] In a first mill. Egalkurra incantation we read: "door and bolt, may you be happy (to see) my face!",[310] and similarly in a late cosmological text: "Oh Sun-god, when you enter Heaven's Interior, may the bolt of the clear heavens say 'hello!', may the doors of the heavens bless you".[311] A similar literary motif is found in Greek literature, where it is called *Paraklausithyron*, "lament at the door (by a lover)".[312]

8–9: For the hendiadys *sikkūrum-iṣum*, see Wasserman 2003, 11. – The stylistic device of direct speeches to objects is rare in OB literature. Another clear example of it is found in A 7478 i 5 (№ 1), where the woman is exchanging words with a washbasin (*murammiktum*). One may also mention here Enkidu speaking bitterly to the door which was made of the tree that he and Gilgameš cut in the cedar forest (SB Gilg. VII: 37ff.), and Enki's revealing the secret of the coming flood to Atraḫsis by talking to the wall (Lambert/Millard 1969, 88: III 20–21).[313]

14: *immallatim* (<*in mallatim*): The attached prep. may indicate an OB layer of composition of the text.

19: *šarrum*: The fact that Dumuzi is referred to as "king" could suggest that the text was performed in the royal court.

20: The rare word *šudād/tum*, "lover", is uncommon as a term for the beloved. It is attested only in this text and in a lexical list where it stands as a synonym of *šunundum*, "hero" (see ll. 15, 18) and of *rāʾimum*, "lover" (cf. CAD Š/3, 193). – *šudātu Ištar*: note the archaic -*u* construct form.

21: Sandals and shoes are rarely mentioned in the OB and MB literary corpus. Note that the two references to *šēnum* in the corpus (this text and the bilingual proverb VS 24, 113: 4) employ the same expression: *šēna paṭārum*, "to loosen, to take off the shoes/sandals".

---

309 See also Songs 5: 5.

310 Stadhousers 2013, 316, text 11: 6: *daltu u sikkūru ana pānīya lū ḫadâtunu.*

311 Abel-Winkler 59, no. 2 1–6, cited in Horowitz 1998, 248: *Šamaš ana qereb šamê ina erēbika šigār šamê ellûtim šulma liqbûkum dalāt šamê likrubākum* (Akk. only cited).

312 A comparative study of the Akk. and Greek motifs of 'talking to doors' is underway by the author.

313 A nice parallel to the two above Akk. examples is the Classical story of Pyramus and Thisbe, two lovers who were forced to express their mutual affection by talking through a fissure in a brick-wall (Ovid, Metamorphoses IV 55–92). Interestingly, the setting of the story is Babylon (ref. Elyze Zomer).

21ff.: Ištar's address to Dumuzi to take off his shoes is an invitation to make love. Though not refusing her directly, he refrains from joining her and continues to be busy with his flocks. When Ištar comes to the sheepfold (l. 36), Dumuzi and his sheep are gone.

38–39: The text ends with a rhyming couplet serving as doxology. Similar cases were treated in Wasserman 2003, 157–17

# № 8 She Is Luscious like a Flower of the Field (KAL 3, 75)

Copy: KAL 3, 75
Tablet Siglum: VAT 10825+10597+11218[314]
Photo: -/-
Edition: Frahm 2009, 143–145
Collection: Vorderasiatisches Museum, Berlin
Provenance: Assur
Measurements: 6.3x4.9 cm
Period: MA

**Introduction**
As summarized by Frahm (2009, 144), this text presents a broken dialogue between a man and a woman, probably the king and the "daughter of Assur". The setting of the text is urban, probably the court itself (note the mention of the palace in ll. ii 3 and ii 9, and perhaps also the "city" in l. iii 6'). Recently, Stefan Jakob was able to join this tablet to two small fragments which continue the lines of the reverse. His new copy will be published as KAL 7, 33. The present edition is based on Frahm 2009, but the line numbers on the reverse were altered to match Jakob's forthcoming edition.[315]

Obv.
col. i
i 1 [… … … … … …] *man*?
i 2 [… … … … … …] (blank)
i 3 [… … … … … …]-*te*
i 4 [… … … … … …] (blank)
i 5 [… … … … … …] PÀR$^{meš}$-*ki*
i 6 [… … … … … …*ka*]-⌈*a*⌉-*ši*
i 7 [… … … … … …] (blank)
i 8 [… … … … … …] x
i 9 [… … … … … …] x
(Rest broken)

col. ii
ii 1 *i+na* $u_4$*-me-*[*š*]*u-ma sinništu*(MUNUS) *ba-ni-t*[*u*…]
ii 2 *ḫa-di-a nišū*(UN$^{meš}$) *ri-šu bal-ṭ*[*ú*?...]
ii 3 *ri-*⌈*šat*⌉ *ekal*(É.GAL)*-ni* / *lí ḫa-a-di* […]

314 The correct inventory number of KAL 3, 75 is VAT 10825, not 10404. (Stefan Jakob, private communication, 12.8.2014). Cf. Frahm's (2009, 20) remark regarding the inventory number of the tablet.
315 Lines rev. iii 11'–13' are published with Jakob's kind permission.

| | |
|---|---|
| ii 4 | *gišimmaru*($^{giš}$G[IŠ]IMMAR) ⌈*ú*⌉-*ḫi?-ni a-na-ku* ⌈*a*⌉-[…] |
| ii 5 | *é*/*ú*? [… …] |
| ii 6 | *i-*[*r*]*i-šu tal-ta-lu* ⌈*ia*⌉-⌈*a*⌉-*t*[*i*?... ...] |
| ii 7 | [*a*]*l*!?-⌈*la*⌉-*ak* [… … …] |
| ii 8 | *i*?-*ḫ*[*a*?-*nu*?]-*ba-ma* $^{giš?}$*a-š*[*u*?-*ḫu*?... ...] |
| ii 9 | [(x)] *ekallu*(É.GAL)-*lu*$_4$ *ri-*[*šat*?...] |
| ii 10 | [*ši*?]-*kin*? *pānī*(IGI$^{meš}$)-*ka* ⌈DINGIR?⌉ […] |
| ii 11 | [*na*]*m-ra-ku* ⌈*ú*⌉ […] |
| ii 12 | [(x)] x x [… …. …] |
| | |
| Rev. | |
| col. iii | |
| iii 1'–7' | (To be published by Stefan Jakob) |
| iii 8' | [x x] *ku*? ⌈*u*⌉ *m*[*i*?-… …] |
| iii 9' | [*a*]*r*?-*ki bu-uk-r*[*i*?... …] |
| iii 10' | [(blank)] *lamassata*($^{d}$LAMMA)-*ta* [… …] |
| iii 11' | *as-mat ki-i il-lu-ur ṣēri*(EDIN) *ki-i šu-bi*[*l-te ša*] [$^{d}$INNIN?] |
| iii 12' | *ša si-ma-a-ni bu-ni ri-šat* ⌈*ru*⌉-*púš*? *kibrāti*(UB$^{meš}$) |
| iii 13' | *šalummatu*(SU.LIM)-*ma a-na-ku a-na šumēli*(GÙB) TE RA ŠI T[E? DING]IR?$^{meš}$ *ni-bit Aš-šur* |
| ---- | |
| iii 14' | [x] ⌈*ur*?⌉-*qar mārat*(DUMU.MUNUS) *Aš-šur ta-kar-rab a-*[*na*?...] |
| iii 15' | x *ka-ak-ki bēl*(EN) *šarrāni*(MAN$^{meš}$)-*ni* $^{d}$*I*[*š*?-*tar*? ...] |
| iii 16' | [x] ⌈*ta*⌉-*ši-it ḫa-si-is ta-ši-i*[*m*?-*te*? …] |
| iii 17' | x x *le-*ʾ*u-ti-ka* ⌈DINGIR?⌉ [… …] |
| | |
| Up. Ed. | |
| Up.ed 1' | […] *lìb-bi-ia mam-ma* [… … …] |
| Up.ed 2' | x x [… …] x x x [(x)] *sa-ap-pi-ḫu* […] |
| Up.ed 3' | [… …] *la* [… …] |
| ---- | |
| Up.ed 4' | 109 *šumī*(MU[$^{meš}$]) |
| | (Rest uninscribed) |

**Translation**

| | |
|---|---|
| col. i | |
| | (too broken to translate) |
| col. ii | |
| ii 1 | On this very day the beautiful woman […], |
| ii 2 | They were joyful, the people. The […] were exultant, *saf*[*e and sound*]. |
| ii 3 | The celebration of (our?) palace, the joy of [...], |
| ii 4 | I will […] the fresh dates (from?) the date-palm. |

| | |
|---|---|
| ii 5 | ... |
| ii 6 | The scent, the pollen of date-palm, over me […] |
| ii 7 | I shall *g*[*o*…] |
| ii 8 | The pine trees are thri[v]ing [….] |
| ii 9 | The palace, the *cel*[*ebration* of…] |
| ii 10 | The appearance of your face, *Oh god*! […] |
| ii 11 | I am shining .. [ ] |
| ii 12 | [(x)] x x] |

Rev.
col. iii

| | |
|---|---|
| iii 1'–7' | (To be published by Stefan Jakob) |
| iii 8' | … |
| iii 9' | *Behind the son of* [… …] |
| iii 10' | A protecting goddess [… …] |
| iii 11' | She is luscious like an *illūru*-flower of the field, like an ea[r of barley of] Ištar, |
| iii 12' | (an ear) of appropriate time, (of) beauty, the joy of the *width*(?) of the (four) quarters of the world! |
| iii 13' | *There is* radiance. I will *approach* to the left(?) … the gods invoked by Aššur. |

----

| | |
|---|---|
| iii 14' | […] the daughter of Aššur gives blessings to […] |
| iii 15' | […] the weapons of the lord of kings, Ištar [will…] |
| iii 16' | […] … wise in discernme[nt…] |
| iii 17' | … your power, *of god* […] |

Up. Ed.

| | |
|---|---|
| Up.ed 1' | […] my heart, whoever/nobody […] |
| Up.ed 2' | … […] wasteful […] |
| Up.ed 3' | … |

----

| | |
|---|---|
| Up.ed 4' | 109 lines. |

**Commentary**

ii 2: The subject at the beginning of the line is *nišū* (pl. f.). Hence, *rīšū* and *balṭ*[*ū*] (pl. m.) must relate to another subject.

ii 3: The celebration (*rīštum*) in this line (and probably also in ll. ii 9 and iii 12') brings to mind the repeated refrain *rīšātumma išdum ana ālim*, "Celebration is a foundation for the city!" in the MB text Or. 60, 340 (№ 12).

ii 7: [*a*]*l*!?-[*la*]-*ak*, as suggested by Frahm (2009, 144), seems possible epigraphically and contextually (note *anāku* in ll. ii 4 and iii 13').

ii 10: Reading ⌈DINGIR?⌉ at the end of the line is tentative. As a support to this cf. CUSAS 10, 9: 12 (№ 3): "I who am blooming, my fate (lit.: god) is with you!".[316]

iii 11': Frahm (2009, 145) hesitates between *asmat*, 3 sg. f. stative, or *asmāt*(*a*), a shortened 2 sg. m. stative form. The simile *kī illūr ṣēri* "like a flower of the field" (following the new fragment of Jakob), makes it more plausible that a woman is the intended subject of the verb. Note further that *illūrum* is so far found only in Assyrian love-related compositions, cf. LKA 15: 3 (№ 9): "On the treetops *illūru*-flower blossoms to him (= Dumuzi)".[317]

iii 12': *ša simāni*: The adjective *simānum* describing an ear of barley is found also in another text, only in the negative. A 7478 i 14 (№ 1) reads: "(the lover appeared) as an ear of barley not in its proper time".[318] The quasi-homonym *simānum*, the third month of the Babylonian year is found in Fs. Renger 192–193 i 4 (№ 6): "like apples of *the month of Simān*(?)".[319] – ⌈*ru*⌉-*púš*? *kibrāti*(UB$^{meš}$): The sign after *ru-* is tentatively restored (MPS).

iii 13': Frahm's reading is now improved by Jakob's new join.

316 CUSAS 10, 9: 12 (№ 18): *ša šummuḫāk ilī ittika*.
317 LKA 15: 3 (№ 9): *ina appāte ša iṣi iḫtannubamma illūru*.
318 A 7478 i 14 (№ 1): *kīma šubultim ša la sí-ma-ni-im*.
319 Fs. Renger 192–193 i 4 (№ 6): *kīma ḫašḫūri* ⌈*si*?⌉-⌈*ma*?⌉-*ni*.

# № 9 It Is Dumuzi Whom Ištar Keeps Searching (LKA 15)

Copy: Ebeling LKA 15, Meinhold 2009, Pl. 12
Tablet Siglum: VAT 14039
Photo: -/-
Collection: Vorderasiatisches Museum, Berlin
Edition: Meinhold 2009 301–312, Parpola apud Nissinen 2001, 118–119
Studies: Groneberg 1987, 188, Nissinen 2001, Lapinkivi 2004, 30, 57, Foster 2005, 1025
Provenance: Assur
Measurements: ?
Period: MA (Shalmaneser)

**Introduction**

The obverse of the tablet contains an eclogue and idyllic description of Ištar looking for Dumuzi. The god Aššur is also mentioned, but he does not seem to have an active role in the story. The tone of the text recalls the Babylonian ballad JAOS 103, 26–27 (№ 7), yet its setting is not domestic but pastoral. On the reverse appears a short supplication of Shalmaneser to Ištar, accompanied by a list of edible commodities, on the occasion of the acceptance of his hand-lifting prayer to the goddess (or, perhaps, ritual instuctions, as by the end of PRAK1 B 472 = № 13). It remains unclear whether the two sides of the tablet originally belonged to the same composition. An exclamation in the 1 pl. voice, "we have sung", is found by the end of the reverse, and a short colophon which mentions that it is the "fourth tablet" seals the text.

Obv.

1 $^{d}$*Dumu-zi* $^{d}$*Iš*$_{8}$*-tár iš-te-né-ʾi re-i-ia i-*⌈ *še*$_{20}$⌉*-ʾi ri-i-*⌈*ta*⌉

2 *it-te-ner-ru bu-la-šu i-sa-hur-ma ri-*⌈*ta*⌉ *a-šar di-šu up-ta-ṣa-na nu-ru-*[*u*]*m?-m*[*e?*]

3 *i+na ap-pa-*{PA}*-te ša iṣi*(GIŠ) *iḫ-ta-nu-ba-ma il-lu-ru*

4 *īnā*(IGI$^{meš}$)*-šu ri-ta qer-bi-ta i-bir-ra-ma ina na-mé-e qí-ša-ta šadê*(KUR$^{meš}$) *i-še*$_{20}$ {KU} ⌈*ku-up*⌉*-pi*

5 *i-mur-ma* $^{d}$*Iš*$_{8}$*-tár na-ra-ma i-še*$_{20}$*-ʾu a-na gu-up-ri bēl*(⌈EN) *ta*⌉*-ma-ti-ma is-sà-qar-šu*

----

6 [*at-t*]*a al-ka re-i aš-ra-ni lu-ru-ku re-i-ia re-i-ʾi bu-ul-ka*

7 [DUMU?.(MUNU]S?) *Aš-šur iddina*(SUM*-na*) *burāša*(LI) *a-na ri-ti-ni-ma ša šam-ha-at*

8 [*a*]*t?-ta-ma ta-*⌈*mi*⌉*-ir-ta-ni ta-re-ʾi ter-*⌈*te?-ne?*⌉*-iʾ ú-šal-li-ni-ma ša šam-*⌈*ḫa-at*⌉

9 [(x) x] ⌈x⌉ IA-[x x (x)] ⌈x x⌉*-e* [D]U SI?(-)BAL*-te ša iš-*⌈*ru-ka*⌉ *a-ba-ia-ma* ⌈x⌉ [x x] x

10 [x x x x x x x x (x x x)] ⌈x x⌉ *ri-te ri-*⌈*piš*⌉ ⌈x⌉[x (x)] ⌈x x (x)⌉ [x (x)]*-zu?*

(Broken: more than half the tablet is missing)

Rev.

1' [x x x x x x x (x x)] ⌈x x⌉ [x x (x)] ⌈*lu*!- *na*!⌉-*ad* *karānu*(GEŠTIN) *ša be-la-*⌈*ti*?⌉

2' [x x x x (x x) *kunāšu*(ZÍ]Z.AN.NA? text: UD) *ù* *kakkû*(⌈GÚ⌉.T[UR]) *ḫallūru*[GÚ].GAL *kibtu*(GIG) *ù in-ni-nu*

3' [x x x x (x x)]-*še* PI(-)Aʾ-*ša n*[*a*]*m*?-*ḫa-ri ṭu-ub ši-ka-ri*

4' ⌈*īn*(IGI)-*ša*?⌉ [x x (x)] ⌈*pár*?⌉-*ṣi ka-li-ku-nu* ⌈*li*⌉-*riš* $^{d}$*Iš*$_{8}$.*tár a-na pa-ni-ku-nu*

5' *ṣu-lu-l*[*u*? *li*]*b-ši elī*(UGU)-*ku-nu* ⌈LI?⌉ A LU *pá-ri a-bu-re-e* A ⌈x⌉ [(x)]

6' ⌈*ša* $^{md}$*Salmānu*(DI⌉-*m*[*a-n*]*u-ašarēd*(SAG) *ni-iš qa-*⌈*ta*⌉-*ti-šu im-ta-ḫar*

7' *id-di-na-*⌈*šu ša*⌉ *e-ri-šu* ⌈*za-ma*⌉-*ru ša at-tu-ia mim-ma ni-iz-za-mur*

----

MAN
MAN

----

8' *tup-pí* 4.KÁM.MA

**Translation**

Obv.

1 It is Dumuzi whom Ištar keeps searching; – "Oh my shepherd!", she searches the pasture.

2 His cattle enters all the time, looking for pasture, where the grass veils itself with *pomegranates*,

3 (where) on the treetops *illūru*-flower blossoms to him.

4 His eyes examine the pasture and the meadow; in the steppe and in the mountain forests he seeks water holes.

4 Ištar saw the beloved which she was seeking *in*(!) the hut of the 'Lord of Oath' and said to him:

5 – "Oh you, come to me, my shepherd! Let me lead you to the place, Oh my shepherd! Direct your cattle (to that place)!"

6 "[*The daughte*]*r*(?) of Aššur bestowed juniper(s) on our pasture which is abundant".

7 "It is you who shall shepherd our meadow, you shall constantly shepherd our river-flat which is abundant".

8 "[……] (*junipers*?) which my father granted […]"

10 "[……] *widen* the pasture [….]!"

Rev.

1' "[…] *may I praise* the wine of the lady",

2' "[…] emmer, lentils, peas, wheat and barley",

3' "[...] …*the beer-jar of* the best of beer",

4' *Her eye* [...] the rites of all of you! May Ištar rejoice in your(pl.) presence!

5' May there be protection for you! ... *hymns of pasture* [...]"

6' She accepted the hand-lifting of Shalmaneser.

7' She gave him what he asked for. As for the song, which is mine, we have sung it in its entirety.

====

8' Fourth tablet

**Commentary**

1: *rē'īya*: With Meinhold (2009, 304) this form is understood as a literary vocative (similarly CAD Š/2, 359 and CAD R 307a 1c). Support for Meinhold's argument can be found in the use of *rē'īya* alongside *rē'ī* as the incipits of poems in KAR 158 viii 5 (№ 19): *iškar rē'i*(SIPA)*-ía iškar rē'i*(SIPA).

2: *it-te-ner-ru bu-la-šu*: Meinhold (2009, 304–335) derived the verbal form *it-te-ner-ru* from *warûm*-Gtn, "Er (=Dumuzi) führt fortwährend sein Vieh". This analysis, however, is difficult, semantically and especially morphologically, since, as noted by Meinhold in her commentary, *warûm* is never attested with the *e*-vowel; only *ittanarrû*, *ittarrû* etc. A possible solution is that this form presents a sandhi spelling: *ītenerrub būlašu*, where *būlašu* is not acc., but a literary st. cstr. of the type *ṭēmašu*, namely the subject of the sentence (MPS). – *nu-ru-*[*u*]*m*?*-m*[*e*?]: Parpola apud Nissinen (2001, 118) read *nu-ru-*[*b*]*a*?-[*ti*?] from *nurbu*, "soft, tender parts", but this reading does not accord with the traces by the end of the line. Meinhold does not commit herself and reads NU RU [(x) x ME?]. A possible reading is *nu-ru-*[*u*]*m*!*-me* from *nurmû* (in Nuzi also *nurumû*), "pomegranates".[320] Pomegranates feature in Mesopotamian love incantations, notably in ŠÀ.ZI.GA: "Incantation. The beautiful woman has brought forth love. Inanna, who loves apples and pomegranates, has brought forth potency..." and the ritual which follows: "either to an apple or to a pomegranate you recite the incantation three times. You give (the fruit) to the woman (and) have her suck the juices. That woman will come to you: you can make love to her".[321] More on pomegranates in love literature, see Paul 2002 491. – *up-ta-ṣa-na*: Reading follows Parpola apud Nissinen (2001, 118). The verb *paṣānum*, "to cover, veil" (CAD P 217f.) fits well with the subject "grass" (*dīšu*).

3: Following CAD I/J 88a 2. Note the grammatical incongruence between *appātu* (pl.) and *iṣi* (sg.).

---

320 Reading suggested to me in a seminar by Peter Zilberg and Yakir Paz.

321 Biggs 1967, 70: 1–3, 8–10: [é]n munus-sig$_5$-sig$_5$-ga ág- ba-ra-è $^{d}$Innin ág giš-ḫašḫur giš-nu-úr-ma šà-zi-ga ba-ra-è... *kikiṭṭûšu lū* <*ana*> *ḫašḫūri lū ana nurmi šipta šalašišu tanaddi ana sinnilti tadan mêšunu tušamzaqši sinniltu ši illak*(*u*) *arkiši*.

5: *bēl*(EN) *tamâti*: Reading follows Meinhold (2009, 307f.). – Dumuzi is sitting in a reed hut used by herdsmen. A similar scene is found in OB Gilg. II: 75 where Šamḫat leads Enkidu *ana gupri ša rēʾīm*. – The preposition *ana* is difficult: one expects *ina*.

6: Meinhold (2009, 302) reads [*a*?]-[*ta*?]-*al-ka*, "[Ich] bin gekommen", but the previous reading of Parpola apud Nissinen (2001, 118) [*at-t*]*a al-ka* seems better (cf. beginning of l. 8). – *áš-ra-ni* is understood by Meinhold as *ašrani*, "an unseren Ort", but the text does not have the preposition "to". A solution to this was mentioned by Meinhold herself (2009, 308): parsing this word as *ašrāni*, namely ending with the term. adv. *-āni*, "*to* the place". For more cases of *-āni* in this function in OB, see Wasserman 2003, 116 n. 105 (with previous literature).

7: Parpola apud Nissinen (2001, 118) suggested [DUM]U? *Aš-šur*, "the son of Aššur". Meinhold (2009, 308) concluded that DUMU at beginning of the line is not tenable, without offering an alternative. However, another love-related text from Assur, lends support to the suggestion of Parpola apud Nissinen. KAL 3, 75 iii 14' (№ 8) reads: "the daughter of Assur will pray/bless the…".[322] "The offspring of Assur" may therefore suit here well . – Juniper trees, *burāšum* (LI), appear elsewhere in divine love poetry. So in the love dialogue of Nabû and Tašmetu, where the scent of holy juniper (ŠEM.LI) fills the dais and the shade of juniper (GIŠ.LI) offers shelter to Nabû,[323] and the NB composition about Banitu (designating Ištar) and her consort, where a chariot is joyously brought to a garden of junipers (*kirî burašî*).[324]

7–8: The plural forms in these lines can be assigned to the stylistic device of "plural of ecstasy", as defined by Paul 1995. – Note the end-rhyme *ša šamḫat*, not a common stylistic device in Akk. literature. End-rhymes may indicate oral performance (as in Or. 60, 340 = № 12). On rhyming in OB literature, see Wasserman 2003, 157–173.

9: I follow Parpola apud Nissinen (2001, 118) in reading *iš*-[*ru-ka*], "he granted", against Meinhold's *iš-ru-ur* whose meaning in this context is hard to establish. – I see no alternative but to follow Parpola apud Nissinen (2001, 118–119) in taking *a-ba-ia,* "my father", as the subject of this broken sentence (despite the objections of Meinhold 2009, 310). – The sequence SI-BAL-TE read by Meinhold (2009, 302) might be read *si-pala-te,* from *supālu* (also *sipālu*), "juniper" (CAD S 390f.).[325] A pl. f. form of *su*/*ipālu* is, however, not attested.

10: *ri-te ri*-[*piš*]: Reading follows Parpola apud Nissinen (2001, 118). Meinhold (2009, 302) has RI TE RI GIR.

322 KAL 3, 75 iii 14' (№ 8): *mārat*(DUMU.MUNUS) *Aššur takarrab*.
323 Livingstone 1989 (= SAA 3) rev. 14: 8–11.
324 STT 366: 14–20 = Deller 1983.
325 Reading suggested by Peter Zilberg and Yaqir Paz.

1': [*lu*!-*na*!]-*ad*: a form of *nâdum*, "to praise, extol". Though the line is only partially preserved, it may describe the king's praising the wine of his lady, Ištar.

3': Parpola apud Nissinen (2001, 118), who overlooked *ša*, took *pi-*ʾ*i* to stand for *pīḫu*, "beer-jar". But, as noted by Meinhold (2009, 310), the sequence *pīḫu ša namḫāri,* "the beer-jar of the beer-vessel" makes little sense. Meinhold reads PI Aʾ *ša*, suggesting that PI Aʾ might stand for *pû*, "mouth or opening". This reading is orthographically problematic as there is no attestation of a similar spelling of *pû* ending with a glottal stop. Yet *pīša*, "her (Ištar's) mouth", is a tempting reading. It forms a good parallel to *īnša*, "her eye" in the following line, and would result in: "[may I serve to] her mouth a beer-jar of the best beer".

4': Meinhold (2009, 310) reads IGI. I suggest reading IGI-*ša*, probably "her eye".

5': The second half of this line is unclear. Parpola apud Nissinen (2001, 118) read *li-a lu-ba-ri a-bu-re-e-a* [x], without a translation. Meinhold (2009, 310) reads [I] ŠA A LU BA RI A BU RE E A [x] [(x)]. A possible reading would be … *pá-ri a-bu-re-e a-* [x] [(x)], with *pá-ri* derived from *pārum*, "hymn", and *a-bu-re-e* deriving from *aburrē*, "water-meadow, pasture" which fits well in this context (and cf. the term *zamāru* in l. 7').

8': "Fourth tablet": This short scribal note is typical of post-OB love lyric texts. Cf. the colophons in the end of JAOS 103, 26–27 (№ 7) and Or. 60, 340 (№ 12). – Two MAN marks are found also in the end of KBo 36, 27 (№ 21).

# № 10 Let Me Be Sated with Your Charms (MIO 12, 52–53)

Copy: Lambert 1966, 52–53
Tablet Siglum: VAT 17347 (Bab. 40294)
Photo: -/-
Edition: Lambert 1966, 48–50
Collection: Vorderasiatisches Museum, Berlin
Studies: Hecker 1989, 741–743, Wasserman 2003, Cat. No.106, Foster 2005, 160–161, Hecker 2005, 173–175
Provenance: Babylon
Measurements: 10.5x9.0x1.8 cm
Period: Late OB (Abī-ešuḫ)

**Introduction**
A carefully written descriptive hymnal text, accompanied by direct speeches. King Abī-ešūḫ is mentioned in connection with amatory relations of the divine couple Nanāya and Muʾati. The setting of the text is the city of Babylon, probably the royal court (see l. 3'). There is some difficulty determining what side of the tablet is the obverse and what the reverse (see Hecker 2005, 173 n. 54). The tablet was collated on 01/02/2011.

Obv. ?

1 *[lu]-u[š-ba la]-la-ki* $^{d}$*Na-na-a ša-ap-t[a]-ki du-u[š-šu-pa ...]*

2 [...] x *da-di-ki šu-um-š[u? ...]*

----

3 [... *r]i-tu-ma-am* $^{d}$*Na-na-a ra* [x x] x *ḫi a li? ur? lu-ur-ta-a-ma*

4 [...] x *[t]u a-la na-me-er lu-uš-te-eb-ri*

----

5 [...] x [...] x x *ma-al* x x x *šu šu-ul-ma a-na da-a-ar li-re um-ma-an-šu*

6 [...] x x *A-bi-e-[š]u-uḫ lu-te-ep-pu-uš*

====

7 *[be?-l]i a-ta-ú ra-[i]-mi-iš-ša re-ša-tim li-ib-[ba-š]*u *tu-ša-am-la el-ṣi-iš*

----

8 *[mu-ùʾ-a-t]i [a-t]a-ú ra-i-mi-iš-ša re-ša-tim li-i[b-ba-šu] tu-ša-am-la el-ṣi-iš*

----

9 *[be?-li?] du-uš-šu-pu da-du-ú-ka di-iš-pa i-še-e[b-bi ku-zu-u]b ra-mi-ka*

----

10 *mu-ùʾ-a-ti du-uš-šu-pu da-du-ú-ka di-iš-pa i-š[e-eb-bi ku-zu]-ub ra-mi-ka*

----

11 *ṣa-al-mu ša ta-ab-ra i-ši-nu-ú ka-ia-an ú-ul iš-še-e[b-bi* ...]

----

12 *lu-uš-te-eṣ-bu ša-qí-a-am la-an-ka re-ša-ti ma-li* […]

----

13 *mu-ù᾽-a-ti ša-qí-a-am la-an-ka re-ša-ti ma-li* x [...]

----

14 *šar-rum lu da-ri i-na qá-bé-e-ki A-bi-e-šu-*[*uḫ lu*] *da-r*[*i i-na qá-be-ki*]

====

15 *ša-am-ḫu mu-ù᾽-a-ti-ni* $u_4$*-ma-am ek-le-e-t*[*a*?*-am*?] *ta-*[x x] x [....]

16 (traces only)

Rev. ?

1' (traces only)

2' [.....] x *re-eš-tam ṭa-a-ba ni* x [...]

----

3' *ta-ap-pa-l*[*i-is* K]Á.DINGIR.RA$^{ki}$ *i-na i-ni-ša dam-*[*qá-tim* ...]

4' *ta-ak-ru-ub-*[*šu t*]*a-aq-ta-bi du-mu-uq-šu* [.....]

----

5' $u_4$*-mi-ša ba-la-ṭ*[*am a-na*] *šar-ri a-ši-bi šu-p*[*a-at ne-eḫ-ti* ?...]

6' $^{d}$*Na-na-a ba-la-ṭ*[*am a-n*]*a šar-ri A-bi-e-š*[*u-uḫ* ...] x x [...]

7' *tu-šu-ši-ib-šu i-na šu-pa-at ne-eḫ-ti li-i*[*š*?/*ta*/*da*...*i*]*m-m*[*a* ...]

====

8' *in-bu in-bu si-ma-at pa-ni* ni x [x x] x x [(x)] x x *ú šu*/*ma ma-za* x

9' $^{d}$*Na-na*!?(Text: IA)*-a* {AŠ} *ša re-*[*š*]*a-tim-*[*ma*]

----

10' *ša-am-ḫa mu-ù᾽-a-ti tu-ka-an-na ši-i tu-še-ši-ib-šu pa-ra-ku-ú ra-b*[*i*?*-ú*?...]

11' *ki-ma na-aš-ši i-ri-mu i-za-an-na-an*

----

12' [*it-ta-na-a*]*k-ku-ú bu-nu-ša*!?(Text: TA) *ša-ni-iš iḫ-ta-aš-šu-ús-si ki-ma me-e ṣa-mi mi-im-mu-ú-š*[*a*]

13' [x x x] *dam-qá ra-ma-a-ta du-uš-šu-um-ma*

----

14' [... ...] x x x x [*fi*]*t*?*-ta ku-uz-bi an-nu-ú ti-bi lu-ur-ta-a-ma*

15' [... ...] x *la-la-a-ki lu-uš-bi*

----

16' [… …] x x x x *e*!?*-ma mi-im-ma* [*li-ib-bu-u*]*k ub-ba-la-*[*am*?] *iš-ti-ša*

17' [… ...] x *ma ṭe-ma* x [x x (x)*-ḫ*]*u-un-ma*

----

18' [… …] x *ša ḫa ip t*[*u*] x x x x [....] x x *ra-a-ma li-*[*ma*?]*-li*

19' [… … *l*]*i ḫu-ur* x x *lu-ut*-[...

20' [… …] *ú ga ḫu* x x [...

====

21' [… …] x *ni* x [......

22' [… …] *a ra-am-ki ki-ma ši-it-ti* [....]

23' [… …] *ki-ma ṣe-eḫ-ri pa-ṣa-na ú*-x [...]

**Translation**

Obv.?

1 Let me be sated with your charms, Nanāya – your lips are very sw[eet…]

2 [… *your*] passion is .. […]

----

3 […] lovemaking, Nanāya, .... let us make love,

4 […] May I always be lustrous.

----

5 […] ... well-being, let him shepherd his men forever.

6 [The…] ... (for?) Abī-Ešūh, may I perform again and again.

====

7 [*My lord*], I will speak to her lover, so that she will gladly fill his heart with joy,

----

8 [Muʾati], I will speak to her lover, so that she will gladly fill his heart with joy.

----

9 [*My lord*], so sweet is your passion, the appeal of your love is sated with honey,

----

10 Muʾati, so sweet is your passion, the appeal of your love is sated with honey.

----

11 The image(s), the one(s) which *you have looked* (*at*), is/are constant *festival(s)*. It/they will not *be sat*[*ed*…].

----

12 Let me gaze at your body, so tall, filled with joy […]

----

13 Muʾati, (let me gaze at) your body, so tall, filled with joy […]

----

14 At you command may the king live forever! [At your command] may Abī-Ešūh live forever!

====

15 The exuberant, our Muʾati, in daylight and *darkness* […]

16 …

Rev.?

1' …
2' […] prime, good [….]
----
3' She looked on Babylon with her kind eyes […]
4' She blessed it, she decreed its well-being […]
----
5' Daily lif[e for] the king who dwells in s[ecurity …]
6' Nanāya, life for the king Abī-E[šūh (will provide)...]
7' She let him dwell in security [… …].
----
8' Passion, passion, (as) befits the face of [… …]
9' *Nanāya* of j[o]y.
----
10' She treats kindly elated Muʾati; she seated him *on a large* dais […]
11' Like dew charms (of love) rain down (on him).
----
12' [*They make lov*]*e repeatedly*. In her appearance he repeatedly rejoiced on her; whatever is hers is like water (for the) thirsty.
13' [Your ...] are beautiful. You are loveable....]. He is so sweet!
----
14' […] this appeal of mine, rise, I want to make love (to you).
15' […] let me be sated with your attractiveness.
----
16' […] *wherever*, I will bring *you* whatever your [*heart*] desires from her.
17' […] … […]
----
18' [……] let him *be filled* with love.
19' …
20' …
21' …
22' […] … your(f.) love like a sleep […]
23' […] quickly […] to veil […]

**Commentary**

3: *lurtāmā*: Lambert (1966, 49) suggested that this verbal form (whose exact parallel is found in PRAK 1 B 472 i 3' = № 13) is to be analyzed as precative 1 du. form, "let us two make love together". Support for this suggestion comes from YOS 11, 24 i 22 (№ 15), where *lu-uḫ-ta-al-ṣa* is found (see also Hecker 2005, 173).

7: *a-ta-ú*: I follow Lambert's (1966, 51) translation and take *a-ta-ú* as 1 sg. form (cf. ll. 3, 4), against Hecker (1989, 741) who takes it as an imp. – "Her lover" refers most probably to the king, who was a personification of Muʾati.

9: [*be*?-*li*?]: Restoration already in CAD K 614b.

10: Reading follows Hecker 1989, 743.

11: *ṣalmu ša ta-ab-ra*: With Lambert (1966, 51), I take *tabrâ*(*m*) as a form of *barûm*, "to look at". – *i-ši-nu-ú* is understood as *iššinnu*/*isinnu*, "festival". Both nouns in this sentence may be in pl.

12: *ša-qí-a-am la-an-ka*: The alternative reading *ša ki-a-am la-an-ka* is difficult: *šaqīam lānka*, "your tall body", is preferred.

15: *ūmam ek-le-e-t*[*a*?-*am*?]: The somewhat rare merismatic pair *ūmum-ekletum* is found also in OB Gilg. Schøyen$_2$: 35: "The day (*ūmu*) shrouded itself, darkness (*ekletum*) went forth",[326] paralleled in SB Gilg. IV 102: "The day grew still, darkness went forth".[327]

3': Another example of a city which is loved by a god comes from the Zimrī-līm epic. Terqa is called there *narāmat Dagan*, "beloved by Dagan (Guichard 2014, 23 iv 9).

7': *tušūšib* is an early OB form, but note the more recent form *tušēšib* in l. 10'.

9': $^{d}$*Na-na*!?-*a* {AŠ} *ša re*-[*š*]*a-tim*-[*ma*]: The sign *aš* could be a glide connecting *Nanāya* and *ša rēšātim* (which would hint that the scribe was writing by dictation). Note a similar case of a badly written Nanāya in Fs. Renger 192–193 i 20 (№ 6).

10': *tukannâ šī*: Reading follows Hecker 1989, 743 n. 10a. – *parakku rabû*: Reading seems certain and goes well with *wašābum*-Š. The syntax suggests a loc. adv.

11': *našši* (< *nalši*): The assimilation *šš* < *lš* is a clear post-OB feature, but can be found already in OB (see GAG § 34). See also YOS 11, 12a: 6 which reads *libbi annanna mār annanna ša iš-šu* (*iššu* < *ilšu*) *annanna*, "The heart of so-and-so, whose god is so-and-so".

12': *bu-nu-ša*!?: Instead of the non-attested lemma *bunūtum* (or taking *bunūtum* for *banūtum*), I suggest to emend *ta* to *ša*, arriving to the well attested *būnu*, "outward appearance, face" (attested also in KAL 3, 75 iii 12' = № 8) – The collocation of *šanîš* and *hašāšum* "to swell, be happy" is perhaps also found in a hymn to Nanāya: "Nanāya […] – he (the king) *repeatedly* rejoices over her".[328] – [*it-ta-na-a*]*k-ku-ú*: Restoring the verb *niākum* is questionable, due to the negative nuance it usually carries: "having illicit intercourse" (see Overview § 4.4). – *mimmûša*: Previously I took this form as a loc. adv. (Wasserman 2003, 126 "thirsting for her stuff as for water"; so already Lambert 1966, 51, Foster 2005, 161 and Hecker 1989). Now I consider that taking this form in the nom. is

326 OB Gilg. Schøyen2: 35 (= George 2003, 234 ): *ūmu iʾapir ūṣi ekletum*.
327 SB Gilg. IV 102 (= George 2003, 592): *ūmu ušḫarrir ūṣa ekletum*.
328 VS 10, 215: 42 (= Streck/Wasserman 2012, 188): Nanāya [*ša*?]-⌈*ni*!?-*iš*?⌉ *iḫtaššuš*. Note that in their edition Streck and Wasserman (2012, 188) read […]-⌈*ri*?-*iš*?⌉.

simpler (so CAD M/2, 81a-b: "Her possessions are (as desirable) as water for the thirst"). In this way *mimmûša* is the subject of an elliptic nominal phrase whose predicate is *kīma mê ṣāmi*.

13': *duššumma*: Contra Hecker 1989, 743 n. 13a, with Lambert 1966, 51, this form is derived from *duššup*, "very sweet", not a form of *dešûm*-D (as in l. 10).

14': *lurtāmā*: See note to l. 3 above and cf. Mayer 2003, 234.

18': *râma li-*[*ma*?]*-li*: Lambert's copy is accurate (confirmed by collation). The form can be *limmali* (*malûm*-N) or *limalli* (*malûm*-D).

22': *râmki kīma šitti*: Reading follows Hecker 1989, 743. (Reading *a-ra-am-ki ki-ma ši-it-ti*, "I love you like a sleep…", is not excluded). – Overcoming Lambert's (1966, 50–51) hesitations, *ši-it-ti* by the end of line is to be taken from *šittum*, "sleep", a common motif in love lyrics (see Overview § 6.1).

23': *kīma ṣeḫri pa-ṣa-na*: I take *kīma ṣeḫri* as an adv. "quickly, immediately" (AHw 1089a, B3). For a similar use in ALL of *paṣānum*, "to veil", cf. ZA 49, 168–169 iii 14 (№ 16): *lu pa-aṣ*!*-ma an-sú-ur-ri ú-ul* [x x x].

# № 11 My Heart Is Awake Though I am Sleeping (The Moussaieff Love Song)[329]

Tablet Siglum: -/-
Photo: Figs. 14–16 (by NW)
Edition: below (Figs. 11–13)
Collection: The Shlomo Moussaieff Collection
Provenance: Nippur?
Measurements: 10x5.2x1.5 cm
Period: MB (based on OB origin?)

**Introduction**

The text, published here for the first time, presents back-and-forth amatory speeches of two lovers, conveying their desire for each other. Occasionally a narrative voice – a 'chorus' for lack of a better term – intervenes, describing the male lover. The tone of the text is passionate and devotional, its language supple, expressive and prolific with floral and avifaunal imagery. This composition duly deserves the appellation 'love lyric'.

The whitish tablet is in good condition. Only its corners are chipped off. As immediately noticed, the tablet is horizontally oriented. This landscape orientation – uncharacteristic to OB texts in general and to OB literary texts in particular – caused the lines to be significantly longer than other texts in ALL (and, indeed, longer than other OB literary texts). Consequently, both the man's and the woman's talk appear together in some lines.[330] The original provenance of the tablet is unknown, but based on grammatical, orthographical and epigraphical arguments, I suggest that the text was written, or at least copied, in Nippur.

The Moussaieff text shows a mixture of OB and MB features:

(a) The shape of the tablet: As mentioned, the Moussaieff tablet is horizontally arranged. Only one other text in the corpus shows a similar landscape orientation: Or. 60, 340 (№ 12), a MB text unearthed in Nippur and now housed in Jena. The two tablets are almost

329 This dialogue amounts to part of the private collection of the late Shlomo Moussaieff (1925–2015). Since the tablets in the Moussaieff collection bear no numbers, I follow the owner's wish and refer to the text as the Moussaieff Love Song. The existence of the tablet was made known to me by Jakob Klein, who passed me excellent photos of the tablet and arranged a meeting with its owner. In this meeting Shlomo Moussaieff generously loaned the tablet to me and granted me rights of publication. I am grateful to Mr. Roi Ram, Moussaieff's personal assistant and to Jakob Klein for their help and cooperation. Shlomo Moussaieff passed away in June 2015 before seeing this tablet published. While working on the Moussaieff Love Song I consulted two colleagues: Uri Gabbay read my preliminary edition and offered valuable suggestions, and M. P. Streck with whom I re-read the text and whose readings and interpretations are integrated into my edition. I thank them cordially.

330 As the discussion below will show, it is very likely that this horizontal arrangement of the tablet, with its long lines, was the decision of a later copyist. In any case, it is unusual in OB literary texts to switch between speakers within the same line.

identical in size: The Moussaieff Love Song measures 10x5.2 cm while the Jena tablet is 10x6.5 cm. But the similarity between the two tablets does not end here.

(b) Epigraphy: The Moussaieff text is beautifully written with a confident and accurate hand. The signs are elaborate, almost lapidary (see specifically the signs *ma*, *ud*, *ḫi*, *bi* and *še*). But interestingly, regular cursive signs appear side-by-side with the elaborate forms of the same signs. The clearest example is that of *na* which is found in its archaic and elaborate form (rev. 6 (2x), rev. 8, rev. 14) and in its cursive, regular OB sign form (obv. 2, obv. 4, obv. 6, obv. 9, rev. 4, rev. 7). Similarly, the star-like, archaic *an* sign (obv. 1 and rev. 2) stands next to the cursive forms of the same sign (obv. 14 and rev. 14). This mixture of old and later signs indicates that a later scribe made a deliberate effort to produce a tablet in an archaic style.[331]

Curiously, a similar amalgam of archaic, lapidary and cursive signs is found in the Jena tablet. In Or. 60, 340 (№ 12) too, the archaic *an* sign[332] coincides with the cursive form of this sign.[333] The situation with the *na* sign is even more revealing: all the *na* signs in the main part of Or. 60, 340 (№ 12) are archaically written, while the *na* signs in the rhymes which seal each line in the text are written cursively. Hence, the scribe of the Jena tablet also made an intentional effort to produce an old-looking tablet – but he too was not careful enough and let the cursive way of writing some of the more common signs intrude, thus betraying the true date of the tablet.[334]

(c) Orthography: The Moussaieff Love Song uses, unexceptionally, the signs *pi* and *sa*. This very same usage is found in Or. 60, 340 (№ 12). CV and VC-signs predominate while CVC-signs occur mainly in final position (where mimation is required).[335] Occasionally the text uses archaic syllabic values: *ù* for a verbal prefix (rev. 5, rev. 8), and *qà* (rev. 8). What is important, however, is that together with regular OB orthography, there are syllabic values which are found only in post-OB texts: *šúm*(SUM) and *tar* (both in rev. 8). These values prove that the text was copied in post-OB times.

(d) Grammar: The Moussaieff Love Song shows a mixture of OB and post-OB grammatical features. Mimation is mostly kept.[336] The change of *w* > *m* is not attested,[337] and uncontracted vowels are common.[338] Some cases of "broken"-spellings (see Groneberg

331 Scribes, at least some, could produce texts with archaic signs. This phenomenon is found, e.g., in the short OB drafts for seal inscriptions which were written in quasi-lapidary style, see Beckman 1998 and Feingold 2002 (refs. Dominique Charpin).

332 Or. 60, 340: obv. 2, rev. 2 (№ 12).

333 Or. 60, 340: rev. 4 (№ 12).

334 Another example of MB Nippur scribe employing both archaic and cursive sign forms when copying an OB original was noted by Lambert (BWL 276).

335 *tim*, *tam*, *tum*, *dam*, *kum*, *lam*, *lum*, *rum*, and *ḫar* (obv. 5 in a verbal form). Note especially *lam-mi* (rev. 2) in initial position.

336 But see [*ṭa*?]-*bu rē'um* obv. 13, *na-ši-ap-pa* rev. 4 and *ta-ma-ra-tu* rev. 6.

337 *na-wa-ar-tum* obv. 1, *li-wi-ir* rev. 3, *na-wa-ar* rev. 7, *ta-wi-ra-ti-šu* rev. 9, *it-ta-wi-ir* rev. 10. (See Hess 2012, 87–89).

338 *ta-*⌈*am*?⌉*-ṣi-a-tim* obv. 3, *ṣi-a-am* obv. 8, *lu-ú-ša-li-a-am* obv. 15, *um-mi-a-ni-im* rev. 6, *ma-ni-a-šu* rev. 9.

1980) exist,[339] and bridging vowels (glides) are also found.[340] Some hymnic-epic features can also be found: a shortened attached personal pronoun,[341] an archaic construct form in -*u*,[342] a loc. adv.,[343] and the preposition *an*(*a*) attached to the following noun.[344] But here too, to this set of OB features, younger traits are joined: third-weak verbs are spelled with the ultimate vowel lengthened, even when no attached pronoun follows,[345] and long vowels occur where grammatically they are not required,[346] notably in precative forms.[347] These are orthographical convention which occur in OB, but become more prominent in MB texts.[348] The clearest post-OB signs are found in the pronomina: -*ki* standing for -*kim*.[349]

(e) Lexicon: At least two lemmas in the Moussaieff Love Song are so far attested only in post-OB texts: *lammum* (rev. 2) *ṣurrum* (rev. 3).

Weighing all the evidence, it is hard to avoid the conclusion that the Moussaieff Love Song is an MB copy of an OB, perhaps even early OB original, which the scribe strove to present as an old text. The similarities to the Nippur tablet Or. 60, 340 (№ 12) suggest that our text was very likely written in Nippur as well.

The copying process can be identified by scribal mistakes (whose number grows towards the end of the tablet): an omitted sign,[350] a wrong – but similar – sign used,[351] and signs mistakenly copied from the preceding line.[352]

The rulings that separate the text into sections with different numbers of lines must be addressed.[353] What is clear is that the different sections do not mark a change of speaker, for 'He' and 'She' appear not only in the same sections, but at times also in the same line.[354] Do the rulings mark separate units in a single composition, or is it possible that we are dealing with different compositions written one after the other on the same tablet? Since the text bears no colophon, the answer to this question must remain conjectural, but my impression is that the obv. of the tablet consists of only one composition (ending in obv. 15 – where a happy union of the couple is described), while the reverse, which is thematically

339 *na-ši-ap-pa* rev. 4, *ṣi-ip-pi-a-tim* rev. 12.

340 *a-*⌈*we*⌉*-er* (for *â'er*) obv. 4 and *pi ú-ṣi-ia ra-*⌈*ab*⌉*-bu?-tim-ma* (< *pī ūṣi a*(*n*)*-rabbûtim*) obv. 7 – but cf. s obv. 4.

341 [*li?*]-⌈*bu*⌉*-uk* obv. 7.

342 ⌈*ra-ma*⌉*-ka* obv. 3.

343 *a-ru-ur-tu-ú-a* obv. 4.

344 *a-ma-ni-šu* rev. 7 and perhaps also *pi ú-ṣi-ia ra-*⌈*ab*⌉*-bu?-tim-ma* (< *pī ūṣi a*(*n*)*-rabbûtim*) obv. 7.

345 *ú-ma-al-li-i* obv. 7, *ir-de-e-ši* obv. 9, *im-ḫi-i* obv. 10, *i-ma-lu-ú* (pl.) obv. 14, ⌈*hu-di?*⌉*-a-an-ni* rev. 2.

346 *ri-bu-ú!-um* obv. 4, *-ku-ú-um* obv. 5, *ú-úr-ri-iš* obv. 9, *tu-ú-ub-ba-lam* rev. 1.

347 *lu-ú-ra-am-ki* obv. 1, *lu-ú-ša-li-a-am lu-ú-ud-bu-u*[*b...*] obv. 15, *lu-ú-ba-a-ma* rev. 3, *lu-ú-ḫa-ad-di* rev. 4, *lu-ú-ma-ḫi-ir-ka* rev. 7.

348 See Hess 2012, 164–165.

349 obv. 3 and rev. 9 (2x), but cf. rev. 6 and note that the distinction *-ka* vs. *-kum* is kept (obv. 5, rev. 8 (See Hess 2012, 122).

350 ⌈*i?*⌉*-na* <*bu*>*-sú-ur-ra-tim* obv. 6.

351 "*ba-ak*!(Text: AZ)-*ki* rev. 5. (if needed AZ is a mistake)"

352 *ḫa-ar-pi-iš*!(Text: LUM) rev. 11, taken erroneously from *-lum* in the previous line. It is also possible that *ṣi-a-am ši-it-tum* (obv. 8) is a copying mistake. One expects imp. 2 sg. f. (*ṣīm*), in correct congruence with *šittum*.

353 On the obv.: 3 ll. / 3 ll. / 4 ll. / 2 ll. / 3 ll. On the rev.: 3 ll. / 3 ll. / 3 ll. / 1 ll. / 2 ll. // 2 ll.

354 See obv. 1, obv. 2, obv. 5.

less coherent, may contain another composition which culminates in another "happy end" (rev. 1 – rev. 10), or even more than one composition.[355] Finally, none of the lines in the Moussaieff Love Song appears in the incipits of the Assur catalogue KAR 158 (№ 19).

Obv.

1 *⌈i⌉-⌈na⌉ ⌈a⌉-⌈la⌉-ki-⌈šu iš⌉-ša-ka-an na-wa-ar-tum ki lu-di-ir-ka ki lu-ú-ra-am-ki*

2 *[ḫa]-(⌈ab?⌉)-bi-li-iš da-di-ka lu-um-šu-úḫ i-na ma-ti ap-pi la-le-ki lu-ú-⌈sú⌉-⌈ḫa⌉-[a]m?*

3 [x x *e*]*p?-te*$_9$*-ki ta-⌈am?⌉-ṣi-a-tim ù mi-iṣ-ra-tim ša-la-lam ⌈ra-ma⌉-ka šu-ul-li-⌈il?⌉ aš-ši*

----

4 *⌈a-ku-ud⌉ a-ru-ur-tu-ú-a ri-bu-ú!-um na-ši ši-it-ti a-⌈we⌉-er bi-tam a-du-ul as-ḫu-ur*

5 *mi-im-ma ú-ul ⌈ú⌉-ta-ḫa!-di te-e-er-ma ur-ri ⌈im⌉-⌈ta⌉-⌈ḫar⌉ ⌈ša⌉ a-qú-ul-la-ku-ú-um*

6 *pi-ia a-na-aṣ-ṣa-ar ka-at-ma ⌈i⌉-⌈na⌉-⌈ia?⌉ li-ib-bi e-er ṣa-al-la-⌈ku⌉ ⌈i?⌉-na <bu>-sú-ur-ra-tim* / *i[ḫ]-[d]u-ú li-ib-bi*

----

7 *pi ú-ṣi-ia ra-⌈ab⌉-bu?-tim-ma ⌈an?⌉-⌈nu?⌉ ⌈li?⌉-⌈bu⌉-uk ⌈da⌉-⌈di⌉ ú-ma-al-li-i*

8 *⌈a?⌉-na pa-ru-uš-ši-im e-er-*⌈x?⌉ *ú-te-er-ra-am al-ki-im-mi ši-it-tum ⌈la-ḫi?-iš⌉ ṣi-a-am? ši-it-tum*

9 *⌈a-la⌉-lu-ú pa-as-pa-sí-im ú-úr-ri-iš mu-ši-⌈tum⌉ ⌈il?⌉-li-ik-ma a-na-ku er-de-e-ši*

10 *⌈úr?⌉-ši ki-i-ma ṣa-ab-[ra?]-a-tim ka-ba-at-ti im-ḫi-i*

----

11 *[ti?-i?]-⌈bi⌉ et-pe-er ti-⌈i-bi⌉ et-pe-er ṣi-ḫa-ti-ia sú-ú-ni ki-i-ma ul-[ša?]-[ni-i]m*

12 *[ú/ù]-ra-ab-ba-kum in-ba-am eš-ša-a[m]*

Lo. Ed.

13 [*ṭa?* or: *in*]*-bu rēʾûm*(SIPA) *il-lu-ru-um na-as-qum ša ša-di-šu ša-ru-ú-ru li-ib-bi-ni ša* ⌈x⌉-[x x x]

14 *⌈sú?⌉-ma-ti* NI *id-ra-an-ni i-ma-lu-ú ta-⌈wa-tum?⌉ ša ṣú-uḫ-ra-ti-⌈im?⌉* [x x]

15 *ga-a-na lu-ú-ša-li-a-am lu-ú-ud-bu-u*[*b* x x x (x)]*-nu?*

Rev.

1 *[qà?]-⌈ab?⌉-li-tam mi-nam tu-ú-ub-ba-lam ia-ši-im šu-um-ṣi mi-iḫ-ḫu-ri ù ki* x [

2 *[du?]-mi-iq ma-di-iš šu-um-mi-ḫa-an-ni ⌈ḫu-di?⌉-a-an-ni lu-*

355 Note the double ruling line after rev. 12.

*mu-ur kirî*($^{\text{giš}}$KIRI$_6$) *lam*!*-mi* ⌈x⌉-[…]

3 *[li-i]b-bi li-wi-ir ṣú-ur-ri lu-ri-iš lu-uḫ-du lu-ú-ba-a-ma ṣú-ú-ḫi-*⌈*iš*⌉ *ri-bi-*⌈*it*⌉ ⌈x?⌉ ⌈*a*⌉*-lim*

----

4 ⌈*ú/ù?*⌉*-la a-ma-ni-šu lu-ub-lam li-ib-ba-ki lu-ú-ḫa-ad-di na-ši-ap-pa ru-um-mi lu-mi-id-ki*

5 [*pi?*] *šu-ul-mi ba-AZ-ki pa-as-pa-sí kirûm*($^{\text{giš}}$KIRI$_6$) *i-ni-ib-šu eqlum*(A.ŠÀ*-lum*) *še'*(ŠE)*-a-šu ù-ša-ar-ba-ni* (x?)

6 ⌈*ḫi-mé*⌉*-tam li-iš-dam na-šu-ki-im ma-ri um-mi-a-ni-im ta-ma-ra-tu na-šu la-le-e-ki*

----

7 ⌈*a*⌉*-na*!*-ku i-na bi-tim lu-ú-ma-ḫi-ir-ka na-wa-ar ka-ba-at-tim ku-uz-ba-am ta-ar-ta-ma-am*

8 *ù-tar pa-pa-am qà-ta-tam el-ka ša* ⌈*ta*⌉*-ra-am-mu ú-ri na-di*!*-kum* ⌈*bābum*⌉(⌈KÁ?⌉) *ra-ap-šúm*(SUM) *šu-ud-du-lum*

9 *ú-ga-rum e-ri-iš-ki ti-i-di ma-ni-a-ti-šu ḫa-ar-pi-iš e-ri-iš-ki ta-wi-ra-ti-šu*

----

10 *i-li-lam le-e-lam li-ib-bi it-ta-wi-ir e-re-ed-de u*$_4$*-mi*

----

11 *ni-*⌈*kur*⌉*-ru-um up-pu-la?-ka nap-pi-*⌈*il*⌉*-lum ḫa-ar-šu-ú el-la-a-ku ú-ma-*⌈*ša*⌉*-aš du-um ṣú-uḫ-ḫu-um*

12 ni ib *bu-nu-ú la?-lu ṣi-ip-pi-a-tim ḫa-ar-pi-iš*!(Text: LUM) *kasap*(KÙ.BABBAR) *ša-di-šu wu-ud-di la re-ḫa-tum*!(Text: TIM) *uk-ku-la* / *šu-lu-um-mu-*⌈*um?*⌉ *ik-kí-ir*

====

13 [*ni-*(*i*)*-ir*] *i-mi-it-ti-ka ù ni-i-ir šu-m*[*e*]-⌈*li*⌉-⌈*ka*⌉ *šu-ta-ta-a na-ag-bi bé-e-li ú-*⌈*du?*⌉*-ul* x

14 [*da*⌉*at*([$^{\text{giš}}$I]G) ⌈*ša?*⌉ *ú-li i-mi-it-tim* ⌈*ù šu-me-lim la*⌉*-ṭá-a-ma ti-i-di ši-ib-qì-ši-na-*⌈*ma?*⌉ / *sa-an-ta-ak*

**Translation**

Obv.

1 (Chorus:) [In] his *coming* brightness is brought about. (She:) – How I want to embrace you! He: – How I want to love you!

2 (She:) – Like *a* [*robb*]*er* I want to plunder your attractiveness! (He:) – When may I *pull out* your *clitoris* (lit. "the nose of your desire")!

3 (He?:) [*…I have ope*]*ned for you entrances*(?) and borders. (She?:) Take (me) captive by your love! (He?:) I carried away.

----

4 (She?:) I got worried in my hunger, trembling has carried away my sleep. I woke up, I went through the house, searched around.

5 (He?:) Do not get worried at all! (She:) Return (it to me)! My day has arrived in which *I am paying attention* to you.

6 (He?:) I avoid talking, my eyes are drawn, my heart is awake (though) I am sleeping. My heart rejoiced in the *good news*.

----

7 (She:) My speech turned to tenderness. *Indeed*: I filled your hea[rt] with attractiveness.

8 (He:) *Because of*(?) the goad I am (Text: he is) awake. I repeat: 'Oh sleep, come to me like to a baby! Go out from me, Oh sleep!'

9 (He:) By day-light – there are joyful calls of the duck. When the night has gone I have pursued her.

10 (He?:) My bedroom (is) like twittering (birds); my mind went crazy.

----

11 (She:) [*Become er*]*ect*! Feed yourself! Become erect! Feed yourself with my lovemaking! My lap is like *best of oils*.

12 (She:) I will grow for you a new fruit!

13 (Chorus:) [*Fru*]*it*, shepherd, the chosen flower of the mountain, gleaming of our heart which …

14 (She?:) My dove, ... embrace me! (Even if) the (malicious) speeches of the young girls will fill the…

15 (He:) Come on! I want to plunge (into your love)! Let me tal[k (sweet words to you!)]

Rev.

1 (She:) *In the middle watch of the night*, what do you carry for me? (He:?) Let me attain the offering and …

2 (She:) [Ma]ke (me) beautiful! Make me greatly flourish! Make me happy! (He?:) Let me see the orchard of the *almond* trees!

3 (She?:) May my [he]art be bright! May I be happy in my inside! May I rejoice! May I walk along with laughter in the street of the city.

----

4 (He:) To whom should I bring the *best oil*? May I make your heart rejoice! Leave aside the reed-basket! Let me lean upon you!

5 (She:) *A word of* greeting (is) the squalling of the ducks. (As) the orchard – its fruit, the field – its grain, (so) did he make me grow.

6 (He:) The craftsmen carry for you butter and ghee. Audience-gifts – they are carrying for your pleasure.

----

7 (She:) I, in the house, let me make you accept happy mood, attractiveness, mutual love.

8 (She:) I make excessive the thin curl *over you*. That which you love, my vulva, is laid down for you: wide, spacious gate.

9 (He:) The field is plowed up for you. You know its dimensions; it is plowed early for you; (You know) its meadows.

----

10 (He?:) Hurrah! At evening time my heart became pure for me, turned bright! I will continue my day.

====

11 (She?:) *What was denied is paid back to you. Compensated...* I am pure, I am wiping clean. The smile is darkened.

12 (Chorus?/He?:) ... the pleasures of the orchards are pleasant in early time. (Chorus?/He?:) Distinguish the silver of its mountain, (even if) *the slag* (lit. leftovers*) is not darkened.* What (formerly) was favorable has become hostile.

----

13 (She:) [The yoke] of your right and the yoke of your left are facing each other; My source, Oh my lord, is *locked…*

14 (She:) The *u.*-door of the right and (the *u.*-door) of the left are curbed. You know their (= the rival women?) plans regularly.

**Commentary**

obv. 1: Restoring *ina alākišu* at the beginning is likely but uncertain. – *nawartum*: a by-form of *namirtum*/*nawirtum* (unattested hitherto).

obv. 2: [*ḫa*]-(⌈*ab*?⌉)-*bi-li-iš*: This spelling of *ḫābiliš*, "like a robber", is typically post-OB, but it is not impossible that the text has only [*ḫa*]-*bi-li-iš*. – The verb *mašā'um* in its sexual meaning is found also in CUSAS 10, 12: 10 (№ 18): "She is taken by force regarding her vulva".[356] – *appi lalêki*: This compound is unknown elsewhere, but *appum* designates often the tip, or the crown of different body parts (e.g. *appi išāri* = *glans penis* or *appi tulê* = *papillis*).[357] I find it hard to imagine that *appi lalêki* refers here literally to the nose of the woman, hence I cautiously postulate that the "tip of desire" refers euphemistically to the clitoris (MPS). – Reading the verbal form at the end of the line, *lu-ú*-[*sú*?]-[*ḫa*?]-[*a*]*m*?, is possible but not certain. If correct, *nasāḫum* "to tear out, pull out", is used here metaphorically, in parallel to *mašā'um* "to plunder", in the first part of the line.

obv. 3: *ta-am-ṣi-a-tim*: This *taPRĪSt* pattern pl. form (unattested elsewhere), deriving in all likelihood from *wuṣṣûm*, "to spread", is semantically related to *miṣrātim*, "borders", thus "apertures" or "entrances" is exptected. – ⌈*ra-ma*⌉-*ka*: a poetical long construct form

356 CUSAS 10, 12: 10 (№ 18): *ūraša mašḫat*.

357 See Böck 2000, 49 and CAD A/2, 187–188, 2a-b.

(instead of *rāmka*). – *ša-la-lam šu-ul-li-*[*il*]: The *figura etymologica* (standing for the more common idiom *šallatam šalālum*) continues the metaphors in the previous line where *mašāʾum* and perhaps also *nasāḫum* are used. – It is not clear who is the subject of the verbal form *aššī* which ends this line. I assume it is the man who responds positively to the encouragement of the woman: "I have carried (your booty)".

obv. 4: Another attestation of the uncommon motif of hunger (here, *arurtum*) is found in A 7478 i 3–4 (№ 1): "I entered into the pantry, lying to sleep without eating".[358] Hunger leads to sleeplessness, and the speaker (the woman, I believe) goes out and walks around the house of her beloved. Encircling the beloved (or, as in this line, his house), in order to catch his or her attention, or to prevent competitors from gaining access to him or her, is found also in other texts.[359] – *a-*[*we*]*-er*: Formally this verb can be analyzed as deriving from *nawārum*, but *awʾēr* (standing for *aʾēr* with a glide), deriving from *êrum*, "to be awake" makes better sense here (MPS).

obv. 5: [*ú*]*-ta-ḫa*!*-di*: This is the first attestation of *naʾādum*-Dt-imp. 2 sg. f.[360] The expected form is *utaʾʾidī*, but the sign looks more like a squeezed ḪA than ḪI. – The possessive suffix in "my day", refers to the subject, the speaker of this phrase, as described by Stol 1996.

obv. 6: *pi-ia*: Syntax requires that this noun is in acc. (*pī* is expected), hence *-ia* is yet another glide, bridging *pī* to *anaṣṣar*. – *pâ naṣārum*: With AHw 755b, 12a and CAD N/2, 39a 6a this idiom means "to avoid talking, refraining from expressing verbally what is on one's mind". A fine example of this expression comes from a physiognomical omen: "If he is (able to) guard his mouth, the respect of the people (to him) is made clear/given to him".[361] – *libbī ēr ṣallāku*: The Biblical parallel "I was asleep, but my heart was wakeful. Hark, my beloved knocks!" (Songs 5: 2) is remarkable, proving that Mesopotamian and biblical love literature drew from a common pool of stock-phrases. – *<bu>-sú-ur-ra-tim*: This emendation seems unavoidable. Reading *ina sú-ur-ra-tim iḫdu libbī*, "my heart rejoiced in lies", though possible grammatically, is thematically unsustainable.

obv. 7: *pi(-)ú-ṣi-ia(-)ra-*[*ab*]*-bu-tim-ma*: Sandhi spelling for *pî ūṣi arrabbūtim* (< *an*(*a*) *rabbūtim*). Words and utterances are described as "coming out" from the mouth, as, e.g.: "I execute (whatever) order comes (*ittaṣi*) from the mouth of the king, my lord".[362]

obv. 8: *paruššum*: The exact meaning of this rare word for "staff, goad, spike" (CAD P 211a – attested only in bilingual texts and once in *Ludlul* II 101: "The rod was piercing me,

---

358 A 7478 i3–4 (№ 1): *ērub iḫḫuršim ibbalum akālim ṣallāku.*

359 MAD 5, 8: 21–24 (№ 22), MS 3062: 14–15 (№ 23), CUSAS 10, 9: 13(№ 23). Cf. also Songs 2: 9.

360 For the elision of the initial *n-* in D and Dt forms of prima-Nun verbs, see GAG § 102e and Kouwenberg 2010, 470.

361 Böck 2000, 134: 61: *šumma nāṣir pīšu* (var. *pīšum*) *kabattu nišī namuršu* (var: *šakinšu*), and similarly, the advice in the Counsels of Wisdom (BWL 104: 131): *ē tumaṣṣi pīka uṣur šaptīka*, "Do not talk exessively, guard your lips".

362 EA 160: 11, 16: *ša ittaṣi ištu pī šarri bēliya uševšer* (cited in CAD A/2, 366a).

it was covered with thorn”[363] – is not clear. Is a phallic nuance intended? – *ēr*: The text presents a 3 sg. m stative form, but 1 sg. *ērēku* would make better sense. – The request that sleep will go away is found also in the incipit KAR 158 vi 19' (№ 19): “Go away sleep!”.[364]

obv. 9: *alālū paspasim*: This line gives, for the first time it seems, a description of the duck’s quacking.[365] In the second mill. roosters were not yet domesticated in Mesopotamia,[366] hence the quacking of ducks was the characteristic sound of daybreak.[367] – *urriš*: This rare temp. adv., is found twice only in Enūma eliš, in the merismatic couple *urriš–mūšiš*.[368]

obv. 10: *ṣab*[*r*]*ātim*: If correctly restored, the pl. f. adj. *ṣab*[*r*]*ātim* refers elliptically to twittering birds,[369] which the love-stricken man hears in his bed chamber. A similar situation is described in CUSAS 10, 8 (№ 2): “I (Text: he) awoke to the noise of swallows, writhed in (my) bedroom on the bed”.[370]

obv. 11: *etper*: A similar reflexive form of *epērum*-Gt is found in YOS 11, 24 (№ 15): “Be mingled with fruits and desires! Be capped with vitality!”.[371]

obv. 12: A similar collocation joining “fresh” and “fruit” is found in CUSAS 10, 8: 8–10 (№ 2).

obv. 13: Only one sign is missing in the beginning of the line: [*in*]*bu* or [*ṭā*]*bu* are both possible.[372]

obv. 14: [*sú*?]*-ma-ti* NI *id-ra-an-ni* remains unclear to me. Reading *summatini* is difficult, as the correct form should be *summatni*. Joining the NI sign to the verbal form which follows (*ì-id-ra-an-ni*) is difficult orthographically. Assuming that *summatī* is the correct reading, then a parallel to this line can be offered: “I have thrown my coop on the young

363 Oshima 2014, 92–93: 101 (= BWL 44: 101): *paruššu usaḫḫilanni ziqta labšat.*

364 KAR 158 vi 19' (№ 19): *šittu atlaki*:

365 In the Sultantepe birdcall text (Lambert 1970b, 114: 10) the duck’s call is recorded as *kingu-kingu*. Black/Al-Rawi (1987, 122) raise the possibility that those bird names in Akk. which are based on a reduplicated stem (as *kirkarrum*, *šiqšiqqum*, *paspasum*), are onomatopoeic and describe the birds’ call.

366 For the common opinion reg. the domestication of cocks and hens in the ancient Near East, see Black/Al-Rawi 1987, 119 n. 6, and more recently Perry-Gal et al. 2015. Note the appearance of the DAR.LUGAL$^{\text{mušen}}$ in the first line of the OB bird text published Black/Al-Rawi (1987) and again by Al-Rawi/Dalley (2000).

367 The legend of the Capitoline geese of Juno, whose clamor in the last watch of night saved Rome from the nocturnal attack of the Gauls, comes to mind.

368 Lambert 2013, 52 i 38, i 50, and cf. CAD U/W 243a.

369 For the sexual overtones of the verb *ṣabārum*, cf. Groneberg 1986.

370 CUSAS 10, 8: 20–21 (№ 2): [*arrig*]*im šinūnūtim iggeltâm* [*in*]*a uršima agrur ina mayyālim.*

371 YOS 11, 24 i 23 (№ 15): *itablal eli inbī u dādī balāṭam etper.*

372 Cf. Songs 2: 16 where a shepherd and a flower are mentioned together.

man, so that I may catch the 'dove'; (The coop) of my delights Nanāya will fill for me"![373] A "dove" (this time *sukannīnum*) is a metaphor for the male lover, perhaps even for his male member (see Overview § 4.6). – *imallû tāwītum* poses also difficulty, as the verb is in m. pl. while its supposed subj. is in f. pl. – The topos of the gossiping girls who try to separate the two lovers are mentioned also in CUSAS 10, 9: 29 (№ 3) and ZA 49, 168–169 i 11–12 (№ 16).

obv. 15: The verb *šalûm*, "to submerge, immerse in water", designating the total immersion in love, is found also in CUSAS 10, 8: 4–5 (№ 2): "My mood plunged into the infesting heart".[374]

rev. 2: *lammī*: For the identification of the *lammu*-tree (so far attested from MB times onwards) as "almond tree", see CAD L 67f. AHw 533 is more cautious and suggests "ein Baum" (adding, based on lexical equations, "eine Platane?"). Nesbitt/Postgate (1998–2001, 635) take *lammum* to be a kind of nut-tree, and Postgate/Hepper/Streck 2011–2013 discuss the possibility that *lammum* belongs to the genus *Pistacia*. Whatever the identification of this tree, other love-related texts use this tree as a metaphor for the male lover (see, SAA 3, 41: 14–16, and cf. Songs 6:11).

rev. 3: *ṣurrī*: The parallelism *libbum* // *ṣurrum* in this line has a direct counterpart in Malku = šarru V: 6 (Hrůša 2010, 395). The lemma *ṣurrum* is clearly dated to post-OB texts. – For another attestation of *ṣūḫiš*, "laughingly", in OB literary texts, see Wasserman 1992.

rev. 4: *ammannišu*: *ammannišu* (< *ana mānišu*) opens a rhetorical question, in which the pronominal suffix stresses that the speaker wants to bring the gift only to his expecting lover, cf. CAD M/1, 216b (MPS). – [*ú*/*ù*?]-*la*: *ulûm*, "best of oil" is restored, continuing *ul*-[*ša*?]-[*ni-im*] (obv. 11) and *ḫimētam lišdam* (rev. 6). – *na-ši-ap-pa*: from *našappu*, "a reed basket" (CAD N/2, 56). A similar "broken"-spelling in the text is *ṣi-ip-pi-a-tim* (rev. 12). – *rummî*: The verb *ramûm*-D, "to release, to let loose, to remove", when referring to a woman in amorous context, carries sexual innuendo. In the seduction scene in SB Gilg. I, Šamḫat removes her clothes in front of Enkidu: "Uncradle your bosom; bare your sex so he may take in your charms!",[375] and the epic continues: "Šamḫat let loose her skirts, she bared her sex and he took in her charms"[376] (trans. George). A similar appeal of a love struck man to the woman to drop what is in her hand and pay attention to him is found in YOS 11, 87: 14–17 (№ 26): "May the dough fall (out) of her hands, (as well as) the little one on her arms."[377]

---

373 Fs. Renger i 16–20 (№ 6): *quppī addi eṭlamma u sukannīna luṣbatma ša ṣīḫātiya* ᵈ*Nanāya tumallam.*
374 CUSAS 10, 8: 4–5 (№ 2): *kabtatī išalli libbam muḫattitam.*
375 SB Gilg. I 180–181 ( = George 2003, 548): *rummî kirimmīki ūrki pitêma kuzubki lilqe.*
376 SB Gilg. I 188–189 (= George 2003, 548): *urtammi Šamḫat dīdaša ūrša iptēma kuzubša ilqe.*
377 YOS 11, 87: 14–17 (№ 26): *<li>imqut līšum* [*ša*] *qātiša limqut* [*ṣ*]*uḫārum ša aḫiša.*

rev. 5: The first half of the line mentions again the ducks. Their sound is perceived this time not as a "joyful song", but as the hitherto unknown *baZkum*.[378] – The second half of the line echoes the vegetal motif in obv. 12 (*urabbâkkum inbam eššam*).

rev. 6: *mārī ummiānim*: This term is the subject of the sentence, hence one expects *mārū ummiānim*. Other examples of pl. m. nom. ending in *-ī* are known, as, e.g. *ilī mātim ekallam ireddû* (YOS 10, 24: 10. MPS). The appearance of craftsmen in this context is surprising. Perhaps a cultic scene is described, where devotees bring gifts to the temple. – *ta-ma-ra-tu*: This form of *tāmartum*, "gift" (CAD T 113f.) is syntactically difficult, as the form, *tāmarātim*, is expected.

rev. 7: *tartāmam*: For *tartāmum*, "mutual love", see Streck 2012b. Note that this lemma is in sg., while CAD T 245a lists only pl. forms.

rev. 8: *pappam*: The "curl" (the pl. of which can be m. or f., see AHw 824b) is declined here as f., as the adj. *qatattam* (<*qatantam*) proves. – *bābum rapšum šuddulum*: Wide vagina, metaphorically called "gate", is mentioned also in a physiognomical omen: "If a woman has a wide vagina…"[379] The opposite image, that of "locked gates", is found in ZA 75, 198–204h 117 (№ 33): "I have opened for you(m.) – Oh Erra-bāni – my seven gates!".[380]

rev. 9: *ugārum* and *tawirtum*: In a number of OB records *tawirtum* qualifies *ugārum* (CAT T 121b, 2'). Here these two terms for cultivated field are separated. – Plowing a field is a known metaphor in ALL for sexual intercourse.[381] An example can be brought from CUSAS 10, 10 (№ 4), where the man is mocking his ex-lover: "Do not place (me?) in the salt, your field is all too well known!".[382] Similarly, the cultivator (*errēšum*) is an appellation for the one who takes the woman sexually, as seen in an incipit from Babylon, CUSAS 10, 12: 20–21: "(One) is going out(f.), (another) is open(f.) – two are their(f. pl.) plowmen. [...] to the second of her plowmen (she says): '(You are) not the shepherd!'".[383]

rev. 10: This single line sentence marks, it seems, the end of a thematic unit, or a composition. Happy ending: having made love in the evening, the man's heart was happy (*īlilam ittawir*) and he is ready to continue his day.

378 Another option is to emend *ba-AZ-ki* to *ba-ak*!-*ki*. The adj. *bakkûm*, "crying", attested only in post-OB references (CAD B 35), would then refer to the continuous quacking of the ducks. If so, *ba-ak*!(Text: AZ)-*ki* is a copying mistake caused by *pa-as-pa-sí* which follows.

379 Böck 2000, 160: 153: *šumma sinništu ḫurdatam rapšat*.

380 ZA 75, 198–204i 117 (№ 34): *uptettīkum sebet bābiya*.

381 See Livingstone 1991 who discusses the seeder plow as a metaphor for the male organ (with previous bibliography).

382 CUSAS 10, 10: 38–39 (№ 4): *ina ṭabtim lā tašakkani*<*ni*?> *eqelki ḫukkum*.

383 CUSAS 10, 12: 20–21 (№ 18): [*wā*]*ṣiat pētât šina errēšāšina* […] *ana šanîm errēšiša ul rē'ûm*.

rev. 11–12: In these two challenging lines, which might have been corrupted in the process of copying, love is described in terms of valuable goods or a debt. In addition, what previously was shining and complete becomes dark.

rev. 11: I cannot untangle most of this line. The word *ni-kur-ru-um* (signs are clear) is tentatively understood as an unattested by-form of *nukurrûm*, "denial, denied amount of silver". – The following *up-pu-la?-ka* is perhaps *uppulakka*, stative of *apālum*-D, "to pay a debt, to satisfy" (but the pron. *-ka* is hard to explain). – *nap-pi-il-lum* is understood, with reservations, as an awkwardly spelled *nāpilum* (< *napālum* II, "to pay balance"). – I have no solution for *ḫa-ar-šu-ú* which follows, and *du-um* is parsed as *dūm*, a stative of *da'āmum*-D. The smile, envisioned as light, is suddenly darkened. (MPS).

rev. 12: The first two signs in the line elude me. – *ṣi-ip-pi-a-tim*: Another example of vowel breaking (as *na-ši-ap-pa* in rev. 4). – *ḫa-ar-pi*-LUM: This must be emended to *ḫa-ar-pi-iš*!, "early, in good time". The mistake was triggered by the *lum* sign in the preceding line, another copying mistake. – The second part of the line contrasts *kaspum* and *rēḫātum*, a juxtaposition known from daily-life texts, notably OA records (CAD R 338 b) 1'). As I understand it, the male lover is compared to precious silver ore, hidden in the mountain,[384] which should not be thrown away with the slag, the other, unworthy lovers. The woman is advised to distinguish between the two,[385] even if the slag is not yet dark in color. The syntax, however, is perplexing. First, *rēḫātum* is never negated (MPS), and second, if, as I believe, *ukkulā* is the predicate of the sentence, one expects *rēḫātum* in nom. I see no other option, but to analyze *lā* as negating the entire sentence, and emending *reḫātim* to *reḫātum*. – Note that, albeit less likely, *ik-kí-ir* can also be read *iq-qi-ir* (and then: "well-being is precious").

rev. 13–14: This couplet, separated by a double dividing line, contains probably a short new composition. At the beginning of the line, read perhaps [$^{giš}$I]G, namely *dalat ulli immitim/šumēlim*, attested so far only in lexical lists (CAD U/W 82a).[386]

rev. 13: *nagbī bēlī ú-*[*du?*]*-ul*: Deriving the verbal form from *edēlum*-D, offers a striking parallel to Songs 4: 12: "A garden locked is my own, my bride, a fountain locked, a sealed-up spring". The same verbal form, however, can be understood as *naṭālum*-imp., and then "Look (*uṭul*), Oh lord, at my source!".

---

384 Silver and its mountain is found in Lipšur Litanies: *arnī kīma kaspi ḫurāṣi ša ištu šadîšu ibbabla ana ašrišu ay itūr*, "May my sin, like silver and gold mined from its mountain, never return to its home" (CAD Š/1, 53 d). See also the incipit from the Assur catalogue KAR 158 vii 49' (№ 19): *re-bi-<it>-ka ša uqnî šadî*, "Your genitals are lapis-lazuli of the mountain.

385 *wu-ud-di* must be *wuddî* (*wadûm*-D imp.), not the modal particle *wuddi* (or *wadi*, following Kouwenberg's 2013, 331–334 convincing remarks), since the modal particle is never spelled with geminated dd (Wasserman 2012, 65 and Kouwenberg 2013, 331).

386 Alternatively, the beauty of the woman is praised by her beloved in terms of sumptuous equine equipment, as in Songs 1: 9–11.

rev. 14: *šibqīšina*: The woman is complaining against the tricks of her rivals. She expresses her confidence that the man knows these tricks and will not change his mind because of them. The same term, *šibqū*, is found in ZA 49, 168–169 (№16), another love dialogue, where the man tells the woman: "I remember more than you your tricks of the past".[387]

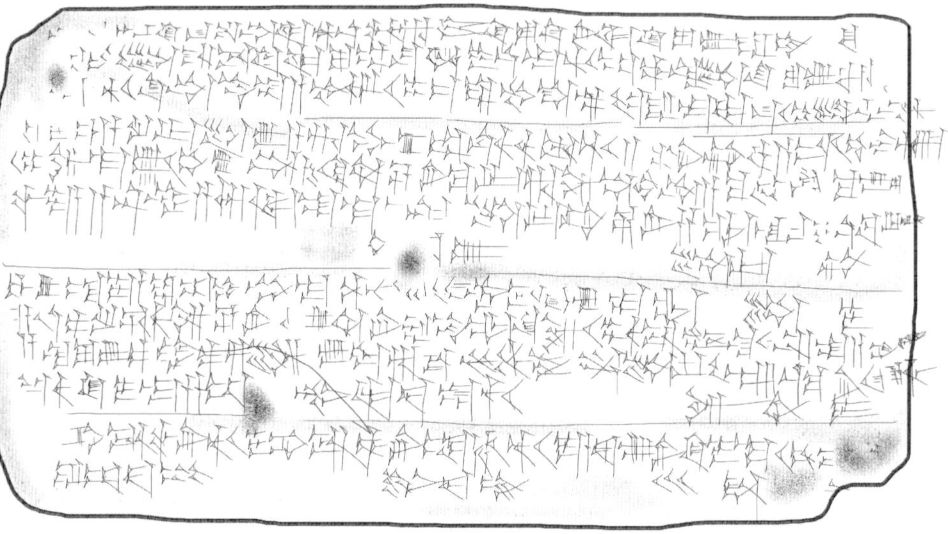

Fig. 11: The Moussaieff Love Song Obv.

387 ZA 49, 168–169 i 17–18 (№ 16): elīki ḫassāku ana šibqīki ša panānum.

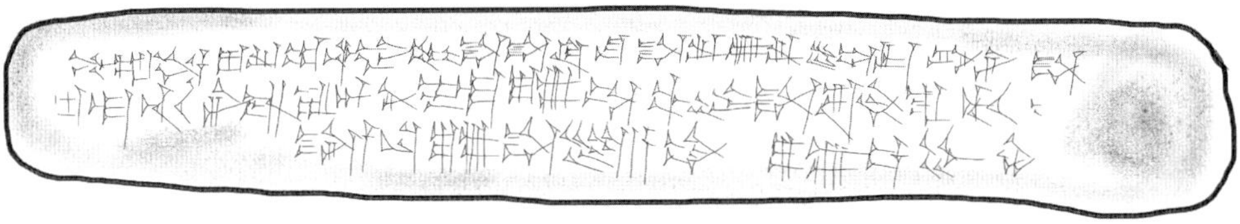

Fig. 12: The Moussaieff Love Song Lower Edge

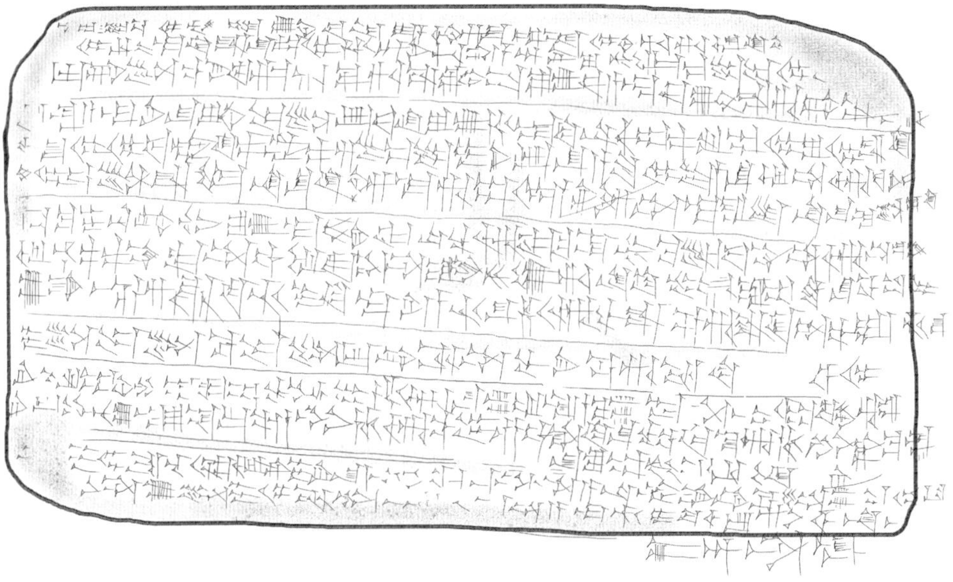

Fig. 13: The Moussaieff Love Song Rev.

Fig. 14: The Moussaieff Love Song Obv.

Fig. 15: The Moussaieff Love Song Lower Edge

Fig. 16: The Moussaieff Love Song Rev.

## № 12 Celebration Is a Foundation for the City! (Or. 60, 340)

Copy: -/-
Tablet Siglum: HS 1879
Photo: von Soden/Oelsner 1991, Pl. CVI
Edition: von Soden/Oelsner 1991, 340–341
Collection: Hilprecht Sammlung, Jena
Studies: Hurowitz 1995
Provenance: Nippur?
Measurements: 10.0x6.5 cm
Period: MB

**Introduction**
The text can be dated to MB period based on grammar and its physical characteristics. Noticeable first are the lapidary-like signs which are clearly archaized. Some grammatical points reveal undeniable MB characteristics: the dissimilation of *gg* > *ng* in *a-ma-an-gu-ru-ku-nu-ši* (l. 12), the verbal theme (a/u) in this verb, instead of the verbal theme (a) as in OB, and the dative suffix *-kunūši*, instead of the acc. suffix *-kunūti* in OB (see von Soden/Oelsner 1991, 339). Note further the nasalized form of *bamtum*, appearing here as *pa-an-ti-ša* (l. 15) with *nt* < *mt* change (similar to *ṣindu* < OB *ṣimdum*), and the spelling *Iš-tar* (l. 21) which is also atypical to OB. Another indication of the MB dating of the text is the colophon (which mentions the first regnal year of Hammurāpi, again, an archaizing feature). Colophons are uncommon in OB texts. In our corpus only late-OB and MB texts contain colophons: Fs. Renger 192–193 (№ 6), a late-OB text, and JAOS 103, 26–27 (№ 7) and LKA 15 (№ 9), two MB/MA texts. (More on the orthographical peculiarities of this text and its resemblance to the Moussaieff Love Song, see Introduction to the Moussaieff Love Song = № 11 above).
The text is one of the more explicit ones in the corpus, describing orgiastic sexual activity in bold and non-metaphorical language. Interestingly this activity, though connected to a celebration in the city, which probably had political significance, does not involve the king – at least not in the parts of it which we hold in our hands. The only reference to the palace or the king is in the colophon.

Obv.
1 *ri-ša-tu-m[a] iš-dum a-na* URU.KI
2 $^{d}$*Tēlitum*(ZÍB) [*be-le-e*]*t* [*d*]*a?-a-nim ri-ša-tu-ma iš-dum a-na* URU.KI
3 *i-ša?-*[*al? ri-ša-t*]*u-ma iš-dum a-na* URU.KI
4 *ku-u*[*l-ma-ši-tum ri-ša-tu-m*]*a iš-dum a-na* URU.KI
5 *eṭ-*[*lu-tum ri-ša-tu-m*]*a iš-dum a-na* URU.KI
6 *ar-*[*d*]*a-tum ri-ša-tu-m*]*a iš-dum a-na* URU.KI
7 *i-ša-a*[*l ri-ša-tu-m*]*a iš-dum a-na* URU.KI
8 *iš-te-en i*[*l-li-ka-aš-ši-im-ma ri-ša-t*]*u-ma iš-dum a-na*

URU.KI
9 *al-ki mu-ug-ri-i*[*n*]-*n*[*i ri-ša-t*]*u-ma iš-dum a-na* URU.KI
10 *ù ša-nu-ú il-li-ka-aš-ši-im-ma ri-ša-tu-ma iš-dum a-na* URU.KI
11 *al-ki lu-la-ap-pi-it ḫur-da-at-ki ri-ša-tu-ma iš-dum a-na* URU.KI
12 *iš-tu-ma a-ma-an-gu-ru-ku-nu-ši ri-ša-tu-ma iš-dum a-na* URU.KI
13 *eṭ-lu-ut a-li-ku-nu pu-uḫ-ḫi-ra-nim-ma ri-ša-tu-ma iš-dum a-na* URU.KI

----

Rev.
14 *a-na ṣi-il-li du-ri-im i ni-i-lik ri-ša-tu-ma iš-dum a-na* URU.KI
15 7 *pa-an-ti-ša* 7 *qá-ab-li-ša ri-ša-tu-ma iš-dum a-na* URU.KI
16 1 *šu-ši ù* 1 *šu-ši ip-ta-na-aš-ša-ḫu a-na ú-ri-ša ri-ša-tu-ma iš-dum a-na* URU.KI
17 *i-ta-an-ḫu eṭ-lu-tum ul in-na-aḫ Iš-tar ri-ša-tu-ma iš-dum a-na* URU.KI
18 *šu-uk-na eṭ-lu-tum a-na ḫur-da-ti da-mi-iq-ti-im-ma ri-ša-tu-ma iš-dum a-na* URU.KI
19 *ar-da-tum i-na qá-bé-e-ša ri-ša-tu-ma iš-dum a-na* URU.KI
20 *eṭ-lu-tum iš-mu-ú im-gu-ru a-ma-as-sa ri-ša-tu-ma iš-dum a-na* URU.KI

----

21 *napḫar* (PAP) 20 *pa-rum ša Iš-tar* MU LUGAL *Ḫa-am-mu-ra-pí-im*
22 $^{md}$ŠEG$_5$.ŠEG$_5$-*bēlu*(EN)-*rēṣū*(Á.DAḪ)-*šu*(A.NI) LUGAL-E
23 *mār*(DUMU) $^{m}$*Šumu*(MU)-*libši*(ḪÉ.GÁL)
24 *išṭur*(IN-SAR)

**Translation**

Obv.
1 Celebration is a foundation for the city!
2 *Telītum*, [lad]y of... ...
Celebration is a foundation for the city!
3 ... ...[
Celebratio]n is a foundation for the city!
4 *Ku*[*lmašitum* …
Celebratio]n is a foundation for the city!
5 The young m[en …

Celebratio]n is a foundation for the city!
6 The young [women …
Celebratio]n is a foundation for the city!
7 … …[
Celebratio]n is a foundation for the city!
8 One c[ame to her (saying):
Celebrati]on is a foundation for the city!
9 "Come, yield to m[e!]"
Celebrati]on is a foundation for the city!
10 Also a second came to her (saying):
Celebration is a foundation for the city!
11 "Come; let me fondle your vulva"
Celebration is a foundation for the city!
12 "After I yield to you,
Celebration is a foundation for the city!
13 Gather around me the men of your city
Celebration is a foundation for the city!
---

Rev.
14 Let us go to the shadow of the city-wall!"
Celebration is a foundation for the city!
15 Seven to her front, seven to her loins:
Celebration is a foundation for the city!
16 Sixty and sixty relieve themselves repeatedly in her vagina.
Celebration is a foundation for the city!
17 The men got tired, Ištar did not tire
Celebration is a foundation for the city!
18 "Place (it), guys, *in* the pretty vulva!"
Celebration is a foundation for the city!
19 As the young woman was speaking,
Celebration is a foundation for the city!
20 The young men heard and yielded to her order.
Celebration is a foundation for the city!
---
21 Total 20 (lines). *Pārum* of Ištar. Year: Hammurāpi became king.
22–24 $^{md}$ŠEG$_5$.ŠEG$_5$–*bēlu–rēṣūšu* son of *Šumu-libši* wrote.

**Commentary**

1: The syntax of the repetitive rhyme can be that of a nominal sentence, in which case the enclitic *-ma* serves as a copula. Alternatively, it can be understood as an apposition: "Celebration! A Foundation for the city!"

9: *alkī mugrīnni*: The same sequence of verbs, but in opposite order is found in ZA 49, 168–169 i 19 (№ 16): *mugrī atalkī.*

13: The idiom *ḫurdatam lupputum* is found also in PRAK 1 B 472 i 13' (№ 13): "Stretch your(m.) left hand and touch our vulva!",[388] and in SB Gilg. VI 69: "Put out your hand and stroke our vulva!".[389]

14: The image of the prostitute standing by the city-wall is well known. An interesting Sum. parallel would not be out of place. In Inanna H, the goddess states: "When I'm standing at the wall it is one shekel, when I'm bending over, it is one and a half".[390]

16: On Ištar's insatiable sexual appetetite reflected in this composition, see Cooper 2006–2008, 18.

20: There is a hierarchical shift between the young men of the city and the female protagonist of the text, Ištar. In l. 9 it was she who was ordered to "yield" (*magārum*), but in l. 20 the men of the city "yielded" to her (*magārum* again).

21: *Ḫa-am-mu-ra-pí-im*: The mimation at the end of the royal name is a hyper-correction (adding mimation automatically after every noun) – a clear sign of the archaizing effort in this colophon.

388 PRAK 1 B 472 i 13' (№ 13): *bilamma šumēlek luppitma ḫurdatni.*

389 Gilg. VI 69 (= George 2003, 622–623: 69): *u qātka šūṣâmma luput ḫurdatni.*

390 Sjöberg 1977, 17: 19f. (with Attinger 1998): é-gar$_8$-da gub-bu-gu$_{10}$ 1 gig$_4$-àm gurum-e-gu$_{10}$ 1½ gig$_4$-àm. This line is discussed in Cooper 2006–2008, 14 (refs. Jana Matuszak). More on the wages of a prostitute in wisdom literature, see Y. Cohen 2015.

## № 13 The Beating of Your Heart – A Pleasant Tune (PRAK 1 B 472)

Copy: de Genouillac 1924, Pl. 38
Tablet Siglum: Ki. 1063
Photo: Goodnick Westenholz 1987, 418–419
Edition: Goodnick Westenholz 1987, 422–424
Collection: Arkeoloji Müzeleri, Istanbul
Studies: Römer 1989, 635, Foster 2005, 169
Provenance: Kiš
Measurements: ?
Period: early OB (Ur III?)

**Introduction**
The text shows archaic traits, placing it chronologically in the early OB period, if not earlier, in the Ur III period.[391] Note the following: the usage of syllabic values *šà* and *àm* (rev. 3'), and perhaps also *úš* (ii 10'); the inclined relative pronoun *ši munāmāti* (i 5'); the shortened and attached prepositions *i-nu-ut* (i 4') and *i-nu-uḫ-ši* (rev. 5'); the archaic verbal form *tušūdi*, instead of regular OB *tušēdi* (ii 11');[392] the shortened possessive suffixes *šu-me-le-ek* (i 13') and *ši-ip-ru-uk* (ii 8', ii 9'). Mimation, however, is often lacking: *ra?-ab-bi?* (i 4'), *mu-na-ma-ti* (i 5') – both forms at the end of a line, *ka-na-ka-ti* (i 8') – where the initial *m* in the next word *mūnī* may explain the absence of mimation, $u_4$*-mi* (ii 4', ii 6') – unless pl., *ar-ḫu-ti* (ii 5') and perhaps also *šu-ri-ni* (ii 13'). Thematically the text seems close to the OAkk love incantation MAD 5, 8 (№ 22), also from Kiš. The very broken passage at the end of the text might include ritual instructions. Another possible case of a ritual that follows a love-related text is LKA 15 (№ 9).

Obv.
col. i
i 1' [...] ⌈x⌉ *ki* [*n*]*i a-na-ku* ⌈x⌉ [...]
i 2' [*tu-ru-uk*] ⌈*li*⌉*-bi-ka ni-gu-*[*tu*/*ta*/*ti*...]
i 3' *ti-bé-ma lu-*⌈*ur*⌉*-ta-ma-*[*ka-ma*]
i 4' *i-nu-ut-li-ka ra?-ab-bi?*
i 5' *ši mu-na-ma-ti*
i 6' *da-du-*⌈*ka*⌉ *ṭà-a-bu*
i 7' *mu-úḫ!-ta-an-bu in-bu-ka*
i 8' *šà ka-na-ka-ti mu-ni-i ba-lu-ku-ú*
i 9' *me-<a>-mu re-ši-ni in-ṣa-bu uz-ni-ni*
i 10' *šà-di-i bu-di-ni ù* ⌈*la*⌉*-lu i-ir-ti-ni*

391 Goodnick Westenholz (1987, 416) opts for the OB period: "The exact date of the tablet is difficult to determine. From the internal evidence, there is no doubt that the text belongs to the Old Babylonian period. The sign forms generally are those of the pre-Hammurabi period" (Goodnick Westenholz 1987, 416 n. 6).

392 See GAG §§ 103s-t and 106q, and Kouwenberg 2010, 454–456.

| | |
|---|---|
| i 11' | *sí-in-s*[*í*]*-nu* ⌈*qá*⌉*-ti-ni* |
| i 12' | *ḫu-du-šu qá-ab-li-ni* |
| i 13' | *bi-la-ma šu-me-le-ek lu-pí-it-ma ḫu-ur-da-at-ni* |
| i 14' | *me-li-il tu-li-i-ni* |
| i 15' | [*er-ba ḫa-al*⌉*-la ap-ti* |
| i 16' | [...] ⌈x⌉ *ti* |

col. ii

| | |
|---|---|
| ii 1' | [...] ⌈x⌉ [...] |
| ii 2' | [...] *bi*? *ma* [...] |
| ii 3' | [*k*]*i* ⌈*wa*⌉*-ar-ḫi-ka ab/p-*[...] |
| ii 4' | *ki* $u_4$*-mi a-ma-ru-ma ši-ma-*[*at*..] |
| ii 5' | *ar-ḫu-ti ù še-ra-a-an* [...] |
| ii 6' | *ki* $u_4$*-mi ta-ḫa-a-zu i-*[...] |
| ii 7' | *an-na ši-tu-um ta-re-*[...] |
| ii 8' | *ši-ip-ru-uk li-li-ka-*[...] |
| ii 9' | *ši-ip-ru-uk li-li-kam-m*[*a* ...] |
| ii 10' | *lu-úš-me šu-ul-ma-ka a-na-*[*ku* ...] |
| ii 11' | *i-ṣú-ru-um tu-šu-di li-*[*ša*?*-na*?*-am*?] |
| ii 12' | *qá-ti ta* x x x *da-mi-iq*!-[*ta-am*] |
| ii 13' | *šu-ri-ni ù* x *ni iḫ* [...] |
| ii 14' | *ep-pu-ú*[*š* ...] |
| ii 15' | *ù da-mi-*[*iq-ta-ka*] |
| ii 16' | *na-aḫ-šu* [...] |

Rev.

| | |
|---|---|
| 1' | *ta-sà-*⌈*ra*⌉*-*[*aq* ....] |
| 2' | *ṣuḫārum*(?)(DI$_4$.DI$_4$.L[A]?) [...] |
| 3' | *šiptam*?(ÉN?-*àm*?) ⌈*ka*?⌉-[...] |
| 4' | *ta-sà-ra-aq* [...] |
| 5' | *i-nu-uḫ-ši i-*[...] |
| 6' | x *ni* x [...] |

**Translation**

Obv.

col. i

| | |
|---|---|
| i 1' | [...] …I am.. [...] |
| i 2' | [*The beating*] of your heart – a pleasant tu[ne]. |
| i 3' | Rise and let me make love [with you (or: together)]. |
| i 4' | In your(m.) soft lap, |
| i 5' | that of waking-time, |
| i 6' | how sweet is your(m.) lovemaking. |
| i 7' | Your(m.) fruits are profuse! |
| i 8' | Of incense is my bed, (smelling of) *ballukku*-plant. |
| i 9' | Oh the crowns of our heads, the rings of our ears, |

| | |
|---|---|
| i 10' | the hills of our shoulders, the attraction of our chests, |
| i 11' | the 'spadix' of our hands, |
| i 12' | The '*frog*' of our waist. |
| i 13' | Stretch your(m.) left hand and touch our vulva! |
| i 14' | Play(m.) with our breasts! |
| i 15' | [Enter], I have opened (my) thigh(s)! |
| i 16' | [...]... |

col. ii

| | |
|---|---|
| ii 1' | [...] … [...] |
| ii 2' | [...] ... [...] |
| ii 3' | [W]hen your(m.) moon (is visible?) *I will* […], |
| ii 4' | In the (or: my) day when I will see the signs of […], signs (or: destiny?) of… |
| ii 5' | … and in the morning […], |
| ii 6' | In the (or: my) day when you will grasp … […] |
| ii 7' | Indeed, sleep will *po*[*ur*(?)…] |
| ii 8' | May your(m.) message arrive [to me…], |
| ii 9' | May your(m.) message come to me, |
| ii 10' | so that I, Oh I, will hear your(m.) well-being. |
| ii 11' | The bird *made known*(?) the *n*[*ews*(?)] |
| ii 12' | My hand will… fav[or], |
| ii 13' | Our eyebrows and… […], |
| ii 14' | I will d[o…]. |
| ii 15' | and your(m.) fa[vor…]. |
| ii 16' | Oh lusty one […]. |

Rev.

| | |
|---|---|
| 1' | You(m.) will sprin[kle…] |
| 2' | *servant*(?) […] |
| 3' | *incantation*(?) …[…] |
| 4' | You(m.) will sprinkle [...] |
| 5' | In abundance [...] |
| 6' | … [...] |

**Commentary**

i 3': *lu*-[*ur*]-*ta-ma*-[*ka-ma*]: the same verbal form also in MIO 12, 52–53: 3 (№ 10) *lu-ur-ta-a-ma*. Another restitution, however, may be considered: in KAR 158 i 5' (№ 19) we find *lu-ur-ta-ma-nu*, 1 du. verbal form with the ventive -*nu* (see Kouwenberg 2010, 364 n. 32). The form could therefore be *lu*-[*ur*]-*ta-ma*-[*nu*-(*ma*)].

i 4': *inutlika ra*?-*ab-bi*?: See Mayer 2003, 231.

i 6'–7': Note the chiasmus *dādūka ṭābū* | *muḫtanbū inbūka*.

i 7': *mu-úḫ!-ta-an-bu*: Reading *úḫ*! is easier than *uḫ*-[x] in the *editio princeps*. The form *muḫtanbū* instead of *muḫtannibū* is a shortened Gtn part. A similar form is found in the SB text LSS 2/4, 23:3 (cited in CAD M/2, 177b. The correction of AHw 319b [*m*]*u-uḫ-ta-an-*<*ni-*>*bu* is not warranted).

i 8': *ba-lu-ku-ú*: judging by the copy, the last sign could be *-um*. Note the anticipatory genitive construction, a rare syntactic and stylistic device in OB. – The incense bearing plant *kanaktum* is mentioned in MAD 5, 8: 5 (№ 22), also from Kiš.

i 9'–14': This rhythmic enumeration of body parts, arranged *a capite ad calcem*, offers a fine example of the "plural of ecstasy" (see Paul 1995).

i 10': *šadî*: It is hard to see why this form is not in the nom., as the other body parts in this section.

i 12': *ḫuduššu qablini*: Goodnick Westenholz (1987, 423) translates: "the belt hung with (lapis-lazuli) frog charms of our wrists", taking *ḫudušu* to render "frog", or a special kind of a belt (AHw 353a). A Mari letter (ARM 26/1, p. 263 no. 98 n. c) shows that *ḫudušum* – an animal or a stone – was dark in color (*tarik*).[393] The fact that the *ḫudušu* is found in the area of the waist, and that *ḫurdatum*, "female pudenda", appears in the next line, does not leave much choice: I suggest that the "frog", which other sources say is "dark", is a euphemistic designation for the female sex organ. For more on euphemistic expressions, see Overview § 4.6.

i 13': *šumēlek*: On the acc. *-em*, resulting from a progressive vowel harmony see Wasserman 2003, 166 n. 43. – 'A stretched hand' could be a euphemism for the erect penis, see Paul 2002, 491. – The idiom *ḫurdatam lupputum*[394] is found also in Or. 60, 340: 11 (№ 12), and in SB Gilg. VI 69 (= George 2003, 622).

ii 5': *še-ra-a-an*: The morpheme *-ān* is known to be attached to other diurnal terms (as, e.g., *šimētān*, "(in the) evening time"). Yet, this text (as other Kiš texts, e.g. PRAK 2 C 3, PRAK 2 C 30) uses the syllabic value *àm*(A-AN) (rev. 3'), so reading *še-ra-àm* is not excluded.

ii 7': *an-na ši-tu-um ta-re-*[...]: So, contra Goodnick Westenholz (1987, 422) who reads *an-na-ši tu-um-ta-ri* [...], "I have been carried away (?)". The defective spelling *ši-tu-um* for *šittum*, "sleep", is found also in *i-ṣú-ru-um* for *iṣṣūrum* (ii 11'). – *ta-re-*[...]: at the end of the line one could restore a form of *reḫûm*, "to pour", typically said of sleep.

ii 10'–11': For birds bringing news to the lovers, see Overview § 6.3. Note that *iṣṣūrum* here is f., as attested rarely in OB (AHw 390a 1a).

393 The term *ḫudušum* was not taken up in Arkhipov 2012.

394 Correct Hecker 2005, 165 n. 9 who transliterates the line with *luput* instead of *luppit*.

rev. 3': *šiptam*(?)(ÉN?-*àm*?) [*ka*?]-[...]: Goodnick Westenholz (1987, 423) reads *šà-a-an-*[*ka*?]-[...

## № 14a–f The Kiš Fragments Mentioning Šu-Sîn PRAK 2 C 3, PRAK 2 C 30, PRAK 2 C 41, PRAK 2 C 125, PRAK 2 C 134, PRAK 2 C 135

Copy: PRAK 2 C 3, PRAK 2 C 30, PRAK 2 C 41, PRAK 2 C 125, PRAK 2 C 134, PRAK 2 C 135
Tablet Sigla: AO 10623, AO 10650, AO 10661, AO 10741, AO 10750, AO 10751
Photos: Figs. 17–24 (Courtesy Béatrice André-Salvini)
Edition: below
Collection: Louvre, Paris
Provenance: Kiš
Period: Early OB (Ur III?)

**Introduction**
While working on literary material from Kiš housed in the Louvre, I identified a small group of fragments that contain key words which are typical of ALL (*inbum*, *sūnum*, *mārum*, *ḫāwirum*, and *narāmum*).[395] It turned out that the fragments, most of them broken with only a few decipherable words, mention the goddesses Ištar and Nanāya, the gods Anum and Šamaš, the couple Sîn and Ningal, and most unexpectedly, Šu-Sîn, who can only be the fourth king of the Ur dynasty.[396]

Besides the mention of the name of Šu-Sîn and the unmistakable archaic sign forms used in the fragments, a crucial indication for the early date of this group is the syllabic values *šà*[397] and *àm* (found also in the larger fragment PRAK 1 B 472 = № 13). As for the reading *sin* of the sign EŠ (30), this usage is characteristic of first mill. texts, but is found also in OAkk personal names.[398] As a rule, the royal name Šu-Sîn's is spelled $^{(d)}$*šu*-$^{d}$EN.ZU – in the king's own monumental and hymnal writings,[399] and in administrative texts written in his reign. The spelling *šu*-30 for the royal name Šu-Sîn is therefore uncommon. A parallel to this spelling, however, is found in a duplicate of the letter of Šarrum-bāni to Šu-Sîn,[400] proving that this spelling is not unique in late Ur III texts and in early OB times.

395 This group of fragments is not mentioned in Hilgert's 2002 extensive study of Ur III Akk.
396 Although the Kiš fragments resemble each other, both epigraphically and orthographically, I was unable to tell whether they belong originally to the same tablet. Note that two Kiš fragments, PRAK 2 C 114 + PRAK 2 C 136, which thematically are not related to love, were joined by Antoine Cavigneaux. More joins, I believe, are possible.
397 For the syllabic value *šà* in Ur III Akk., see Hilgert 2002, 117 (no. 224).
398 See Akk. Syll. no. 275
399 Including his sole Akk. inscription (= FAOS 7, 343).
400 OECT 5, 26 = AN1922-163, = ms. X1 in Michalowski 2011, letter no. 18 = 404: 1 (ref. Piotr Michalowski).

Thematically, what singles out this group of fragments is the interaction between the king and the gods in ritual setting.[401] Such an interaction – as far as the broken context of the fragments allows one to say – is unknown elsewhere in ALL. The loose border between the human and the divine, set in cult and ritual, brings this group of texts closer to the tradition of Sum. love lyrics[402] than any other text in ALL (and consequently strengthens the proposal that this group should be dated to the very early OB period, if not to Ur III period).

401 See esp. PRAK 2 C 30 (№ 14), PRAK 2 C 41: 5' (№ 14c), PRAK 2 C 134: 3' (№ 14e).
402 See Klein/Sefati 2008.

## № 14a = PRAK 2 C 3 (AO 10623)

Measurements: 8.2x4.6 cm

Obv.

1' *Šu-S*[*în*(30)?] ⌈*ri*⌉ [...]
2' x-*i*!-GI ⌈x⌉ [...
3' *ḫa-ṭá-àm* ⌈*ta*⌉-⌈x⌉-[...]
4' $^{d}$[*N*]*in*?*-gal* DINGIR DA [...]
5' *šarrum*(LUGAL) *li*-⌈*di*?⌉-*n*[*a*- ...]
6' *na-bi šar-r*[*u-um*?...]
7' *zi-ik-ri-š*[*u* ...]
8' *Šu-Sîn*(30) *mé-le-e*[*l*? ...]
9' *ki Šamši*($^{d}$UTU-*ši*) *li*-⌈*ip*?⌉-⌈*pu*?⌉-[*uḫ*?]
10' *ṣe*!(Text: AD)*-ru-šu el-ši-na* x [...]
11' *iš*$_7$?*-ri-iḫ*?*-ma ma-tum*? *ba-n*[*i*? ...]
12' *šà ru-uq* ⌈x⌉-DU?/UŠ RU-x ...]
13' *šà ta-na-*[*ad*?*-di*?] *ta-*[...]
14' *u*$_4$*-mi-šu S*[*în*(30) *ù* $^{d}$*Nin*]*-gal l*[*i*?-...]
15' *ḫa-ṭá-àm* ⌈*ù parakkam*(BÁRA)⌉*-àm-*[...]
16' *i-ti*$_4$*-qú-ma a-*⌈*pí*?*-ir*?⌉ [...]
17' *re-ši-iš ka-ak-*<*ka*>*-bu-u*[*m*?]
18' *ip-pu-uḫ-ri I-g*[*i*$_4$*-gi*$_4$]
19' *qé-er-bu* UD-*ri* [...]
20' $^{d}$*Nin-gal ù Sîn*(30) x
21' *ra-mi-*[*š*]*u mi-ig-r*[*i*?]

Rev.

1 *a-la-ak šar-r*[*i*?*-im*?...]
2 *ù* x še ka š[u ...]
3 ⌈*šà*?⌉*-ti-*$^{d}$*En-líl* [...]
4 *im-mu-ti-*⌈x⌉ [...]
5 *àm-su-k*[*a*? ]
6 *me-a-a*[*t*? ]
7 *ip-pu-uḫ-r*[*i I-gi*$_4$*-gi*$_4$]
8 *ù E-nu-n*[*a-ki* DN *iltum*]
9 *ra-bi-t*[*u*?*-um*?]
10 *ir*?-[...]

**Translation**

Obv.

| | |
|---|---|
| 1' | Š[u-Sîn(?)] ...[...] |
| 2' | .... [...] |
| 3' | *You will...* the scepter... [...] |
| 4' | Ningal, the god... [...] |
| 5' | May the king *give*(?) [...] |
| 6' | The ki[ng] was summoned [...] |
| 7' | Hi[s] utterances [...] |
| 8' | Šu-Sîn! *Pla[y with* [...] |
| 9' | Like the sun *let him shine* [...] |
| 10' | *Towards him,* more than them(pl. f.) .[...] |
| 11' | The land *took pride*, the creat[or...] |
| 12' | Which ... [...] |
| 13' | Which you have ... you...[...] |
| 14' | *At this day* may S[în and Nin]gal [...] |
| 15' | Scepter and *throne* [...] |
| 16' | *They moved along*, he is *crowned* [...] |
| 17' | On (his?) head a sta[r...] |
| 18' | In the assembly of the *Ig[igi*-gods |
| 19' | in the midst of *the day* [...] |
| 20' | Ningal and Sîn [...] |
| 21' | His love, his favora[ble...] |

Rev.

| | |
|---|---|
| 1 | The going of the ki[ng...] |
| 2 | ... [...] |
| 3 | *Šâti-Enlil* [...] |
| 4 | In the front of ...[...] |
| 5 | ... [...] |
| 6 | *Hundred(s) of* [...] |
| 7 | In the assembl[y of the Igigi] |
| 8 | and of the Anun[aki, DN] |
| 9 | The great [goddess ...] |
| 10 | ... [...] |

**Commentary**

This fragment, the largest of the group, describes a mythical scene involving Sîn, Ningal, the assembly of the gods and king Šu-Sîn. Only ll. 8'–10' show characteristics of ALL. No other text in the corpus is contextualized in such a mythical setup, and it is not impossible that the text is based on some unknown Sum. origin.

3': *ḫa-ṭá-àm*: The same defective spelling of *ḫaṭṭum* is found in l. 15'.

5': A similar LI sign (looking as ŠE+NA) is found in l. 9'.

8': *mé-le-e*[*l*]: If correctly restored this form of *mēlulum* parallels PRAK 1 B 472: 14' (№ 13): *melil tulîni*, "Play(m.) with our breasts!", and PRAK 2 C 125: 4 (№ 14d) (*me-le-e*[*l*]). Note, however, that the fragment distinguishes between *mi* and *me* (l. 6'), so MI is not easily read *mé*. Perhaps restore *mi-li-i*[*k*]?

11': This line eludes me: *ab-ri-iḫ?-ma ma-tum*, or *ab-ri-im?-ma ma-tum* yields no good reading (one expects a 3 sg. verb coordinated with *mātum*, presumably the subject of the sentence). Hard-pressed, I suggest reading *iš*$_7$*?-ri-iḫ?*, from *šarāḫum*, "to take pride, make splendid", although this verb is attested in G only in the statives *šaruḫ* and *šarḫat*, and probably is *išruḫ* in the pret. Another difficulty against this reading is that *iš* is attested in l. 17'.

12': *šà ru-uq* [x]-DU?/UŠ RU-x … : The beginning of this line might be restored *šà ru-uq-ti*, from *ruqtum*, a by-form of *ruʾtum*, "spittle", as in MAD 5, 8: 5, 10, 12 (№ 22) and ZA 75, 198–204a 18 (№ 27).

18': *ip-pu-uh-ri*: This lemma is cited in CAD P 487a 2' ("OB lit."). Cf. l. 7.

3: [*šà?*]-*ti*-$^{d}$*En-líl*: Probably a feminine PN. Although a certain *šât*-$^{d}$*Enlil* is mentioned in ASJ 11, 332, 4 r. 3 as owning a field,[403] one imagines here another lady, with a homonymic name, from the higher echelons of Ur III society.

403 Ref. Uri Gabbay.

Fig. 17: PRAK 2 C 3 (AO 10623) Obv.

Fig. 18: PRAK 2 C 3 (AO 10623) Rev.

### № 14b = PRAK 2 C 30 (AO 10650)

Measurements: 4.1x3.0 cm

| | |
|---|---|
| 1' | *šu-n*[*u*?... ...] |
| 2' | *lu-pí-*[*it-ma*...] |
| 3' | *i-na su*?-[*ni*?... ...] |
| --- | |
| 4' | *be-le-et* [... ...] |
| 5' | *tu-àm-ša* [... ...] |
| 6' | dINNIN *ma*?-[*ša*?]-[*àm*?...] |
| 7' | *Šu-Sîn*(30) *in-*[x] [... ...] |
| 8' | *ta-za-am-m*[*a-ar*...] |
| 9' | [*ta*]-*za-ma-*[*ar*...] |
| 10' | [d]INNIN [... ...] |

**Translation**

| | |
|---|---|
| 1' | The[y? ... ...] |
| 2' | To[uch my(?) ...] |

3' In (my?) la[p(?) …]
---
4' Lady [… …]
5' Her twin-brother [… …]
6' Ištar, the twin-bro[ther(?) ...]
7' Šu-Sîn ... [ ]
8' You/She will si[ng…]
9' You/She will si[ng…]
10' Ištar [… …]

**Commentary**

2': For the restoration *luppit* see PRAK 1 B 472: 13' (№ 13). Restoring a first person precative form *lūbi*[*l*…], "let me carry", is also possible.

5', 6': *tū'amum* and *māšum*: These two synonyms for twin-brother refer to Ištar's twin, Šamaš.

Fig. 19: PRAK 2 C 30 (AO 10650)

## № 14c = PRAK 2 C 41 (AO 10661)

Measurements: ?

Obv.

| | |
|---|---|
| 1' | [...*i*]*d*?-*du* [...] |
| 2' | [*q*]*é-er-bu-u*[*š*...] |
| 3' | *Iš*$_8$-*tár ù A-nu-u*[*m*...] |
| 4' | *ḫa-wi*!-*ir-š*[*a*...] |
| 5' | *pé-el-lu-*[*du-*...] |
| 6' | *A-nu-um* [*ù*] [*Iš*$_8$-*tár*...] |
| 7' | *Iš*$_8$-*tár ù A*-[*nu-um*...] |
| 8' | *ši-ma* x [...] |
| 9' | *š*[*u*?-*Sîn*(30) [...] |
| 10' | x [...] |

Rev.
traces only.

**Translation**

Obv.

| | |
|---|---|
| 1' | [ ]... [...] |
| 2' | [A]mong th[em ...] |
| 3' | Ištar and Anu[m...] |
| 4' | H[er] beloved ...] |
| 5' | Rit[ual...] |
| 6' | Anum and [Ištar ...] |
| 7' | Ištar and A[num...] |
| 8' | She... [...] |
| 9' | Š[u-Sîn?? ...] |
| 10' | ...[...] |

Rev.
traces only.

**Commentary**

4': *ḫa-wi*!-*ir-š*[*a*...]: This designation indicates that this fragment also concerns love. Ištar and Anum are known to have a couple-like relationship.

5': *pilludû*/*pelludû*: This word for "ritual" is common in SB texts, but is attested in OB Lexical lists (CAD P 377b).

Fig. 20: PRAK 2 C 41 (AO 10661) Obv.

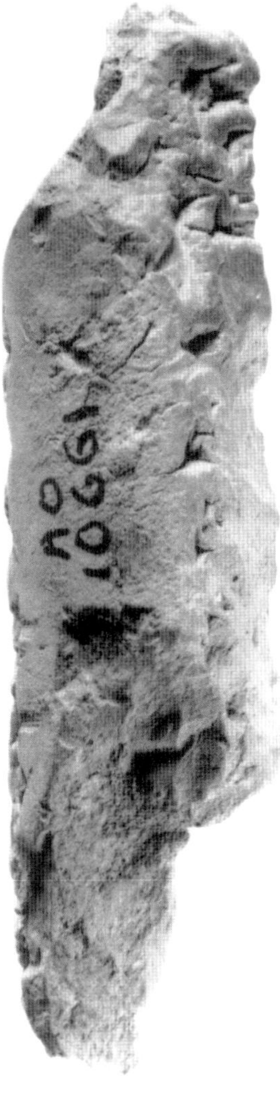


Fig. 21: PRAK 2 C 41 (AO 10661) Edge

## № 14d = PRAK 2 C 125 (AO 10741)

Measurements: ?

1 [… …] x *nu-úr-k*[*a* …]
2 [*be*]-[*li*?] x x *šu*? *ḫu*? *ir-ti-qù-ma* x …]
3 *ak-ki-ma še-ri-ma li-p*[*u*?-*ḫa*?-*am*?...]
4 *be-li*! *še-ri me-le-e*[*l* …]
5 *li*-[x] x (x) [*m*]*a*?-*ru-um li*?-[…]
6 *lu-ul*-[x x x x] x *su*?-*ni*-[…]
7 [… …] x x […]

**Translation**

1 […… y]our light(?) …
2 *My lord… … they went far away.*
3 Just like dawn let (*the sun*?/*light*?) *s*[*hine on me*(?)...]
4 My lord (*at*?) dawn play [with my…]
5 May the *boy*…, may he […]
6 Let me… (in my?) *lap* […]
7 (traces)

**Commentary**

2: *ir-ti-qù-ma*: I take this verbal from *rêqum*, "to be distant, go far off", as in two other love-related compositions: CUSAS 10, 8: 13 (№ 2) and ZA 49, 168–169 iv 14 (№ 16).

4: *me-le-e*[*l*]: The imperative *mēlulum* is attested in № 14a = PRAK 2 C 3: 8' (*mé-le-e*[*l*]) and in PRAK 1 B 472 i 13'–14' (№ 13) (*me-li-il*).

Fig. 22: PRAK 2 C 125 (AO 10741)

## № 14e = PRAK 2 C 134 (AO 10750)

Measurements: 2.3x1.8 cm

col. i

| | |
|---|---|
| i 1' | [… … …] |
| i 2' | [… …]-AD? |
| i 3' | [… …]-*ni*? |
| i 4' | [… …]-(*ti*) |
| i 5' | [… …]-(*li me* [x]) |
| i 6' | […] (⌈x⌉ *Šu-Sîn*(30) *na-ra*?-*mi*) |
| i 7' | [… …]-(x) |

col. ii

| | |
|---|---|
| ii 1' | [*úr*?]-x [... ...] |
| ii 2' | *šu-nu* WI?-x [… …] |
| ii 3' | *i-pár-ṣí* [… …] |
| ii 4' | *iš-še*-K[I? … …] |
| ii 5' | x-*šu-nu* [… …] |
| ii 6' | *pí-šu ù* [… …] |
| ii 7' | x [… …] |

**Translation**

col. i

| | |
|---|---|
| i 1'-5' | … |
| i 6' | […] Šu-Sîn my beloved, |
| i 7' | … |

col. ii

| | |
|---|---|
| ii 1' | ... |
| ii 2' | They … |
| ii 3' | In the ritual … |
| ii 4' | In the? … |
| ii 5' | Their… |
| ii 6' | His mouth and … |
| ii 7' | … |

**Commentary**

The lower left part of this small fragment was further broken since it was copied by de Genouillac. Signs in brackets transcribe those signs that are found in the copy, but now entirely lost.

i 2': The last sign was not accurately copied by de Genouillac. It is not I and not MI. If AD is correct (the vertical stroke is hiding at the end of the column?), then it is probably the end of a verbal form.

ii 4': Similarly to *i-pár-ṣí* in the preceding line, *iš-še*-K[I?] is perhaps also a nominal phrase with the attached prep. *in*(*a*).

ii 5': The first sign might be HUR or BIR.

Fig. 23: PRAK 2 C 134 (AO 10750)

## № 14f = PRAK 2 C 135 (AO 10751)

Measurements: 2.8x3.1 cm

col. i

| | |
|---|---|
| i 1 | [… …]-⌈*ka*⌉-*ma* |
| i 2 | [… …]-*ka* |
| i 3 | [… …]-⌈x⌉ |

col. ii

| | |
|---|---|
| ii 1 | *ia Na-na-ia* […] |
| ii 2 | *šu-ma la ia*-⌈*ti*?⌉ […] |
| ii 3 | *aq-bi-i* […] |
| ii 4 | *i-na ti-ma*?-*l*[*i*?..] |

**Translation**

col. i

| | |
|---|---|
| i 1 | Your(m.) […] |
| i 2 | Your(m.) […] |
| i 3 | … |

col.ii

2010).[404] In the same direction it is possible that IA is to be read *ay* (for which see Streck 2014, 15 § 30), with the meaning "alas" (AHw 23b, s.v. *ai* II and CAD A/1, 220–221).

ii 2: *šu-ma*: Probably an unusual orthography for *šumma*, "if" (not *šū-ma*).

ii 4: *i-na ti-ma*?-*l*[*i*?..]: If read correctly, this expression opens a temporal clause, "yesterday…" (but note that in OB only *timāli* is attested, while *ina timāli* is typical of NA texts).

Fig. 24: PRAK 2 C 135 (AO 10751)

404 Such a vocable is found in KAR 158 iii 11' (№ 19): e-ia lu-gal-gu kìri-za-al [...], "eya! My king, joy […]".

# № 15 The Vigorous Sun Keeps Overcoming Me (YOS 11, 24)

Copy: YOS 11, 24
Tablet Siglum: YBC 4643
Photo: Sigrist/Goodnick Westenholz 2008, 680
Edition: Sigrist/Goodnick Westenholz 2008, 679–683
Collection: Yale Babylonian Collection, New Haven
Studies: Römer/Hecker 1989, 747–750, Groneberg 1999, 174, Groneberg 2002, 166, Mayer 2003, 234, Wasserman 2003, Cat. No. 254, Foster 2005, 162–164, Hecker 2005, 171–173
Provenance: Larsa
Measurements: 17.3x13.1x3.0 cm
Period: OB (Rīm-Sîn)

**Introduction**

Although written on a large tablet with two columns, the text seems to be a draft (or even a school text).[405] It is clumsily written, with missing signs or signs written over erasures (i 2, i 4, i 5(?), i 7, i 8, i 9, i 11, ii 9), superfluous signs (i 14, i 16, i 28, ii 4, ii 7), and erroneous division into lines (i 18–19, i 20–21). The text lacks cohesion and does not read as a homogeneous composition, but rather as an accumulation of phrases typical of love lyrics. Different voices alternate, even within a single line: 'She', 'He', and a 'Chorus' (1 pl. voice) – but a coherent dialogue does not emerge. The text ends abruptly with two signs at the beginning of ii 10. Errant signs follow the empty space left (see copy). A possible explanation to the above is that YOS 11, 24 is a failed attempt to translate a Sum. love composition into Akkadian.

Based on a paleographical examination, the text can be safely dated as OB. This date is underscored by the mention of king Rīm-Sîn of Larsa. The present edition makes use of collations done by the late Aaron Shaffer in the early 1990's (marked °).

col. i

| | |
|---|---|
| i 1 | [*a-na eš-še*$_{20}$*-t*]*im ša-tim a-ri-a-tum it-ba-la ḫi-ib-ši* |
| i 2 | [*e-re*]-⌈*ma*⌉*-am zi-ib-ba-sú il-te-qé mu-di-tum*° |
| i 3 | [$^{d}$UTU *ši*]*-it-mu-rum ḫi-ta-pu-ut e-li-ia* |
| i 4 | [*ši-mi*] *me-ḫi-ir*! *ṣí-ḫa-ti-ia i-na sú-pi-im i-li-a-ni-ma* |
| i 5 | *ta-ma*!?*-ṣí ra-mi la ta-qi*$_{4}$*-ip-pí-šu* |
| i 6 | *da-an-ni-iš ta-ma-ḫi la ta-ta-ka-li-šum at-ti* |
| i 7 | *lu*°(ras.)*-ma-an iš-ti-ti te-eš*$_{15}$*-me-ma ra-i-mi ta-qú-lam* |
| i 8 | *te-el-qé un-ne*!*-ni-ia li-ib-*<*ba*>*-ka li-ip-pa-aš-ra-am* |
| i 9 | *i-na pu-úḫ-ri-im* <*ša*> *a-li ù ni-š*[*i*] *ba-aš-tim* |
| i 10 | *šu-mi dam-qá-am ta-az-kur-ma* |
| i 11 | *qá-qá-di tu-ka-ab-bi-*⌈*it*°⌉(ras.) *be-lí* |
| i 12 | *ki ma-ṣí-ma-an tu-ša-*[*qí-*(*a*)]*-an-ni* |

405 Hecker 2005, 169.

| | |
|---|---|
| i 13 | *i-na i-in ta-ap-pa-ti-*[*ia e-li š*]*a pa-na* / *e-*[*qì-ir da-an*]*-ni-iš* |
| i 14 | *an-na ni-sa-nu-um ša ni-nu* {NU} *ni-ik-ta-na-ra-bu-šum* |
| i 15 | *a-na a-ma-ri-šu ni-za-me-ru iš-tu ul-lam* |
| i 16 | *ú-mi ma-du-tim a-na da-ar ba-la-*{ṬÙ}*-ṭam* |
| i 17 | *na-ši me-le-eṣ li-ib-bi-im a-na* $^{d}$*Ri-im-*$^{d}$EN.ZU $^{d}$UTU*-ši-ni* |
| i 18 | *a-na ša-tim eš-še*$_{20}$*-tim ka-ra-nam* |
| i 19 | *i-qí-a-ši-im-ma ša ta-ṣa-ru-ra im-ni* |
| i 20 | *al-kam lu-un-ne-ed-ra-am ki-ma li-ib-bi* / *iq-bi-a-am i ni-pu-uš* |
| i 21 | *ši-ip-ra-am ša mu-ur-ta-mi ka-al mu-ši-im* / *e ni-iṣ-la-al* |
| i 22 | *lu-uḫ-ta-al-ṣa ṣú-ḫi-iš i-na ma-a-a-li-im* / *ki-la-al-la-ni* |
| i 23 | *i-ta-ab-la-al e-li in-bi ù da-di* / *ba-la-ṭam et-pi-ir* |
| i 24 | *i-na ṣe-ri-ia ṣú-ru-up la-la-ka* |
| i 25 | *ta-bi-ik-kum ra-mi ta-ap-ḫa-ra-am* / *li-qí ma-la ḫa-aš-ḫa-ti* |
| i 26 | *ia-tam ù ša ra-*{I}*-mi-ia ku-uš-di-im* |
| i 27 | *ša-li šar-ra-tum* $^{d}$*Na-na-a* |
| i 28 | *ú-ta-ak-*{AL}*-ki-la-an-ni ú-ul i-li-kam* |
| i 29 | [*e°-re°*]*-eš-šu* |
| i 30 | [*ra-i-*]*mi-i! at°-ta° ra-ma-a ka-ši ni-a-tu* |
| i 31 | [x-x-x-x *da-di*]*-i-ka ù i-in-bi-i-ka* |
| i 32 | [*ba-la-ṭam te*]*-e-pi-ra-ni šu-la-a-*[*ku*? x (x)] |
| i 33 | [...] x [.] x [...] |
| (break) | |

col. ii

| | |
|---|---|
| Up. Ed. | |
| ii 1 | *lu-uš-te-mi-iq-šum-ma-an* |
| ii 2 | *a-na be-li-ia* |
| ii 3 | (ras. over the whole line) |
| ii 4 | *da-an-ni-iš kam-šat ù qú-ud-di-*x-x / {LI} *i-ša-ak-ka-na-an-ni a-ḫi-tam* |
| ii 5 | *at-ta at-tu-li-im ma-aḫ-ri-am* / *ta-ṣa-al-ma* |
| ii 6 | *tu-ša iṣ-ṣé-ri-ia sú-up-pa-am te-li-ia* |
| ii 7 | *ma wa!-aš-ra ša-ap-ta-ša ub-lam ṭé-e-ma* / {Ù-LI} *ù le-ʾu*$_{5}$*-tam šu-uk-lu-la-at* |
| ii 8 | *zi-mi-i-ka iṭ-ṭù-ul* |
| ii 9 | *ir-te-ed*!(Text: DA)*-du-kum la ta-ka-aš-ši-ṭa-an-ni* |
| ii 10 | *in-na* |
| | (Rest uninscribed) |

**Translation**

col. i

| | |
|---|---|
| i 1 | (<u>Chorus</u>:) [*For the n*]*ew year, the pregnant (women) carried the …* |
| i 2 | The love-charm – the expert (goddess) took its tail. |

| | |
|---|---|
| i 3 | (She:) The vigor[ous sun] keeps overcoming me. |
| i 4 | [Hear] the resound of my laughs of delight! They rise to you in supplication. |
| i 5 | (She:) *Are you able*, my love? (Chorus:) do not trust(f.) him! |
| i 6 | (She:) You are so ecstatic! (Chorus:) do not put(f.) your confidence in him! |
| i 6–7 | (He:) Would you only be my one and only! (She:) You have heard, Oh my beloved(m.), you have listened to me. |
| i 8 | (She:) You have accepted my prayer, may your(m.) heart be satisfied. |
| i 9–11 | In the assembly (of) the city, and among the people of consequence you(m.) have mentioned my good name and honored me, my lord. |
| i 12 | How much more could you have exalted me? |
| i 13 | I have gained so much value in my girlfriends' eye! |
| i 14–15 | (Chorus:) Indeed, it is (in) the month of Nisan that we regularly give blessings to him, praising his appearance (since) ancient times in order to see him: |
| i 16–17 | 'Numerous days, life for ever (it = the month of Nisan) carries joy of heart to Rīm-Sîn, our sun!' |
| i 18–19 | (Chorus:) For the New Year, he poured wine for her, (*with his*) right (hand) which oozes. |
| i 20 | (She:) Come to me! I want to be embraced as my heart told me. |
| i 20–21 | Let us practice the work of lovers all the night, let us not sleep! |
| i 22 | Let the two of us *clinch*(?) passionately together in bed! |
| i 23 | Be mingled *over* fruits and desires! *Provide* (*me*?) with vitality! |
| i 24 | Burn your craving upon me! |
| i 25 | My love is poured on you(m.) entirely. Take(m.!) as much as you desire! |
| i 26 | (*He:*) Reach 'mine' and 'that of my *love*'! |
| i 27 | (Chorus:) Rejoice, Oh queen Nanāya! |
| i 28 | (She:) He has encouraged me (but) did not come |
| i 29 | to his awakening. |
| i 30 | … … … ours. |
| i 31 | […] your [des]ires and your fruits. |
| i 32 | [*Pro*]*vide* me [with vitality], [I am(?)] *happy*. |
| i 33 | … |

(break)

| | |
|---|---|
| col. ii | |
| ii 1–2 | (She:) If I could only pray to him, to my master! |
| ii 3… | |
| ii 4 | (He?:) She *kneels* and *prostrates*(?) a lot. She will put me aside. |
| ii 5 | (She:) You fought against an opponent for …. |
| ii 6 | assuming (wrongly) that you could pray in my presence. |
| ii 7 | (Chorus:) Indeed, her lips are relaxed; she carries (good) news. She is perfect in her competence! |
| ii 8 | She looked on your(m.) features. |
| ii 9 | (She:) They(m.) have escorted (me) to you(m.). Do not cut me off! |
| ii 10 | … |

**Commentary**

i 1: Reading follows Hecker (2005, 172 n. 45) who suggested restoring the first line after i18.

i 2: The description of the "love-charm" as having a tail has a parallel in YOS 11, 87: 1–3 (№ 26): *eremmum eremmum qarnāšu hurāṣum zibbassi uqnum ellum*, where a scorpion-like figure comes to mind (see there commentary to this line).

i 5: *ta-ma*!-*ṣí*: Both copy and a photo show clear BA, not MA. And yet, *ta-ba-zi* offers no good meaning, especially as *bazā'um* is attested only in the D-stem. With hesitation I emend the form to *ta-ma*!-*ṣí* from *maṣûm*, "to be able to, to be sufficient".

i 5–6: I understand these two lines as starting with a question of the woman, followed by the cautious advice of the chorus (Sigrist/Goodnick Westenholz 2008, 681f. differently).

i 6–7: *attī lūman ištēti*: *attī*, squeezed in at the end of i 6, goes with the sentence in i 7. Note that *lu*! is over erasure.

i 8–13: See Hecker 2005, 171.

i 8: *li-ib-<ba>-ka*: Correction following Hecker 1989, 748, 7a.

i 9: *ina puḫrim āli u nišī bāštim*: Difficult. This construction must be a scrambled result of either *ina puḫur ālim u nišī bāštim*, or simpler (as suggested by Hecker 2005, 171) of *ina puḫrim <ša> āli u nišī bāštim*.

i 14–19: See Hecker 2005, 172.

i 14: *karābum*: Reading with Hecker (1989, 748) (not *qerēbum*, as suggested by Sigrist/Goodnick Westenholz).

i 17: $^{d}$UTU-*ši-ni*: Another instance of "plural of ecstasy" (see Paul 1995).

i 18–19, i 20–21: The enjambment in these couplets has no literary rationale and is a result of miscalculation of the division of lines. – The end of i 19 is very difficult: *imnu* is m. while *taṣarrura* is f. (– perhaps *idum* was intended?). Besides, *imni* is not nom. but gen. (– or maybe read *imnī*?)

i 19, i 20–25: Reading and interpretation follow Hecker 2005, 172.

i 22: *luḫtalṣā*: Similarly to Lambert (1966, 49 ad 3) who analyzed *lu-ur-ta-a-ma* in MIO 12, 52–53: 3 (№ 10) as *lurtāmā*, 1 du. precative, I suggest that *lu-uh-ta-al-ṣa* is also 1 du. precative: *luḫtalṣā*, "Let the two of us clinch passionately together". Note, however, that elsewhere *ḫalāṣum* means "to press out liquid" and connecting this verb to persons is not easy.

i 23: *i-ta-ab-la-al*: From *balālum* (contra Hecker 1989, 749, who probably had in mind *i-ta-ap-la-al*, "Halte Aufsicht über…"). – *etpir*: A similar imp. form of *epērum*-Gt with reflexive meaning is found in Moussaieff Love Song i 11 (see also i 32).

i 25: *ḫašḫāti*: With Hecker 2005, 172 n. 49, this is a 2. m stative form. Similar case is found in ZA 75, 198–204d 53 (№ 30): *da-an-na-ti*.

i 26: I interpret this line as spoken by the man, calling the woman in his ecstasy to reach him (*yâtam*) and 'that of my love', namely his sexual member (see also Overview § 4.6). – *ša ra-*{I}*-mi-ia*: This slight emendation to *ša râmiya*, "that of my love", seems preferable to *ša ra-i-mi-ia*, since *ša rāʾimiya*, "that of my beloved", is not clear (see the deliberation of Sigrist/Goodnick Westenholz 2008, 699f.).

i 27: *šâlum*: Following Sigrist/Goodnick Westenholz 2008, 700.

i 28: *ú-ta-ak-*{AL}*-ki-la-an-ni ul illikam*: Following Sigrist/Goodnick Westenholz 2008, 700.

i 29: [*e*°*-re*°]*-eš-šu*: Following Sigrist/Goodnick Westenholz 2008, 700: *êrum+iš+šu*, "to/for his awakening". On the meaning of sleep vs. being awake in ALL, see Overview § 6.1.

i 31–32: This couplet resonates i 23. – *šu-la-a-*[*ku*?] may derive from the rare verb *šiʾālum*/*šâlum*-Dt, "to rejoice", attested so far only in JAOS 103, 26–27: 4 (= № 7), or, more simply from the *elûm*-Š, "I am elevated" (MPS).

ii 4: *kam-šat ù qú-ud-di*-x-x: Difficult. Assuming a syllabic value *šat* for KUR, which is not common in OB, I suggest reading *kamšat* as a (non-attested) by-from of *kamāsum*, "to kneel". The continuation may perhaps be connected to *qadādum*, "to bow down". – {LI} *i-ša-ak-ka-na-an-ni a-ḫi-tam*: I follow Hecker (1989, 749 n. 4a) in assuming that {LI} is a mistake. Sigrist/Goodnick Westenholz 2008, 681 and 702 read: *da-an-ni-iš qù-lam lu-ud-di ù-/li i-ša-ak-ka-na-an-ni a-ḫi-tam*, "Let me cast firmly (over her?) a calm so that she will not set me aside".

ii 5: *at-tu-li-im*: Not clear. Sigrist/Goodnick Westenholz 2008, 681 and 683 suggest "for (my) breast" (< *an*(*a*) *tulîm*). One may perhaps consider also the infinitive *itūlum*, "to sleep" (< *an*(*a*) *itūlim*), in which case an emendation *ta-ṣa-*<*la*>*-al-ma*, "you are lying down to sleep" comes to mind.

ii 6: *tuša*: For this particle see Wasserman 2012, Chap. 5 (but reading *tu-ta*, *tūta*, "you have found" is not excluded).

ii 7: *ṭēmam wabālum*: This idiom appears in a difficult phrase in another love-related composition, CUSAS 10, 10: 40–41 (№ 4). If understood correctly, "the news" refers to a birth of a child. This may be also the meaning here too: the woman is "perfect in her competence" because she is ready and able to conceive. – {Ù-LI} *ù le-ʾ*$u_5$*-tam šu-uk-lu-la-at*: Reading follows Hecker (1989, 750 n. 8a). This correction seems preferable to me to the heavily restored suggestion of Sigrist/Goodnick Westenholz 2008, 681 and 703: Ù-LI Ù-LI *ḫu-ud* <*li-ib-bi-im*> *šu*!*-uk-lu-la-at*.

ii 9: *la ta-ka-aš-ši-ṭa-an-ni* cannot be derived from *kašādum* (a/u), as understood by Sigrist/Goodnick Westenholz 2008, 683 ("Why do you not approach me"?), but, as noticed by Hecker (1989, 750), from *kašāṭum* (i/i), "to cut off".

# № 16 I Will Not Change for You a Word! (ZA 49, 168–169)

Copy: -/-
Tablet Siglum: Si 57
Photo: von Soden 1950, 168–169
Edition: von Soden 1950, 162–173, Held 1961, 6–9, Ponchia 1996, 115–119
Collection: Arkeoloji Müzeleri, Istanbul
Studies: Held 1962, Stolarczyk 1986, Hecker 1989, 743–747, Groneberg 2002, Wasserman 2003, Cat. No. 265, Foster 2005, 155–159, Klein/Sefati 2008, 623–624
Provenance: Sippar
Measurements: 11.5x16.8 cm
Period: Late OB (Hammurāpi)

**Introduction**

This dialogue between an obnoxious man and the loyal female lover whom he rejects is probably the best known piece of Akk. love literature in the corpus. This two-column text has a partial parallel in a one-column text, CUSAS 10, 10 (№ 4). It can be safely dated to the OB period based on epigraphical and grammatical criteria, as well as on the fact that king Hammurāpi is mentioned in it (iv 6).

In August 2013 Marten Stol kindly sent me a list of collations made by Fritz R. Kraus on 23.05.1961 while he was in Istanbul, preparing his AbB 5 volume. These collations – which are mostly of historical interest now – are mentioned occasionally in the commentary.

Obv.
col. i

| | |
|---|---|
| i 1 | *[ṣ]u-úr-pí tu-ur-ki ez-bi* |
| i 2 | *la ma-ga-al da-ba-bu-um* |
| i 3 | *qá-bé-e qá-bu-ú-um-ma* |
| i 4 | *ú-ul e-ni-a-ak-ki-im* |
| i 5 | *at-wa-a-am ma-li ṣa-ab-⸢ta⸣-a-ku* |
| i 6 | *ša a-na sí-in-ni-iš-tim ip-pa-ra-qá-du* |
| i 7 | *sà-ma-an ⸢du⸣-ri-im* |
| i 8 | *šum-ma la it-*KU*-ud ú-ul a-wi-lum mi-ḫi-ir-šu* |
| ---- | |
| i 9 | *li-iz-zi-iz ki-it-ti* |
| i 10 | *i-na ma-ḫa-ar Iš*$_8$*-tár šar-ra-tim* |
| i 11 | *li-iḫ-pí-it ra-mi li-ba-aš* |
| i 12 | *ka-ar-ri-iš-ti* |
| i 13 | *k[a-t]i? pa-la-ḫa-am ku-uz-zu-ba-am* |
| i 14 | *i-ta-ás-ḫu-ur ma-ri-im* |
| i 15 | *i-na qá-bé-e* $^{d}$*Na-na-a-a ub*!*-lam*! *da-ri-iš* |
| i 16 | *a-li me-ḫi-ir-ti* |
| ---- | |

i 17 e-li-ki ḫa-as-sà-a-ku
i 18 a-na ši-ib-qì-ki ša pa-na-nu-um
i 19 mu-ug-ri a-ta-al-ki
i 20 a-na ma-li-ik-ti-ki šu-un-ni-i
i 21 ki-ma e-re-nu
----
i 22 ú-ṣa-ab-ba-at-ka-ma $u_{4}$-ma-am
i 23 ra-am-ka ù ra-mi uš-ta-ma-ga-ar
i 24 us-sé-ne-el-le-ma a-na $^{d}$Na-na-a-a
i 25 sa-li-im-ka be-lí da-ri-a-am e-le-eq-qé
i 26 na-ad-nam
----
i 27 a-la-wi-ki ni-tam i-na ṣe-ri-ki
i 28 ur-pí-a a-ka-aṣ-ṣa-ar
i 29 mu-ta-ak-ki-il-ta-ki li-il-qé-e
i 30 ru-ʾà-am-<ki?> ti-ki-a-ti-ki ḫu-ul-li-q[í]
i 31 li-qé-e ki-na-tim
----
i 32 (traces)
(gap of c. 5–6 lines)

col.ii
ii 1 […]-i ig-gi-[il?-tu?]
ii 2 ú-ul i-ba-aš-ši-i-[ma]
ii 3 mi-im-ma ú-ul i-na li-ib-bi-ia [x]
ii 4 iš-ša-aq-qá-al-ši-im [x]-x-el-[x]
ii 5 ú-za-am-ma [ra]-mi
----
ii 6 e-li la ra-im-ti-ka mi-ši-tam li-[it-bu-uk]
ii 7 šar-ra-tum $Iš_{8}$-tár
ii 8 ki-ma ia-ti la ṣa-la-lum [lu e-mi-is-si]
ii 9 ka-li mu-ši-im li-ku-úr [li-id-li-ip]
----
ii 10 e-ze-er la mu-se-ep-p[í-(it)-tam]
ii 11 ú-ul a-ḫa-aš-še-eḫ la [mu-ka-zi-ib-tam]
ii 12 ú-ul a-na-ad-di-iš-ši-im [i-ri-mi]
ii 13 da-ba-bu-um a-na la [ma-ga-ri-im]
ii 14 mi-nam i-[ba-aš-ši]
ii 15 ú-ša-ak-la [da]-bi-ba-[ti-ša/ia]
ii 16 ú-ul e-še-em-me(-)ša […]
ii 17 a-ša-ar li?-[ib-bi ek-le-tim]
ii 18 ra-mi [x] at-ta-di
ii 19 mi-nam tu-sa-an-na-qá-ni-i[n-ni]
----

ii 20 *it[-ta]-tu?-ia ú-la-ap-<pa>-ta-ni-[in-ni]*
ii 21 *ša-a[p]-ti e-li-tum i-la-[ab-bi-ik]*
ii 22 *lu ša-ap-li-tum-ma i-ru-ub-[ba-am]*
ii 23 *e-di-ir-šu a-na-aš-ši-iq-[šu]*
ii 24 *at-ta-na-ap-la-ás el-[šu]*
ii 25 *a-ka-aš-ša-ad er-ni-it-ti* [x x]
ii 26 *e-li da-[bi-ba-ti-ia]*
ii 27 *ù dam-qí-iš ar-r[a-i-mi-ia x x x]*
ii 28 *i-nu-ma ši-it-ta-n[i* x x x x x]
ii 29 *ni-ka-aš-ša-a[d ernittam?]*
----
ii 30 (traces)
(gap of c. 14 lines)

Rev.
col. iii
iii 1 [...]
iii 2 *i-na* [...]
iii 3 *ar-wi-[ia?* x x x x]
iii 4 *a-la-súm ú-ul e-li-i k[a-ša-sú]*
iii 5 *a-na Iš*$_8$*-tár id-di-na-aš-šu a-na q[í-iš-tim]*
----
iii 6 *a-na ša iq-ta-na-ab-bi-a-ni-ik-[ki-im]*
iii 7 *ú-la-mi et-tum a[t-ti]*
iii 8 *ki-le-e at-ba-al ra-mi ú-ul* [x x]
iii 9 *ut-te-es-sí i-na zu-um-ri-k[i]*
iii 10 *ki-ma ša-ar bi-ri in-bi-ia ur?-ti?-iq?*
----
iii 11 *a-sa-aḫ-ḫu-ur in-bi-[ka]*
iii 12 *be-lí zu-um-ma-a-ku ra-am-[ka]*
iii 13 *iq-qá-at ṣí-ḫa-tu-ka šu-*[x (x)]
iii 14 *lu pa-aṣ*!(Text: I)*-ma an-sú-ur-ri ú-ul* [x x x]
iii 15 *ur-ri ù mu-ši a-da-ab-bu-ub [it-ti-ka]*
----
iii 16 *lu-tu-úr ù lu-tu-ur-ma lu-uš-[lu-uš]*
iii 17 *a-na pí-ia ṭà-ba-am la ú-še-eb?-b[u?* x x]
iii 18 *a-na ú-pa* (-) *a-ap-tim ti-iṣ-ba-ti* x x
iii 19 *ku-uš-di ga-na ra-mi*
----
iii 20 *an-ḫa?*(Text: N[A]) *i-na-ia da-an-ni-iš* {IŠ}
iii 21 *da-al-pa-a-ku i-na i-ta-ap-lu-si-šu*
iii 22 *tu-ša i-ba-a ba-ab-[t]i*
iii 23 *u*$_4$*-mu-um it-ta-la-ak a-li [ma-ri or: be-lí]*
(gap of c. 15 lines)

col. iv
iv1 *[a-n]a ka-[ša?-di?-šu?* x x x x x]
iv2 *iš-té-na[m* x x x x x]
iv3 *mi-nam* [x x x x]
iv4 *ga-na lu-uṣ-ba-at bi-[ir?-ke?-šu?*]
iv5 *lu-ši-ib lu-te-eq-qí šum-ma ša gir-ri-ia*
---
iv 6 *at-ma-ki-im* $^{d}$*Na-na-a-a ù Ḫa-am-mu-ra-pí šarram*(LUGAL)
iv 7 *ša ki-na-ti-ia lu a-qá-ab-bi-ki-im*
iv 8 *ra-am-ki e-li di-li-ip-tim*
iv 9 *ù a-šu-uš-tim la wa-at-ru i-na ṣe-ri-ia*
----
iv 10 *e-ra-da-nim*° *aš-šum qí-pa-a-ku ra-i-mi*
iv 11 *da-bi-ba-tu-ia*
iv 12 *e-li ka-ka-ab ša-me-e ma-da*
iv 13 *li-ir-[q]í-a li-ta-aq-ra*
iv 14 *ša-ar i-na-an-na-ma li-it-ta-*<*ar*>*-qí-a*
iv 15 *a-na-ku uš-ba-am-ma*
iv 16 [*pí*]*-i be-lí-ia eš-te-ne-em-me*
----
iv 17 *et-ti la ma-ás-ku*
iv 18 [*š*]*a pa-na zi-mu-ki*
iv 19 [*az*]*-zi-iz-ki-im-ma*
iv 20 [*pu-d*]*i-ki te-te-en-di* {DI}
iv 21 [*ma-g*]*i-ir-tum šum-ki*
iv 22 [*be-l*]*e-et mi-il-ki-i na-ba-ki*
iv 23 *ša-ni-tum-ma*!(Text: MI) *lu le-mu-ut-ta-ni*
iv 24 [*ma*]*-ḫa-ar Iš*$_{8}$*-tár*
----
Ed.
iv 25 [*dam?-qí?-i*]*š? ta-ap-pa-al*
----

**Translation**
Obv.
col. i
i 1 (He:) Yell! Do not bother to reply!
i 2 Not so much talking!
i 3 My decision is made,
i 4–5 I will not change for you a word, anything I said.
i 6–7 He who lies on his back for a woman is a weevil from the city wall.
i 8 If he is not *serious* he is no match for a man.
----

i 9–10 (She:) May my righteousness appear before Ištar the queen!
i 11–12 May my love prevail, may my slanderer come to shame!
i 13–15 At Nanāya's command I have always (taken upon me) to adore you, to charm you, to take care of (my) baby!
i 16 Where is my match?!

----

i 17–18 (He:) I remember more than you your tricks of the past.
i 19–21 Give up! Go away! Report to your counselor that we are (now) awake!

----

i 22–23 (She:) I will catch you, and this very day I shall reconcile your love with mine.
i 24 I keep on praying to Nanāya;
i 25–26 (So that) I shall accept your peace, my lord, forever, as a gift.

----

i 27 (He:) I shall lay siege upon you,
i 28 I shall gather my clouds on you.
i 29–30 May your supporter take away your seductiveness, put an end to your complaint!
i 31 Accept the truth!
i 32 …
(gap of c. 5–6 lines)

col. ii
ii 1 (He:) […] she/he was *aw*[*ake*(?)]
ii 2 *and* does not exist.
ii 3–4 Nothing is in my heart
ii 4 ... will be paid out to her.
ii 5 I yearn for my [lo]ve.

----

ii 6–7 (She:) May queen Ištar [*pour*] confusion over the one who loves you not!
ii 8 May she, like me, [be afflicted] with sleeplessness!
ii 9 May she be dazed and [restless] all night long!

----

ii 10 (He:) I despise the girl who does not wo[rship (me)].
ii 11 I do not desire for the girl who does not [fawn].
ii 12 I shall not give her [my love-charm].
ii 13 Talking in order to dis[agree]
ii 14 Why [does it exist?]
ii 15 I shall stop [*her*/*my*] slanderers,
ii 16 I shall not hear what […]
ii 17–18 To the m[idst of darkness] I have thrown away my love:
ii 19 Why do you keep bothering [me]?

----

ii 20 (She:) My (ominous) signs trouble me:
ii 21 My upper lip becomes moist,
ii 22 While my lower lip trembles!
ii 23 I shall embrace him, I shall kiss him,
ii 24 I shall gaze at [him],
ii 25–26 I shall achieve my victory […] over [my slanderers],
ii 27 And to my lover [*I shall*] gracefully […]
ii 28 When our sleep […]
ii 29 We shall achieve [*victory*]
----
ii 30 …
(gap of c. 14 lines)

Rev.
col. iii
iii 1 (She:) …
iii 2 In […]
iii 3 [*My*(?)] *gazelle* […]
iii 4 I run but I cannot [reach him],
iii 5 She gave him to Ištar as a gift.
----
iii 6 (He:) As for those (women) who keep telling you:
iii 7 "Y[ou] are not the only one!"
iii 8 Stop! I have taken my love away, and will not [*return* (*it*)].
iii 9 I have removed [it] from your body,
iii 10 I have taken my charms thousands of miles away.
----
iii 11 (She:) I seek [your] pleasures,
iii 12 My lord, I yearn for [your] love.
iii 13 Because *in* your delights […]
iii 14 *Let them be veiled*, would they never […]
iii 15 I shall talk [to you] day and night.
----
iii 16 (He:) Let me repeat it twice and thrice;
iii 17 I *swear* not to say anything kind to you (lit. satisfy my mouth with *kindness*),
iii 18 Take your place by the window orifice:
iii 19 Come on, catch my love!
----
iii 20 (She:) My eyes are very tired,
iii 21 I am sleepless from gazing at him,
iii 22 It seems that he walked across my street?

| | |
|---|---|
| iii 23 | The day has gone by, where is [my darling (or: my lord)]?<br>(gap of c. 15 lines) |

col. iv

| | |
|---|---|
| iv 1 | (<u>She:</u>) To catch him [...] |
| iv 2 | The one [...] |
| iv 3 | What [...] |
| iv 4 | Come on, let me hold [his] *k*[*nees*], |
| iv 5 | I shall sit and wait maybe he is on his way to me! |
| ---- | |
| iv 6 | (<u>He:</u>) I have sworn to you by Nanāya and Hammurāpi the king; |
| iv 7 | Indeed, I am telling to you the truth; |
| iv 8–9 | Your love is nothing more to me than agony and grief. |
| ---- | |
| iv 10 | (<u>She:</u>) They(f.) ... because I trust my loved one. |
| iv 11–12 | My slanderers outnumber the stars of heaven. |
| iv 13 | May they hide! May they be scarce! |
| iv 14 | May they hide themselves forever right now! |
| iv 15–16 | And as for me, I sat down, listening to the words of my lord. |
| ---- | |
| iv 17–18 | (<u>He:</u>) My one, not ugly are your features – (they are) as before, |
| iv 19 | (When) I stood by you, |
| iv 20 | And you leaned your *sh*[*oulders*] (against me). |
| iv 21 | [*Mag*]*irtum* ("Favorable") is your name, |
| iv 22 | "Wise la[dy]"– your title. |
| iv 23 | The other woman is indeed our misfortune, |
| iv 24 | *By* Ištar! |

Ed.

| | |
|---|---|
| iv 25 | [...*Nice*]*ly* you reply. |

**Commentary**

i 1: [*ṣ*]*u-úr-pí*: Reading with AHw 268, 7a and 1373b, 2 s.v. *tūru* and Hecker 1989, 743, 1a. Groneberg 2002, 168 suggests [*k*]*urbī*, "bend down". (Note Kraus' collations: "1. Zeichen nach Koll. nicht [K]U; 2. Zeichen kaum ÚR; 3. Zeichen nach Photo nicht BI; viell. *-am*?").

i 7: *sà-ma-an* ⌈*du*⌉*-ri-im*: Previous readings were *sà-ki-il* ⌈*ša*⌉*-ri-im* (CAD S 68b 1a), or *ṣa-*⌈*ri*!⌉*-*[*i*]*m* ⌈*ša-*⌉*ri-im* (Groneberg 2002, 168, 175). Now, with CUSAS 10, 10: 14 (№ 4) George's reading *sà-ma-an* ⌈*du*⌉*-ri-im* is secured. (Kraus' collations did not solve the riddle. His reading *za-ki-el* lead to *sà-ki-il* of the CAD. Alternatively he read *za-*[*b*]*a-al*?).

i 8: *it*-KU-*ud*: CAD I/J 298 hesitates between a derivation from *naqādum* and *ekēdum*. CAD N/1, 153–154. s.v. *nakādum* does not list this line. AHw 1552b stresses: not from *ekēdum*! Mayer (in Deller/Mayer/Sommerfeld 1987, 198) analyses this form as *nakādum*-Gt, and translates "besorgt sein", which is roughly followed here.

i 13: *k*[*a-t*]*i*?: Reading follows Wilcke 1985, 195 (improving on Held: *k*[*a-a-a*]*m*). Groneberg 2002, 169 suggests reading *ka*[*nâ*]*m*, "preening".

i 15: *ub*!-*lam*!: Contra Groneberg 2002, 169 who reads *bêlam*? *dāriš*, "I am asked (to do this) forever".

i 19: *mugrī atalkī*: For verb-couples (Koppelungen) as this one, see Wasserman 2003, 22. The same couple of verbs, in opposite order (*alkī mugrīnni*) is found in Or. 60, 340: 9 (№ 12). – *atalkī*: OA Imp. of *alākum*-Gt. In OB one expects *atlakī*.

i 21: *kīma êrēnu*: For the motif of sleep and wakefulness in ALL, see Overview § 6.1.

i 24: *us-sé-ne-el-li-ma*: With AHw 1056a: *sullûm*-Dtn. The suggestion of Groneberg 2002, 176 to read *uṣ-ṣé-ne-el-le-ma* should be rejected, as *ṣullûm*-Dtn shows no coloring to -*e*.

i 27–28: *alawwīki nītam ina ṣēriki urpīya akaṣṣar*: Reading with AHw 456b 4a and 1432b 3, CAD K 261a 3a, and Hecker 1989, 744 ("Gewölk"). The meaning of the idiom "to gather cloud(s) against..." is made clear by Maqlû V 83–84: *urpata ikṣuramma*, "(The sorceress) has gathered the cloud against me". Hence, Wilcke's (1985, 195) suggestion to read *alawwi qinītam ina ṣēriki urabīja akaṣṣar*, "Ich schliesse das Vermögen ein und verschliesse deinetwegen mein Einkommen", is not helpful contextually and cannot be accepted.

i 30: *ḫu-ul-li-q*[*í*]: So, although Groneberg (2002, 176) reads *ḫu-ul-li-*[*ki*], from *ḫullum*, "neck ring". (Kraus' collations: "Ende *ḫu-ul-li-q*[*í*] zieml. deutl. nicht -*ma*").

i 31: *kīnātim leqûm*, "to accept the truth". It is not impossible that the same expression is found in the OB wisdom dialogue CBS 1399: 7: *KI-in-na-tim l*[*e-qí*]-*i* <*la*?> *s*[*ar*?-*r*]*a*?-*tim ṣú-ub-bi-it*, although the reading *qinnatum*, "buttocks", was preferred in Streck/Wasserman 2011, 117–119.

ii 1: *ig-gi-*[*il*?-*tu*?]: If correctly restored, this form derives from the verb *negeltûm*/*nagaltûm*, "to awake, wake (up)", and follows thematically i 21: *kīma êrēnu* "that we are (now) awake!".

ii 5: *ú-za-am-ma* [*ra*]-*mi*: With AHw 1536b 1 and CAD Z 156a, "to be deprived of". See also CUSAS 10, 9: 16 (№ 3): *šanîš uzammīka*, "Again I yearned for you". By contrast, Hecker 1989, 744 traslates "Es kommt heraus" (*waṣûm*) and Groneberg 2002, 176, similarly: *ú-ṣa-am-ma*, "Ich werde herausgehen".

ii 6–7: *mi-ši-tam li-[it-bu-uk]*: I follow CAD M/2, 126, s.v. *mīšītu*, "confusion, blindness" (from *ešûm*), but *mišītu* (from *mašûm*) may also fit the context and remind of CUSAS 10, 9: 23 (№ 3): "My fruits are unforgettable".[406]

ii 10–19: As noted by George, these lines have near parallel in CUSAS 10, 10: 1–8 (№ 4).

ii 10: *e-ze-er:* Reading follows CAD Z 98a 2'. (Groneberg 2002, 179 prefers *e-sé-er*, "Ich setze die fest, die [mich] nicht anfle[ht]", probably following i 27 *alawwīki nītam*).

ii 14: *mi-nam i-[ba-aš-ši]*: George translates the parallel line in CUSAS 10, 10: 6 (№ 4): "how can that be shameful [on] her(?) account", but understanding *mīnam ibašši* from *bašûm* – here and in the parallel text – seems better: the man cannot fathom why the woman continues disobeying him.

ii 18: *attadi*: The parallel lines in CUSAS 10, 10: 7–8 (№ 4) have [*anan*]*din rāmī*. The man declares that his love is now thrown away to *ašar li*[*bbi ekletim*] "midst of darkness", which is echoed in iii 10: *kīma šār bīrī inbīya urtīq*, "I have taken my charms thousands of miles away". For the metaphorical meaning of light and darkness in ALL, see Overview § 6.2.

ii 21–22: This description of the upper and lower lips leans, no doubt, on physiognomic signs but the material collected by Böck (2000) does not offer a direct parallel to them.

ii 24: *attanaplas el*[*šu*]: Restoration based on CUSAS 10, 9: 4 (№ 3): "The boy is not aware of the (girl) watching him".[407] (Groneberg 2002, 177 suggests: *el-*[*ṣi-iš*?]).

ii 28: For sleep in ALL, see Overview § 6.1.

ii 29: *nikašša*[*d ernittam*?]: Restoration based on ii 25. If correct, *ernittam kašādum* in this context would refer to sexual climax (see Overview § 4.5).

iii 10: *kīma šār bīrī*: A similar expression is found in a wisdom dialogue Fs. Reiner, 384: 4'–5' (= Streck/Wasserman 2011, 119). – The reading *ur*?*-ti*?*-iq*? is questionable. Groneberg 2002, 177 suggested *in-bi-ia aḫ-ri-*[*iš*?], "eil[ig] meine "Frucht"!". (Kraus' collations: "nicht *urtiq*").

iii 12: *zu-um-ma-a-ku*: Reading with AHw 1536b 2 and CAD Z 156a 1a which takes its form from *zummûm*, "to be deprived of" (cf. ii 5). Hecker 1989, 746 prefers *ṣummûm*, "ich dürste...".

iii 13: *šu-*[x (x)]: Groneberg 2002, 171 restores the end of the line to *šu-*[*li*], "Get an erection by laughing happily". However, euphemistic references to the male erection do not

406 CUSAS 10, 9: 23 (№ 3): *inbūa ul ša mīši*.
407 CUSAS 10, 9: 4 (№ 3): *ul īde* [*m*]*ārum* [*na*]*-ṭì-*<*la*>*-*[*sú*].

employ *elûm* (but rather *tebûm*, or images of hard stone, see Paul 2002, 489 and Overview § 4.6) – For the prepositional phrase *iq-qá-at*, see the OB myth about Bēlet-ilī CT 15, 2 viii 5': $^{d}$*Ištar i-qá-tu gi-ni-i-ša.*

iii 14: *lu pa-aṣ*!(Text: I)-*ma*: Groneberg 2002, 171 reads *lu-pa-i-ma* (*lūpaʾima*, "I shall appear"), but *wapûm* is not characteristic of love lyrics, whereas a similar expression with *paṣām/num*, "to veil, to cover", regrettably also in a broken context, is found in MIO 12, 52–53: 23' (№ 10): "[…] quickly […] to veil ...".[408]

iii 17: *ana pīya ḫi-ba-am*: I follow Groneberg 2002, 177 in reading *ṭà-ba-am* (– but not her suggestion to read the end of the line *la ú-še-*[*re-eb-kī*?]). The syllabic value *ṭà* is rare in OB literary texts, but can be found sporadically.[409] The expression *ana pîya ṭābam šebûm* would mean "to satisfy the mouth with (something) sweet" ≈ "to say something kind". Hecker (1989, 746) prefers to read *ḫi-ba-am* (from *ḫībum*, verb. Adj. of *ḫâbum*, "to love", AHw 344b).

iv 6: *atmākim*, "I have sworn to you...": The past tense serves as a performative (see Mayer 1992 and Wasserman 2003, 168–169).

iv 10: *e-ra-da-nim*: Groneberg (2002, 181 n. 18) takes this form from *râdum*, "to quake, shake", but if so the form should have been *iruddānim* (see CAD R, 62 a: "uncert.").

iv 13: *li-ta-aq-ra*: With CAD A/2, 205b 1a, from *waqārum*. Groneberg's suggestion (2002, 178) to read *li-ta-ak-ra*, "sie sollen miteinander streiten" (from *nakārum*), is not convincing.

iv 14: *li-it-ta-*<*ar*>*-qí-a*: I take this slightly emended form from *rêqum*, "to be distant, go far off" (similarly to Maqlû V 166ff.), against Groneberg's (2002, 178) suggestion *li-it-ta-qí-a*, "Gerade jetzt sollen sie unendlich viele Opfer bringen" (from *naqûm*).

iv 17: *ettī*: Reading follows Held's original interpretation ("My one and only"), against Groneberg, 2002, 181: "Mein Omen" (from *ittum*).

iv 19: [*az*]*zizkimma*: The verb *izuzzum* creates a contrastive closure with *lizziz kittī* in i 9.

iv 20: [*pu-d*]*i-ki te-te-en-di* {DI}: The signs are questionable. CAD Q 104b 10' follows Held's reading [*qá-qá-a*]*d-ki* (and so also Hecker 1989, 746).

iv 21: [*mag*]*irtum*: Another contrastive closure with *mugrī atalkī* (i 19) and *râmka u râmī uštamaggar* (i 23).

---

408 MIO 12, 52–53: 23' (№ 10): [...] *kīma ṣeḫri pa-ṣa-na ú-*x [...].

409 E.g. AbB 12, 99: 15 (literary letter to Amurrum), JAOS 103, 205f.: 9 (literary letter to Nabû), YOS 11, 16a // YOS 11, 77b 1//10 (incantation against scorpion?).

iv 23: *šanītumma lū lemuttani*: Against Groneberg (2002, 178) who reads entirely differently: [*ta*]-*ni-tum mé-lu*?-*li*? *mu-ut-ta-ni*?, "[Lobpre]is ist mein? Spielen vor uns".

iv 24: [*ma*]*ḫar Ištar*: Yet another closure with *ina maḫar Ištar šarratim* in i 10.

iv 25 (Edge): Reading and translation follow Groneberg 2002, 178.

# II. Incipits of Akkadian Love Literature: Catalogues

## № 17 Like Pure Oil Your Message Is Sweet (ASJ 10, 18)

Copy: Finkel 1988, 18
Tablet Siglum: BM 59484 = A.H. 82-7-14 3893
Photo: -/-
Edition: Finkel 1988, 17–18
Studies: Wasserman 2003, Cat. No. 37
Collection: The British Museum, London
Provenance: Sippar?
Measurements: 5.6x3.4x1.8 cm
Period: Late OB (Ammī-ṣaduqa)

**Introduction**
A broken catalogue, mentioning Ammī-ṣaduqa. Each two lines (unindented) stand for one incipit, as proven by the total in l. 11. None of the incipits was identified.

| | |
|---|---|
| Obv. | |
| 1–3 | (broken) |
| 4 | [x (x)] x-*a tap-pa-tu* x [...] |
| ---- | |
| 5 | [x-l]*a*?-*ni* [.....] |
| 6 | *Iš*$_8$-*tár bu-ul-li-ṭi-i-šu* [...] |
| ---- | |
| 7 | *ra-i-mi* [(…?)] |
| 8 | *Am-mi-ṣa-du-qá šu-n*[*un*?-*dum*?] |
| ---- | |
| 9 | *ki-i ša-am-*[*ni-im el-li-im*] |
| 10 | *lu-ú ṭa-ba-at ši-pí-ir-t*[*a-ka*] |
| ---- | |
| | |
| Lo. Ed. | |
| 11 | [*napḫa*]*rum*([PA]P) 5 *ir-túm* |
| ---- | |
| | |
| Rev. | |
| 12 | *ú-te-ek-ki-da-an-ni ra-am-k*[*a*] |
| 13 | *be-lí gu-um-me-ra-am da-di-k*[*a*] |
| ---- | |
| 14 | *me-eḫ-ru-um* |
| ---- | |
| 15 | *ka-ṣi ša-a-ru* [(...)] |
| 16 | *ad-du* [*liš-ta-mi*] x x [...] |
| | (rest broken) |

**Translation**

Obv.

| | |
|---|---|
| 1–2 | (broken) |
| 3–4 | " ... companion-girls ...[...]" |
| ---- | |
| 5–6 | "Our(?)... ... Ištar, recover him back to life! [...]" |
| ---- | |
| 7–8 | "My beloved, Ammī-ṣaduqa the *il*[*lustrious*(?)]" |
| ---- | |
| 9–10 | "Indeed, like [pure o]il your mess[age] is sweet." |
| ---- | |
| 11 | A total of five *irtum* songs. |
| ---- | |

Rev.

| | |
|---|---|
| 12–13 | "Your(m.) love has spoken ill of me; My lord, grant me all your favors!" |
| ---- | |
| 14 | Refrain. |
| ---- | |
| 15–16 | "Cold is the wind ... a thunder may be heard ..." (rest broken) |

**Commentary**

8: *Am-mi-ṣa-du-qá šu-n*[*un*?-*dum*?] : Note that by the end of the line there is an upper horizontal broken wedge after the *šu*-, hence the possible restoration *šunundum*, a MB form of *šunūdum* can be offered. For this lemma see JAOS 103, 26–27: 15 (№ 7): "The illustrious one is worried about the dogs and shepherds".[410]

12 : *ūtekkidanni* : the first occurrence of OB *ekēdum*-D outside of lexical lists.

16: [*liš-ta-mi*]: Note that *šemûm*-D is very rare and no attestation of Dt is found so far, and yet parsing this form from *šemûm*-Gtn, "May Addu hear constantly" is difficult.

410 JAOS 103, 26–27: 15 (№ 7): *ana kalbī u rē'ī mariṣ šunundum*, and also l. 18.

# № 18 Stand in the Light of the Window (CUSAS 10, 12)

Copy: George 2009, Pls. XXXIV, XXXVI
Tablet Siglum: MS 3391
Photo: George 2009, Pls. XXXIII, XXXV, CDLI no. P252332
Edition: George 2009, 71–75
Collection: Schøyen Collection, Oslo
Provenance: ?
Measurements: 10.5x6.2x2.2 cm
Period: OB

**Introduction**

This catalogue lists mostly love related compositions (none of which is identified). Usually each line stands for a separate incipit, but occasionally enjambment occurs and some incipits are divided between the lines (ll. 12–14, 27–28, 29–30). Like KAR 158 (№ 19), this catalogue also mixes incipits of love-related compositions and texts of other genres (cf. ll. 11, 31). The incipits in this catalogue are bold, even vulgar in tone, compared to the Assur catalogue (see ll. 4, 5, 8, 9, 10, 13–14, 16, 19, 20, 27–28; other incipits may also contain sexual insinuations which elude us today, as ll. 36–37).

Obv.

| | |
|---|---|
| 1 | *[i]-na nu-úr a-pa-[ti-im] i-zi-iz-z[i]* |
| 2 | *šum-ma aṣ-ṣa-la-al [di]-ke-en-ni [at-ti]* |
| 3 | *ak-ku-uš di-pi-ir la te-sé-ḫe-e-ma* |
| 4 | *mu-ta-[al]-li-[ik-ti] ta-ta-la-ak a-la-la-ni* |
| 5 | *ra-bu-um ra-bu-[um] la te-te-bé-e-ma* |
| 6 | *lu-up-pa-al-sà-[ak]-ka in-nu-[úr] a-pa-ti-im* |
| 7 | *i nu-[uš-ta]-aq-ti [ne!-pi-iš!]-tu ra-mi-im-ma* |
| 8 | *a-bu-un-ti lu-uš-tu-uḫ-m[a]* |
| 9 | *ar-ra-ak ša? pi-ri-im iṣ-ṣé-eḫ!-ra-*{AM?}*-k[a]* |
| ---- | |
| 10 | *i ni-iq-ri ki-sà/ṣa-al-l[a] [ú]-ra-ša [ma]-aš-ḫa-at* |
| 11 | *gu-ga-al-la i-la-am ša-[al-ma?] i-lam* [x-*ša?*]-*a*-[*ni*] |
| 12 | *ri-mu-um ul* {ras.} *iz-za-az-ma ar-mu-ú [sa]-mu-tu* |
| 13 | *li-ṣú?!*(Text: MA)*-ni-im?* {ras.} *i-im-ta-šu-uḫ?* x x x {ras.} |
| 14 | *iš-[ku]-un-ma i-qá-al* |
| ---- | |
| 15 | *iš-ša-a a-bu-ba-am i-ša-[ka]-an mi-na-am* |
| 16 | *lu-pí-iš ši-ip-[r]a-am ṭù-li-ma-am pī*(KA) *na-ap-ša-ri* |
| 17 | *ka-bu-ut al-pi-im še-er-a-ni qá-at-nu-ti* |
| 18 | *pa-at-ra-am ù me-ši-il-ta-am a-na-iš-ša-a* {A} |
| 19 | *lu-[ub?-la?]* x *ti ri ri a-ḫa-at a-bi-ki! lu-ni-ik* |
| ---- | |

20 [*wa-a*]-⌈*ṣí*⌉-*at pe-te-at ši-na e-re-ša-ši-na*
21 [x x] x x *a-na ša*{ras.}*-ni-im e-re-ši-ša ul rēʾûm*(SIPA)
22 [x x x] x *li-ṣú-ni a-na*! *bi-ti e-mi-ka* / x x-*ra-šu-nu* x x

Rev.
23 [x x x] *ni* x [...] x-*kum* ⌈*ub*?/*ma*?⌉-*lu*
24 *a-n*[*a wa*?]-*ar-du*-⌈*ú-tim*? *ú*⌉-*ul a-ba-a*[*š*]-⌈*ka*⌉
25 ⌈*ú-ul*⌉ *az-za-az ma-ḫa-ar ib-ri*-⌈*ia*⌉
26 ⌈*i*⌉-*ir-ti ra-qá*-⌈*at*⌉ *i-na-a pu-ṣa*-⌈*tim*!(Text: T[UM]) *ma*⌉-*li-a*(Text: IḪ)
27 [*na*?]-*di-at ú-ba-ni ṣe-ḫe-er-tum pe-er-di*!(Text: IS)
28 *sí*?-*sí-im te-el-li ú tu-ra-ad*
29 *a*-⌈*na*⌉ [*d*]*a-ar ša-na-tim da-ar* ⌈*er-bé*⌉-*et* ⌈*ša*?⌉-*ar*
30 ⌈*ù*⌉ *ḫa-am-še*-⌈*et*!⌉ *lu*?-*ṣí-ku*-⌈*um ka*⌉-*lu-ú*
31 *né*-⌈*me*⌉-*lum ša* ⌈*āli*(URU)$^{ki}$?⌉-*ka iš-qí*?-*ka ša-ḫi-tu*
32 x-*di*-x-*ka i-ša-tu li-ku-ul*
33 *šar*(LUGAL) *mātim*(KALAM) ⌈*a*⌉-*nu-um ki*? *ṭa-ab e-re-nu*
34 ⌈*i*⌉-*na mu-uḫ-ḫi* ⌈*e-re*⌉-*ni-im na-ba*?-*sú wa-ṣa-at*
35 *i-na mu-uḫ-ḫi na-ba-ki lu-qú*-⌈*sú wa-ṣi*⌉-*at*
36 *iš-ta-al la-ma-da e-er-ša at-ta-di-iš ik*!-⌈*ki*⌉-*da*
37 *wa-ṣe-e mu-ṣi-i iš-ta-al la-ma-da*

**Translation**

Obv.
1 "Stand(f.) in the light of the windows!"
2 "If I fall asleep – you(f.), wake me up!"
3 "I am going – move(m.) on! Do not rebel!"
4 "My restless girl was walking to and fro like a hoopoe."
5 "Big one(m.), big one, do not arise!"
6 "Let me look at you(m.) by the light of the windows!"
7 "Let us complete the deed of lovemaking!"
8 "Let me grow long for the girl!"
9 "It is so enlarged! That of an elephant *was* smaller than yours!"

----

10 "Let us invite the ...! She is taken by force regarding her vulva"
11 "Ask the canal-inspector, the god and ... me the god"
12–13 "The wild bull is not standing – let the red gazelles come out!"
13–14 "He has taken by force ... He placed (it) and (now) he is silent"

----

15 "He brought the Flood – achieving what?"
16 "Let me perform the work (of lovemaking?), the spleen, the

| | |
|---|---|
| | “mouth” of the uvula” |
| 17 | “Bull’s shit, thin sinews!” |
| 18 | “I carry a knife and a whetstone” |
| 19 | “Let me carry... let me have sex with your aunt!” |
| ---- | |
| 20 | “(One) is going out(f.), (another) is open(f.) – two are their(f. pl.) plowmen” |
| 21 | “[...] to the second of her plowmen: ‘(You are) not the Shepherd!’” |
| 22 | “[...] may they come out to your(m.) father-in-law’s house, their(m.) [...]” |
| | |
| Rev. | |
| 23 | “[...] ... [...] to you, they brought(?)” |
| 24 | “To slavery I shall not degrade myself before you(m.)” |
| 25 | “I shell not serve before my friend” |
| 26 | “My breast is *thin*, my eyes are speckled with white spots!” |
| 27 | “My little finger is [tw]isted” |
| 27–28 | “A *mare*(?) of a horse – she goes up and down” |
| 29–30 | “For eternity of years, an eternity, (for) four eons (of years), indeed five (eons of years), I will come out to you(m.), the *kalû*!” |
| 31 | “The profit of your city: a sow gave you a drink” |
| 32 | “May fire consume your [...]!” |
| 33 | “It is the king of the land! How sweet is the cedar!” |
| 34–35 | “On top of the cedar his ... comes out. On top of your(f.) ... his merchandise(?) comes out!” |
| 36–37 | “He asked (to?) know (sexually), (and) I set down a bed for him *outside*. While getting out, the one going out, asked (to?) know (sexually)”. |

**Commentary**
2: *i-zi-iz-z*[*i*]: So, not *iz-zi-iz-z*[*i*] as in George, 2009, 72.

3: *di-pi-ir*: With George this form is the imp. of the hitherto unattested verb *dapārum*-G, connected to *ṭapārum* (see CAD Ṭ 48, AHw 1380a, CDA 413a and SB Gilg. I 111, cf. George 2003, 790 ad l.).

4: The *allallum*-bird, tentatively translated (following George, 2009, 73) as “hoopoe”, is mentioned in the OB bird name text (Black/Al-Rawi 1987, 124 iii 3 = Al-Rawi/Dalley 2000, 106 iii 56).

9: *iṣ-ṣé-eḫ*!-*ra*-{AM?}-*k*[*a*]: The text seems to distinguish between ḪI and IḪ signs (see l. 3 vs. the sign in this line) and therefore I prefer reading here *iṣ-ṣé-eḫ*!-*ra*-{AM?}-*k*[*a*], a G-perfect form, rather than *iṣ-ṣé-ḫe-ra-*{AM?}*-k*[*a*], as George suggested (N stem is elsewhere not attested).

8: *abbunti*: The attached preposition (*an*(*a*) *bunti*) is an archaized feature. Mimation, on the other hand, is lacking.

10: *ī niqri ki-sà/ṣa-al-l*[*a*]: *qerûm* is used once in a context where a woman is invited by a man to have sexual intercourse,[411] hence *qerûm* is preferred over *gerûm*. The verb *qerûm* takes a direct obj. so *ki-sà/ṣa-al-l*[*a*] could fit grammatically, but neither *kisallum*, "court", nor *kiṣallum*, "ankle", offer a solution. The continuation of the line has clear sexual connotations: *mašāḫum/mašā'um*, "to take by force", is used in the Laws of Ešnunna § 26 where a woman is abducted and taken sexually by force (cf. CAD M/1, 361a 1', and see also l. 13). The same verb, *mašāḫum*, is found in the Moussaieff Love Song obv. 2 (№ 11): "Like *a* [*robb*]*er* I want to plunder your attractiveness![412]

12–14: These lines contain two incipits with faultily divided lines. The first incipit is *rīmum ul izzazma armū līṣûnim* and the second *imtaššuḫ iškunma iqâl*. I suggest that the first incipit pictures metaphorically an opportunity for her suitors (the red gazelles) to approach the woman sexually, when her husband (wild bull) is absent. The second incipit *imtašuḫ… iškunma iqâl* describes sexual intercourse. The verb *šakānum* is used here as in Or. 60, 340: 18 (№ 12), where Ištar encourages the boys "Place (it) (*šuknā*), guys, *in* the pretty vulva!".[413] (More on this in Overview § 4.4).

15: *iššâ abūbum*: The devastating force of the flood is mentioned in ŠÀ.ZI.GA with reference to the enormous sexual potency of a stallion: "A furious horse whose arousal is a devastating (flood)".[414]

16: *lūpiš ši-ip-ra-am*: George's (2009, 73) correction (*lu-pí-iš-ši a*!*-a*!*-*[*r*]*a-am*, "I shall deck her out with flours(?)") is not necessary: the signs are clear and *šiprum*, "work", refers here to the act of lovemaking. The line continues by listing two organs which are not easily connected to amatory imagery: *ṭulīmum*, spleen and *pî napšāri*, "uvula(?)", which perhaps were meant to insult.

17: *kabūt alpim*, "ox's dung", is attested in magico-medical context, probably designating a certain stone (CAD K 29a 2'). In this line, however, it is more likely that this compound should be taken literally, as an insult in a quarrel between angry lovers.

18: The image of the knife on the whetstone, with the inherent actions of lubrication and friction, carries clear sexual connotations.

---

411 RA 69, 121, No. 8: 10, cited in CAD Q 242c.

412 Love Song obv. 2 (№ 11): [*ḫā*]*biliš dādīki lumšuḫ*.

413 Or. 60, 340: 18 (№ 12): *šuknā eṭlūtum ana ḫurdati damiqtimma*.

414 Biggs 1967, 17: 13 *sisû ezzu ša tībušu našpandi*.

24: Love as submission or slavery, is found in CUSAS 10, 9: 21, 25 (№ 3).

26: *irtī ra-qá-at*: George (2009, 73) translates "my chest is undeveloped". The form can be analyzed as *rāqat* (from *râqum*, "to be empty"), or *raqqat* (from *raqāqum*, "to be(come) thin"). However, *rāqu* occurs only in Assyrian, whereas Babylonian has regularly *rīqu*, which makes this derivation preferable (MPS). Be it as it may, the image is probably that of prepubescent breasts (as in Songs 8: 8, 10). – *īnāya pūṣātim maliā*: Reading follows George. White spots in the eyes are mentioned in physiognomical omens (Böck 2000, 112: 65–66): "If he is covered with white spots in his right eye – poverty and misfortune is destined for him; If he is covered with white spots in his left eye – wealth will follow him".[415] Eyes are also a locus where love takes its toll. In ZA 49, 168–169 iii 20 (№ 16) the waiting woman says: "My eyes are very tired".[416] This incipit describes physiognomical signs of love – but their exact meaning is not clear.

27: *nadiat ubānī ṣeḫertum*: Very likely another physiognomical symptom of being in love.

27–28: The incipit begins with the last word of 27. There are not many words which begin with *pe-er*: The clearest candidates are *pērtum*, "hair" (so probably George who translates: "the mane(?) of a horse(?)"), or *perdum*, "a kind of equid". Although *perdum* is attested so far mostly in OA texts, the powerful picture of horses mating is known in Akk. literature. See, e.g. the SB fable, which begins: "When an excited horse was mounting a jenny-ass...".[417] (See also the reference from ŠÀ.ZI.GA in commentary to l. 15 above).

29–30: As the sequence *erbēt šar u ḫamš*[*et*!] indicates, the two lines form one incipit (MPS). – The mentioning of *kalû* in love lyric composition is noteworthy. It is perhaps the sole attestation in the corpus which refers to sexual rapport that is not purely heterosexual.

31: A "sow" is probably a derogatory reference to a woman, as "bitch" in CUSAS 10, 10: 43 (№ 4).

33: A similar incipit is found in KAR 158 vii 28' (№ 19): "The one who goes down to the garden, Oh king, the cutter of cedar (branches)".[418]

36–37: Reading differs from George. The expression *ištāl lamāda* is understood as referring to a man asking a woman for sexual favours.

---

415 Böck 2000, 112: 65–66: *šumma imitti īnišu pūṣa ediḫ lupnu u lā magāru šakinšu, šumma šumēli īnišu* MIN(*pūṣa ediḫ*) *mašrû ireddēšu.*

416 ZA 49, 168–169 iii 20: *anḫā īnāya danniš.*

417 BWL 218: 15–18: *sīsû tibû ina muḫḫi atāni parê kî elû.*

418 KAR 158 vii 28' (№ 19): *ārid kirî šarru ḫāṣibu erēni.*

# № 19 My Love Is the Light that Illuminates the Eclipse (KAR 158)

Copy: KAR 158
Tablet Siglum: VAT 10101
Photo: CDLI no. P282615
Edition: Ebeling 1922 (Figs. 25–29)
Studies: Loretz 1964, Limet 1996, Hecker 2005, 170–171, Klein/Sefati 2008, Hecker 2013
Collection: Vorderasiatisches Museum, Berlin
Provenance: Assur
Measurements: c. 18.0x20.0x3.5 cm
Period: MA

**Introduction**

KAR 158 (VAT 10101), now kept in Berlin, a meticulously compiled tablet with tiny and accurate script, is probably the longest of all catalogues of Akk. literary texts to reach us,[419] listing 152 different Akk. and 32 Sum. compositions by their first lines.[420] Dozens of other incipits in it were broken away. Its beautiful script, very few mistakes, the careful organization of the catalogue into sections, each tagged with a generic label[421] and arithmetically summarized, the detailed sub-totals and the long grand total section at the end of the tablet, and finally the fact that the tablet was baked in antiquity, all prove that it was written by an accomplished scribe and attest to the importance of this catalogue in the eyes of Assyrian librarians.[422]

KAR 158 was copied by Erich Ebeling in 1922. Ebeling also published the first and so-far only complete edition of the text. Recently a new German translation of the catalogue was published by Hecker (2013). Though treated sporadically, and cited extensively in the dictionaries, no modern edition of this text, so crucial for the study of

419 Another extensive catalogue is the Catalogue of Texts and Authors (Lambert 1962). For catalogues in general see Krecher (1976–1980). But what does a "catalogue" mean? Is it simply a text which lists the inventory of a specific library? Gordin (2011, 192 n. 66), following Christiansen 2008, suggests that, in the realm of Hittite scribal practices, "certain shelf lists can be seen as bibliographical notes (Literaturverzeichnisse) referring to texts that are to be rewritten, relocated or otherwise used for specific reasons, such as cultic events etc." Potentially, the function of a tablet listing the titles of different compositions can be more complex than merely listing what exists in the library.

420 Hecker (2013, 54) sums up: "Der Katalog umfaßte ursprünglich etwa 400 Liedanfänge bzw. die mit diesen identischen Liedtitel, von denen rund 275 erhalten sind, allerdings teilweise beschädigt". These figures ean probably on Black (1983, 25) who gives the same exact numbers. Similar calculation is found in Hecker 2005, 170. Klein/Sefati 2008, 619 give even higher numbers: "The tablet originally contained incipits of ca. 410 songs, of which 275 items were preserved. Approximately 60 songs were Sum., and the rest were Akkadian". The number of preserved incipits (not including sub-summaries and summaries!) is, however, lower.

421 The rich generic terminology found in KAR 158 will not be discussed here. This terminology was treated extensively by Draffkorn Kilmer 1965, Groneberg 2003, and Shehata 2009.

422 The tablet (Fund Nr. Ass. 3915) was unearthed in the Assur-temple and is part of what is inaccurately still called "the Tiglathpileser library" (Hecker 2013, 54). Further on the finding spot of the tablet, cf. Klein/Sefati 2008, 619–620, with n. 22.

Akk. literature, exists today. Almost a century after Ebeling's *editio princeps*, an up-to-date edition of the catalogue and a comprehensive study of its contents are merited.[423]

*Collations of KAR 158*

KAR 158 was collated by the present author in December 2013. The tablet, much due to the fact that it was baked in antiquity, is presently in a good state of preservation. Ebeling's 1922 copy proves on the whole to be accurate, but few readings were corrected (all marked with °, cf. esp. ii 48').[424] What, however, was badly lacking in Ebeling's copy was a general drawing of the tablet, showing its shape and the arrangement of its different columns and sections (Figs. 25–26). Based on the detached copies of each of the columns separately, it was very difficult to assess the original size of the tablet when complete, and the number of lines that were broken away.

Judging by the thickness of VAT 10101 and its curvature (Fig. 27), it is clear that the original tablet was *larger* than previously assumed, and that the remaining fragment makes up only c. 50% of the original catalogue (Figs. 28–29). Estimating the original size of the tablet is possible if one calculates the missing lines in the two first columns of the tablet, taking into consideration the following points:

The first complete section of the catalogue (i 4'–9') lists 11 incipits. This means that c. 6 lines were broken away before the blessing to Ea (i 1'–3'). However, it is not impossible that a few more lines which served as a header (as e.g., "These are the hymns that are…" *vel sim*) preceded the first section, making the broken upper part of the tablet a little bit longer.

Line i 44' of the catalogue summarizes 31 incipits and ii 48' of the catalogue summarizes 93(!) incipits.[425] This means that each *iškaru* had 31 incipits. And therefore, from i 45' (where a new *iškaru* starts) until ii 1' (where the first 5 incipits of the third *iškaru* are already summarized) one should place 31 incipits which, together with the sub-summaries and the blessing formulae to Ea, make c. 50 lines. Hence, the length of the first column was originally c. 100 lines. (c. 6 broken lines at the upper part of col. i + c. 44 existing lines of the first *iškaru* + c. 50 broken lines of the second *iškaru*).

423 Cf. "KAR 158, that was published by Ebeling… ca. 88 years ago… is still awaiting a fully revised edition" (Klein/Sefati 2008, 619).

424 Curiously, the small holes which punctuate the surface of the tablet (the function of which is commonly assumed to prevent its cracking while being baked – though, following Joachim Marzahn in a private communication, this supposition was never proven) were not reproduced systematically by Ebeling: about half of them are missing in his copy. They are now marked in the edition as ○.

425 The scribe wrote erroneously 153, cf. commentary to ii 48'.

# KAR 158 Obv.

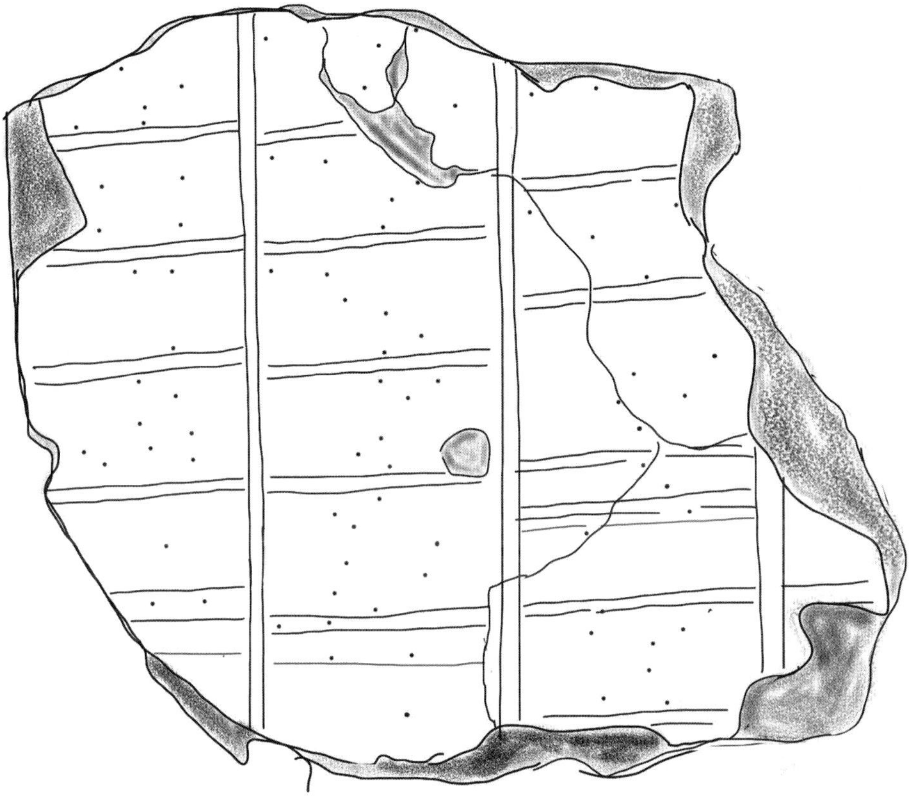

Fig. 25: KAR 158 Obv. General View

KAR 158 Rev.

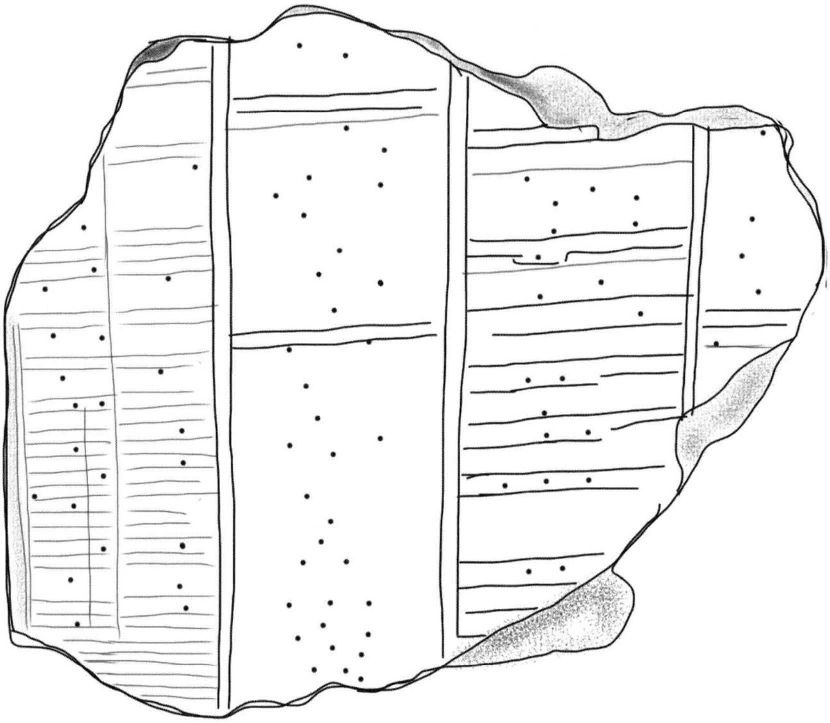

Fig. 26: KAR 158 Rev. General View

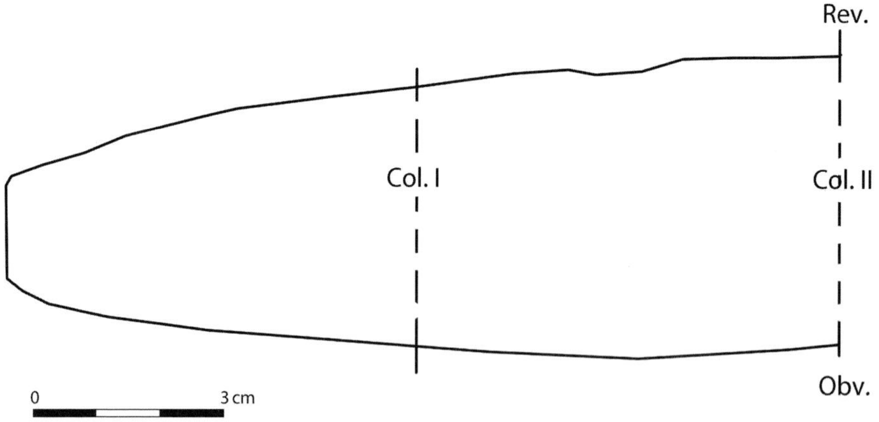


Fig. 27: KAR 158 Side View

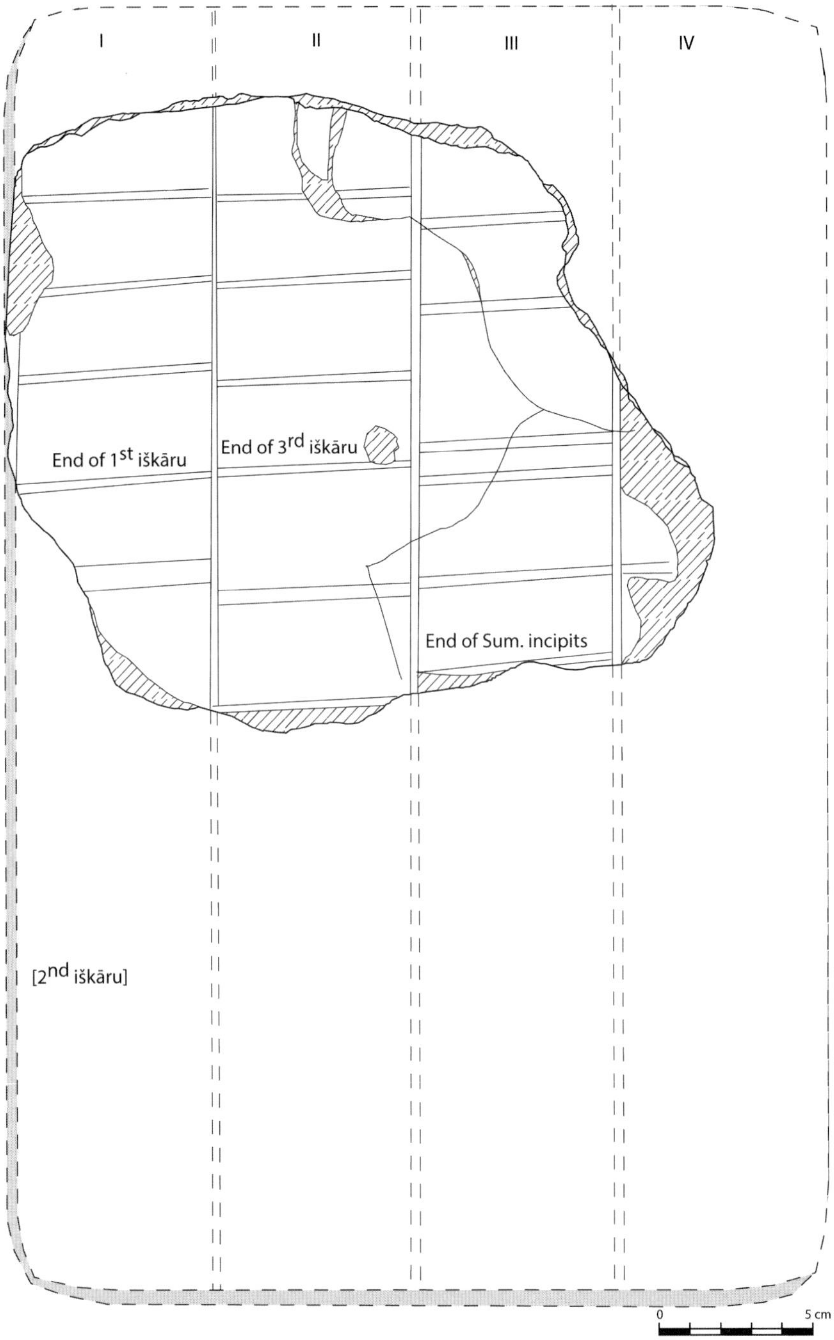


Fig. 28: KAR 158 Obv. Reconstructed

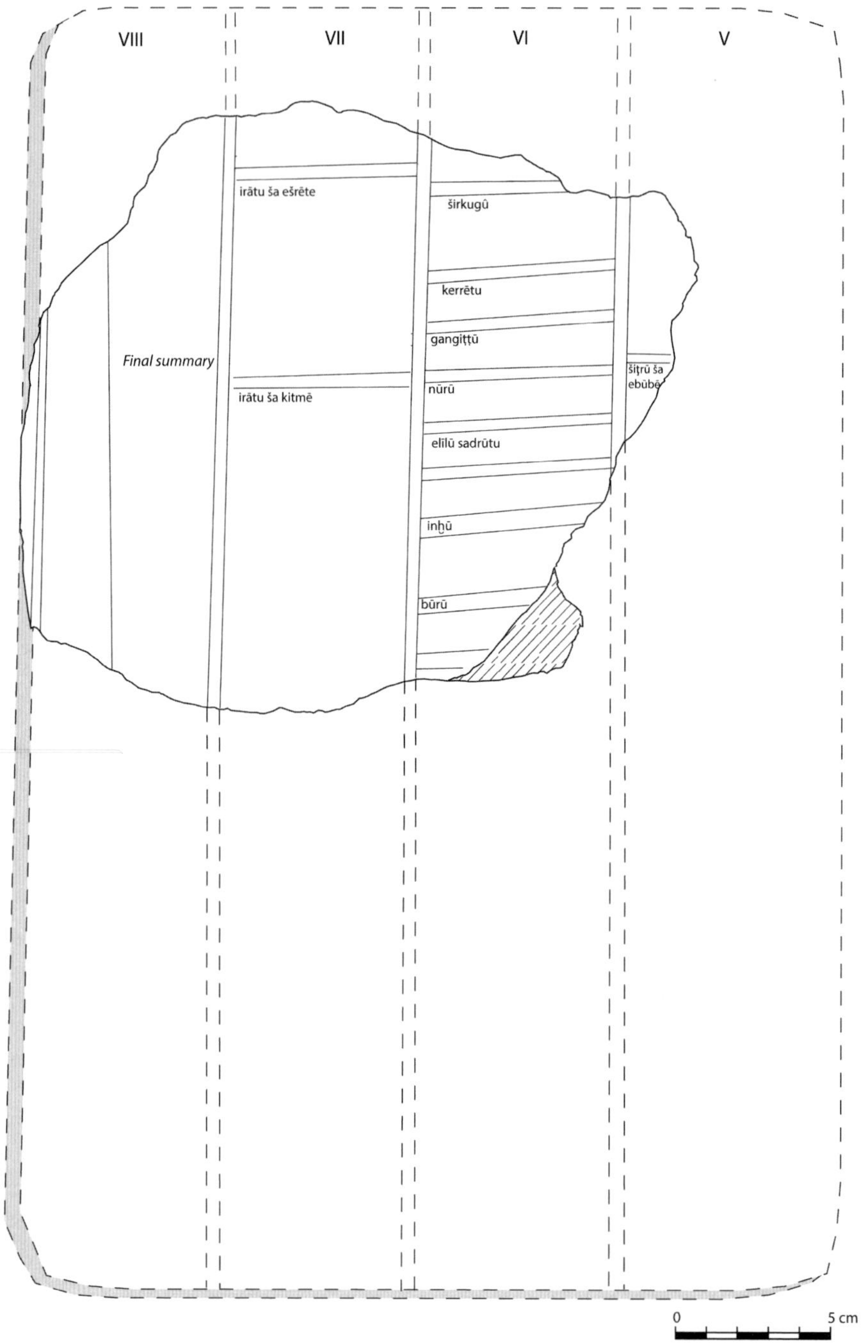


Fig. 29: KAR 158 Rev. Reconstructed

*The Generic Definition of the Catalogue*

Not all the compositions listed in KAR 158 belong to love literature.[426] The Sum. incipits certainly do not belong to it, while the last part of the catalogue (vii 1'–55') lists compositions that clearly deal with love. The thematic definition of a number of incipits in the catalogue is unclear. For instance, the five consecutive incipits that focus on the god Erra[427] cannot concern sex and love, but what about the incipit "Jubilate, land!" (ii 41'), or "Honor the god! Love the god!" (ii 42')? At first glance they seem not to be connected to love literature, but rather to be laudatory hymns. And yet, this observation may prove wrong once we note that these two incipits contain verbs that are known to be productive in love literature: *riāšum*, "to rejoice, be happy"[428] and *râmum*, "to love". And what about "The mountain(s) – it is (/they are) so high! Moreover, the summit(s) – it is (/they are) so immense!" (ii 38'–39')? Again, it seems as if there is nothing amorous in this long incipit, but if taken metaphorically it is not impossible that the "mountains" and "summits" in this incipit refer to female body parts.[429] And so, since it is risky, or even impossible in many cases, to decide whether a lost composition is part of love literature (a category not easily defined), based only on its first line, I prefer (unlike Groneberg 2003) to treat the Assur catalogue in its entirety and avoid generic and semantic dissection which cannot be anything but arbitrary.[430]

*The Literary Tradition Reflected in KAR 158 and its Origin*

So far, only one Akk. incipit from the Assur catalogue was identified as matching a known composition: BM 47507, the 'ballad' published by Black (JAOS 103, 26–27 = № 7). This text corresponds to i 6' in the catalogue. Interestingly, this MB composition – unearthed in Babylonia, not in Assur – ends with a catch line to another, still unknown, composition which corresponds to the next incipit in the Assur catalogue, in i 7'. This finding allows for the conclusion that there was a cycle, or a sequence of compositions, dealing with love which was copied, perhaps even performed, in a fixed order. What is remarkable, however, is that this cycle of love compositions from Babylonia is known and maintained by the Assur catalogue (at least as far as the beginning of the tablet goes).[431]

---

426 Cf. Hecker 2013, 55.

427 "Oh first born, the son of An, let me praise your power!", "Let me praise Erra! His power let me extol!", "Lord, let me sing the praise of your divinity!", "He went out, Šarrabu, the lord of battles", "The guard of Erra, who observes (all)" (i 20'–24').

428 Passim in Or. 60, 340 (№ 12).

429 As in PRAK 1 B 472 i 10' (№ 13). See commentary to these lines.

430 Klein/Sefati (2008, 620) conclude that "in view of the cultic-mythological character of [the] 'ballad' [JAOS 103, 26–27 =№ 7], it may be assumed that *all* [italics in origin] the love songs included in the first three series of the catalog… were cultic-mythological love songs until at least one other song is identified as popular and 'secular'". I cannot concur with this conclusion. The remaining parts of the tablet leave no doubt that KAR 158 was a heterogenous catalogue, comprising different sorts of literary composition, many of which, but not all, relate to different aspects of love – private or public. It is impossible to draw a conclusion regarding the entirety of a tablet as large as KAR 158 based only on one incipit.

431 Other types of literary compositions were also arranged in cycles, as hinted by the the fact that, e.g, a

A crucial point regarding the Assur catalogue is that the origin of the literary tradition it records is in Babylonia, namely KAR 158 mirrors non-Assyrian scribal activity. This idea is not new: Weidner (1952–53, 199–200, 207) has already raised this possibility. Here I offer arguments in support of this suggestion.

Two successive incipits offer indisputable reference to southern Mesopotamia: "On the exact day, in Larsa, impishness wafted at me" (vii 36'–37') and "Rejoice Nanāya in the orchard of Ebabbar which you love" (vii 38'). Further, the goddess Namṣat (i 16') is probably connected to *Namṣium*, an unknown location in southern Mesopotamia.[432]

None of the gods mentioned in the catalogue (Ea, Enlil, Erra, Gušaya, Ištar, Labbatu, Lamassum, Namṣat, Nanāya, Ningišzida, Sîn, Šamaš, Šarrabu,[433] and Dumuzi[434]) are specifically Assyrian, or connected directly to the city of Aššur.[435] Had the catalogue been based on Assyrian material, is it plausible that it would not include even one god which characterizes the Assyrian pantheon in particular?[436]

It is also hard to imagine that the section of Sum. incipits found in the middle of the catalogue (ii 49'–iii 43') does not draw on the southern tradition, especially as three of the incipits in this group are known OB Sum. hymns.[437] The fact that many of the Sum. incipits in the catalogue are written in syllabic orthography also points to the southern background of this section of the catalogue, since it indicates that the hymns were at some point recited orally,[438] and this is far more likely to happen in Babylonia than in Assur.

There are few undisputed Assyrian forms in KAR 158: *mērī* and *mērtum* (i 45', ii 22', vii 39') *ēnum*, not *īnum* (ii 22', vii 8'), *nīru*, instead of the all-Akk. *nūru* (ii 5', vii 45'), and *daššuptu*, not *duššuptu* (vii 18'). Their number, however, is not high. The sole verb which could be considered Assyrian (*tu-te-e*, vi 25') may just as well be taken as an archaic Babylonian form. No vowel harmony or Assyrian attached pronouns are attested.

Thus, though found in the city of Assur,[439] the Babylonian origin of KAR 158 is clear, and it is safe to say that the tablet – written by a confident Assyrian scribe with a beautiful Assyrian ductus – is an Assyrian copy of a catalogue originating in Babylon, or a catalogue compiled by an Assyrian scribe based on a collection of texts brought to Assur from Babylon.

---

catch line to the Great Šamaš hymn, *mušnammir gimir šamê*, was found at the end a Marduk prayer (see Lambert 1959–1960, 48 and 60: 208).

432 See Stol, 1998–2001, 142.

433 For this demon see Krebernik, 2009–2010, 70–71.

434 Dumuzi appears indirectly, called the "shepherd" and "Ištar's lover" (i 6').

435 Note *ḫamru* (vii 51'), "holy place", which according to AHw 318a might be connected specifically to Assur.

436 Indeed, in LKA 15 (№ 9), a love lyric text mentioning Shalmaneser, Assur is mentioned (7). Similarly in KAL 3, 75 (№ 8), also from Assur, one finds the "daughter of Assur" (iii 14').

437 ii 52' is a Balbale of Inanna, iii 11' is an Adab to An for Lipit-Ištar, iii 36' is an Adab to An for Ur-Ninurta.

438 See Civil 1967, 209.

439 KAR 158 (Ass. 3915 = VAT 10101) was found in library N1 at the Assur Temple, together with lexical and literary texts, many of them of the NA period (Pedersén 1986, 17, 21 no. 26).

*From Babylon to Assur*

The mutual suspicion between Babylon and Assur during the second half of the second mill., and the growing geo-political animosity which led to sporadic military outbursts, nonethless did not bring cultural contact between the two Akkadian-speaking kingdoms to a complete halt. Throughout the Middle Assyrian period Babylon remained the cultural center of Mesopotamia, and Babylonian scribes reached Assur (as well as other polities) already in the 14th cent., from the time of Aššur-uballiṭ I. These scribes served as cultural agents who planted and cultivated in Assur the rich and complex Babylonian knowledge accumulated for centuries in the urban centers of southern Mesopotamia.[440]

A particular historical event can be singled out as a turning point in this complex (and mostly hidden) transfer of knowledge: the invasion of Babylonia by Tukultī-Ninurta I who led a successful military campaign against the Kassite king Kaštiliaš IV at the end of the 13th cent. The highpoint of this campaign was the takeover of the capital, Babylon, itself. As a result of this war, chronicled in the historiographical-literary source commonly known as the Epic of Tukultī-Ninurta, a critical mass of Babylonian texts reached Assur as booty.[441] In a regrettably broken passage which enumerates the plunder from the conquered city, the Epic tells of texts belonging to different branches of Mesopotamian wisdom which were carried off to Assur: "secret knowledge" (*niṣirtu*), "tablets of..." (*tuppāt* [...]), "astronomical series" (*tupšarūtu*), "medico-magical manuals" (*āšipūtu*), "penitential prayers" (*eršaḫunga*), "series of divination by extispicy (which reveal) the plans of heaven (and) earth" (*bārûtu ... uṣurāt šamê erṣeti*), "medical manuals (accompanied with) their procedures of bandages" (*malṭarāt asûti, nēpeš naṣmadāti*).[442] The last term in the list of looted texts is the least clear: *maḫrâti māšarāt abbēšu ša* ... Machinist (1978, 129) translated: "the earlier inventories of his fathers which...", similarly Foster (2005, 315): "the muster lists of his ancestors...".[443] What these old inventories, or lists, enumerated (possibly administrative items?) remains unknown. It is, however, not impossible that they included lists of literary oeuvres, namely catalogues. There is no indication, certainly no proof, that one of the *māšarātu* was our KAR 158, but the fact that some kinds of list were mentioned in connection to different kinds of literary text allows us to assume that catalogues were part of the massive influx of literary and scientific texts brought from Kassite Babylon to Assur.

*KAR 158 and the Lost Tradition of Love Literature*

As mentioned already, of the 152 incipits presently existing in the catalogue – which represent roughly half the original number of incipits listed when the tablet was complete –

440 See Wiggermann 2008, Heeßel 2009.

441 Weidner 1952–1953, 199–200, 207. A number of the Babylonian texts reaching Assur after this event were medical, see *inter alia* BAM 2, 159 iv 22', SpTU 2, 50: 12, BAM 4, 382: rev. 3, BAM 4, 322:1–28 // BAM 4, 321, and BAM 4, 322: 29 ("copy of of Hammurāpi's palace"). See in general Farber 2014, 16.

442 Machinist 1978, 128: 2'–9' and 367–373.

443 CAD M/1, 358: "the former [...], the musters of his father".

only one Akk. composition has been identified as corresponding to a line in the Assur catalogue:[444] JAOS 103, 26–27 (№ 7). How to interpret this fact? The easy way is to see here yet another case of bad luck which caused the virtual disappearance of the literary tradition mirrored by KAR 158. Indeed, the chance of discovery is a crucial factor in Assyriology, as in other fields based on the study of ancient written sources, and one must never forget the arbitrariness of the material available. What we have in our hands is often so incomplete that any general conclusion needs to be formulated with extreme caution. But to remain on the safe bank of the river of existing knowledge, never daring to cross the stormy water of hypothesis, inhibits scholarship. Caution and risk must be weighed against each other.

With these methodological reflections in mind I present my thoughts about the literary tradition of KAR 158 and its unlucky fate.

A good starting point is to compare KAR 158 to another Akk. catalogue of literary texts, the first mill. Nineveh Catalogue of Texts and Authors published by Lambert (1962). Unlike KAR 158 the Nineveh catalogue contains quite a number of compositions that can be identified by their first lines, or titles. Along with divination and ritual texts, medical lists as Sag-gig-ga and astronomical series as Enūma Anu Enlil, a number of key literary compositions – the myths of Erra, Etana and Lugal-e, the epic of Gilgameš, and the wisdom hymn Theodicy – are listed in this catalogue as well. Not all the incipits in the Nineveh catalogue can be identified, but it is clear that the Catalogue of Texts and Authors mirrors substantial parts of the Ninevite literary tradition as we know it from other sources. In this respect KAR 158 is different. To date – so long as new findings from museums in Berlin or Istanbul do not alter the picture – there seems to be no connection between the bulk of Akk. compositions that are recorded in KAR 158 and the actual literary tradition in Assur at the time of the redaction of the catalogue. Interestingly, this statement concerns the Akk. incipits, much less the Sum. incipits in KAR 158, since as mentioned already, 3 of the 32 Sum. incipits outlined in the catalogue were identified successfully, whereas only 1 of the 152 Akk. incipits matches a known Akk. composition. All this leads to the conclusion that the Assur catalogue reflects a literary tradition – a significant part of which could be labeled love literature – that was discontinued, perhaps even deliberately aborted. This break in the tradition took place in Assur, either after the compilation of KAR 158 or before it (in which case the catalogue was copied from an earlier copy when the texts listed in it were already out of circulation).

If this suggestion holds true, the next question is what caused the discontinuation of the literary tradition emulated by KAR 158? A wealth of theoretical answers present themselves. One may postulate an intentional decision to discontinue this tradition because of its sexual audacity,[445] similar to the debates concerning the inclusion of Songs in the Masoretic Canon, reflected in the Rabbinic tradition.[446] And yet, a simpler, and thus preferable, scenario can be offered. Unlike other texts that were brought to Assur from

---

444 Frahm (2009, 144) raises the possibility that KAL 3, 75 (№ 8) could have been found in KAR 158 had its first line been preserved.

445 See especially the texts listed in CUSAS 10, 12 (№ 18).

446 See, however, Barton 2005 where doubt regarding the existence of this presumed debate is presented (with previous literature).

Babylon – series of omens, medical manuals, prayers, hymns and rituals – the texts recorded by KAR 158 did not find their way into the local curriculum and were not considered integral to the Assyrian scribal school. The reason for this is simple: love literature was not considered as important as scientific texts, and thus not essential in the eyes of the Assyrian scribes. These texts subsequently stopped being copied and eventually fell into oblivion. Their quasi-total disappearance – again, as far as our present data goes – not only from Assur but also from Babylonia, proves that even in their original Babylonian setting, love-related compositions were probably preserved in single manuscripts, and when no longer copied, doomed to extinction.

But it would be wrong to say that Assyrian scribes found no interest in love literature: a local tradition of amorous poetry was developed in Assur, modeled perhaps after some of the texts brought from Babylon. Two such texts exist in the corpus: KAL 3, 75 (№ 8) and LKA 15 (№ 9). The latter text shows thematic resemblance to the Babylonian text JAOS 103, 26–27 (№ 7).

Finally, there is yet another angle to the lost tradition of love-related texts reflected by KAR 158. Not only does the Assur catalogue list compositions that are mostly unknown to us, but there is also a split between the love-related compositions that *are* known and those mentioned as incipits in KAR 158 and in the Babylonian catalogues (ASJ 10, 18 = № 17 and CUSAS 10, 12 = № 18). In other words, two separate channels of Akk. love literature have reached us: a catalogued tradition and a non-catalogued tradition. The catalogued tradition can be described as hymnal in character, while the non-catalogued tradition which we have in our hands consists of monologues and dialogues. The former is more official, with ties to the cultic sphere; the latter more colloquial and conversational, perhaps performative in nature. Interestingly, it is the official tradition, the one which was kept and copied by scribes, which eventually was lost, while the other, more fluid tradition, reached us in part.

### *Possible Dating of KAR 158*

A number of grammatical features indicate that the Assur catalogue is dependent on early layers of OB literary Akk. Forms with loc. adv. abound,[447] as well as forms with the archaic construct forms in *-u*.[448] One case of a prep. attached to the following noun is found.[449]

Other features, however, point towards an MB dating. Mimation is not used in the catalogue. The consonant change *št* > *lt* or *ld* appears twice,[450] and the consonantal change *mt* > *md* also occurs.[451] The dropping of the initial *w* is also attested.[452] The change of intervocalic *w* > *m* can perhaps also be found.[453]

---

447 *ta-ni-tu-uk-ka* (ii 43'), *ma-an-nu ba-lu-uk-ki* (vi 23'), *ep-šu pi-i-ka* (vii 5' and vii 47' – But cf. von Soden 1931, 212 for a different view), *e-bir-tu nāri* (vii 30'), *áš-ru-un-ni ta-gu-ša* (vii 31').

448 *be-lu a-nu-na-ti* (i 23'), *bu-kur-tu* ᵈ*A-nim* (ii 32'), *ḫa-ṣi-bu e-re-ni* (vii 28'), *ma-an-su kibrāti* (v 9'), *a-šu-ú ka-lu ālāni* (vi 12'), *ḫu-du ka-bat-ti* (vii 4'), *ra-i-mu da-di-ni* (vii 29'), *a-lu me-li-li* (vii 30'), *muš-na-me-ru atallî* (vii 45'), and perhaps also *bēl*/*bēlum*(EN) *a-ši-bu…* (v 5'). See von Soden 1931, 212–213.

449 *an-ni-ri* (iiv 5'). See von Soden 1933, 135 n. 2.

450 *ma-al-da-ḫi* (ii 14'), *il-ta-a-at* (iii 37').

451 *im-da-la* (< *imtalâ* vii 42'), see GAG § 31f.

Based on the above, I suggest that the early layer of at least some of the incipits in KAR 158 can be dated to the OB or late OB period. Later, in the MB period, a secondary redactory phase occurred – probably as a result of copying which modernized some of the older forms. The Assyrian scribe who produced the tablet in our hands did not significantly alter the Babylonian text that he received.

Obv.
col. i

| | |
|---|---|
| | (c. 5–7 lines missing) |
| i 0' | [1 *iš-ka-ra-a-tu*] |
| i 1' | [6 *za-ma-ru*$^{\text{meš}}$ *il-ta-a*]-*a*[*t*] *iškari*(ÉŠ.GÀR) |
| i 2' | [...*ak-ka-di-ta*] *am-nu* |
| i 3' | [$^{\text{d}}$*É-a ba*]-*la-aṭ-ka li-iq-bi* |
| i 4' | [...] ⸢*šu*°⸣ ○ *tu-li-da-an-ni-ma* |
| i 5' | [x] ⸢x⸣-*ku-ú ra-a ki-la-ma lu-ur-ta-ma-nu* |
| i 6' | [*er-ba-a*]*m-ma rēʾû*($^{\text{lú}}$SIPA) *ḫar-mi* ○ $^{\text{d}}$*Iš*$_{8}$-*tár-ma* |
| i 7' | [*ur?-ša?-a*]*n*°-*na rēʾâ*($^{\text{lú}}$SIPA) ○ *az-za-am-mu-ur-ma* |
| i 8' | [(x?)] ○ *rēʾâ*($^{\text{lú}}$SIPA) ○ *šú-a-ti* |
| i 9' | [2(?) *iš*]-*ka-ra-a-tu* 11 *za-ma-ru*$^{\text{meš}}$ |
| i 10' | [*ak-k*]*a-di-ta* *am-nu* |
| i 11' | [$^{\text{d}}$*É*]-*a ba-la-aṭ-ka li-iq-bi* |
| i 12' | [*be-le-*]*et* ○ *ka-lu* ○ *parakkī*(BARAG$^{\text{meš}}$) |
| i 13' | [$^{\text{d}}$*Iš*$_{8}$-*tár*] *du-un-na-at ilta*(DINGIR) *la-ab-ba-ta* |
| i 14' | [x x x x x] $^{\text{d}}$*I-gi-gi ma-al-ka-ta* |
| i 15' | [$^{\text{d}}$*Iš*$_{8}$-*tár?*] ○ *le-a-at* ○ *a-bi-ša* |
| i 16' | [...]-*tu* $^{\text{d}}$*Nam-ṣa-at na-di-na-at lamassāti*($^{\text{d}}$LAMMA$^{\text{meš}}$) |
| i 17' | [3]*iš-ka-ra-a-tu* 16 *za-ma-ru*$^{\text{meš}}$ |
| i 18' | *ak-ka-di-ta* ○ ○ *am-nu* |
| i 19' | $^{\text{d}}$*É-a* ○ *ba-la-aṭ-ka li-iq-bi* |
| i 20' | *bu-kur bi-in* $^{\text{d}}$*A-nim lu-uz-mur du-un-na-ka* |
| i 21' | *lu-uz-mur* $^{\text{d}}$*Èr-ra du-un-na-šu lu-ul-li* |
| i 22' | *be-e-lu lu-uz-mu-ur za-mar i-lu-ti-ka* |
| i 23' | *it-ta-ṣi* $^{\text{d}}$*Šar-ra-bu be-lu a-nu-na-ti* |
| i 24' | *ma-ṣa-ra-at* ○ $^{\text{d}}$*Èr-ra* ○ *ḫa-i-ṭù* |
| i 25' | 4 *iš-ka-ra-a-tu* ○ 21 *za-ma-ru*$^{\text{meš}}$ |
| i 26' | *ak-ka-di-ta am-nu* |
| i 27' | ○ $^{\text{d}}$*É-a* ○ *ba-la-aṭ-ka* ○ *li-iq-bi* |
| i 28' | *ta-ni-it qu-ra-di Adad*($^{\text{d}}$IM) *lu-sa-qar* |
| i 29' | *i-la* ○ ○ *mu-ur-ta-aṣ-na* |
| i 30' | [*lu*]-*uz-za-mur at-ḫe-e bi-nu-ut* ○ $^{\text{d}}$*A-nim* |
| i 31' | [*ga-áš*]-*ra* ○ *a-li-la* ○ *bu-kur* $^{\text{d}}$*A-nim* |
| i 32' | [x-x]-*ra-ka* ○ *šar*(XX) *ilāni*(DINGIR$^{\text{meš}}$) ○ *Adad*($^{\text{d}}$IM) |

452 *as-ma* (< *wasma* vii 26').
453 *namārītu* < *nawārītu* (ii 21') and *ḫamru* < *ḫawru* (vii 51' – but see commentary to this line).

| | |
|---|---|
| i 33' | [*Adad*($^{d}$IM)?] *bu-kur* $^{d}$*A-nim ša e-zi-za ila*(DINGIR) *ga-áš-ra* |
| i 34' | [5] *iš-ka-ra-a-tu* 26 *za-ma-ru*$^{meš}$ |
| i 35' | [*ak*]-*ka-di-ta am-nu* |
| i 36' | [$^{d}$]*É-a* ○ *ba-al-aṭ-ka li-iq-bi* |
| i 37' | [$^{d}$(?)x-x-(x) *t*]*i*°? *e-ri-ši im-nu-ši* $^{d}$*En-líl* |
| i 38' | [...] ○ $^{d}$*Šá-maš* ○ *ki-it-tu* |
| i 39' | [...] *gi-it-ma-lu na-ra-am* $^{d}$*En-líl* |
| i 40' | [...][$^{d}$]*I-gi-gi man-sa-a ila*(DINGIR) *qar-da* |
| i 41' | [*m*]*aturra*($^{gi}$]$^{š}$MÁ.TUR) *lu-uz-mur a-na Sîn*($^{d}$XXX) |
| | [○ ] ○ ○ |
| i 42' | [6 *iš-ka-ra*]-[*a*]-*tu* 31 *za-ma-ru*$^{meš}$ |
| i 43' | [*iškar*(ÉŠ.GÀR) *ma-ru-ma*] [*ra*]-*im-ni ak-ka-di-ta* |
| i 44' | [$^{d}$*É-a ba-la-a*]*ṭ-ka li-iq-bi* |
| ==== | |
| i 45' | [… *me*]-*ri ù me-er-te* |
| i 46' | […] *em-qu mer'ukunu*(DUMU-*ku-nu*) |
| i 47' | [...*du*(?)]-*un-na-a-at* |
| i 48' | [...] *aqru*(KAL°-*ru*) |
| i 49' | […] [x] x |

col. ii

| | |
|---|---|
| ii 0' | [1 *iš-ka-ra-tu]* |
| ii 1' | 5 *za-ma-r*[*u*$^{meš}$ *il-ta-a-at iškari*(ÉŠ.GÀR)] |
| ii 2' | $^{d}$*Iš*$_{8}$*-tár-ú-ta* [*am-nu*] |
| ii 3' | ○ $^{d}$*É-a ba-la-aṭ-ka* [*li-iq-bi*] |
| ii 4' | *ḫar-mi it-ta-ka* ○ *ur-gu-la* |
| ii 5' | *an-ni-ri a*[*l*]-*ta-mi r*[*ē*]*'u*($^{lú}$[SI]PA) *e-mu-ú*-[…] |
| ii 6' | *za-mar* $^{d}$*Iš*$_{8}$*-tár šar-ra-*[*ti*] *a-za-am-mu-ur* |
| ii 7' | *a-na na-aḫ-ši* ○ *rē'i*($^{lú}$SIPA) *a-ṣa-ia-aḫ* |
| ii 8' | *ù re-'-i* [*a*?-*n*]*a*? *bīti*(É) *ru-'-a-am* |
| ii 9' | *a-ra-am*-[…]-x-*ia* ○ - *ma* |
| ii 10' | 2 *iš-ka-ra-a-tu*[10 *za-*]*ma-ru*$^{meš}$ |
| ii 11' | ○ $^{d}$*Iš*$_{8}$*-tár-ú-ta* [(vac.)] *am-nu* |
| ii 12' | $^{d}$*É-a* ○ *ba-la-aṭ-k*[*al*]*i-iq-bi* |
| ii 13' | *ši-it-mar-tu na-ba-a-a*[*ṭ* *nu-u*]*r*? -*ša* |
| ii 14' | *ba-'-i* *ma-al-da-ḫi* [...] [*lu-ṣi*?!(Text: I°)] |
| ii 15' | *šar-rat me-le-ṣi* ○ *ra-ṣu-um-ta* |
| ii 16' | *qa-ri-it-ta mērat*(DUMU.MUNUS) *Sîn*($^{d}$XXX) *ilta*(DINGIR) *te-le-ta* |
| ii 17' | *ḫa-an-na-ma-tu-um-ma* ○ MIN (*ḫannamātumma*) *dam-qa-a-tu* |
| ii 18' | 3 *iš-ka-ra-a-tu* 15 *za-ma-ru*$^{meš}$ |
| ii 19' | $^{d}$*Iš*$_{8}$*-tár-ú-ta* ○ *am-nu* |
| ii 20' | ○ $^{d}$*É-a* ○ *ba-la-aṭ-k li-iq-bi* |
| ii 21' | *ti-iš-ma-ri ila*(DINGIR)-*at-ni na-ma-ri-tu* |

| | |
|---|---|
| ii 22' | *me-er-tu* ○ *lìb-ba-ša ni-gu-ta* |
| ii 23' | $^{d}$*Na-na-a* ○ [*a*]*t*!-*ti-ma* |
| ii 24' | *šul-ma a-na šarri*(LUGAL) *ki-i ta-ši-mi* |
| ii 25' | *tuk-te-en-ni šar-ra-tu* ○ $^{d}$*Na-na-a* |
| ii 26' | *am-ma-rat kal nišī*(UN$^{meš}$) ○ *ra-*ʾ*-um-ta* |
| ii 27' | 4 *iš-ka-ra-a-tu* 20 *za-ma-ru*$^{meš}$ |
| ii 28' | $^{d}$*Iš*$_8$*-tár-ú-ta* ○ *am-nu* |
| ii 29' | ○ $^{d}$*É-a* ○ *ba-la-aṭ-ka* ○ *li-iq-bi* |
| ii 30' | $^{d}$*Iš*$_8$*-tár am-ma-ra-ta lu-ú-še lu-ú*[*s*]*-qur-ma* |
| ii 31' | *at-mar-ti* $^{d}$*I-gi-gi ša-nu-da-a-*[*at i*]*-la-ti* |
| ii 32' | *bu-kur-tu* $^{d}$*A-nim* ○ *rabītu*(GAL-*t*[*u*) x x] |
| ii 33' | *lu-uz-mu-ur* ○ *ta*$_8$(ḪI)*-šim-*[*ti* DN (3 signs missing)] |
| ii 34' | *ú-ta-al-li-i*○ *ra-*[*šu*]-[*ub-tu/ti* …] |
| ii 35' | 5 *iš-ka-ra-a-tu* 25 *za-ma-ru*$^{meš}$ |
| ii 36' | $^{d}$*Iš*$_8$*-tár-ú-ta* ○ *am-nu* |
| ii 37' | ○ $^{d}$*É-a* ○ *ba-la-aṭ-ka li-iq-bi* |
| ii 38' | *ša-du-ú lu-ú e-lu-ú-ma* |
| ii 39' | *ḫur-ša-an-nu ap-pu-na-ma lu-ú še-e-ḫu* |
| ii 40' | *e-nu-ma tu-ra-aq-qi-du* ○ *an-ta* |
| ii 41' | *ri-i-iš*°(sic) ○ *ma-a-tu* |
| ii 42' | *i-la ku-un-na-a i-la* ○ *ra-a-ma* |
| ii 43' | *šar-ri* ○ *ta-ni-tu-uk-ka* |
| ii 44' | $^{d}$*Na-na-a lìb-ba-ša* ○ *ḫa-da-a ub-lam-ma* |
| | ○ ○ ○ ○ |
| ii 45' | ŠU.NÍGIN 6 *iš-ka-ra-a-tu* 31 *za-ma-ru*$^{meš}$ |
| ii 46' | *iškar*(ÉŠ.GÀR) *re-*ʾ*-i re-*ʾ*-i* $^{d}$*Iš*$_8$*-tár-ú-ta am-nu* |
| ii 47' | $^{d}$*É-a* ○ *ba-la-aṭ-ka* ○ *li-iq-bi* |
| ii 48' | ŠU.NIGIN 60!+30+3(Text: 2x60° + 3x10 + 3) *za-ma-ru ak-ka-du-ú* |
| ==== | |
| ii 49' | ni-gál-le dingir al-la-am-ma a-ma gu-un-na-ki |
| ii 50' | lá-le lá-le lá-le im-du-ud |
| ii 51' | ma-a-al-lu ki nam-al-la ma-a-an-gu |
| ii 52' | ba-lam ba-lá-li ḫi-iz-za-me-e pa-x (x)] |
| ii 53' | [*i*]*n-du-ra ku*$_8$*-ru-um-ma-ta*$_8$ *id-n*[*a*… ] |

col. iii

| | |
|---|---|
| iii 0' | [*za-ma-ru il-ta-a-at iškari*(ÉŠ.GÀR)] |
| iii 1' | [... *te-g*]*i-e š*[*u-me-ra am-nu*] |
| iii 2' | ○ $^{d}$*É-a ba-l*[*a-a*]*ṭ-k*[*ali-iq-bi*] |
| iii 3' | im-me lil-ma du-ur-[r]a!?-š[e?/l[i?...] |
| iii 4' | im-me e-si-ge nu-du e-tu-[...] |
| iii 5' | lu-gal me-le-em-zu ni-x [...] |
| iii 6' | en ni-im-gu-ru an-ki me-g[al?...] |
| iii 7' | ur-sag me-ni me-en-ni(-) [...] |

| | |
|---|---|
| iii 8' | 2 *iš-ka-ra-a-tu* 10 [*za-ma-ru*$^{meš}$] |
| iii 9' | *te-gi-e šu-me-ra*[*am-nu*] |
| iii 10' | ○$^{d}$*É-a ba-la-aṭ-ka* ○ [*li-iq-bi*] |
| iii 11' | e-ia lu-gal-gu kìri-za-al [...] |
| iii 12' | i[b]-⌈gìr za ḫi?⌉ ○ ku-ub-ba a-ab-[...] |
| iii 13' | en-na ⌈$^{d}$En⌉-líl pa-è nir-gá[l...] |
| iii 14' | en pìrig?-gal ZU.AB E-ri-du-g[a...] |
| iii 15' | ur-sag-gu-zal-ma ○ e-a-x [...] |
| iii 16' | 3 *iš-ka-ra-a-tu* 15 *za-ma*-r[*u*$^{meš}$] |
| iii 17' | *te-gi-e šu-me-ra*[*am-nu*] |
| iii 18' | $^{d}$*É-a ba-la-aṭ-ka li-i*[*q-bi*] |
| iii 19' | en-gal ○ an-ki-a sag-íl-[la] |
| iii 20' | me a-ia di-im-gi-ir-e-n[e] |
| iii 21' | en sag-íl maḫ-e lu-nun-gal ○ -e-n[e] |
| iii 22' | ur-sag ga-ar-ga ○ mud-gal-dinger-e-n[e] |
| iii 23' | $^{d}$En-líl a-lim pirig gi-iš-tug ir-me-[...] |
| iii 24' | en sa lil-ma-○ su ga- ○ le-eš d[u-ga?...] |
| iii 25' | ur-sag a-lim pirig zag-dib kin-gál $^{d}$En-líl-l[e] |
| iii 26' | lu-gal nir-gál maḫ-e ○ en an-ki-bi-[da-ke$_{4}$] |
| iii 27' | nir-gál du-kù-ga giš-lá-bi ur$_{4}$-ur$_{4}$-[ra? ...] |
| iii 28' | 4 *iš-ka-ra-a-tu* ○ 23 *za-ma-ru*$^{meš}$ |
| iii 29' | *te-gi-e* ○ *šu-me-ra am-nu* |
| iii 30' | $^{d}$*É-a ba-la-aṭ-ka* ○ *li-iq-bi* |
| iii 31' | ŠU.NÍGIN 23 *te-gu-ú* ○ *šu-me-ru* |
| ==== | |
| iii 32' | a-an-še ○ me-zi-da(-)gu(-)nam-a-ni |
| iii 33' | en-gal an-ki eš-maḫ sag-ge in-di-ib |
| iii 34' | en-gal maḫ-dí-ib di-im-gi-ir-e-ne |
| iii 35' | en-na an su-ul-la ga-li-im si-ga |
| iii 36' | an-nu ú-ru un-gal di-im-gi-ir-e-ne |
| iii 37' | 5 *za-ma-ru* ○ *il-ta-a-at* ○ *iškāri*(ÉŠ.GÀR) |
| iii 38' | *a-da-pa šu-me-ra am-nu* |
| iii 39' | ○ $^{d}$*É-a* ○ *ba-la-aṭ-ka li-iq-bi* |
| iii 40' | lu-gal an-za-gi-na ○ ta-al-lu-ra-áš-še |
| iii 41' | en-né ú-šúm-gal di-im-gi-ir-e-ne |
| iii 42' | nu-un gal-di sag-še ○ lu-ga-la-ak-ki |
| iii 43' | nin sukkal gal-an-zu an-na me-e-eš-še |
| iii 44' | *pa-qi-id* ○ *ma-ḫar* $^{d}$*A-ni*[*m*] |
| iii 45' | *ilū*(DINGIR) $^{d}$*A-nun-na-ki* ○ *ra-bu-ú*-[*ti*] |
| iii 46' | [2 *iš-ka-ra-a-tu*] 10 *za-ma-ru*[$^{meš}$] |

col. iv

| | |
|---|---|
| iv 1' | *e*?-[... ...] |
| iv 2' | *ma-an*-s[*u*?-... ...] |

iv 3' *ḫi-ri-it* [... ...]
iv 4' *muš-na-me-er* [... ...]
iv 5' *gi-šar* [… …]
iv 6' *mu-ma-ʾ-*⌈*e*⌉-⌈*ru*?... …]
iv 7' […] (UN°) ○ [… …]
iv 8' [… …]
iv 9' [… …]
iv 10' x [… …]
iv 11' *še*? [… …]
iv 12' x [… …]

Rev.
col. v
v 1' *ilāni*(DINGIR$^{\text{meš}}$) ○ […]
v 2' *zu-ʾ-ú-*[*na-at* … …]
v 3' *ku-un-na-*[*at* …]
v 4' *bīt*/*bītum*(É) *e-ri-mi*(-) […]
v 5' *bēl*/*bēlum*(EN) *a-ši-bu* […]
v 6' *bēl*(EN) *ḫa-si-si* ME […]
v 7' *i-la el-la* [……]
v 8' *i-la* ○ *an-za-a*[ ]
v 9' *ma-an-su kibrāti*(UB$^{\text{meš}}$) *š*[*u-*…]
v 10' *ma-an-su šu-a-ti ta*?-[… …]
v 11' *a-pal* ○ *bi-in* […]
v 12' *ma-li-ka* ○ [……]
v 13' *i-la-at ta-áš-me-e* [……]
v 14' *be-e-la* ○ ○ […]
v 15' *ma-a-ar* [……]
v 16' ŠU.NÍGIN 13 *ši-iṭ-*[*ru ša eb-bu-be* …]
v 17' ○ *ak-ka-*[*di-i*]
====
v 18' *bi-in* [……]
v 19' TA [……]
v 20' *i-*Š[I……]
v 21' ⌈x⌉ [……]
(rest broken)

col. vi
vi 1' EN ZI K[U? ……]
vi 2' *le-i-tu* [……]
vi 3' *be-le-t*[*u*……]
vi 4' ŠU.NÍGIN 8 *šu-me-ru* 3 *ak-ka-du-ú*
vi 5' ŠU.NÍGIN–*ma* 11 *šìr-ku-gu-ú*
====
vi 6' *ḫu-di-i* ○ *be-le-et-ni* ○ *šu-li-li*

| | |
|---|---|
| vi 7' | *e-muq-ti em-qe*!(Text: IQ)-*ti* ○ *am-ma-rat nišī*(UN$^{\text{meš}}$) |
| vi 8' | *ra-šu-ub-tu* ○ *i-na ilāni*(DINGIR$^{\text{meš}}$) ○ *a-na-ku* |
| vi 9' | *su-ú-qa a-ba-ʾ-ma* 2 *sekrēti*(SAL.UŠ$^{\text{meš}}$) *ú-ta* |
| vi 10' | *ra-šu-ub-tu* ○ *i-na ilāni*(DINGIR$^{\text{meš}}$) ○ *a-na-ku* |
| vi 11' | ŠU.NÍGIN 5 ○ *ke-er- re-e-tu* |
| ==== | |
| vi 12' | *da-i-iš kibrāti*(UB$^{\text{meš}}$) *a-šu-ú ka-lu ālāni*(URU.URU) |
| vi 13' | *ga-áš-ra ila*(DINGIR) *šar-ra* ○ *lu-uz-za-mu-ur* |
| vi 14' | *i-la* ○ *da-ap-na* |
| vi 15' | ŠU.NÍGIN 2 *ga-an-gi-iṭ-* ○ *ṭu* |
| ==== | |
| vi 16' | *ša-a-ar* ○*ṣi-il-li la-a te-zi-ni* |
| vi 17' | *ma-an-nu bēl*(EN) *eleppi*($^{\text{giš}}$MÁ) *ma-an-nu bēl*(EN) *makurri*($^{\text{giš}}$MÁ.GUR) |
| vi 18' | ŠU.NÍGIN 2 ○ ○ *nu-ú-ru*$^{\text{meš}}$ |
| ==== | |
| vi 19' | *ši-it-tu at-la-ki ma-a-ra lu-di-ir* |
| vi 20' | *a-šap-pa-ar* ○ *a-na mērʾati*(DUMU.SAL-*ti*) *e-me-ia* |
| vi 21' | 2 *el-le-lu* ○ ○ *sad-ru-ú-tu* |
| ==== | |
| vi 22' | $^{\text{d}}$*Iš*$_8$-*tár šar-rat nišī*(UN$^{\text{meš}}$) *ra-ʾ-um-tu* |
| vi 23' | $^{\text{d}}$*Iš*$_8$-*tár ma-an-nu ba-lu-uk-ki be-le-ti* |
| vi 24' | 2 ○ ○ ○ *in-ḫu*$^{\text{meš}}$ |
| ==== | |
| vi 25' | *ša-a-ma-ri-tu tu-te-e* ○ *tu-te-e-ma* |
| vi 26' | *eṭ-lu* ○ *iš-tu a-mu-ru-*[*ka*] |
| vi 27' | *šur-bu-ta a-na nišī*(UN$^{\text{meš}}$) ○ *a-za-am-m*[*u-ur*] |
| vi 28' | *ṣi-il-lu-lu* ○ *ša nišī*(UN$^{\text{meš}}$) ○ *a-*[*za-am-mu-ur*] |
| vi 29' | *i-na šu-bat bēl*(EN) *ilāni*(DINGIR$^{\text{meš}}$) *i-za-mu-ra* x x (x)] |
| vi 30' | ŠU.NÍGIN 5 ○ ○ *b*[*u-ru-ú*] |
| ==== | |
| vi 31' | $^{\text{d}}$*Gu-ša-ia* [… …] |
| vi 32' | $^{\text{d}}$*Gu-ša-ia* [… …] |
| vi 33' | 2 [$^{\text{d}}$*Gu-ša-a-tu* … …] |
| ==== | |
| | (rest broken) |
| col. vii | |
| vii 1' | [*na*?-*ap*?]-*lu-us-ka-ma* [...] |
| vii 2' | *up-ḫa ki-i kakkab*(MUL) *še-*[*e-ri*] |
| vii 3' | *i-na ṣi-iḫ-ti* ○ *ša ṣe-e-*[*ri*] |
| vii 4' | *an-nu-u ṣi-bu-tu ša ḫu-du ka-bat-ti* |
| vii 5' | *ep-šu pi-i-ka ad mu-ti-ia šúm-me-ḫa-ni-ma* |
| vii 6' | ŠU.NÍGIN 23 *i-ra-a-tu ša e-šèr-te* |
| ==== | |

| | |
|---|---|
| vii 7' | *ke-e ṣi-ḫa-a-ku* ○ *a-na na-aḫ-ši* |
| vii 8' | $u_4$*-um e-en im-ni-ia iš-ḫi-ṭa-an-ni* |
| vii 9' | *i-le-qe a-ma-aṣ-ṣi* ○ *a-na ma-a-ri* |
| vii 10' | *ma-te-ma be-lu te-ru-ba i-na-an-na* |
| vii 11' | *ḫi°-i°-pa-a-ku* ○ *a-na da-di-ka* |
| vii 12' | *it-ti* ○ *il-ta-a-at* ○ *mu-ši-ti* |
| vii 13' | *mu-ú-ša ma-a-ru ú-šàm-ša-a-ku* |
| vii 14' | *a-am-mar* ○ *ša-ma-an erṣeti*(KI-*ti*) |
| vii 15' | $u_4$*-mu ub-la bu-su-ra-tu-ma ḫu-ud lìb-bi* |
| vii 16' | *e-la-ia ma-a-ru lu na-me-er er-ba* |
| vii 17' | *la-a me-ḫe-er-ti* ○ *iš-nu-na-an-ni* |
| vii 18' | $^{uru}$*Ni-ip-pu-ri-ti la-ḫa-na-tu da-šu-up-tu* |
| vii 19' | *šu-up-pi* ○ *ḫu-ul-li* |
| vii 20' | *ša-am-ša áš-ni* ○ *be-la-ni* |
| vii 21' | *sa-am-mu-ut e-re-ni ra-am-ka be-lu* |
| vii 22' | *a-na bāb*(KÁ) *e-ni* ○ *ta-al-li-ka-am-ma* |
| vii 23' | *a-na mu-ši-ti an-ni-ti a-na li-la-ti an-na-ti* |
| vii 24' | ŠU.NÍGIN 17 ○ *i-ra-a-tu* ○ *ša ki-it-me* |
| ==== | |
| vii 25' | *ke-e na-aḫ-ša-at ke-e nam-ra-at* |
| vii 26' | *i-še-ʾi as°-ma kirî*($^{giš}$KIRI$_6$) *la-li-ka* |
| vii 27' | $u_4$*-ma lìb-bi* ○ *me-lu-la ni-gu-ta* |
| vii 28' | *a-ri-id kirî*($^{giš}$KIRI$_6$) *šarru*(LUGAL) *ḫa-ṣi-bu e-re-ni* |
| vii 29' | *at-ta ma-a-ru ra-i-mu* ○ *da-di-ni* |
| vii 30' | *e-bir-tu nāri*(ÍD) ○ *a-lu me-li-li* |
| vii 31' | *áš-ru-un-ni ta-gu-ša araḫ*(ITU) *ṣi-ḫa-ti* |
| vii 32' | *ul-la* ○ *a-li-ik* ○ *ma-a-ru* |
| vii 33' | *ki-i sà-ra-at* ○ *ša-at ḫa-aṭ-ṭi* |
| vii 34' | *iṣ-ṣur-tu ti-it-ku-ur-ri lal-la-ru ri-gim-ki* |
| vii 35' | *ša-an-da-na-ak* ○ *kirî*($^{giš}$KIRI$_6$) *ṣi-ḫa-ti* |
| vii 36' | $u_4$*-um-du i-na* $^{uru}$*La-ar-sa-an* |
| vii 37' | *ṣi-ḫa-tu* ○ ○ *i-zi-qa* |
| vii 38' | *ri-ši* $^{d}$*Na-na-a i-na kirî*($^{giš}$KIRI$_6$) É.BABBAR *ša ta-ra-mi* |
| vii 39' | *me-er-tu ub-la* ○ *lìb-ba-ša* ○*šu-a-ra* |
| vii 40' | *ka-ia-nam-ma ki-i sak-ta-ku-ma* |
| vii 41' | *a-ṣi-iḫ-ku* ○ (-)*ma-an mārī*(DUMU) *mārī*(DUMU) |
| vii 42' | *bar-ma-a-tu īnā*(IGI$^{meš}$)*-ia im-da-la-a ši-it-ta* |
| vii 43' | *ra-am-ka* ○ ○ *lu-ú ṣurru*($^{NA}{}_4$ZÚ) |
| vii 44' | *ṣi-ḫa-tu-ka lu-ú ḫurāṣu*(KUG.GI) |
| vii 45' | *ra-a-mi ni-i-ru muš-na-me-ru atallî*(AN.MI) |
| vii 46' | *mu-u-ša* ○ *aḫ-su-us-ka-ma* |
| vii 47' | *ep-šu* ○ ○ ○ *pi-i-ka* |
| vii 48' | *iš-tu ṣa-al-la-ku i-na su-un ma-a-ri* |
| vii 49' | *re-bi-<it>-ka* ○ *ša uqnî* ($^{na4}$ZA.GÌN) *šadî*(KUR) |
| vii 50' | *ḫa-di-iš* ○ *ak-ša* ○ *šar-ru* |

vii 51' *mi-ig-ru* ○ *ḫa-am-ru*
vii 52' *i-na la-li-ki* ○ *ḫu-un-bi*
vii 53' *ú-ka-a-al* ○ ○ *ra-am-*[*ka*]
vii 54' *i-na ša-a-ar* ○ [*mu-ú*]-[*ši*]
vii 55' TI x [... ...]
(rest broken)

col. viii
(at least 2–3 lines are missing)
viii 1' [… …] *re-du-ú*
====
viii 2' [… …]^meš^ *um-ma-ni*
====
viii 3' [… …] *iškar*(ÉŠ.GÀR) *ma-ru-ma ra-im-ni*
viii 4' [… …] *iškar*(ÉŠ.GÀR) *mur-ta-mi*
viii 5' [… …] *iškar*(ÉŠ.GÀR) *rē'i*(SIPA)*-ía* MIN(=*iškar*) *rē'î*(SIPA)
viii 6' [… …] *ak-ka-du-ú*
====
viii 7' [… …] | n a - a m - b a l - e d u $_{10}$ *šu-me-ru*
====
viii 8' [… …] | *te-gu-ú šu-me-ru*
====
viii 9' [… …] x | *šu-me-ru*^meš^ ○
viii 10' [… …] x | *ak-ka-du-ú*
viii 11' [… …] x | *za-ma-ru a-da-pu*^meš^
====
viii 12' [(vac.?)] | | š i r - g í d - d a^meš^ *šu-me-ru*
viii 13' [(vac.?)] | ○ | š i r - d i n g i r - g a l - l a - k u *šu-me-ru*
====
viii 14' [(vac.)] | 3 | | *ši-iṭ-ru ša eb-bu-be akkadî*(URI^KI^)
====
viii 15' 2 | | | KIMIN(*šiṭru*) *ša pi-i-te akkadî*(URI^KI^)
====
viii 16' 5 | | ○ | *pa-a-ru ak-ka-du-ú*
====
viii 17' ○ | | 1 | *šu-me* ○*-ru*
viii 18' | | 10 | *ak-ka-du-ú*
====
viii 19' | ŠU.NÍGIN | 11 | *za-mar še-e-ri*
====
viii 20' | 11 | | *za-mar a-la-li akkadî*(URI^KI^)
====
viii 21' | ○ | 9 ○ | *šu-me-ru*^meš^
viii 22' | | 1 | *ak-ka-du-ú*^meš^
viii 23' | ŠU.NÍGIN | 10 | *za-mar* ^d^*Nin-giš-zi-da*

====
viii 24' | 12 | | *za-mar šarru*(LUGAL) *ak-ka-du-ú*
====
viii 25' | ○ | 8 | *šu-me-*○*ru*$^{meš}$
viii 26' | | 3 | *ak-ka-du-ú*$^{meš}$
viii 27' | ŠU.NÍGIN | 11 | *šìr-ku-gu-ú*$^{meš}$
====
viii 28' | 5 ○ | ○ | *kér-re-tu ak-ka-du-ú*
====
viii 29' | 2° | | *ga-an-gíṭ-ṭu*$^{meš}$ KIMIN(*akkadû*)
====
viii 30' | 2 | | *nu-ú-ru* ○KIMIN(*akkadû*)
====
viii 31' | 2 ○ | | *e-le-lu sad-ru-tu* KIMIN(*akkadû*)
====
viii 32' | 2 | | *in-ḫu* ○KIMIN(*akkadû*)

viii 33' | 5 | ○ | *bu-ú-ru* KIMIN(*akkadû*)
====
viii 34' ○ | 2 | | $^{d}$*Gu-ša-a-tu* KIMIN(*akkadû*)
====
viii | 1 | *a-ra-aḫ-ḫu šu-me-ru*
====
viii 36' | 1 | | *šu-ta-ni-du-ú* KIMIN(*šumerū*)
====
viii 37' | 2 | | *ši-qa-tu* ⌈*šu-me-ru*⌉
====
viii 38' | 2 | ○ | *pi-ša-a-tu* ○ ⌈KI?⌉.MIN?
====
viii 39' | 2 | | *ri-ip-qu* KIMIN(*šumerū?*)
====
viii 40' | ○ | 2 | *šu-me-ru*$^{meš}$
viii 41' | | 3 | *ak-ka-du-ú*
viii 42' | ŠU.NÍGIN 5 | | *qu-ur-du*
====
viii 43' | 1 | | *kar-su-ú akaddû*(URI$^{KI}$)
====
viii 44' | 4 ○ | | *me-e-ru šu-me-ru*
====
viii 45' | | 23 | *irātu*(GABA$^{meš}$) *ša e-šèr-te akaddê*(URI$^{KI}$)
viii 46' | | 17 | *irātu*(GABA$^{meš}$) *ša ki-it-me*
viii 47' | | 24 | *irātu*(GABA$^{meš}$) *ša e-bu-be*
viii 48' [(vac.)] | | 4 | *irātu*(GABA$^{meš}$) *ša pi-it-te*
viii 49' [(vac.?) | | ] x | *irātu*(GABA$^{meš}$) *ša ni-id qabli*(MÚRU)
viii 50' [(vac.?) | | ] | *irātu*(GABA$^{meš}$)] *ša ni-iš! tuḫ-ri*

| | |
|---|---|
| viii 51' | [(vac.?) \| \| *irātu*(GABA$^{\text{meš}}$) *š*]*a qabli*(MÚRU)-*te* |
| viii 52' | [(vac.?) \| \| \| ] KIMIN(??) |
| | (rest broken) |

**Translation**

col. i

| | |
|---|---|
| i 0' | [1$^{st}$ *section*:] |
| i 1'–2' | [6 hymns of the *fir*]*st* series [in Akkadian-style] I listed. |
| i 3' | – May [Ea] command your [he]alth! |
| i 4' | "[…] … you bore me" |
| i 5' | "[…].. Oh shepherd! Hang on and let's, the two of us, make love!" |
| i 6' | "[*Ent*]*er*, shepherd – Ištar's lover" |
| i 7' | "[*The warri*]*or*, the shepherd, I repeatedly praised" |
| i 8' | "[…] that shepherd!" |
| i 9'–10' | [2$^{nd}$ of the se]ctions: 11 hymns in Akkadian-style I listed. |
| i 11' | – May Ea command your health! |
| i 12' | "[Mist]ress of all daises" |
| i 13' | "[Ištar] is powerful, the lioness-deity" |
| i 14' | "[…] of the Igigi, the queen" |
| i 15' | "[Ištar(?)], the competent of her father" |
| i 16' | "Namṣat [the…] who provides protective spirits" |
| i 17'–18' | 3$^{rd}$ of the sections: 16 hymns in Akkadian-style I listed. |
| i 19' | – May Ea command your health! |
| i 20' | "Oh first born, the son of An, let me praise your power!" |
| i 21' | "Let me praise Erra! His power let me extol!" |
| i 22' | "Lord, let me sing the praise of your divinity!" |
| i 23' | "He went out, Šarrabu, the lord of battles" |
| i 24' | "The guard of Erra, who observes (all)" |
| i 25'–26' | 4$^{th}$ of the sections: 21 hymns in Akkadian-style I listed. |
| i 27' | – May Ea command your health! |
| i 28'–29' | "Let me proclaim the praise of Adad the hero, the thunderous god!" |
| i 30' | "Let [me] praise repeatedly the companions, An's creation!" |
| i 31' | "The mighty, the powerful, the first born of An" |
| i 32' | "[*I will* …] *you*, the king of the gods, Adad!" |
| i 33' | "[Adad(?)], the first born of An who rages, the mighty god" |
| i 34'–35' | [5$^{th}$] of the sections: 26 hymns in Akkadian-style I listed. |
| i 36' | – May Ea command your health! |
| i 37' | "[DN(?)] has conceived her, Enlil grew fond of her" |
| i 38' | "[…] Šamaš, justice" |
| i 39' | "[… …] the perfect one, beloved of Enlil" |
| i 40' | "[Let me praise DN, the …] of the Igigi, the leader, a heroic god!" |
| i 41' | "[… The small (processional) b]oat let me praise, to Sîn!" |
| i 42' | [6$^{th}$ of the section]s: 31 hymns |

| | |
|---|---|
| i 43' | [of the series "Young man loving me"] in Akkadian-style. |
| i 44' | [– May Ea] command your [hea]lth! |
| ---- | |
| i 45' | "[… …] my son and my daughter" |
| i 46' | "[… …] the wise, your(pl. m.) son" |
| i 47' | "[… … she(?) is s]trong(?)" |
| i 48' | "… …] precious" |
| i 49' | "[… …] ..." |
| | |
| col.ii | |
| i 0' | [1st *of the sections:*] |
| ii 1'–2' | 5 hym[ns of a *first*(?) series] in the *ištarūtu*-style [I listed]. |
| ii 3' | – May Ea command your health! |
| ii 4' | "My consort, your *sign* is the *Urgulû*-instrument" |
| ii 5' | "To the tavern's light, Oh shepherd, I have(?)…[…]" |
| ii 6' | "I will sing the praise of Ištar, the queen" |
| ii 7' | "To the lusty shepherd I will smile" |
| ii 8'–9' | "Verily my shepherd, lead me to the house. I love… my only…" |
| ii 10'–11' | 2nd of the sections: [10 hy]mns in the *ištarūtu*-style I listed. |
| ii 12' | – May Ea command your health! |
| ii 13' | "Impetuous, the shining of her [… li]ght" |
| ii 14' | "Go(f.) along the processional road of […], let me come out!" |
| ii 15' | "(Praise) the queen of joy, the powerful one!" |
| ii 16' | "(Praise) the valiant one, the daughter of Sîn, the competent deity!" |
| ii 17' | "So luxuriant are they, so luxuriant are they – the beautiful (women)" |
| ii 18'–19' | 3rd of the sections: 15 hymns in the *ištarūtu*-style I listed. |
| ii 20' | – May Ea command your health! |
| ii 21' | "Hail(f.) our goddess, Oh the dawn-watch!" |
| ii 22' | "The girl – her heart, a joyful song" |
| ii 23'–24' | "Oh Nanāya, it is you (who has) thus decreed the well-being for the king!" |
| ii 25' | "You will be treated with honor, Oh queen Nanāya!" |
| ii 26' | "The overseer(f.) of all the people, the beloved one" |
| ii 27'–28' | 4th of the sections: 20 hymns in the *ištarūtu*-style I listed. |
| ii 29' | – May Ea command your health! |
| ii 30' | "Ištar, the overseer(f.), let me…, let me proclaim!" |
| ii 31' | "All-seeing among the Igigi, most famous among the goddesses" |
| ii 32' | "First born(f.) of An, the great one(f.)" |
| ii 33' | "Let me praise the sagacity of [DN!]" |
| ii 34' | "Be repeatedly extolled, the *te*[*rrifying*…!]" |
| ii 35'–36' | 5th of the sections: 25 hymns in the *ištarūtu*-style I listed. |

| | |
|---|---|
| ii 37' | – May Ea command your health! |
| ii 38'–39' | "The mountain(s) – it is (/they are) so high! Moreover, the summit(s) – it is (/they are) so immense!" |
| ii 40' | "When you made the battles dance" |
| ii 41' | "Jubilate, land!" |
| ii 42' | "Honor(pl.) the god! Love(pl.) the god!" |
| ii 43' | "Oh my king, in your praise" |
| ii 44' | "Nanāya had a joyous thought" |
| ii 45'–46' | Altogether 6 sections: 31 hymns of the series "My shepherd, my shepherd" in the *ištarūtu*-style I listed. |
| ii 47' | – May Ea command your health! |
| ii 48' | Altogether *93* Akkadian hymns. |
| ==== | |
| ii 49' | "Awe-inspiring, important god, mother(?) of the limits of heaven and earth" |
| ii 50' | "Love-charms, love-charms, love-charms he ..." |
| ii 51' | … |
| ii 52' | "He has sprouted, he has burgeoned, he is well-watered lettuce" |
| ii 53' | "Water skin (and) food ration *give* [*me*…]"; |
| col. iii | |
| iii 0'–1' | [1st *section*: 5] Su[merian *teg*]*û* [hymns of the *first* series I listed]. |
| iii 2' | – May Ea [command y]our health! |
| iii 3' | "*Wind, a phantom*(?), *sitting*(?)… …" |
| iii 4' | "Wind which does not … a silent house …" |
| iii 5' | "King, your shining aura…" |
| iii 6' | "Lord, lightning (or: herald of) heaven and earth …" |
| iii 7' | "A Hero, *his warfare, his warfare…*" |
| iii 8'–9' | 2nd section: 10 Sumerian *tegû* [hymns] [I listed]. |
| iii 10' | – May Ea [command] your health! |
| iii 11' | "*eya*! My king, joy […]" |
| iii 12' | "… … standing… [ ]" |
| iii 13' | "*Lord Enlil, appearing prince* […]" |
| iii 14' | "Lord, great leopard, the Apsû of Eridu" |
| iii 15' | "My hero, *passing*, coming out …." |
| iii 16'–17' | 3rd section: 15 Sum. *tegû* hym[ns] [I listed]. |
| iii 18' | – May Ea com[mand] your health! |
| iii 19'–20' | "Great lord, most high in heaven and earth you are! Father of the gods" |
| iii 21' | "Lord most high, noble, the one of the princely gods" |
| iii 22' | "Hero, strong one, creator of the gods" |
| iii 23' | "Enlil, the honored one, leopard, … wisdom…" |
| iii 24' | "Lord… leader, greatly…." |

| | |
|---|---|
| iii 25' | "Hero, the honored one, leopard, surpassing, overseer, Enlil" |
| iii 26' | "King, noble prince, lord of both heaven and earth" |
| iii 27' | "Prince, in the holy mound, its silence is *overwhelming*" |
| iii 28'–29' | 4th section: 23 hymns of the Sumerian *tegû* I listed. |
| iii 30' | – May Ea command your health! |
| iii 31' | Altogether 23 Sumerian *tegû.* |
| ==== | |
| iii 32' | "To heaven, the just rite, his…." |
| iii 33' | "Great lord (of) heaven and earth, going in front the noble temple" |
| iii 34' | "Great lord, the exalted among the gods" |
| iii 35' | "Lord of vigor, complete with skill" |
| iii 36' | "An, the exalted one, the great among the gods" |
| iii 37'–38' | 5 adab Sumerian hymns of the first series I listed. |
| iii 39' | – May Ea command your health! |
| iii 40' | "Lord of the lapis-lazuli skies, hovering over the earth" |
| iii 41' | "Lord, dragon among the gods" |
| iii 42' | "Exalted prince (going) upwards, king of heaven and earth" |
| iii 43' | "Lady, the wise vizier, in heaven you are (or: she is)" |
| iii 44'–45' | "The provider in front of Anu (and) the great Anunnaki gods" |
| iii 46' | [2nd *series*(?)] 10 hymn[s *I listed*] |

col. iv

| | |
|---|---|
| iv 1' | … [... ...] |
| iv 2' | "*lead*[*er*?]" |
| iv 3' | *The wife of* [... ...]" |
| iv 4' | The illuminator of [... ...]" |
| iv 5'–6' | ... [… …] *commande*[r(?)]" |
| iv 7'–12' | (broken) |

col. v

| | |
|---|---|
| v 1' | "Gods [... ...] " |
| v 2'–3' | "She is adorn[ed], she is hon[ored]" |
| v 4' | "The house of *love-charms*(?) [... ...]" |
| v 5' | "The lord, *sitting*… [... ...]" |
| v 6' | "Lord of wisdom ... [...]" |
| v 7' | "(Praise) the pure god [... ...]" |
| v 8' | "(Praise) the god *Anzû*(?) [... ...]" |
| v 9' | "Leader of the entire world ...[...]" |
| v 10' | "Oh leader, him you will… [...]" |
| v 11'–12' | "First born, offspring of [...] *advisor*(?) [...]" |
| v 13' | "The goddess of listening [of prayers]" |
| v 14' | "The lord … [...]" |
| v 15' | "The son of [...]" |
| v 16'– v17' | Altogether 13 so[ngs of the *modus*(?) of the Akkadian flute] |

| | |
|---|---|
| ==== | |
| v 18' | "Offspring of [... ...]" |
| v 19'–21' | (broken) |
| | |
| col. vi | |
| vi 1' | "Lord(?) … [...]" |
| vi 2' | "The able one(f.) [...]" |
| vi 3' | "Lady...[...]" |
| vi 4' | Altogether 8 Sum. (hymns) 3 Akkadian (hymns). |
| vi 5' | Altogether 11 *šerkugû*-hymns. |
| ==== | |
| vi 6' | "Rejoice, our lady, celebrate!" |
| vi 7' | "The cleverest(f.) of the clever, the overseer(f.) of the people" |
| vi 8' | "The terrifying among the gods, I am" |
| vi 9' | "Passing in the street, I found two *sekrētum*-women" |
| vi 10' | "The terrifying among the gods, I am" |
| vi 11' | Altogether 5 *marching*(?)-hymns. |
| ==== | |
| vi 12' | "Thresher of the entire world, who throws all cities into confusion" |
| vi 13'–14' | "Let me constantly praise the strong god, the king, the aggressive god" |
| vi 15' | Altogether 2 *gangiṭṭu*-hymns. |
| ==== | |
| vi 16' | "The spirit of (my) protection – do not be angry (with me)!" |
| vi 17' | "Who is the owner of the ship? Who is the owner of the processional boat?" |
| vi 18' | Altogether 2 *nūru*-hymns. |
| ==== | |
| vi 19' | "Go away sleep, let me embrace my darling!" |
| vi 20' | "I will send a message to (my) sister-in-law" |
| vi 21' | 2 *elēlu*-hymns in sections. |
| ==== | |
| vi 22' | "Ištar the queen of people, the beloved" |
| vi 23' | "Ištar, who (is) besides you? you are a lady!" |
| vi 24' | 2 *inḫu*-hymns |
| ==== | |
| vi 25' | "She has found, the *extolled one* (or: *the impetuous*), indeed she has found" |
| vi 26' | "Lad, since I have seen [you]" |
| vi 27' | "I will sing the praise of the great one (f.) to the people" |
| vi 28' | "The protection of the people – I [will praise (it)]" |
| vi 29' | "In the abode of the lord of the gods they (pl. f.) will praise […]" |
| vi 30' | Altogether 5 *b*[*ūrū*(?)]-hymns. |
| ==== | |

vi 31' “Gušaya [... ...]”
vi 32' “Gušaya [... ...]”
vi 33' 2 hymns [of *whirling dances*(?)].
====

(rest broken)

col. vii
vii 1' “[Lo]oking [at you]”
vii 2' “Shine to me like the star of da[wn]”
vii 3' “In the flirtations of the field”
vii 4' “This is the desire of the joy of the heart”
vii 5' “Make me blossom with your speech, until I die!”
vii 6' Altogether 23 *irtu*-hymns of the temple.
====
vii 7' “Oh, how did I smile to the lusty one!”
vii 8' “The day, when my right eye twinkled”
vii 9' “He will take (me) – I am suitable for the darling!”
vii 10' “Whenever you enter – Oh lord – it is now!”
vii 11' “I am cleaning myself for your(m.) love”
vii 12' “With this single night”
vii 13' “Tonight, Oh darling, I will make you pass the night (with me)”
vii 14' “I will see *the snake*(?) of the earth”
vii 15' “(What) the day brought is truly good news: happiness of the heart”
vii 16' “*Hooray*! (My) darling is shining – come in!”
vii 17' “One who is not of my status pretended to be my equal”
vii 18' “My Nippur-girl, a sweet courtesan”
vii 19' “Come silently(f.), advance(f.)!”
vii 20' “I have competed with the sun, Oh our lord!”
vii 21' “Your love, Oh lord, – fragrance of the cedar tree!”
vii 22' “To the spring gate you(m.) came to me”
vii 23' “To this night, to this evening”
vii 24' Altogether 17 *irtu*-songs of the lyre.
====
vii 25' “How sumptuous is she! How shining is she!”
vii 26' “She seeks your ripe garden of pleasures”
vii 27' “Today, my heart, (let us have) dancing (and) singing!”
vii 28' “The one who goes down to the garden, Oh king, the cutter of cedar (branches)”
vii 29' “You, darling, who loves our lovemaking”
vii 30' “On the other side of the river – the city of dancing”
vii 31' “To our place you(m.) sped, Oh month of delights”
vii 32' “No! Darling, go!”
vii 33' “How deceiving is she, that of the scepter”

| | |
|---|---|
| vii 34' | “Oh bird, my mourning dove, your(f.) voice is (like that of) a wailer” |
| vii 35' | “Oh chief gardener of the date-palm orchard of delights” |
| vii 36'–37' | “On the day, in Larsa, impishness wafted at me” |
| vii 38' | “Rejoice Nanāya in the orchard of Ebabbar which you love” |
| vii 39' | “The girl, her heart desires dancing” |
| vii 40' | “How am I to remain silent constantly?” |
| vii 41' | “Had I only shown my charms to you, Oh my darling, darling” |
| vii 42' | “My flickering eyes are filled with sleep” |
| vii 43'–44' | “Your love is an obsidian-blade, your lovemaking is golden” |
| vii 45' | “My love is the light that illuminates the eclipse” |
| vii 46' | “I was thinking about you at night” |
| vii 47' | “At your command” |
| vii 48' | “Since I was sleeping in (my) darling’s lap” |
| vii 49' | “Your genitals are lapis-lazuli of the mountain” |
| vii 50' | “Come here joyfully, Oh king!” |
| vii 51' | “Favorable one, *chosen one*(?)” |
| vii 52' | “Start blooming in your desire!” |
| vii 53' | “I *remember* [your] love” |
| vii 54' | “In the breeze of the night” |
| vii 55' | traces |
| | (rest broken) |

col. viii

| | |
|---|---|
| vii 1' | “[… …] *soldier*” |
| ==== | |
| viii 2' | “[… …] (*of*) the *army*” |
| ==== | |
| viii 3' | “[… …] the series “Young man loving me” |
| viii 4' | “[… …] the series “The lovers” |
| viii 5' | “[… …] the series “My shepherd, my shepherd” |
| viii 6' | [… …] (in) Akkadian. |
| ==== | |
| viii 7' | “[… …] Sumerian na-am-bal-e-du-hymns. |
| ==== | |
| viii 8' | [… …] Sumerian *tegû*-hymns. |
| ==== | |
| viii 9' | [… …] (in) Sumerian. |
| viii 10' | [… …] (in) Akkadian: |
| viii 11' | [*Altogether*…] adab hymns. |
| ==== | |
| viii 12' | [… …] Sumerian šir-gid-da-hymns. |
| viii 13' | [… …] Sumerian šir-dingir-gal-la-ku-hymns. |
| ==== | |

viii 14' 3 (songs of) the *modus*(?) of the Akkadian flute.

====

viii 15' 2 (songs) in the modus of the Akkadian *harp*(?).

====

viii 16' 5 Akkadian *pāru*-hymns.

====

viii 17' 1 (in) Sumerian

viii 18' 10 (in) Akkadian:

====

viii 19' Altogether 11 hymns of the *šēru-string*.

====

viii 20' 11 Akkadian hymns of ululation.

====

viii 21' 9 (in) Sumerian

viii 22' 1 (in) Akkadian:

viii 23' Altogether 10 Ningišzida hymns.

====

viii 24' 12 hymns (for?/of?) the king, Akkadian.

====

viii 25' 8 (in) Sumerian

viii 26' 3 (in) Akkadian:

viii 27' Altogether 11 šir-ku-gu-hymns.

====

viii 28' 5 Akkadian *marching*(?) songs.

====

viii 29' 2! Akkadian *gangiṭṭu*-song.

====

viii 30' 2 Akkadian *nūru*-songs.

====

viii 31' 2 Akkadian *cheerful* songs arranged in sections.

====

viii 32' 2 Akkadian *inḫu*-hymns.

viii 33' 5 Akkadian *būru*-hymns.

====

viii 34' 2 Akkadian *whirling dances*(?).

====

viii 35' 1 Sumerian *araḫḫu*-hymn.

====

viii 36' 1 Sumerian hymn with antiphons.

====

viii 37' 2 Sumerian *irrigation*(?)-songs.

====

viii 38' 2 Sumerian 'rude'-songs.

====

| | |
|---|---|
| viii 39' | 2 Sumerian *hoeing*-songs. |
| ==== | |
| viii 40' | 2 Sumerian |
| viii 41' | 3 Akkadian: |
| viii 42' | Altogether 5 heroic-songs. |
| ==== | |
| viii 43' | 1 Akkadian *karsû*-song. |
| ==== | |
| viii 44' | 4 Sumerian *merru*-songs. |
| ==== | |
| viii 45' | 23 (hymns in) the Akkadian *ešertu* tone-scale. |
| viii 46' | 17 (hymns in) the lyre tone-scale. |
| viii 47' | 24 (hymns in) the flute tone-scale. |
| viii 48' | 4 (hymns in) the harp tone-scale. |
| viii 49' | […] (hymns in) the "descending" tone-scale. |
| viii 50' | […] (hymns in) the "ascending" tone-scale. |
| viii 51' | […] (hymns in) the "middle" tone-scale. |
| viii 52' | […] ditto. |
| | (rest broken) |

**Commentary**[454]

i 0': In the broken part at the beginning of col. i 6 incipits are missing, as proven by the summary i 9'–10' which mentions 11 compositions.

i 5': *ra-a*: The form can be parsed as *rāʾâ*, the uncontracted form of *rūʾûm*, or *râ*, the contracted form of this lemma. Syntactically it is either acc. or voc. – *lurtāmānu*: For the ventive *-nu*, see GAG § 82d (where this morpheme is qualified as "n/spB"). More on 1 du. verbal forms, typically found in reciprocal verbs as *râmum*-Gt, see Kouwenberg 2010, 364 n. 32 (see also commentaries to PRAK 1 B 472 i 3' (№ 13) and YOS 11, 24 i 20–22 (№ 15).

i 6': [*er-ba-a*]*m*°*-ma*°: Restitution JAOS 103, 26–27 (№ 7).

i 7': [*ur*?*-ša*?*-a*]*n*?*-na rēʾa*($^{\text{lú}}$SIPA): Following Black 1983, 28.

i 14': *malkatum*: "Queen" is an epithet of Ištar.

i 23': See Krebernik 2009–2010, 71: "'Š. Herr der Kämpfe' oder vielleicht besser 'Zwistigkeiten'", "lord of disputations".

454 Many lines of KAR 158 are fully or partially cited in the CAD and the AHw. I refrain from bringing these references unless they have direct bearing on the discussion. In the same vein, I do not comment on the section of the catalogue which lists incipits of Sum. hymns (ii 49'–iii 43'), as theses compositions do not belong to love literature.

i 38': Hecker 2013, 56 restores: “[Bei dir] o Šamaš, ist Recht”.

i 43': [*iškar ma-ru-ma*] *rāʾimni akkadīta*: This colophon is recapitulated in viii 3'. Klein/Sefati 2008, 620 suggest that “the songs listed in the series *māruma rāʾimni* are distinct in that they mostly deal with the love between Tammuz and Ištar, similar to the Sumerain Dumuzi-Inana songs”. Note, however, that although the first third of this *iškarum* Ištar is mentioned, in the rest of it other gods predominate.

i 45': [*me*]-*ri u mērte*: Assyrian forms (cf. also ii 22').

i 45'–49': These lines list the next 5 incipits of the 7th section. The column probably ends with 3 lines of the ŠU.NÍGIN summary formula (as in ii 45'–47').

ii 0': In the broken part at the beginning of col. ii there are 5 incipits missing.

ii 5': Hecker 2013, 56 (with AHw 85a, and CAD A/2, 473b) translates: “Zum Licht des Gasthauses, Hirte ..[…]”. This reading is followed here, but another should also be considered, namely deriving *altami* from *law/mûm*, “to surround, besiege”, cf. CUSAS 10, 9: 13 (№ 3) and ZA 49, 168–169 i 27 (№ 16). – *nīru*: This word for “light”, a by-form of the common *nūru*, is attested only in Assyrian sources (see also vii 45' and cf. ii 13' where *nūru* is restored).

ii 7': Similar incipit in vii 7'.

ii 8'–9': *ù re-ʾ-i* [*a-n*]*a bīti*(É) *ru-ʾ-a-am a-ra-am-*[*mu?* …]-x-*ia-ma*: Contra Black 1983, 28 and Hecker 2013, 56, the two lines belong to one incipit, as demonstrated by the indentation of ii 9' and the count of the incipits in this section (ii 4'–9'). Following Hecker 2005, 171 (“Mein Hirte, nun bring mich ins Haus!”) and Hecker 2013, 56 (“Und bring mich nach Hause, mein Hirte”) *ru-ʾ-a-am* is understood as *warûm*-G imp.

ii 13': *na-ba-a-a*[*t*]: Reading with Hecker 2013, 56: “… strahlend ist ihr [Lich]t”.

ii 14': [*lu-ṣi*?!(Text: I°)]: Though *lu-ṣi* presents itself as a plausible restoration, collation does not support *ṣi*. The wedges look like a simple I sign.

ii 15': Hecker 2013, 56: “Die wohlklingende Königin des Frohsinns”.

ii 17': A similar collocation is found in MAD 5, 8: 6–7 (№ 22): “You, Oh two beautiful maidens, are blooming!”.[455]

ii 21': CAD Š/1, 297b and CAD N/1, 208b, translate: “praise the dawn, O our goddess”. Hecker (2013, 57) similarly: “Preise, o unsere Göttin, die Morgenröte”. The acc., however,

455 MAD 5, 8: 6–7 (№ 22): *wa*[*rd*]*atā damiqtā tuḫtannamā*.

is kept in catalogue, so it is the goddess who is the object of *tišmarī*, while *namārītu*, the third watch, stands in a vocative.

ii 22': Similar incipit in vii 39'.

ii 23'–24': Hecker 2013, 57 ignores the indentation of ii 24', translating the two lines as separate incipits: "DN, mein Merkmal ist" (following Ebeling in reading *it-ti-ma*), and "Wie weist du dem König Heil zu". (Cf. CAD Š/3, 247b 1a and Sigrist/Goodnick Westenholz 2008, 671).

ii 25': *tuk-te-en-ni*: Contra CAD K 167f. which cites this line under *kânum*-D, I take this verb as deriving from *kanûm*-Dt (not in CAD K 542a 3), similarly to ii 42' and v 3'.

ii 30': *lu-ú-še*: Remains unclear: perhaps from *šeʾûm*?

ii 33': *ta*$_8$(ḪI)-*šim*-[*ti*]: The syllabic value *ta*$_8$(ḪI) is difficult but is found in ii 53' as well. In my mind this reading is preferable to Hecker's 2013, 57: "Ich will [deinen] süßen Duft besingen", which must be based on the logographic spelling DÙ ŠIM. – By the end of the line c. 3 signs are missing; I assume a DN.

ii 34': Possible restoration *ra*-[*šu*]-[*ub-tu/ti* …] after vi 8' (MPS).

ii 38'–39': If this incipit concerns love (and this is questionable, given the next incipits) then "mountains" refer metaphorically to bodily curves, as in PRAK 1 B 472 i 10' (№ 13): "The mountains of our shoulders, the attraction of our chests".[456]

ii 40'–46': This section contains 6, not 5 incipits, as usual. Another section of 6 incipits must have been found at the first lines of the tablet, which are now lost (see commentary to i 0'). The grand total in ii 48', which numbers 93 incipits (31+31+[31]), corroborates this calculation.

ii 40': As already noted by von Soden (1933, 154–155), the motif of the battle as an ecstatic dance or feast is found also in Agš A iii 7–8 // 11–12: "Her festival is battle, dance-making the *frays*".[457] Hecker (2013, 57) translates differently: "Als du oben tanztest" which is based on the logographic reading AN.TA = *eliš*. Again, as in ii 33', I consider such purely logographic spelling unlikely in this text.

ii 41': *ri-i-iš*°: Interestingly *mātu* is exceptionally treated here as m. (Or, should one emend *ri-i-iš* to *ri-i-ši*?). – This incipit recalls the repeated refrain in Or. 60, 340 (№ 12): *rīšātumma išdum ana āli*.

---

456 PRAK 1 B 472 i 10' (№ 13): *šadî būdīni u lalû irtīni*.

457 Agš A iii 7–8 // 11–12: *isinša tamḫāru šutraqqudu antī*.

ii 45'–46': The expected sub-summary formula (“X[th] of the sections enumerating the Y first hymns in the *ištarūtu*-manner I listed”) does not appear: either omitted by mistake, or left out because of the grand total which follows.

ii 48': Collation shows that the number summarizing the incipits of the two first columns is not 93, as in Ebeling’s copy, but 153 (= 2x60 + 3x10 + 3); namely the numeral begins with two vertical strokes, not with one. Up to this point the tablet lists 31+31 incipits, plus the 31 incipits that originally were found in the part of the tablet which is now broken away after i 49'. (These 31 incipits are summarized as *iškar murtāmī* in viii 4' by the end of the tablet.) The number 153 is therefore impossible and must be an ancient scribal mistake for 93.

ii 49'–iii 43': This section of the catalogue contains non-orthographic (“syllabic”) incipits of Sum. hyms which are not related to love and sex. Only a few of the incipits were identified with known compositions. As this section of the catalogue does not deal with the subject of this study, no running commentary is given.

ii 52': Civil (1967, 208 n. 28, followed by Black 1983, 25, n. 4) identified this incipit as the opening of a Balbale of Inanna (= ETCSL t.4.08.05). See also Klein/Sefati 2008, 619 n. 18.

ii 53': [*i*]*n-du-ra ku*$_8$*-ru-um-ma-ta*$_8$ *id-n*[*a*?]: Though found surrounded by Sum. incipits, this line is in Akk. (A similar situation is found in iii 44'–45'.) – Note the rare word *indūru*, “Wassersack?” (AHw 382a) and the unusual syllabic value *ta*$_8$ (found also in ii 33', see above). The key word, joining this incipit to the previous one, is probably “water”.

iii 36': This incipit was identified as the opening line of Adab to An for Ur-Ninurta (= ETCSL c.2.5.6.5). See Falkenstein 1950, 88 and Klein/Sefati 2008, 619 n. 18).

iii 44'–45': This two-line incipit joins the four previous Sum. incipits (as in ii 53').

iii 46': [2 *iš-ka-ra-a-tu*] 10 *za-ma-ru*[$^{meš}$]: Restoration based on iii 37'–38'.

iv 2': *ma-an-s*[*u*?]: *massû*, “leader” (with CAD M/1, 327b) is found also in v 9' and iii 24' (Sum. incipit). An alternative restitution is *ma-an-n*[*u*] (see vi 17').

iv 3': *ḫi-ri-it*: Taken from *ḫirītum*, “wife”, although the known construct form is *ḫīrat.*

iv 4': *mušnammer*: A part. of *namārum*-ŠD is found also in vii 45' (but reading *še-ri na-me-er*, “My dawn is shining”, is not excluded).

iv 6': *mu-ma-*ʾ-x [...]: Read *mummaʾʾerum*?

iv 7': The sign UN copied by Ebeling is now lost.

v 4': É *e-ri-mi*(-) [...]: *irʾemum*/*irimmum*, “love-charm” is not attested with *bītum*, but no other reading presents itself (and see the following incipit).

v 5': *bēl/bēlum*(EN) *a-ši-bu* [...]: The part. *āšibu*, "sitting" (probably with an archaic const. form with *-u*) continues nicely the previous incipit where "house of love-charms" is mentioned.

v 8'–12': This section may focus on Anzu. The winged creature is mentioned explicitly in v 8' (so also CAD A/2, 154b), and indirectly in the next incipits, where he is *mansû kibrāti* (v 9') and *apal bīn* (v 11'–12') which recalls the opening of the Anzû myth, *bīn šar dadmē*.

vi 2': *le-i-tu*: *lē'ûm*, "powerful, competent", or *lītum*, "victory"? The spelling *le-a-at* is found in i 15' (for which see von Soden 1931, 225).

vi 7': *emuqti em-qe*!(Text: IQ)*-ti ammarat nišī*: Reading with CAD E 152a and Limet 1996, 153 (Groneberg 2003, 64 reads: *e-ni-ti emqītī amarat nišē*, "my wise punishment watches over the people", noting in n. 76: "The sign NI is partly erased (collated)"). – *ammaratu:* Also in ii 26'.

vi 10': *rašubtu ina ilāni anāku*: Repeated in vi 8'. This mistake was unnoticed by the scribe who counted it twice in the summary of total incipits.

vi 19': *šittu atlakī*: A similar phrase is found in the Moussaieff Love Song obv. 8 (№ 11): "Oh sleep, come to me like to a baby! Go out from me, Oh sleep!"[458] For the theme of sleep in ALL, see Overview § 6.1 (and cf. vii 42').

vi 23': ᵈ*Ištar mannu balukki be-le-ti*: CAD B 72a 2' translates: "who is the lady apart from you, Ištar?", but the ending *-ēti* in *be-le-ti* cannot be construed as a 3 sg. f. stative. This incipit is to be analyzed as a direct call to the goddess in 2 sg. f., with an inserted comment *mannu balukki*. A different view is found in von Soden 1931, 226: *bēletī* is a poetic form of *bēltī*, "my lady" (and so: "Ištar, who is besides you, my lady?").

vi 25': *šāmarītu*: This f. adj. is a hapax (CAD Š/1, 295b, AHw 1154a). I derive it from *šamārum* B, mainly attested in the Gt stem, "to extol" (but see, however, ii 13' where I translate "impetuous", leaning on *šamārum* A "to rage", and cf. CAD B 343a, s.v. *būru* D: "O untamed lady…").

vii 1': [*nap*?]*-lu-us-ka-ma*: So, contra Groneberg 2003, 66 ([x x *ul*?]*luṣkama*, "… swollen to you…").

vii 2': *upḫa kī kakkab še-*[*e-ri*]: Reading with CAD N/1, 266a (Groneberg 2003, 66 reads: (*an*(coll.)!*-ḫa ki-i mul*-BU, "they are weary like…").The Morning star is Venus, Ištar.

vii 3': *ina ṣiḫti ša ṣēri*: This incipit also refers to Ištar, presenting her as making love with Dumuzi in the steppe. A similar image is found in Fs. Renger 192–193 i 11–13 (№ 6): "My

---

458 Moussaieff Love Song obv 8 (№ 11): *alkīmmi šittum* [*la-ḫi*?*-iš*] *ṣīam šittum*.

love of the steppe, may the trappers return (him) back to me! You will *embrace* my delights".[459]

vii 4': *annû ṣibûtu ša ḫūdu kabatti*: CAD Ṣ 168a 4': "Here he is! a request (whose fulfillment brings) happiness!". CAD A/2, 140f., more accurately: "This one is what a happy heart wishes for".

vii 5': *epšu pīka: epiš* appended with loc. adv., serving as *instrumentalis* (cf. vii 47' andCAD I/J 170b, CAD Š/l, 290b). – *ad mūtiya*: Contra AHw 691, s.v. *mutu*(*m*), who reads *abi mutija* "father of my husband". Hecker 2013, 60 translated only the first half of the line: "Der Ausspruch deines Mundes". (Note finally Groneberg 2003, 66 which is not clear to me: *epšu* [*p*]*īka atmu pi*?(sign: *ti*)-*ja summe hanimma*, "speak! interrupt the speech of my mouth(!): he is blooming").

vii 7': A similar incipit is found in ii 7'. (Cf. CAD K 32lb, CAD S 65a, and Klein/Sefati 2008, 621).

vii 8': *ūm ēn imniya išḫiṭanni*: Another case of a somatic reaction of a lovesick woman is ZA 49, 168–169 ii 21–22 (№ 16): "My (ominous) signs trouble me: my upper lip becomes moist, while my lower lip trembles!"[460]

vii 9': *ileqqe amaṣṣi ana māri*: Contra CAD M/1, 345a 1 which reads *ilik*, "go (away)! I am worthy of the lover": but *i-li-ik* cannot be the imp. of *alākum*-G, and the sign in question is QI, (cf. ii 40' and iii 44'), not IQ (cf. ii 47' and passim).

vii 10': *matēma bēlu terruba inanna*: Paul 1995: "When, O darling? Just now you have arrived!", Groneberg 2003, 66: "When, Oh lord? you will now come in!", and Hecker 2013, 60: "Wann, Herr, kommst du herein? Jetzt". – *te-ru-ba*: a present of the Babylonian form of *erēbum* (the Assyrian form would be *terraba*).

vii 11': *ḫi-i-pa-a-ku ana dādīka*: With Hecker (2005, 171) and AHw 306a, s.v. *ḫâb*/*pu*, "säubern, reinigen": "bin geputzt für deine Liebe" (contra CAD Ḫ 21a: "I am consecrated for your love"). Groneberg 2003, 66 took *ḫi-i* together as one sign, ḪAR: "I am early (quick) [*harpāku*] for your 'darlings'"). Collation ascertains two separate signs *ḫi* and *i*.

vii 12': *itti iltat mušīti*: Reading with CAD M/2, 271f. and von Soden 1933, 131. (Groneberg 2003, 66: "with the …(?) of the night", reading *šimtāt*, not *iltât*).

vii 13': *mūša māru ušamšâkku*: A similar invitation of a woman to her lover to pass the night with her is found in JAOS 103, 26–27: 1–2 (№ 7): "Come in, shepherd, Ištar's lover; Spend the night here, shepherd, Ištar's lover".[461] – *ú-šàm-ša-a-ku*: von Soden (1931, 176)

459 Fs. Renger i 11–13 (№ 6): *râmi ša ṣēri ḫābilū literrūnimma ṣīḫātiya talammi.*

460 ZA 49 ii 21–22 (№ 16): *ittātūa ulap*<*pa*>*tāni*[*inni*] *šaptī elītum ila*[*bbik*] *lū šaplītumma irub*[*bam*].

461 JAOS 103, 26–27: 1–2 (№ 7): *erbamma rēʾû ḫ*[*aram* ᵈ*Ištarma*] *māšamma rēʾû ḫar*[am ᵈ*Ištar*].

takes the dative suffix *-ku* (not the later *-ka*) as an indication of an older ms. before the copyist's eyes.

vii 14': *ammar šamān erṣeti*: A difficult line. CAD Š/1, 328b k) translates: "I find(?) oil from the earth". The enigmatic "oil from the earth", *šaman erṣeti*, could refer to bitumen, but such a designation is unknown (not in Stol 2012a) and does not fit the context. Somewhat better would be *šammān erṣeti*, "the snake of the earth "(CAD Š/1, 314, s.v. *šammānu*), but this too remains obscure.

vii 16': *e-la-ia māru lū namer erba*: AHw 203b, lists this incipit s.v. *ellēʾa*, "nein, keinesfalls", offering no translation ("unkl."). Previously, however, von Soden (1933, 137) took *ela* as a form of *eli*, translating (n. 4): "Über mir (oder „mehr als ich"?) möge der Sohn „glänzen"; tritt ein zu mir". By contrast, CAD E 10lb, places this incipit under *ellēa*/*ellēama* (*elaja*), "an exclamation of joy": "O youngster, let me light (a light)! come here!", which is accepted here. Groneberg 2003, 66 follows von Soden in the AHw: "Not at all!...". – The description of the lover as full of light follows the key-metaphor of light signifying love, see Overview § 6.2.

vii 18': *Nippurītī laḫannatu daššuptu*: CAD L 38b leaves *laḫannatu* non-translated: "My girl from Nippur, the sweet *l.*", but AHw 528a, s.v. *laḫḫi*/*anatu* translates "eine Angestellte", comparing this lemma to Rabbinic Heb. *lᵉḥēnā*, "concubine". Hecker (2005, 171 and 2013, 60) goes in a different direction: "Mein Mädchen aus Nippur, süßer Spatz", understanding *laḫannatu* as a by-form of *laḫantu*, a rare bird name, attested so far only in lexical lists (CAD L 40a). Yet another solution was suggested by von Soden. In AHw 165a, s.v. *dašpu*, the word is transcribed *laḫanatu* and translated "Müllerin", "milling-girl", to be connected to *alaḫḫinu*, "Müller" (AHw 31a). Namely, for him *laḫ*(*ḫ*)*an*(*n*)*atu* as a variant of **alaḫḫinatu*, "milling-girl". This lemma is attested in an MA letter which reports of 2 MUNUS$^{meš}$ *a-láḫ-ḫi-na-a-tu*, traveling with the queen Qaʾʾīmātu, her two sisters, 13 women of noble blood, and a woman of the eunuch-category. The letter sums up by saying that 6 wagons accompanied this high-ranking group escorting the king.[462] In the context of this letter, the meaning "milling-girl" must be excluded and some kind of high-ranking "concubine" be assumed. – *daššuptu*: an Assyrian form.

vii 19': *šuppī ḫullī*: Cf. CAD Ḫ 34a ("come (addressing a woman) on tiptoe(?)!"), and CAD Š/1, 427b ("walk (addressing a woman), go carefully"). See also AHw 309b s.v. *ḫalālum* IV and AHw 1170a.

vii 20': *šamša ašni bēlani*: Hecker 2013, 60 does not translate this line, but cf. AHw 1158b 3b) and CAD Š/l, 338a. – *ašni*: Cf. CAD Š/l, 400a and AHw 1165b (with hesitation). (Groneberg 2003, 67 translates entirely differently: "our…(?) our tassel [*tillani*]"). – *bēlani*: von Soden 1931, 215 explained this form (and not the usual *bēlni*) as a poetic form. A less

462 Cancik-Kirschbaum 1996, 148 no. 10:8–15 with the note of Postgate 2001. Note further that in the NA legal document Kwasman/Parpola 1991, 63 (= SAA 6, 66) a certain Baḫianu is mentioned as the LÚ.GAL URU$^{meš}$ *ša* $^{mí}$*láḫ-ḫi-ni-te* (ref. Peter Zilberg).

likely explanation is that *-ani* is a poss. suffix known in LB (GAG § 43k n. 12). – For the stylistic function of the plural speaking voice, expressing amorous ecstasy, see Paul 1995, 594–595.

vii 22': *ana bāb ēni tallikamma*: Reading with CAD I/J 158a. (Groneberg 2003, 67, differently: "you approach the doors [*bābēni*]"). – *ēni*: an Assyrian form. – Springs are a preferred locus for amorous activity in love-related literature (cf. in Songs 4: 12, 15).

vii 26': *iše''i asma kirî lalîka*: Reading with CAD A/2, 337b and CAD Š/2, 356 d), and contra Groneberg 2003, 67 (*i-še-'-ì*!(Koll.)*-ma*, "indeed she looks for the garden of your sexuality"), and Limet 1996, 158 (*i-še-e'-as-ma*, "elle languit dans le jardin de ton desir"). Collation proves that the sign in question, though eroded since Ebeling's copy, is AS and not *ì*(NI). Hecker 2013, 60 translates: "Er(*sic*) sucht den angemessenen Garten deines Liebreizes".

vii 27': *ūma libbī mēlula nigûta*: The speaker addresses here his own body. Another example of this rare literary device in Akk. literature is found in YOS 11, 21c 26 (№ 25): "be at peace my heart! Make firm your two foundations ...".[463] In classical Arab. poetry this device, called *iltifāt* or *tağrīd* by Arab commentators, is well known.[464]

vii 28': *ārid kirî šarru ḫāṣibu erēni*: The description of the lover descending to the garden and cutting twigs appears in MAD 5, 8: 8–9 (№ 22): "To the garden you come down, indeed come down to the garden!".[465] A similar incipit is found in the Babylonian catalogue: "It is the king of the land! How sweet is the cedar!".[466]

vii 29': *atta māru rā'imu dādīni*: Note the archaic construct form *rā'imu*. – For the stylistic use of the pl. *dādīni*, see Paul 1995, 594.

vii 30': *ebirtu nāri ālu mēlili*: Note the loc. adv. in *ebirtu* (see von Soden 1933, 92 n. 3) and once more the archaic construct in *ālu*.

vii 31': *ašrunni tagūša araḫ ṣīḫāti* – Again, loc. adv. in *ašrunni* (< *ašrumni*, see von Soden 1933, 97). – *ṣīḫāti*: In pl. (unlike Groneberg 2003, 67).

vii 32': *ulla alik māru*: Understanding this alliterating line depends on the interjection *ulla*. CAD U/W 74b, translates: "now, go, sweet-heart!", but CAD A/l, 302b: "away! [*ullā*]

463 YOS 11, 21c 26 (№ 25): *nūḫ ṣurrī kīn išdīka*.

464 See van Gelder 1982–1984.

465 MAD 5, 8: 8–9 (№ 22): *kirîšum turdā turdāma ana kirîm*. The semantic connection of a king and cedar trees goes beyond love-related literature. A king venturing into the cedar forest reminds anyone versed in Mesopotamian literature of Gilgameš. This scene, so central in Mesopotamian culture, reverberates in other compositions, as in the figure of the lion-king in the Series of the Fox (see Wasserman 2005). The image of the lover descending to the garden is found in Songs 6: 2.

466 CUSAS 10, 12: 33 (№ 18): *šar mātim annûm kī ṭāb erēnu*.

depart, darling". CAD M/l, 314b offers yet another translation: "no! go, darling!", with *ulla* as a negation, which seems to me the simplest and more convincing solution.

vii 33': *ki-i sà-ra-at ša-at ḫa-aṭ-ṭi*: Reading with AHw 1028b and CAD S 184a (Groneberg 2003, 67: *kē i-ṣa-ra-ap*! *šāt hatti*, "how she burns (sexually) that terrifying one"). Equally possible is Hecker 2013, 61, who reads *ṣa-ra-at* and translates: "Wie funkelnd ist die mit dem Stabe". "That of the scepter",[467] deceiving or flashing, is probably Ištar.

vii 35': *šandanak kirî ṣīḫāti*: For the role of the gardener in love-related literature, see Groneberg 1999, 184–185. – Date-palm as a metaphor for the female-lover is found in Songs 7: 8.

vii 36'–37': *ūmdu ina Larsan ṣīḫātu izīqa*: Reading following Sigrist/Goodnick Westenholz 2008 671 who took *u₄-um-du* as a form of *ūmtum*, "day". This reading is preferable to taking DU as a logogram for *izuzzum* or *alākum*, as suggested by CAD Ṣ 186b 2, CAD Z 65b (after Ebeling 1922, 24). (The idea that DU is a short form of Dumuzi, expressed in Groneberg 2003, 67 n. 100, is difficult syntactically and cannot be followed).

vii 38': *rīšī Nanāya ina kirî Ebabbar ša tarammī*: This incipit consists of one line only (against Sigrist/Goodnick Westenholz 2008 671). – For the cult of Nanāya in Larsa, see Stol 1998–2001, 149.

vii 43'–44': *râmka lū ṣurru ṣīḫātuka lū ḫurāṣu*: The couple *ṣurru-ḫurāṣu* is not common in literary texts, and I know only of SB Gilg. VII 157 where it is found.[468] – The phallic allusion of the metaphor "obsidian blade" is hard to miss.

vii 45': *râmī nīru mušnammeru atallî*: For this prime example of the conceptual equation light = love, see Overview § 6.2.

vii 46': *mūša aḫsuskama*: Hecker 2013, 61 takes this line together with the next as one incipit ("Nachts dachte ich an dich (und) was dein Mund sagte"), but vii 47' is not indented and there is no indication that the two lines belong together.

vii47': *epšu pīka*: Von Soden 1931, 212 takes *epšu pīka* as construct form, but loc. adv. makes better sense here (and in vii 5').

vii 48': *ištu ṣallāku ina sūn māri*: For the sleep metaphor, see Overview § 6.1.

---

467 Can the scepter be a euphemism for the erect male member? A *palûm*, "staff", is clearly used in this sense in ZA 75, 198–204i 112–113 (№ 34): *u šumum inašši palâ ramānišu u alpum inašši palâ ramānišu*, "Indeed, even the garlic carries its own staff! Indeed, even the bull carries its own staff!".

468 SB Gilg. VII 157 (= George 2003, 642): *li*[*ddinki*] *ṣurra uqnâ ḫurāṣu*, "May he [give you (= Šamḫat)] obsidian, lapis lazuli and gold".

vii 49': *re-bi-<it>-ka*: The dictionaries and other treatments of this line could not construe the meaning of *re-bi-ka*. AHw 965a, s.v. *rebû* ("vierter, *Viertel*") suggested even reading *re-bi?(kás?)-ka*, and summarizes "unkl.". CAD R 224b, and CAD U/W 201b listed this line without translation. Hecker 2013, 61 n. 35 commented: "Zeilenanfang ist unklar". Groneberg 2003: 68 suggested a verb: *ri-bi kâša…*, "grow big! For you're the lapis lazuli" (but the imp. of *rabûm* is unlikely, and *kâša* is never used as the nom. "you"). The solution to this crux is simple. The scribe omitted by mistake one sign: *re-bi-<it>-ka*, from *ribītum* which CAD R 321a translates: "(a part of the body)". This anatomical term was discussed by Kogan/Militarev 2002, 313–314, who established its meaning as "genitals, groins", perhaps even testicles.[469] – The incipit *rebītka ša uqnîšadî* continues the precious stones imagery found already in vii 43'–44'. These two incipits have a nice parallel in Songs 5: 14: "His hands are rods of gold, studded with beryl; His belly a tablet of ivory, adorned with sapphires".[470]

vii 51': *ḫamru*: AHw 318a lists this incipit under *ḫamru*, "heiliger Bezirk (des Adad)" with the remark "unkl.". CAD M/2, 49b does not translate the word. Hecker 2013, 61 also refrains from translating (see n. 36). Groneberg 2003, 68 has "the favorite, the selected", assuming *ḫamru* < *ḫawru*. This suggestion is followed here with hesitation, since it should be noted that *ḫawru*, the verbal adj. of *ḫiārum*, is not attested, only the participle *ḫāwirum*.

vii 53': *ukāl râm*[*ka*]: I take *kullu* in the sense of "to keep or have in mind", "to remember" (CAD K 513–514). Groneberg 2003, 68 differently: "I (?) control [your] love", and so also Hecker 2013, 61: "Ich halte [deine] Liebe".

viii 1'ff.: For the last part of the catalogue, with its many different designations of hymns and songs, see Groneberg 2003, 61–71.

viii 3': *iškar mārumma rāʾimni*: Recapitulates the incipits summarized in i 43'.

viii 4': *iškar murtāmī*: This is the missing section of 31 incipits (see commentary to ii 48').

viii 5': *iškar rēʾiya rēʾî*: Recapitulates the incipits summarized in ii 46'.

viii 7': This line recapitulates ii 52'.

viii 8': *tegû*: See Shehata 2009, 40ff. – This line recapitulates iii 1', iii 9', iii 17', iii 29', and iii 31'.

viii 11': *zamārū adapu*: See Shehata 2009, 302 n. 1742. – This line recapitulates iii 38'.

viii 12': šìr-gíd-da: See Shehata 2009, 274ff.

469 Cf. Böck 2000, 222: 85 and 304: 27–28.
470 Leonid Kogan turned my attention to this biblical parallel.

viii 13': šìr-dingir-gal-la: See Shehata 2009, 264.

viii 14': *šit/ṭru*: See Shehata 2009, 329f. and CAD Š/3, 146, 3. – This line recapitulates v 16' (but note that the number of songs in v 16' is 13, whereas in this line it is only 3).

viii 19': *zamār šēri*: See Shehata 2009, 227. Tinney 1996, 139 takes *zamār šēri* to designate "song of the morning" (after CAD Z 36b, c).

viii 20': *zamār alāli*: The cheerful, high pitch ululation *alālum* was recently discussed by Mirelman/Sallaberger (2010, 185–186) in their treatment of a Sum. wedding song. Note that the ducks' quacking is also heard as *alālum* in the Moussaieff Love Song obv. 9 (№ 11).

viii 27': šìr-ku-gu: See Shehata 2009, 262ff. – This line recapitulates vi 5'.

viii 28': *kerrētu*: Following AHw 468a "Marschlieder?" (< *girrum*, "way, journey"). – This line recapitulates vi 11'.

viii 29': This line recapitulates vi 15'. Contra to Ebeling's copy the tablet has clear 2° *ga-an-gíṭ-ṭu*$^{meš}$. In addition, Ebeling copied erroneously two round holes which are not there.

viii 30': This line recapitulates vi 18'.

viii 31': This line recapitulates vi 21'.

viii 32': *inḫu*: See Shehata 2009, 316 and passim. – This line recapitulates vi 24'.

viii 33': This line recapitulates vi 30'.

viii 34': This line recapitulates vi 31'–33'.

viii 35': *araḫḫu*: See Shehata 2009, 301–302. Hecker 2013, 62 translates: "Erntelied" (< *araḫḫum*, "storehouse, granary").

viii 37': *šīqātu*: If derived from *šīqu*, "irrigation", then *šīqātu* would be "irrigation-songs" (cf. viii 39' "hoeing-song"). Hecker 2013, 62 n. 39, similarly.

viii 39': *ripqu*: With CAD R 366b: "hoeing-song" (see viii 37' "irrigation-songs").

viii 42': *qurdu*: See Shehata 2009, 324 ("Heldenlieder(?)").

viii 45'–52': For the *irātu*-section, see Draffkorn Kilmer 1965, 267–268, Groneberg 2003, 66–69, Shehata 2009, 329.

viii 45': *irtu*/*irātu*: See Shehata 2009, 328–330. – This line recapitulates vii 6'.

viii 46': This line recapitulates vii 24'.

viii 50': *ni-iš tuḫ-ri*: See Mirelman/Krispijn 2009.

# III. Manipulative Compositions Concerning Love and Sex: Incantations

# № 20 Keep Her Apart! Keep Her Apart! (CUSAS 10, 11)

Copy: George 2009, Pl. XXXII
Tablet Siglum: MS 2920
Photo: George 2009, Pl. XXXI, CDLI no. P252006
Edition: George 2009, 69–70
Collection: Schøyen Collection, Oslo
Provenance: ?
Measurements: 9.5x5.4x2.5 cm
Period: OB

**Introduction**
After a lyric description of dawn as the time of creation of cosmic love, this incantation continues with direct speech: a man is trying to persuade a woman to fall in love with him. As noted by George (2009, 67) this incantation shows thematic similarities, and some verbal parallels, with YOS 11, 87 (№ 26).

Obv.

| | |
|---|---|
| 1 | *[pí-ta-ar-r]a!-as-si pí-ta-ar-ra-as!-<si>* |
| 2 | *[ma-r]a-at A-ni-im ni-pí-iḫ ša-me-e* |
| 3 | *[u*$_4$*?-ma?]-am ú-ul-li-la-a-ma* |
| 4 | *[š]a-me-e ša Anim*(AN.NA) |
| 5 | *i-ba-aš-ši ra-mu-um e-li ni-ši i-[ḫa]-ap-pu-up* |
| 6 | *ra-mu-um li-iḫ-pu-pa-am i-na [ṣe]-ri-[ia]* |
| 7 | *lu-ud-di lu-uq-bi lu-ta-wu-ú [lu-ra-ʾì*(ḪI)*-im* |
| 8 | *ḫu-us-sí-ni-i-ma ki-ma aš-nu-ga-[a]-li* |
| 9 | *li-iḫ-šu-[šu] pa-nu-ki!*(Text: KU) *ki-ma ri-im-ti-i[m]* |
| 10 | *e tu-uš-bi a-na mi-li-ik a-bi-[ki]* |
| 11 | *e te-el-qé-e mi-li-ik um-mi-k[i]* |
| 12 | *šum-ma qá-aš-da-[at] im-da-ša l[i*-x-x] |
| 13 | *šum-ma na-di-a-[at] bi-bi-il-ša l[i*-x-x] |
| 14 | *šum-ma [ke]-ez-re-et li-kà-ap-pí-ir* |
| | */ aš-ta-ma-ša e-li-ia li-im-qú-u[t]* |
| 15 | *ši-i[p-t]um ú-ul ia-tu* |
| 16 | *ši-[pa-at] É-a ù* $^{d}$*Ištar*(INANNA) *iš-ku-nu* |
| | (Rev. uninscribed) |

**Translation**
Obv.

| | |
|---|---|
| 1 | [Keep] her apart! keep [her] apart! |
| 2–4 | [The] daughters of Anu, the lights of heaven, [*in day-ti*]*me*(?) purified the sky of Anu. |
| 5–6 | Love came about, twittering over the people; May Love twitter over me! |

7 Let me cast (a spell), let me speak, let me utter words of love:
8 'Think of me as an *ašnugallum*-snake!
9 May your face rejoice as a wild cow!
10 Do not wait on your father's counsel,
11 Do not heed your mother's advice!'
12 If she is a hierodule may she [...] her support;
13 If she is a cloister-lady may she [...] her gift;
14 If she is a harlot may she clean(?) her tavern, may she throw herself at me!
15 The incantation is not mine:
16 (it is) the incantation (which) Ea and Ištar have created.

**Commentary**

1: *pitarrassi pitarrassi*: The addressee of this imp. is probably the incantation itself, and the attached acc. pronoun *-ši* refers to the woman. Why should the woman be kept apart if, after all, the incantation is about bringing the woman to the man? Perhaps the woman is not free, and the man wishes that she be his, and only his.

3: I restore [*$u_4$?-ma?*]-*am* at the beginning of 3 instead of [*ki-a*]-*am*, as proposed by George. – For the metaphorical relation between love and light, see Overview § 6.2.

4: *šamê ša Anim*: This part of the sky is known in Mesopotamian cosmology as the highest level of the heavens (Horowitz 1998, 244–246).

5–6: *iḫappup... liḫpupam*: On the meaning of the verb *ḫab/āb/pum* in ALL, see commentary to CUSAS 10, 9: 32 (№ 3). Here, where dawn is breaking, *ḫapāpum* refers to the twittering sound of birds, which metaphorically describes the burgeoning of love.

8: *Ašnugal(l)um*: This semi-mythological awe-inspiring snake stands first in a long enumeration of snakes in the incantation TIM 9, 65 // TIM 9, 66. – The Freudian symbolism which connects snakes and male desire is uncommon in ALL.

9: *kīma rīmtim*: The beloved girl is compared to a cow also in YOS 11, 87: 22 (№ 26): "Lick me like (a cow licking) a calf!".[471]

10: *ē tūšbī ana milik abiki*: The idiom *wašābum ana milik* PN can be compared to *wašābum ana pî/qabê...*, "to sit and obey the command/advice of..." (AHw 873a 5, 1482b 5).

10–11: Familial objection to the union of the man and his girl is found also in YOS 11, 87: 14–20 (№. 26). – Note the alliteration in *ḫasāsum* and *ḫašāšum*.

471 YOS 11, 87: 22 (№ 26): *kīma būrim lu''ikīni*.

12–14: After trying to overcome the resistance of the girl's family (8–10), the magician confronts the possibility that the desired female has other, non-familial, reasons for refusing her suitor, namely that she is a member of a social group which forbids coupling with men: *qadištum*, *nadītum*, or a *kezertum*. These lines are paralleled by YOS 11, 87: 7–10 (№. 26).

14: *šumma kezret li-kà-ap-pí-ir aštammaša*: George 2009, 69 reads *li-qá-ab-bi-ir*, "may she wind up her brothel". Orthographically the value *qá* is more common than *kà*, but dwelling places can hardly serve as direct objects of *qebērum*-D. By contrast, *kapārum*-D, "to clear away", is used with houses.

# № 21 I Am Mating You, Oh Nanāya! (KBo 36, 27)

Copy: KBo 36, 27
Tablet siglum: Bo 61/r
Photo: Schwemer 2004, 62–63, Hethitologie Portal, Mainz
Collection: Anadolu Medeniyetleri Müzesi, Ankara
Edition: Schwemer 2004, 61–64
Studies: Laroche 1971, No. 812
Provenance: Ḫattuša
Measurements: ?
Period: MB

**Introduction**

Opaque and abrupt incantation preceded and followed by rituals. Its language, unusually explicit, aims to stimulate and encourage a man to sexual activity. If (ll. 18'–19') are correctly understood, they seem to imply that the man is striving to have sex with a woman who is not his wife.

(Akk. Ritual instructions)

Obv.

15' [tu$_6$] én-é-nu-ru *ag-ra-aḫ-ki Na-na-a*
16' *ag-ra-aḫ-ki Na-na-a* [*ki*]-*ma im-me-ri*
17' *a-la-*[*la*]*-ma* [*ki*]*-ma a-ri-ti ta-nu-qa-tum*!? ([*am*]?)*-ma*
18' *ak*!*-kum bá-*[*ki*]*-ti-ia pí-ta-a-*[*ki*]
19' *ak*!*-kum bá-*[*ki*]*-ti-ia ma-ia-a-al-ki*
20' *a-ra-am* [*Ki-li-li*] *a-na-ak Ki-li-li*
21' *išaru*(GÌŠ) *ṭeḫe*(TE) *išaru*(GÌŠ) *ṭeḫe*([TE) DA].GA.AN.NI
22' DA.ZI.DA.AN.NI (ras.)
23' GÁ.AN.GA DA.[GA].AN.NI [MAḪ].ḪA

----

MAN MAN

----

(Akk. Ritual instructions)

**Translation**

15' Incantation. I am mating you, Oh Nanāya!
16' I am mating you, Oh Nanāya! Like a sheep!
17' Ululation! Like (of) a pregnant woman, a *battle* cry!
18' Instead of my 'wailing woman' – your two openings!
19' Instead of my 'wailing woman' – your bed!
20' I will be making love (to you)! – Oh Kilili! I will have intercourse (with you)! – Oh Kilili!
21' *Penis*! *Approach*! *Penis*! *Approach her bedroom*!

22' *(Approach) her right side*!
23' *Come on*! *(Approach) her exalted bedroom*!

**Commentary**
15'–16': *agraḫki*: With Schwemer (2004, 66) *agraḫki* is a form of the rare verb *garāḫum*, until now attested only as a synonym to *niākum*. (The loan verb from West Semitic, *qarāḫum*, "to become iced up", cf. CAD Q 126–127, makes no sense here). – The past tense of the verb functions as a performative ("right now I am doing so-and-so"). – I find it difficult that the object of this verb is the goddess Nanāya. Human-divine sexual encounters are extremely rare in the corpus, and the only clear case involves Ištar (Or. 60, 340 = № 12). Nanāya, by contrast, is copulating only with the god Muʾāti (MIO 12, 52–53 = № 10). Hard-pressed, I suggest that "Nanāya!" in these lines (and "Kilili!", in 20') serves not as direct object but as a voc., a cry of excitement and self-encouragement (similarly to "Oh god!", or "Christ!", etc.)

17'*: alālum*: "work song, work cry" is mentioned also in The Moussaieff Love Song: obv. 9 (№ 11) and in KAR 158 viii 20' (№ 19).[472] – *tanūqātum*, is "a battle cry" (CAD T 176b). Its etymology is *nâqum* A "to cry, to groan" (CAD N/1, 341a), but a semantic play on the quasi-homonymous *niākum*, "to have (illicit) intercourse", may have been intended. I follow Schwemer (2004, 66) and take the two sonorous expressions in this line – *alālum* and *tanūqātum* – as referring to "Liebesgestöhn". Another sonorous expression in the corpus is *ernittum*, "cry of joy after military triumph". In love incantations *ernittum* many mean the shout of excitement at the peak of sexual activity. Note that *ernittum* is compared to the crying of a child (ZA 75, 198–204d 54, ZA 75, 198–204i 109–110), and that *tanūqātum* is connected to a pregnant woman (probably, as noted by Schwemer (2004, 66), standing for *ālittum*, a woman giving birth.)

18'–19': *ak*!*-kum*: E. Zomer, Leipzig, pointed out to me that the first sign in this couplet is not IM, as read by Schwemer, but probably a malformed AK (compare to IM in 16', as seen in the photos of the tablet in the Hethitologie Portal, Mainz). Accordingly I read *ak-kum* (*ak-ku*₁₃ in first mill. texts), namely *akkū*(*m*) < *an*(*a*) *kûm*, a prepositional phrase meaning "instead of". – *bakkītiya*: *bakkītu*, "wailing woman, mourner", is also attested only in the first mill. (so already Schwemer in his commentary). The "wailing woman" could be a derogatory designation of the man's wife, as opposed to the man's lover. – *pītāki*: If indeed "your two openings", is correctly understood (a suggestion cautiously raised by Schwemer), then this is a euphemistic designation for two erogenous zones of the woman (on "gate" referring to female genitalia, see Overview § 4.6).

20': *arâm*, *anâk*: Unlike *agraḫki* in l. 15' and l. 16' *arâm* and *anâk* are in the present tense. – While *garāḫum* and *râmum* only optionally take a direct object, *niākum* requires an object. Hence, contrary to ll. 15'–16', it is hard to avoid the conclusion that Kilili *is* the direct object of the sexual activity described. However, Schwemer (2004, 68) suggested that a

472 Note that George 2009, 51 finds this lemma also in CUSAS 10, 8: 1 (№ 2), but this reading is not followed here. Instead of *a-la-lí* I read *a-la-ni*.

haplography occurred, namely the writer had in mind *arâmki* and *anâkki* but dropped the attached pronoun *-ki* to avoid the clash with the initial syllable in Kilili. The direct object of the verb *niākum* could therefore be a woman who is not mentioned explicitly (see above ad ll. 15'–16').

21'–23': These lines, which Schwemer takes as abracadabra, are probably written in Sumerograms (I follow here Schwemer's and Zomer's ideas): GÌŠ stands for *išarum*, the male organ; TE for *ṭeḫûm*, "to approach (sexually)"; DA].GA.AN.NI could be interpreted as phonetic spelling of DA.GÁN, "her sleeping chamber"; DA.ZI.DA.AN.NI: perhaps "her right (side)"; and GÁ.AN.GA possibly phonetic spelling for GA.NA. – Two separating MAN marks are found also in the end of LKA 15 (№ 9).

# № 22 Enki Loves the Love-charm (MAD 5, 8)

Copy: Westenholz/Westenholz 1977, 200
Tablet Siglum: Kiš 1930, 143+175 h
Photo: Gelb 1970, Pls. III–IV, CDLI no. P285640
Edition: Westenholz/Westenholz 1977, 198–219, Lambert 2013, 31–32
Collection: Ashmolean Museum, Oxford
Studies: Gelb 1970, 7–12, von Soden 1972, 273–274, Lambert 1987, 37–38 , Wilcke 1991, Lambert 1992, 52–54, Cunningham 1997, Cat. No. 50,
Cavigneaux 1999, 269, Foster 2005, 66–68, Lambert 2013, 31–32
Provenance: Kiš
Measurements: 8.7x4.6x1.1 cm
Period: OAkk

**Introduction**
One of the earliest literary pieces in Akk. literature, this OAkk love incantation shows thematic and stylistic affinities with PRAK 1 B 472 (№ 13), another amatory text from Kiš. The text is written in a confident hand, showing no scribal mistakes. It is therefore not a draft, but a well-prepared composition, ready to be used or studied.

Obv.

| | |
|---|---|
| 1 | $^{d}$EN.KI *ir-e-ma-am* |
| 2 | *è-ra-[?]-am* |
| 3 | *ir-e-mu-um mera'*(DUMU) $^{d}$*Ištar*(INANNA) |
| 4 | *in sà-qì-[śa?/śu? u?-ša?-a]b* |
| 5 | *in ru-úḫ-t[i kà-na]-ak-tim* |
| 6 | *ú-tá-ra wa-a[r-d]a-tá* |
| 7 | *da-mì-iq-tá tu-úḫ-tá-na-ma* |
| 8 | *ki-rí-śum tu-ur*$_4$*-da* |
| 9 | *tu-ur*$_4$*-da-ma a-na kirîm*($^{giš}$KIRI$_6$) |
| 10 | *ru-úḫ-ti kà-na-ak-tim* |
| 11 | *ti-ip-tá-at-qá* |
| 12 | *a-ḫu-uz*$_7$(EŠ) *pá-ki ša ru-qá-tim* |
| 13 | *a-ḫu-uz*$_7$ *bu-ra-ma-ti* |
| 14 | *e-né-ki* |
| 15 | *a-ḫu-uz*$_7$ *ur*$_4$*-ki* |
| 16 | *ša ši-na-tim* |
| 17 | *a-áš-ḫi-iṭ ki-rí-ís* |
| 18 | $^{d}$*Sîn*(EN.ZU) |
| 19 | *ab-tùq ṣarbatam*($^{giš}$ÁSAL) |

Rev.

| | |
|---|---|
| 20 | *u-me-ís-sa* |

21 *du-ri-ni i-tá-as-kà-ri-ni*
22 *ki rā'ium*(SIPA) *ì-du-ru ṣa-nam*
23 *enzum*(ÙZ) *kà-lu-ma-sa laḫrum*(U$_{8}$) *puḫāssa*(SILA$_{4}$-[*sà*])
24 *a-tá-núm mu-ra-aś*
25 *se-er-gu-a i-da-śu*
26 *šamnum*(Ì) *ù ti-bu-ut-tum*
27 *śa-ap-tá-śu*
28 *a-sà-am šamnim*(Ì) *in qá-ti-śu*
29 *a-sà-am i-ri-nim in bu-dì-śu*
30 *ir-e-mu ú-da-bi-bu-śi-ma*
31 *ù iš-ku-nu-śi a-na mu-ḫu-tim*
32 *a-ḫu-uz*$_{7}$ *pá-ki ša da-dì*
33 $^{d}$*Ištar*(INANNA) *ù* $^{d}$*Iš-ḫa-ra*
34 *ù-tám-me-ki*
35 *a-di*$_{4}$ *ṣa-wa-ar-śu*
36 *ù ṣa-wa-ar-ki*
37 *la e-tám-da*
38 *la tá-pá-ša-ḫi-ni*

**Translation**

1–2 Enki loves the love-charm,
3–4 The love-charm, Ištar's son, [sit]ting in [her?/his? l]ap,
5–6 Turning here through the sap of the incense-tree.
6–7 You, Oh two beautiful maidens, are blooming!
8–9 To the garden you come down, indeed come down to the garden!
10–11 You *have drunk*(?) the sap of the incense-tree.
12 I have seized now your(f.) drooling mouth (lit. "mouth of sap"),
13–14 I have seized your(f.) shining eyes,
15–16 I have seized your(f.) urinating vulva (lit. "vulva of urine").
17–18 I leaped to the garden of Sîn,
19–20 I cut the poplar tree *for her day*.
21–22 Encircle(f.) me between the boxwood trees, as the shepherd encircles the flock,
23–24 As the goat (encircles) its kid, the sheep its lamb, the mare its foal!
25 His arms are *adorned*,
26–27 Oil and (the sound of) harp – his lips.
28–29 A cup of oil in his hands, a cup of cedar fragrance *on* his shoulders.
30–31 The love-charms have persuaded her, driven her to ecstasy –
32 Now I have seized your(f.) lustful mouth (lit. "mouth of sexual attraction").
33–34 I conjure you(f.) by the name of Ištar and Išḫara:
35–38 'Until his neck and your(f.) neck are not entwined – you(f.) shall not find peace!'

**Commentary**

1–4: *ir'emum*/*irimmum*: The first four lines form a short historiola about the familial background of the hidden protagonist of this incantation, the love-charm: he is the son of Ištar (– and since Enki loves him, is he the father?). Lambert 2013, 31 translates "cupid".

4: *sāqum* and *uššab*: Reading follows Westenholz/Westenholz 1977, so also Foster 2005, 66, Lambert 2013, 31 and CAD S 169b (Groneberg 2001 differently). – *in sāqi*-[*śa*?/*śu*?]: Either the m. or the f. pron. is possible to restore in the break (see Lambert 1992, 53).

5: *ru-úḫ-t*[*i kà-na*]-*ak-tim*: The incense bearing tree *kanaktum* is mentioned also in PRAK 1 B 472 i 8' (№ 13).

6: *ú-tá-ra*: This form remains difficult. The defective spelling of the text, which does not express unambiguously double consonants, allows two analyses. The verb can be derived from (1) *watārum*-D:[473] either (1a) *uttara* - 1 sg. com., or (1b) 3 sg. m. + ventive, or (1c) *uttarā* - 3 du. com.). Althernatively, the form can stem from (2) *târum*-D: again, either (2a) *utarra* - 1 sg. com., or (2b) 3 sg. m. + ventive, or (2c) *utarrā* - 3 du. com.[474] When deciding whether the form is 1 sg. com. or 3 sg. m. + ventive or 3 du. com. one must take into account that -*am*, not just -*a*, is the expected ventive morpheme. Hence 3 du. com., ending with -*ā*, seems preferable. However, I cannot find two agents that could be the subjects of the verb (Ea and Ištar are unlikely). I follow therefore Sommerfeld's idea (*apud* Groneberg 2001, 104 n. 41) that the subject of *utarra* (*târum*-D 3 sg. m.) is the love-charm *ir'emum*. (Note the lack of mimation also in ll. 6 and 13).

6–7: *wa-a*[*r-d*]*a-tá da-mì-iq-tá* : One expects the ending -*ān* for the du. noun (and the adjective?). The non-appearance of the final -*n* denotes perhaps the absolute state, serving as a voc. (Cf. Hasselbach 2005, 180 n. 101, and Kouwenberg 2010, 179 n. 62). – *tuḫtannamā* (*ḫanāmum*-Dt, 2 du.): See Hasselbach 2005, 59 and 213.

8–9: *kirīśum turdā* | *turdāma ana kirîm*: Note the neat chiastic construction in these lines, probably the earliest attestation of this construction in Akk. literature. – The image of "descending to the garden" is found in KAR 158 vii 28': "Descending to the garden, Oh king, cutter of cedar (branches)".[475] For the erotic meanings of the garden, see Paul 1997, 103–108 and Groneberg 1999, 182–184.

9: *ana kirîm*: As noted by Hasselbach 2005, 167, in Sargonic Akk. the prep. *ana* retains the final vowel -*a*, unlike the prep. *in*(*a*).

473 Sic, and not, as suggested by Lambert 1992, 53, from *watārum*-G whose forms are *īter*/*itter*.

474 See Groneberg 2001, 104 n. 41 with previous literature. Groneberg opted for *târum* ("ist er geleitet"), as did Neumann 2008b.

475 KAR 158 vii 28' (№ 19): *ārid kirî šarru ḫāṣibu erēni*.

11: *ti-ip-tá-at-qá*: There are two problems regarding this crux (see Hasselbach 2005, 191 n. 122): the prefix *ti-* (rather than *ta-/tu-*) for the 2 c. du.,[476] and the question whether the verb is *batāqum* "to break" (so Lambert 2013, 31), or *patāqum*, "to fashion". If *ru-úḫ-ti* (ll. 5, 10), and *ru-qá-tim* (l. 12) mean "sap" or "saliva", it is hard to see how either "to break", or "to fashion" could contextually fit.[477] A possible way out of this limbo is, I suggest, to introduce the verb *patāqum* B, "to drink" (CAD P 275b), a rare verb attested only in a few SB literary texts. Support for this idea is found in the next line, where the speaker says that he has seized the maiden's *drooling mouth* (lit. "mouth of sap", *pâki ša ruqātim*). The *ruʾtum* could perhaps be the material manifestation of the cryptic *irʾemum*.

12: *ru-qá-tim*: For the rendering of *ghain* in Sargonic OAkk, see Lambert 1987, 38, Hasselbach 2005, 85, and Kogan/Markina 2006, 367.

12–13: The preterite forms carry here (and in l. 32) a performative meaning: "Here and now I am seizing…". Similar usage of the preterite (for which cf. Wasserman 2003, 168–169) can be identified in KBo 36, 27: 15'–16' (№ 21): "I am mating you…".[478] – *āḫuz*: For *aḫāzum* in love literature, see Paul 2002, 492.

13–14: *burramāti ēnīki*: Note the lack of mimation. – It is hard to explain why the text chooses here adj. pl. f., not the adj. du, as in *damiqtā(n)* (l. 7).

17: *a-áš-ḫi-it*: The plene spelling of the 1 sg. prefix is not customary in OAkk. (cf. *a-ḫu-uz*$_7$ in ll. 12, 13, and *ab-tùq* (l. 19), and the forms collected in Hasselbach 2005, 195–199).

20: *u-me-ís-sa* : Following Westenholz/Westenholz (1977, 209) this form is understood as ending with the term. adv. *-iš*: "for her day" (so Hasselbach 2005, 48, Neumann 2008b, 10 with n. 65, and CAD U/W 151a, d1', without translation). But what does "her day" mean? Day of love is mentioned also in a broken passage in PRAK 1 B 472 ii 4', ii 6' (№ 13): "In the (or: my) day when I will see the signs of [ …], signs (or: destiny?) of…In the (or: my) day when you will grasp … […]".[479]

21: *du-ri-ni*: With Westenholz/Westenholz 1977, 209, the verb DU-*ri-ni* is derived from √dwr, "to go around". In the same way, CAD T 280, s.v. *taskarinnu*, translates: "go around me (*dūrini*) among the boxwood trees, as the shepherd goes around (*idūru*) his flock". CAD R 307 c), s.v. *rēʾû*, translates "as the shepherd guards (*ì*(?)-*du-ru*) the flock"). AHw 1551b, "schützend umgeben", CDA, 61a, "to surround, enfold", Hasselbach 2005, 59 (with some hesitation) and Neumann 2008b follow this path and accept the verb *duārum*. Another opinion, however, was put forward by Lambert (1987, 38 and 2013, 31) who sees here *târum*, "to turn", and read *tù-ri-ni*, and *ì-tù-ru* (22). This analysis was accepted by Groneberg 2001, 105 and Foster 2005, 67. – *i-tá-as-kà-ri-ni*: The continuation of the line is

476 But note the prefix *ti-* used for the 2 m. sg. in the early OB letter AbB 9, 253: 9, 19 (MPS).
477 Lambert 2013, 31 avoided translating these words.
478 KBo 36, 27: 15'–16' (№ 21): *agraḫki*.
479 PRAK 1 B 472 ii 4', ii 6' (№ 13): *kī ūmi ammaruma ši-ma-*[*aṭ*..] … *kī ūmi taḫḫazu i-*[...].

also a matter of dispute. The common opinion is that *i-tá-as-kà-ri-ni* is to be analyzed from *taskarinnu* "boxwood" (see CAD references above, so also Foster 2005, 67). Krebernik 1996, 18 n. 21, Groneberg 2001, 105 n. 49, and already A. Westenholz (1972) take this form from *zakārum*-Ntn "to mention, call by name" (*i-tá-az-kà-ri-ni*). Since the vegetal metaphors are prevalent in the text I prefer to translate here "boxwood".

25–29: This section describes the body of the male protagonist, so the woman is probably speaking (– or perhaps a female chorus). Another possibility is that the performer of the love ritual, the magician – whose first person voice appears throughout the incantation – is speaking. If so, the magician is praising the attractive physical features of the man, probably the client of the incantation, to the rejecting woman. – A similar stylistic device of enumeration of body parts of the male protagonist is found in the Kiš text PRAK 1 B 472 i 9'–i 12' (№ 13).

25: *se-er-gu-a īdāśu* : I follow AHw 1216b, s.v. *śerg/kûm*, "geschmückt sein", and CAD Š/3, 102b "adorned". So also Neumann (2008b). Foster (2005, 67) translates "his arms are two round bundles of fruit", with *šerkum* (AHw 1217) in mind. (The lack of mimation is not an argument against this suggestion, as mimation is absent also in ll. 6–7, and 13–14.)

26: *timbuttum*: The woman refers to her lover's lips as both kissable and uttering sweet words, like a harp. For this metaphorical use in Akk. literature, see Wasserman 1999.

34–38: As suggested (ad ll. 25–29), the 1 pers. voice in the text (ll. 12, 13, 15, 17, 32) is that of the conjurer, who speaks for the rejected man, his client. In the last section of the incantation (ll. 34–38) the conjurer separates himself from his client, and we are dealing with three separate persons: "I" = the conjurer; "Her" = the unwilling; "His" = the man who turned to the conjurer for help. Since the woman is approached directly, as if she is present in front of the conjurer (l. 36: "your neck", and l. 38: "you shall not find peace"), it is not impossible that the conjurer held in his hand an object which represents her (a tuft of hair, an article of clothing, or any other object which could symbolize her persona), using it as a means of forcing her to fulfill his desires.

# № 23 Look at Me! (MS 3062)

Copy: George, 2016, Pl. LXIX, no. 23b
Tablet Siglum: MS 3062
Photo: George, 2016, Pl. LXIX, Pl. LXIX, CDLI no. 252071
Edition: George, 2016, 148, no. 23b
Studies: George, forthcoming
Collection: Schøyen Collection, Oslo
Provenance: ?
Measurements: ?
Period: OB

**Introduction**

This short Akk. incantation – preceded by a Sum. one dealing with a broken bone and followed by another Sum. incantation mentioning fire – is a real gem: a fine example of the freshness and elasticity of Akk. minor literature. Were it not found in a tablet of other magical texts, little, if anything, would reveal that this lyrical composition had a magical purpose. As discussed by George (2016), the text presents the voice of a young girl, determined to attain her love. A first person speech changes to direct speech, where she addresses her lover: *rāmanni* and *amranni*, "love me!" and "look at me!" (ll. 13 and 16). The imagery is floral (thorn-bush and vine), domestic (fire and water), and bucolic (lamb and flock). The lines seem to be divided arbitrarily on the narrow and elongated tablet, (cf. ll. 9–11: *ana išātim / ezzetim mê / ašpuk*), but it is certainly not accidental that the last line contains only the imperative *amranni*, "look at me!" – a rare stylistic device which George (2010, 212 and forthcoming) calls "a "shocking void".

Obv.

| | |
|---|---|
| 7 | *a-sú-uḫ ba-aš-ta-am* |
| 8 | *a-za-ru-ú ka-ra-na-am* |
| 9 | *a-na i-ša-tim* |
| 10 | *e-ze-tim me-e* |
| 11 | *aš-pu-[u]k* |
| 12 | *ki-ma pu-<ḫa>-di-ka* |
| 13 | *ra-ma-an-[ni]* |
| 14 | *ki-ma ṣe-e-[nim]* |
| 15 | *na-as-ḫi-ra-am-ma* |
| 16 | *am-ra-an-ni* |

**Translation**

| | |
|---|---|
| 7–8 | I have torn the thorn, I will be sowing a vine! |
| 9–11 | I have poured water onto the fierce fire. |
| 12–13 | Love me as your lamb, |
| 14–15 | Encircle me as your small cattle. |
| 16 | Look at me! |

**Commentary**

7: *baštum*: With George (2016), this is a variant of the thorny plant *baltum*. A *jeu de mots* with *bāštum*, "(sexual) dignity", is probably intended.

8: *karānum*: The fruit-bearing vine is a common trope in biblical sources pertaining to love.[480] In the literature of lower Mesopotamia, however, where grapes hardly grow, it is much less at home. Wine – also *karānum* – is found only twice in the corpus of ALL. In the first text the man describes the beloved woman in a sentimental manner as "… sweet as honey, … fresh like wine to the nose".[481] In the hymn glorifying Rīm-Sîn of Larsa, we find: "For the New Year, he (= the king) poured wine for her, (with his) right (hand) which oozes".[482] But the vine, unlike wine, is attested only in this text. The collocation of *zarûm*, "to sow" and *karānum*, "vine" is awkward: vines are planted, not sown. George (forthcoming) explains this strange use as resulting from the ignorance of the young girl of agricultural practices.[483] Perhaps so, but another reason for choosing *karānum* has to do with assonance and sonority. The woman expresses the notion of love by employing alliterating words, all based on the sonorants *r* and *n*: *rāmanni* and *amranni*. Wine, *karānum*, joins this melody.

9: *išātum*: Unlike in modern literature, in ALL fire does not represent passion *per se*, but the agony of unrequited love, the burning anguish of unfulfilled desire (George forthcoming). A colophon of another love incantation points at this direction: KA-inim-ma IZI.ŠÀ.GA, which stands probably for "jelousy" (lit. *išāt libbim*, "fire of the heart", VS 17, 23: 8 = № 24, see Wasserman 2015, 607–608). Since colophons of incantations usually designate the target against which the incantation is intended (as, e.g. "for a dog" or "for a scorpion" which mean "(an incantation) *against* a dog, or *against* a scorpion"), the "fire of the heart" must be a negative thing, namely the suffering of the lover which the incantation tries to relieve. Pouring water on the fire (or anger) of love is known from other texts (see the introduction to ZA 75, 198–204g = № 32). Here the trope of fire fits nicely with the agricultural image of tearing the thorns and planting (lit. sowing) the vine.

12–15: The motif of encircling the lamb and the flock returns to the OAkk love incantation MAD 5, 8: 21–24 (№ 22) which reads: "Encircle me between the boxwood trees, as the shepherd encircles the flock, as the goat (encircles) its kid, the sheep its lamb, the mare its foal!",[484] only that there the man is talking to the woman.

---

480 See, e.g., Songs 6: 11, 7: 9, 13, Psalms 128: 3, and Isaiah 5: 1–2.

481 CUSAS 10, 8: 7–9 (№ 2): *kīma dišpim ṭabat ana appim kīma karānim eššet.*

482 YOS 11, 24 i 18–19 (№15): *ana šattim eššetim karānam iqqiašimma ša taṣarrura imnī.*

483 The reading *ka-ra-na-am … ša ta-ṣa-ru-ra im-ni* (suggested by Hecker in Römer/Hecker 1989, 748 n 19a), is not free of difficulties. Should one perhaps return to the previous reading *ka-ra-na-am i-qí-a-ši-im-ma ša ta-za-ru ra-im-ni*, "he poured wine for her, (he) who sows, our beloved"? If so, this would be another case where *karānum* and *zarûm* are combined!

484 MAD 5, 8: 21–24 (№ 22): *dūrīnni ittaskarinnī kī rā'ium idūru ṣānam enzum kalūmaśśa laḫrum puḫāssa atānum mūraś.*

16: *amranni*: The climax of the incantation is, no doubt, its last line, *amranni*, "look at me!". For the central role of the amatory gaze in the corpus of ALL, see Overview § 6.4.

## № 24 Like an Orchard Fruit Come Out to Him! (VS 17, 23)

Copy: VS 17, 23
Tablet Siglum: VAT 8354
Photo: -/-
Edition: van Dijk 1971, 11, Wasserman 2015
Collection: Vorderasiatisches Museum, Berlin
Studies: Farber 1981 No. 25, Cunningham 1997, Cat. No. 366, Wasserman 2003, 115, Cat. No. 208
Provenance: Larsa?
Measurements: 5.0x7.0x2.0 cm
Period: OB

**Introduction**
Loaded with complex metaphors and images, this short spell, an example of the difficulty and beauty inherent in OB incantations, is treated in full in Wasserman 2015. As its colophon indicates, the text deals with IZI.ŠÀ.GA, lit. "fire of the heart", which designates the burning emotion of jealousy. Similarly to MAD 5, 8 (№ 22), three protagonists can be identified in the text: the unyielding woman, the yearning man (= the client), and the magician (= the speaker). The magician promises the young girl that the man will bring her presents which are meant to soften her heart and overcome her resistance. Somewhat unexpectedly these are raw materials whose prupose was, I suggest (ibid), to serve in the preparation of kohl (ll. 4–7).

Obv.
1 *pa-ar-ki-i[š n]a-ak-ra-at*
2 *ṣú-úḫ-ḫu-ri-iš gi-ri-im-mi-iš*
3 *ki-ma i-ni-ib ki-ri-im e-li-šu wa-a-ṣi-a-ti*!(Text: BI)
4 *li-ib-la-ki-im ú-pe-el-li-a-am*
5 *I-di-ig-la-at*
6 *sà-an-gi-i we-ri-a-am a-ba-ri Šu-ši-im*
7 *li-ib-lam sà-an-gi mu-sà-ḫi-la-at i-né-ki*
----
8 KA-inim-ma IZI.ŠÀ.GA
(Rev. uninscribed)

1–2 Barrier-like she is alienated, (entangled) as a tiny berry-fruit.

| | |
|---|---|
| 3 | Like an orchard fruit come out *over* him! |
| 4–6 | Let the Tigris carry for you(f.) charcoal, *sangû*, copper, lead of Susa! |
| 7 | Let it carry hither *sangû*! Oh you, who pierces your(f.) eyes! |
| ---- | |
| 8 | Incantation (to calm) the *fire of the heart.* |

**Commentary**
Full discussion and commentary of the text is found in Wasserman 2015.

## № 25 You Are Fierce! You Are Furious! (YOS 11, 21c)

Copy: YOS 11, 21: 26–30 (Coll. Farber, YOS 11, p. 65)
Tablet Siglum: YBC 4598
Photo: -/-
Edition: Wilcke 1985, 209 (no translation)
Collection: Yale Babylonian Collection, New Haven
Studies: Cunningham 1997, Cat. No. 399, Wasserman 2003. Cat. No. 253
Provenance: area of Larsa
Measurements: 10.4x6.7x2.8 cm (the entire tablet)
Period: OB (Warad-Sîn – Rīm-Sîn)

**Introduction**
This incantation is the third in a tablet of four incantations. The first (YOS 11, 21a 1–12) is a broken bilingual incantation, mentioning Asarluḫi, ending with ritual instructions; the goal of the second (YOS 11, 21b 13–25) is to gain success in a trial. The third incantation, the one presented here, deals with a woman who is trying to change the heart of her former male lover so that he loves her again. Wilcke (1985, 208–209) noted the resemblance between YOS 11, 21c and one of the incantations from the Isin tablet of love incantations (ZA 75, 198–204d).

The tablet ends with an abracadabra, one of the *Fremdsprachige Beschwörungstexte* treated by van Dijk (1982) and has a long colophon, a rare phenomenon in OB incantations: "On behalf of Ilšu-abušu, the brother of Mannum-kīma-Šamaš, the son of Purratum-[...], at the court(?) of Nūrātum, son of Bēlānu the steward; On behalf of Balāye, the son of Iddin-Ea the accountant of the letters".[485] This colophon allows us to give a chronological framework to the text. Balāye is the grandson of the Balamunamḫe, son of Sîn-nūr-mātim from Larsa, whose archive spans over 38 years, from Warad-Sîn 6 to Rīm-Sîn 31.[486] This is a unique example of a case where a chronological framework can be established.

485 YOS 11, 21: 34–35: *aš-šum* DINGIR-*šu-a-bu-šu* ŠEŠ *Ma-an-nu-um-ki-ma-*$^{d}$UTU DUMU $^{íd}$UD.KÍB.[NUN$^{ki}$] *i-na* KISAL? (van Dijk: É) *nu-ra-tum* DUMU *Be-la-nu abarakkum*(AGRIG) / *aš-šum* BAL-*e* DUMU *I-din-É-a šandabakkum*(GÁ.DUB.BA) *ša un-ne-du-k*[*i*-(*i*)].
486 See Dyckhoff 1998, 117–124, esp. 118.

====

26 *e-ez-ze-ti ša-am-ra-ti ta-al-li-[a? ...] nu-úḫ ṣú-ur-ri ki-in iš-di-i-ka ši?* [x]

27 *lu-ta-ad-di a-na libbika*(ŠÀ-*ka*) *šu-ri-pa-am ta-ak-ṣ[i-a-tim]*

28 *i-na a-ma-ri-ia ki-ma Sé-ra-aš na-ap-še-ra ki-m[a* x]*-le-*[AZ?°] *ru-u[m-mi]*

29 *aš-šum wa-aš-ba-ti-ma kam-sà-a-ku az-za-a-zu i-na mu-ú[ḫ-ḫi- ka]*

30 *lu-ud-di-kum ši-ip-tam ši-pa-at ṣūd pāni* (IGI.NIGÍN.NA) *lu-ul-qé-a-am-[ma?]* / *ša maḫ-ri-[ka]*

====

**Translation**

26 You(m.!) are fierce, you(m.!) are furious, you are *going up*(?) – be at peace my heart! Make firm your(m.) two foundations ...

27 Let me throw on your(m.) heart ice (and) frost!

28 When you see me – be soothed(m.) like (one who drinks) beer, *like a ... rel[ease* (*me*)]!

29–30 Because you(m.?) are sitting while I am kneeling, (because) I am standing at [your s]ervice, let me cast a spell on you(m.), let me take the spell of vertigo that is in *front* of [you].

**Commentary**

26, 29: *ezzēti, šamrāti, wašbāti*: All these are 2 sg. m.(!) stative forms, as the context proves: *libbika*, "your(m.) heart" (l. 27) and *luddīkum*, "let me cast on you (l. 30). Similar -*āti* ending 2 sg. m. stative form exist in the corpus, as, e.g. ZA 75, 198–204d 53 (№ 30): *dannāti*.[487]

26: For the rare stylistic device in which the speaker addresses his body, see commentary to KAR 158 vii 27' (№ 19).

27: *lutaddi ana libbika šurīpam takṣ[i-a-tim]*: A parallel to this phrase is found in ZA 75, 198–204g 81 (№ 32).

29: *aššum… kamsāku azzazu ina mu[ḫ-ḫi-ka]*: A similar submissive statement of the woman is found in CUSAS 10, 9: 21, 25 (№ 3) and YOS 11, 24 ii 4 (№ 15).

30: *maḫ-ri-[ka]*: Examining a photo of the tablet verifies this reading by the end of the line.

487 Cf. see Wilcke 1985, 209.

# № 26 I Raised My Voice to Her (YOS 11, 87)

Copy: YOS 11, 87
Tablet Siglum: MLC 1299
Photo: -/-
Edition: YOS 11, p. 50 (no translation). Cavigneaux 1996, 36 (translation of ll. 5–30)
Collection: Yale Babylonian Collection, New Haven
Studies: Westenholz/Westenholz 1977, Cunningham 1997, Cat. No. 405, Cavigneaux 1998, Wasserman 2003, Cat. No. 263, Foster 2005, 199–200, George 2009, 68
Provenance: area of Larsa
Measurements: 9.5x5.5x2.5 cm
Period: OB

**Introduction**

The incantation – written in cursive and confident OB hand – begins with a short historiola, describing the enigmatic love-charm, *irʾemum*/*irimmum*. The speaker is a desperate man trying to catch the attention of his lover who is busy with house-work and perhaps about to go away. As noted by George (2009, 67), this incantation shows contacts with CUSAS 10, 11.

Obv.
1 *e-re-mu e-re-mu*
2 *qá-ar-na-šu ḫu-ra-ṣum*
3 *zi-ba-sú*!(Text: SÍ) *uq-nu-um e-lu-um*
4 *ša-ki-in i-na li-bi-im ša Eš*$_4$*-tár*
5 *a-s*[*i*]*-ši-im-*[*ma*] *ú-ul i-tu-ra-am*
6 *a-mur-*{MA?!}*-ši-i-ma ú-ul i-pa-al-sà-a*[*m*]
7 *š*[*um*]*-ma qá-áš-da-at li-im-qú-u*[*t*]
8 [*d*]*a-du-ša-a*
9 [*š*]*um-ma na-di-a-at mu-pí-ir-ša*
10 *li-im-qú-ut*
11 *ba-tu-ul-tum ma-ra-tu a-wi-li-im*
12 *a-na ri-ig-mi-ia*
13 *a-na* {RI-IG} *ša-gi-mi-ia*
14 <*li*?>-[*i*]*m-qú-ut li-šu-um*

Rev.
15 [*ša*?] *qá-ti-ša-a*
16 *li-im-qú-ut* [*ṣ*]*ú*!*-ḫa-ru-um*
17 *ša a-ḫi-i-ša*
18 [*e*] [*ta-ar*]*-ku-si-im bi-it-ki*
19 *a-na* [*ri*?]*-ik-si-im* [*ša*?] *qá-ti-ki*
20 [*la*?/*e*?] *t*[*a-ap*]*-pa-*[*la*/*al*]*-sí-i*

21 *ki-ma šu-u*[*m-m*]*a-ni-im i-ta?-ap?-la-si-ni*
22 *ki-ma bu-ri-im lu-i-ki-ni*
23 *a-mi-ni ra-mi ki-ma pa-ar-*[*ši*]*-gi-im*
24 *ta-ar-ku-si re-eš-ki*
25 *ki-ma* [*n*]*é-ba-*[*ḫi*]*-im*
26 *te-z*[*i?-ḫ*]*i-ma? q*[*á-ab-l*]*a-ki*
27 [*ṣí*]-[*ḫa-ti*]*-ia k*[*i-m*]*a ša-am-ni-im*
28 [*n*]*a-ši* [*i?-n*]*i-ki*
29 [*al-k*]*i-ma* [*a-n*]*a ṣe-ri-ia*
30 [x x x] *iš!?-im?-m*[*a? š*]*u-mi-i*[*m*]

**Translation**

Obv.
1 Love-charm! Love-charm!
2–3 His two horns are gold, his(!) tail is pure lapis-lazuli:
4 Placed in the heart of Ištar.
5 I raised my voice to her, but she did not turn to me,
6 I gazed (at her) but she did not look at me.
7–8 If she is a hierodule, may her sweetheart perish.
9–10 If she is a cloister-lady, may her provider perish.
11 May the nubile girl, a daughter of a gentleman
12–14 fall at my cry, at my shout!

Rev.
14–16 May the dough fall (out) of her hands,
16–17 (as well as) the little one on her arms.
18 Do not *attach* your house to me!
19–20 Do not look after *the task under* you hands!
21 Look at me like (a cow held with) a halter!
22 Lick me like (a cow licking) a calf!
23–24 Why, my love, did you cover your head like (with) a *p.*-cover?
25–26 (Why) like (with) a belt did you girdle you loins?
27 My *l*[*ove-making*] is (as good) as oil,
28 ... ... ... you(f.)
29 ... *come forward*, to me!
30 ... ... *name*(?).

**Commentary**

2–3: *qarnāšu... zibassi*: The incongruence of the m. and f. poss. prons. is puzzling. Westenholz/Westenholz (1977, 206) suggested emending *zi-ba-sí* to *zi-iq*!*-nam*!. Cavigneaux (1996, 36 n. 10) proposed that these lines describe two scorpions during lovemaking – the horns referring to the male, the tail to the female. This hypothesis may supply another metaphorical layer to the scene, but since the text's main imagery is bovine, scorpions are of no assistance. Another, also not fully unconvincing, option is to draw on ll. 21–22 and understand the horns as referring to the love-stricken male (the calf), while associating the tail with the desired female (the cow). Considering the above, I opt for the simple solution, emending the text to *qá-ar-na-šu ḫu-ra-ṣum zi-ba-sú*! *uq-nu-um e-lu-um*, taking this description back to the *irʾemum*/*irimmum*. The elusive love-charm had a tail, as proves YOS 11, 24 i 2 (№ 15): "The love-charm – the expert (goddess) took its tail".[488]

6: *a-mur-*{MA?!}*-ši-i-ma*: I follow here Westenholz/Westenholz (1977, 207 n. 13) in correcting *āmurma šīma* to *āmuršima*. The sign *-ma*?!, which in the copy looks like BA, probably triggered Foster (2005, 199) to see here a form of *ḫabābum*, "to murmur, chirp, twitter, to hiss", presumably with *aḫ-bu-ba-ši-i-ma* in mind.[489] A similar situation of ignoring (purposely or unintentionally) the gaze of the lover is found in CUSAS 10, 9: 4 (№ 3): "The boy is not aware of the (girl) watching him".[490]

7–10: *šumma qašdat… šumma nadiat*: The formula *šumma* A.... *šumma* B is known from other incantations of this period. The incantation VS 17, 34: 16–18 reads: "If (the newborn) is a male – like a wild sheep, if it is a female – like a *n*. may it fall to the ground".[491] A parallel to this phrase is found in the OA incantation kt 90-k, 178: 14–17: "If (the newborn) is a male – like a wild sheep, if it is a female – like a ram, if it is a miscarriage (lit. rejected), cast (by) its god – may they (i.e. the daughters of the birth goddess) pick it up (and may he fall to the ground like a vine-snake!)".[492] The same formula in a birth-related context is found, partially broken, in the bilingual incantation RA 70: 54–57: 54 which reads: "[If] it is a boy, *they have* [*look*]*ed* at that (i.e. his) 'weapon'. [If] it is a g[irl], *they have* [*look*]*ed at that* (i.e. her) ['*crucible*']".[493] A new parallel to this formula – expanded to a triplet – is furnished by CUSAS 10, 11: 12–14 (№ 20): "If she is a hierodule may she [...] her support; If she is a cloister-lady may she [...] her gift; If she is a harlot may she purify(?) her tavern, may she throw herself at me!"[494] (George differently).

9: *mu-pí-ir-ša*: Although *mubbirša*, "accuser" is still not impossible (esp. as *abārum*-D is well documented), I follow the new suggestion of George (2009, p. 68 with n. 3) and read *muppirša,* "provider" (notwithstanding that *epērum*-D is not attested, and that "provider" is usually rendered by *ēpir*, or *nāšû*, see CAD N/2, 113a). CH § 18, which deals with the family's obligation to support cloistered women, strengthens George's interpretation. It enumerates *nadītum*, *qadištum*, and *kulmašītum*, a list which resembles closely the three

488 YOS 11, 24 i 2 (№ 15): [*e-re*]-[*ma*]*-am zibbassu ilteqe mūdītum*. On this verb see commentary to CUSAS 10, 9: 32 (№ 3).

489 Note the comment of Cavigneaux 1996, 36: "Je ne sais sur quelle lecture est fondée 'I whistled' de Foster, qui donne un sens excellent".

490 CUSAS 10, 9: 4 (№ 3): *ul īde* [*m*]*ārum* [*na*]-*ṭí*-<*la*>-[*sú*].

491 VS 17, 34: 16–18: *šumma zikar atūdāni šumma sinnišat napṭartāni limqutam qaqqar*[*šu*]*m*.

492 Michel 2004, 396–398: 14–17: *šumma zakar etūdāni šumma sinnišat šappārāni šumma sakpum sakip ilišulišēlâmma*, and see Michel/Wasserman 1997.

493 RA 70: 54–57: 54: [tukum-bi ni]n?-ta x tukul-a-ni igi [mu-u]n-ši-in-bar [tukum-bi munus [x] TUK ga-ri-im-[ma]-a-ni igi [mu-un-ši-in]-bar // [*šumma*] *mār ana kakki šuāši* [*ip-pa*]-[*li-su*] [*šumma mār*]*at ana* [x]-[…*šu*]-*a*-<*ši*> *i*-[*ip-pa*]-[*li-su*].

494 CUSAS 10, 11: 12–14 (№ 20): *šumma qašdat imdaša l*[*i*-x x] *šumma nadiat bibilša l*[*i*-x x] *šumma kezret likappir aštammaša elīya limqu*[*t*].

social categories in our incantation and in CUSAS 10, 11: 12–14 (№ 20) (*qadištum – nadītum – kezertum*).

11: *batultum*, "adolescent, nubile girl" is found in lexical texts as a synonym for (*w*)*ardatum* and *ṣeḫertum* (CAD B 173). It is recorded in dictionaries only in MA, NA, and NB texts, as well as in Ugarit. This distribution could indicate a West Semitic origin (which joins the wide usage of this word in biblical Heb. and in Aram.). YOS 11, 87 proves, however, that this lemma is known already in OB.

14: <*li*>-[*i*]*m-qú-ut*: The missing initial *li-* is due to haplology, because of the initial *li-* in *līšum*. Note *li-im-qú-ut* in l. 16.

15: The copy hardly allows [*i-na*]. Restoring [*ša*] seems safer.

14–17: "May the dough fall (out) of her hands, (as well as) the little one on her arms". Contrary to Foster (2005, 199) and to Cavigneaux (1986, 36) who took these lines as two separate sentences, I prefer to see here two wings of one phrase, a zeugma, whose axis is *limqut*. The young girl is described holding a child, while preparing the dough. A similar picture, in which a male lover addresses a woman, asking her to drop what she has in her hands and turn her full attention to him, is found also in Moussaeiff Love Song rev. 4.

18–20: *ē* [*tar*]*kusīm bītki ana* [*ri*]*iksim* [*ša*] *qātiki* [*ē*/*lā*] *t*[*ap*]*pallasī*/*t*[*ap*]*palsī*: The semantics of *rakāsum* and *riksum* extend towards the abstract terms "arrangement, what attaches one to a place, duty, an assignment, etc.". Cavigneaux (1998) translates similarly: "Ne m'attache pas ta maison! Le lien de tes mains (le paquet que tu as dans les mains?) ne le regarde pas!". The man is annoyed that the desired girl pays more attention to her household duties than to him. He demands that she drop those tasks (the dough and the child in ll. 14 and 16) and follow him.

21: *kīma šummānim itaplasīnni*: The image here is that of a cow led by a halter, forced to look at the person holding it.

22: *kīma būrim lu*ʾʾ*ikīni*: I read with Cavigneaux (1996, 36) *lu*ʾʾ*ikīni*, "lèche moi comme un veau!". Foster (1993, 14) translates, without a note: "Follow me around like a calf!", having perhaps in mind the rare and late verb *lekûm*, "to go". Later, (Foster 2005, 200) joins Cavigneaux and translates: "Lick me over as if I were (your newborn) calf". A bovine comparison with the beloved girl is found in CUSAS 10, 11: 9 (№ 20): "May your face rejoice as a wild cow!".[495]

23–24: *ammīni rāmī kīma paršīgim tarkusī rēški*: A double acc. construction ("why did you cover your head with my love") is not impossible (so Cavigneaux 1996, 36 and Wasserman 2003, 119), but considering the next couplet (ll. 25–26), suggests that *rāmī* is not a direct object but a voc. ("Oh my love!"). The male lover complains that, though the girl is

495 CUSAS 10, 11: 9 (№ 20): *liḫšušū pānūki kīma rīmtim*.

surrounded with his affection, she covers her head and ignores him. Ample evidence from Babylonia, Assur, and Mari relates that women, after marriage, were expected to cover their face with a veil, if not regularly, then at least symbolically, in connection with the marriage ceremony.[496] Still, the head-cover in these lines is *paršīgum* and the verb used with it is *rakāsum*, "to bind" (not *pussunum*/*pussumum*, or *kutummum*, associated with the verbs *pasānum* or *katāmum*, "to veil", as in the marriage ceremony). It is therefore unlikely that the incantation hints that the girl is engaged to another man. The documentation from Mari (now gathered in ARM 30, 78–83) shows that the *paršīgum*-cover is an everyday head cover which can be compared, following Durand, to the modern-day Middle-Eastern *kefieh.*[497] The verbs which describe wearing of the *paršīgum* are *apārum*, *labāšum šakānum*, *ṣamādum*, and also, as in our text, *rakāsum* (CAD P 205a 2'). In conclusion, *paršīgum* head-cover hints that the girl is about to be sent away (to a cloister?), a fact which threatens to bring amorous relations to a bitter end.

496 See van der Toorn 1995 and Michel 1997.

497 Newly published OB letters show that *paršīgum* was also used in the medical context as a kind of bandage, similar to *ṣimdum*, helping with toothache, see Reid/Wagensonner 2014.

# № 27 Place Your Mind with My Mind! (ZA 75, 198–204a)

Copy: -/-
Tablet Siglum: IB 1554
Photo: Wilcke 1985, 208–209
Edition: Wilcke 1985, 198: 9–37
Studies: Scurlock 1989–1990, Cunningham 1997, Cat. No. 315, Wasserman 2003, Cat. No. 3, Foster 2005, 201–202 (a-c), Groneberg 2007, 92, 101–102
Collection: Iraq Museum, Baghdad
Provenance: Isin
Measurements: 25.5x8.0x2.5x4.5 cm (the entire tablet)
Period: OB

**Introduction**
The first incantation in this long tablet of incantations which was found broken in a vase buried in a wall presents a woman trying to manipulate by magic means a male lover to (once again?) feel attracted to her. A rival female lover is mentioned (l. 20). In l. 30 a certain Erra-bāni is mentioned, likely to be the very male lover alluded to before. The two last lines of the incantation (ll. 35–36) seem to be uttered by the man: "May I swell like a dog! Your(f.) two curves are like a halter – do not throw (them away) from me!". If so, the man has changed his mind and is again attracted to the woman.

The incantation contains two short ritual instructions (ll. 23 and 29) which may indicate that the preceding lines belong to separate incantations. Still, since a colophon is found in l. 37, I follow Wilcke and count ll. 9–36 as one long incantation.

9 *e-el-li-a-at ka-al-bi-im* ZU*-mi-im*? *em-ṣú-tim*
10 *me-ḫi-iṣ pa-ni-im ši-pi-ir tu-ú*[*r*?]*-ti i-ni-im*
11 *am-ta-ḫa-aṣ mu-úḫ-ḫa-ka uš-ta-an-ni ṭe-e-em-ka*
12 *šu-uk-nam ṭe-e-em-ka a-na ṭe-e-mi-ia*
13 *šu-uk-nam mi-li-ik-ka a-na mi-il-ki-ia*
14 *a-ka-al-la-ka ki-ma* $^{d}$*Ištar ik-lu-ú* $^{d}$*Dumu-zi*
15 *Sé-e-ra-aš ú-ka-as-sú-ú ša-a-ti-ša*
16 *uk-ta-as-sí-i-ka i-na pī*(KA)*-ia ša ša-ra-a-tim*
17 *i-na ú-ri-ia ša ši-i-na-tim*
18 *i-na pī*(KA)*-ia ša ru-ḫa-tim*
19 *i-na ú-ri-ia ša ši-i-na-tim*
20 *a i-li-ik na-ak-ra-tum i-na ṣe-ri-i-ka*
21 *ra-bi-iṣ ka-al-bu-um ra-bi-iṣ ša-ḫi-ú-um*
22 *at-ta ri-ta-bi-iṣ i-na ḫal-li-ia*

----

23 *ša i-na mu-ḫi nu-ni-im wa-ar-qí-im a-na ša-am-ni-im i-na-an-di ip-pa-aš-ša-aš*

----

24 *am-ra-an-ni-ma ki-ma pi-it-ni-im ḫu-ú-du*
25 *ki-ma [Sé-e]-ra-aš li-ib-ba-ka li-wi-ir*
26 *ki-ma* ᵈ*Šam(a)š-im i-ta-an-pu-ḫa-am*
27 *k[i-m]a* ᵈ*Sîn i-di-ša-am*
28 [x x I]G *ù ra-a[m-k]a li-i-di-iš*
----
29 *[š]a-am-ni-im pa-ša-[a-ši]-im*
----
30 *lu a-li-ka pu-ri-[da-ka]* ᵐ*Èr-ra-ba-ni*
31 *qá-ab-la-ka li-im-mu-š[a]*
32 *lu re-du-ú še-er-ḫa-nu-ka*
33 *li-iḫ-du-ú li-ib-bu-ú-ki*
34 *li-iḫ-šu-ša ka-ab-ta-ta-ki*
35 *lu-ú-bi ki-ma ka-al-bi-im*
36 *ki-ma šu-mu-un-ni-im ḫu-bu-ú-ša-ki e ta-at-bu-ki-im*
----
37 KA-inim-ma ki-ág-gá-kam

**Translation**

9 (With?) saliva of a dog, of thirst(?), of hunger(?),
10 (with?) a blow on the face, (with) "turning of eyes",
11 I have hit your(m.) head, I have changed your(m.) mood.
12 Place your(m.) mind with my mind!
13 Place your(m.) decision with my decision!
14 I hold you(m.) back just like Ištar held back Dumuzi,
15 (Just like) Seraš binds her drinkers,
16 (so) I have bound you(m.) with my hairy mouth,
17 with my urinating vulva,
18 with my drooling mouth,
19 with my urinating vulva.
20 May the enemy-woman not come to you!
21 The dog is lying, the boar is lying –
22 you lie forever in between my thighs.
----
23 What is on the green fish will be thrown to the oil; it will be smeared.
----
24 Look at me and rejoice like a harp!
25 Like (through) Seraš may your heart be bright!
26 Shine on me regularly like Šamaš!
27 Renew (yourself) on me like Sîn!
28 ... and may your love be new!
----
29 [.... in? o]il to rub
----

30 May your(m.) two legs walk, Erra-bāni!
31 May your(m.) loins move!
32 May your ligaments follow!
33 May your(f.) heart rejoice!
34 May your(f.) mood be happy!
35 May I swell like a dog!
36 Your(f.) two curves are like a halter – do not throw (them away) from me!
----
37 Incantation of the lover.

**Commentary**

10: Based on first mill. curses, CAD T 491b takes *tūrti īnim* to be "(an eye disease?)". This meaning suits our line, where other negative descriptions are found. And yet, *tūrti īnim* may also be connected with the designations *mutēr īnim* and *mutērat īnim* which are found in bilingual texts (// lú-igi-bal, lú-nigín-na, igi an-kúr-kúr). CAD M/2, 299b translates them as "false person" (lit. who turns the eyes), based mainly on Civil/Biggs 1960, 6: 5: "she who turns the eye(s) is as false as five".[498] The present context suggests that *īnam turrum* can also carry a non-medical meaning, as in flirting, or a seductive gesture: "giving him the eye", or simply "blinking".

11: *amtaḫaṣ*: The perfect tense forms in this line (and in l. 16) serve as performatives (see Wasserman 2003, 168–169).

14–15: *kīma iklû... ukassû*: The preterite forms in these lines are gnomic past, as defined in Mayer 1992, 387–388.

16: *pīya ša šārātim*: "Hairy mouth" refers to the female sexual organ, as shown by the oppositions "drooling mouth" (lit. "mouth of saliva") and the parallel to "urinating vulva" (lit. "mouth of urine").[499] More on euphemistic terms for sex organs, see Overview § 4.6. For these lines see also Lambert 1987, 37–38 n.7 and Paul 2002, 496.

21–22: *rabiṣ kalbum rabiṣ šaḫium atta ritabbiṣ ina ḫallīya*: The meaning of the pictorial image "The dog is lying, the boar is lying – you lie forever in between my thighs" is made clear by a parallel from the late first mill. love ritual describing Marduk and his consort: "To your vulva which you(f.) guard (lit. in which you trust) I will make *my* dog enter (and) will lock the door".[500] The "dog" in the ritual seems to be a metaphorical appellation for the penis, and the "locked gate" describes the phenomenon known in canines, where after prolonged copulation and ejaculation the bulbous globe of erectile tissue of the dog's penis

498 Civil/Biggs 1966, 6: 5: igi an-kúr-kúr 5 ì-lul // *mutērat ī*[*nim*] *kīma ham*[*iš*] *sarrat*. See Alster 1991–1992, 10: 5.

499 In Akk. both mouth and vulva lips are referred to as *šaptum* (CAD Š/1, 486–487).

500 Lambert 1975, 123: 11: *ana* [*biṣ*]*ṣūriki ša taklāte kalbī ušerreb bāba arakkas*. (Note that the same phrase appears earlier, Lambert 1975, 104: 7, but referring to male genitalia)

swells while the muscles in the female vagina contract, thus preventing the withdrawal of the penis.

24–27: The moon-god and the sun-god are found in a somewhat similar context in a first mill. Egalkurra incantation which uses amatory language. Stadhouders 2013, 320, text 17 reads: "... Oil, oil of Nanāya, oil of Ea, I have anointed myself *with you*. Oh oil, may he (the person who is addressed in the palace) be happy with me as with Sîn, may he rejoice over me as over Šamaš....".[501]

36: *kīma šummunnim ḫu-bu-ú-ša-ki ē tatbukīm*: The context suggests that *ḫubūšu* (unattested hitherto) means some kind of bodily protrusion, referring to the curvaceous parts of the woman, perhaps her breasts. It is expected therefore that the male participant would not want them to be taken away from him. The desired curves are compared to a halter, a rope which holds the animal and which cannot be easily removed. (A similar metaphor in YOS 11, 87: 21 = № 26).

501 Stadhouders 2013, 320, text 17: *šamnu šaman Nanāya šaman Ea appašiška šamnu kīma Sîn liḫdâ kīma Šamaš lirīša.*

# № 28 Be Awake at Night-time! (ZA 75, 198–204b)

Copy: -/-
Tablet Siglum: IB 1554
Photo: Wilcke 1985, 208–209
Edition: Wilcke 1985, 200: 38–41
Studies: Scurlock 1989–1990, Cunningham 1997, Cat. No. 316, Wasserman 2003, Cat. No. 24, Foster 2005, 202 (d)
Collection: Iraq Museum, Baghdad
Provenance: Isin
Measurements: 25.5x8.0x2.5x4.5 cm (the entire tablet)
Period: OB

**Introduction**

A short incantation of the former female lover which aims to deprive the present lover of sleep, namely of love (for the theme of sleep and sleeplessness, see Overview § 6.1).

| | |
|---|---|
| 38 | *di-il-pi mu-ši-i-ta-am* |
| 39 | *ur-ri e ta-aṣ-la-li* |
| 40 | *mu-ši e tu-uš-bi* |
| ---- | |
| 41 | KA-inim-ma *ša* ki-ág-kam |

**Translation**

| | |
|---|---|
| 38 | Be(f.) awake at night-time! |
| 39 | At day-time may you(f.) not sleep! |
| 40 | At night-time may you(f.) not sit down! |
| ---- | |
| 41 | Incantation of the lover. |

# № 29 Loved-one! Loved-one! – Whom Ea and Enlil Have Created (ZA 75, 198–204c)

Copy: -/-
Tablet Siglum: IB 1554
Photo: Wilcke 1985, 208–209
Edition: Wilcke 1985, 200: 42–52
Studies: Scurlock 1989–1990, Cunningham 1997, Cat. No. 317, Wasserman 2003, Cat. No. 25, Foster 2005, 202–203 (e), Groneberg 2007, 104–105
Collection: Iraq Museum, Baghdad
Provenance: Isin
Measurements: 25.5x8.0x2.5x4.5 cm (the entire tablet)
Period: OB

**Introduction**

An incantation of a forsaken female lover destined to gain control over the rejecting lover, but also intent on diminishing the status of her rival, perhaps the lawful wife.

42 *na-ra-mu-um na-ra-mu-um*
43 *ša iš-ku-nu-ka É-a ù* $^{d}$*En-líl*
44 *ki-ma* $^{d}$*Ištar i-na pa-ra-ak-ki-im wa-aš-ba-at*
45 *ki-ma* $^{d}$*Na-na-a i-na šu-tu-mi-im wa-aš-ba-at*
46 *a-la-mi-ka e-né-e-tum ma-aq-li-a-am e-ra-am-ma*
47 *aš-ša-a-tum mu-te-ši-na i-ze-er-ra*
48 *bu-ut-qá-am ap-pa-ša ša-qá-a-am*
49 *šu-uk-na-am ap-pa-ša ša-pa-al še-pí-ia*
50 *ki-ma ra-am-ša iš-qù-ú e-li-ia*
51 *ra-mi li-iš-qá-a-am e-li ra-mi-ša*
----
52 KA-inim-ma ki-ág-gá-kam

**Translation**

42–43 Loved-one! Loved-one! – whom Ea and Enlil have created.
44–45 You(m.) sit like Ištar in (her) dais; You(m.) sit like Nanāya in (her) treasury.
46 I will encircle you!
46–47 The *ēntu*-priestesses love the burning; The wives hate their husbands.
48–49 Cut down her haughty nose! Place her nose under my foot!
50–51 Just as her love is higher than me, may my love get higher than her love!
----
52 Incantation of the lover.

**Commentary**

42–43: *narāmum narāmum ša iškunuka Ea u $^{d}$Enlil*: This opening recalls the opening of YOS 11, 87: 1–4 (№ 26): "Love-charm! Love-charm!... placed in the heart of Ištar".[502] Both incantations start with a repeated appellation to the beloved (*narāmum*, or *erimmum*/*ir'emum*) and continue with the mentioning of its creation (*šakānum*) by a deity. (For this usage of *šakānum*, see also CUSAS 10, 8: 16 = № 2).

44–45: *wašbat*: Wilcke (1985, 201) and Scurlock (1989–1990, 110) take *wašbat* as 3 sg. f. stative, referring to Ištar and Nanāya ("I will surround you(m.) (with a magic circle) just as Ištar sits on a dais (and) Nanāya sits in a sanctuary". Understanding the simile in this way, however, is confusing: how can motionless goddesses be compared to a woman who is moving in circles? There are two ways to look at this problem. One is to assume that it is the surrounded man who is compared to the sitting goddesses, resulting in an elliptical sentence "just as DN is sitting (and surrounded by believers) so I will surround you". Another option is that *wašbat* is not 3 sg. f. stative, but a shortened form of 2 sg. m. stative (<*wašbāta*).[503] Understood in this way the comparison makes better sense: the beloved is described sitting motionless like a statue in a temple and the loving woman can thus encircle him and ensure her control over him. But would a man be compared to female goddesses? Since it is a woman making this comparison, it is not unnatural that she would invoke the two main goddesses of her veneration: Ištar and Nanāya.

46: *alammīka*: The verb *law*/*mûm* in similar context is found in ZA 49, 168–169 i 27 (№ 16): "I shall lay siege to you".[504]

46–47: *enētum... aššātum*: Priestesses of different kinds appear also in YOS 11, 87: 7–10 (№ 26), and CUSAS 10, 11: 12–14 (№ 20). Scurlock (1989–1990, 111 n. 41) points out that CH § 127 also mentions *ēntu*-priestesses and married wives. – Note the use of the prefix *e-* in *erammā* instead of *i-*, and the spelling *mu-te-ši-na* (*mutēšina*) instead of the expected *mutīšina*.

50–51: *kīma râmša išqû elīya râmī lišqâm eli râmiša*: A similar disputant phraseology of "as your X is so-and-so over me, so may my X be so-and-so over you" is found in another incantation, RA 36, 3: 9–12: "Just as the masters are superior to the servants, may my words be superior, in the same way, to your words! Just as the rain is superior to (lit. heavy on) the land, may my words be superior, in the same way, to your words.[505]

---

502 YOS 11, 87: 1–4 (№ 26): *erimmum erimmum … šakin ina libbim ša Ištar*.

503 Such forms are not uncommon in the corpus. See, e.g. CUSAS 10, 13: 7 (№ 5), where *šūturāt* stands for *šūturāt*(*i*), (already George 2009, 77).

504 ZA 49, 168–169 i 27 (№ 16): *alawwīki nītam ina ṣēriki*.

505 RA 36, 3: 9–12: *kīma būlū eli šamkānī ḫabrat kêm qibītī el qibītika lū abrat kīma šamûm el qaqqarim ḫabrat kêm qibītī el qibītika lū ḫabrat*.

# № 30 Why Are You Harsh like a Bramble Bush of the Forest? (ZA 75, 198–204d)

Copy: -/-
Tablet Siglum: IB 1554
Photo: Wilcke 1985, 208–209
Edition: Wilcke 1985, 200: 53–61
Studies: Scurlock 1989–1990, Cunningham 1997, Cat. No. 318, Wasserman 2003, Cat. No. 26, Foster 2005, 203 (f)
Collection: Iraq Museum, Baghdad
Provenance: Isin
Measurements: 25.5x8.0x2.5x4.5 cm (the entire tablet)
Period: OB

**Introduction**
The main question regarding this incantation concerns its topic. Does it deal with love and sex, as Wilcke originally assumed, or was it aimed at "gaining victory or dominance over an opponent", as Scurlock (1989–1990, 107–109) has asserted? Scurlock disputes Wilcke's claim that the Isin tablet was composed by, or for, an *entu*-priestess called Eṭirtum. This priestess – so Wilcke claimed – hoped to increase the sexual desire of a married man called Erra-bāni. Scurlock's main point against this interpretation is that the colophon of the incantation (KA-inim-ma WE-*ṭi-ir-tum*, l. 61) is not connected at all to love. In fact, Scurlock (1989–1990, 108), suggests, this line should be read KA-inim-ma *pi-ṭi-ir-tum*, "incantation of loosening", an incantation which was "designed to give economic control over an adversary".

I agree that Wilcke's suggestion of the love-seeking *entu*-priestess was overstretched (Hecker 2008, similarly). Scurlock is further right in pointing out that this incantation shows strong similarity to Egalkurra incantations, whose goal was to gain victory in court.[506] However, looking at the question from the perspective of ALL, it is hard to avoid the feeling that Scurlock is throwing out the baby with the bath water; this incantation does indeed have much to do with love and sex, even if it borrows from a pool of stock phrases from Mesopotamian magic literature.[507] Can "Why am I lost? (Why) do I not exist (for you)?" (l. 56) be said not to deal with love?[508] The dog-boar motif which follows (ll. 57–58) is also undeniably sexual.[509] As for the act of plucking the hair of the partner (l. 59) – how can this not be intimate?[510] Finally, Scurlock (1989–1990, 108–109) interprets *ša qātika leqeamma ana qātiya šukun* (l. 60) as referring to economic possessions, and compares this to the "open hand" found in rituals of the KA.INIM.MA ŠU.DU$_8$.A.KAM-type. I am not convinced. I prefer to render "what is in your hand" as an elliptical reference to the male sex organ (see Overview § 4.6).

506 And for that one needs not look for first mill. parallels, one can go to YOS 11, 21b 13–25.
507 Cooper 1996, 47 n. 4 similarly.
508 Cf. CUSAS 10, 9: 4 (№ 3), and Overview § 6.4.
509 Cf. ZA 75, 198–204a 21–22 (№ 27) and commentary on these lines.
510 See commentary on this line.

53 *am-mi-ni da-an-na-ti ki-ma mu-ur-di-nu qí-iš-tim*
54 *am-mi-ni ki-ma ṣe-eḫ-ri-im la-ʾì-im er-ni-it-ta-ka le-em-né-et*
55 *a*[*m*]*-mi-ni za-a-wa-nu pa-nu-ú-ki*
56 [*am-m*]*i-ni ḫa-al-qá-ku la a-ba-aš-ši*

Lo. Ed.
57 [*i*]*-na li-ib-bi-ka ni-il ka-al-bu-um*
58 *ni-il ša-ḫi-ú-um*
59 *at-ta i-ti-lam-ma lu-na-as-sí-ḫa-am za-ap-pi-ka*
60 *ša qá-ti-ka le-qè-a-am-ma a-na qá-ti-ia šu-ku-un*
----
61 KA-inim-ma *pi-ṭi-ir-tum*

**Translation**
53 Why are you(m.) harsh like a bramble (bush) of the forest?
54 Why is your(m.) triumph-cry as bad as (that) of a little child?
55 Why is your(f.) face inimical?
56 Why am I lost? (Why) do I not exist (for you)?

Lo. Ed.
57–58 In your(m.) heart lies a dog, lies a boar –
59 You(m.), lay with me so that I may pluck your bristles!
60 What is in your(m.) hand take for me and place in my hand!
----
61 "Loosening" (?) incantation.

**Commentary**
53: *kīma murdinnu qištim* For this simile, see Wasserman 2003, 116 (no. 116). Another floral metaphor of a prickly small fruit to designate the lover is found in VS 17, 23: 2–3 (№ 24): "(entangled) as a tiny berry-fruit. Like an orchard fruit come(f.) *over* him!".[511]

54: *kīma ṣeḫrim lāʾîm ernittaka lemnet*: For this simile see Wasserman 2003, 118 (no. 145).

55: *pānūki*: The incantation is addressed to a man; it is therefore possible that the f. pron. is a mistake.

59: *atta itīlamma lunassiḫam zappīka*: The intimate gesture of plucking the lover's hair is known also in A 7478 iv 1–3 (№ 1): "… in your beard (and) in your hair my two lips are set".[512]

---

511 VS 17, 23: 2–3 (№ 24): *ṣuḫḫuriš girimmiš kīma inib kirîm elīšu waṣiāti.*

512 A 7478: iv 1–3 (№ 1): *izziqnika šārtika šakn*[*ā*] *šaptāya.* (See also the same action in the late love ritual, Lambert 1975, 110: 35).

# № 31 Where Goes Your Heart? (ZA 75, 198–204e)

Copy: -/-
Tablet Siglum: IB 1554
Photo: Wilcke 1985, 208–209
Edition: Wilcke 1985, 202: 62–72
Studies: Scurlock 1989–1990, Cunningham 1997, Cat. No. 319, Wasserman 2003, Cat. No. 27, Foster 2005, 203–204 (g)
Collection: Iraq Museum, Baghdad
Provenance: Isin
Measurements: 25.5x8.0x2.5x4.5 cm (the entire tablet)
Period: OB

**Introduction**
An incantation of a woman trying to secure the love of her male lover. The images compare sexual desire to food and drink.

Rev.
62 *a-i-iš li-ib-b*[*a-k*]*a* [(x x)] *i-il-la-ak*
63 *a-i-iš i-na-*[*aṭ-ṭa-la*] *i-na-*[*a*?*-ka*?]
64 *ia-ši-im l*[*i-*] x x [...] x
65 *ia-ti l*[*i-ip-lu-u*]*s* x x [...] x
66 [*am-r*]*a*?*-an-ni k*[i-m]*a*? x x [...]
67 [*i*]*-ta-ap-la-sà-an-ni* x [x x] x KA ŠI [x x x]
68 *ki-ma a-ka-li-im* [(*te*?)*-le*?]*-mi-*[*a*?]*-an-ni*
69 *ki-ma ši-ka-*[*ri-im* (*te*?)*-le*?/*la*?]*-am-ma-an-ni*
70 *ti-da-ab-ba-a*[*b*? x x x] x x x x*-bi-im*
71 *i-na pī*(KA) x x x x [*u*]*m*?*-ma-at* [ZI] x x*-ma-ni* [(x)]
----
72 KA-ini[m-ma ki-ág-g]á-[kam]

**Translation**
Rev.
62 Where goes your(m.) heart?
63 Whereto l[oo]k your(m.) eyes?
64 To me [may your(m.?) heart go!]
65 At me [may your eyes look!]
66 Look at me as [ ]
67 See me ... [ ]
68 [(You will) cons]ume me like bread,
69 [You will cons]ume me like beer.
70 Speak with me continually [ ] ...
71 In *the mouth*(?)... ...

----

72 Incantation of the lover.

**Commentary**

66: [*am-r*]*a*?-*an-ni*: The desire to be looked at, expressed by the same form *amranni*, is found also in MS 3062: 16 (№ 23).

68–69: [(*te*?)-*le*?]-*mi*-[*a*?]-*an-ni* … [(*te*?)-*le*?/*la*?]-*am-ma-an-ni*: The broken verbal forms at the end of these two parallel lines could well be derived from *lêmum*, "to eat and drink, to consume", or *lemûm*, a verb which alternates with *lêmum* carrying the same meaning – both used with "bread" and "beer" (see CAD L 127a, AHw 543b separates the two verbs). "Eating" is euphemistically used for lovemaking, see Paul 1997, 106 n. 4 and 2002, 495–496.

## № 32 Anger, Anger, Keeps Standing in His Heart! (ZA 75, 198–204g)

Copy:
Tablet Siglum: IB 1554
Photo: Wilcke 1985, 208–209
Edition: Wilcke 1985, 202–204: 73–99
Studies: Scurlock 1989–1990, Cunningham 1997, Cat. No. 320, Wasserman 2003, Cat. No. 28, Foster 2005, 204–205 (h-j), Groneberg 2007, 103–104
Collection: Iraq Museum, Baghdad
Provenance: Isin
Measurements: 25.5x8.0x2.5x4.5 cm (the entire tablet)
Period: OB

**Introduction**
This incantation is divided into three parts, each of which terminates with the call *šeḫiṭ uzzum ša Nanāya*. The close resemblance of this incantation to the small but distinctive group of OB anger incantations[513] is clear. The fact that *uzzum* is systematically referred to here as "anger of Nanāya" (ll. 84, 94, 98) proves that this incantation aims to fight not anger in general, but one in particular, an anger connected to love and sex – for Nanāya is a goddess directly connected to amatory relations. Indeed, as a few scholars have realised (Foster 2005, 204, Walls 2001, 27, Stadhouders 2013, 315), *uzzum* may denote passionate and uncontrolled sexual arousal. So what is the meaning of *šeḫiṭ uzzum ša Nanāya*? Is the incantation trying to drive away the *uzzum*, ordering it to vanish (one of the meanings of *šaḫāṭum*)? In the context of this tablet of love incantations, this would be unlikely since the woman is interested in the virile energy of the male participant. What I believe the incantation aims at here is controlling masculine "anger", the man's sexual arousal, and thus satisfying the speaker's (i.e. the woman's) needs.[514] Different ways of taming this anger are mentioned: crossing over it (ll. 96–97) and using cold fluids (water and maybe also milk in l. 77 in the previous incantation). These methods tell us that anger of love is seen as being connected to fire. The burning effect of love recalls the colophon "fire of the heart" (jealousy),[515] the words of the young girl, resolute to attain her love: "I have poured water onto the fierce fire",[516] as well as the unexpected statement: "the *ēntu*-priestesses love the burning".[517]

Rev.
78 [*uz-zu-um*] *uz-zu-um*
79 [*i*]-*t*[*a*?-*na-za*]-*az i-na li-ib-bi-šu*
80 [*lu-uš-qì-ka*] [*me*]-*e ka-ṣú-ú-tim*

---

513 TIM 9, 72, UET 6/2, 399, Whiting 1985 (= Tell Asmar 1930-T117).
514 See Stadhouders 2013, 315.
515 VS 17, 23: 8 (№ 24): KA-inim-ma IZI.ŠÀ.GA (*išāt libbim*?), and see commentary to this line.
516 MS 3062: 9–11 (№ 23): *ana išātim ezzetim mê ašpuk*.
517 ZA 75, 198–204c: 46 (№ 29): *enētum maliam irammâ*.

| | |
|---|---|
| 81 | *lu-uš-qì-ka šu-ri-pa-am ta-ak-ṣí-a-tim* |
| 82 | *[l]i-ib-ba-ka ki-ma barbarim*(U[R.B]AR.RA) *ba-aš-tum* |
| 83 | *[ki-ma] nēšim*(UR.MAH-*im*) *š[a]-l[um-m]a-tum li-ik-l[a?]-ka* |
| 84 | *še-ḫ[i-i]ṭ uz-zu-u[m š]a $^{d}$Na-na-a* |
| ---- | |
| 85 | *uz-z[u-u]m uz-zu-um* |
| 86 | *i-i[l-la-ka-am] ri-ma-ni-iš* |
| 87 | *iš-t[a!-na-ḫi-ṭa-am] [ka-al-ba]-[n]i-i[š]* |
| 88 | *k[i-ma nēšim*(UR.MAH-*im*) *e-ez] a-l[a?-ka-am]* |
| 89 | *k[i-ma barbarim*(UR.BAR.RA) *la-k]a-ta-am [ú?]-ša-[ar?]* |
| 90 | [x x x x x x x] (-) *me-e ka-ba-at-tim* |
| 91 | *i[ḫ-pi KU-li-a-am] ša li-ib-bi-šu* |
| 92 | *ti-[tu-ra-am lu]-ba e-li-i-šu* |
| 93 | *ša-p[a]-a[l-šu]* $^{\text{⸢íd⸣}}$*Idiglat na-ru-um* |
| 94 | *še-ḫi-iṭ [uz-zu-um] ša $^{d}$Na-na-a* |
| ---- | |
| 95 | *uz-zu-um* [(x x x)] *uz-zu-um* |
| 96 | *ki-ma as-[k]u-u[p-p]a-t[i]m lu-ka-bi-is-k[a]* |
| 97 | *ki-ma qá-aq-[qá-ri-i]m lu-te-et-ti-iq-ka* |
| 98 | *še-ḫi-iṭ [uz]-zu-um ša $^{d}$Na-na-a* |
| ---- | |
| 99 | KA-inim-ma lag-mun-kam |

**Translation**

Rev.

| | |
|---|---|
| 78 | [Anger!], anger! |
| 79 | Keeps s[tand]ing in his heart! |
| 80 | Let me give you(m.) cold water to drink! |
| 81 | Let me give you(m.) ice and cool drinks to drink! |
| 82 | May dignity, like (of) a wolf, (restrain) your heart, |
| 83 | May radiance, like (of) a lion, restrain you(m.)! |
| 84 | Jump! Oh anger of Nanāya! |
| ---- | |
| 85 | Anger! anger! |
| 86 | Co[mes to me] like a wild bull, |
| 87 | Ke[eps jumpin]g on me like a dog. |
| 88 | Like a lion, (anger) is fierce-ranging, |
| 89 | Like a wolf, (anger) breaks into a run. |
| 90 | [...] water(?) of the liver. |
| 91 | I[t has broken the *K*.] of his heart. |
| 92 | Let me cross over the b[ridge], over it (anger)! |
| 93 | Beneath it (anger) is the Tigris, the river! |
| 94 | Jump! Oh anger of Nanāya! |
| ---- | |
| 95 | Anger! anger! |

96 I will trample over you like (over) a threshold!
97 As (I pass over) the soil I will pass back and forth over you!
98 Jump! Oh anger of Nanāya!
----
99 Incantation of the salt-lump.

**Commentary**

82–83: *libbaka kīma barbarim bāštum* [*ki-ma*] *nēšim šal*[*umm*]*atumlikl*[*ā*]*ka*: For the syntax of this couplet, see Wasserman 2003, 118

85–86: *uzz*[*u*]*m uzzum i*[*llakam*] *rīmāniš*: For this simile, see Wasserman 2003, 116.

99: Unlike most of the other incantations in the Isin tablet of love incantations, this colophon does not mentions the objective of the incantation, but refers to the main component of the accompanying ritual (so also in l. 108).

# № 33 Fawn over Me like a Puppy! (ZA 75, 198–204h)

Copy: -/-
Tablet Siglum: IB 1554
Photo: Wilcke 1985, 208–209
Edition: Wilcke 1985, 204: 100–108
Studies: Scurlock 1989–1990, Cunningham 1997, Cat. No. 321, Wasserman 2003, Cat. No. 29, Foster 2005, 205 (k)
Collection: Iraq Museum, Baghdad
Provenance: Isin
Measurements: 25.5x8.0x2.5x4.5 cm (the entire tablet)
Period: OB

**Introduction**

The first incantation of the Isin tablet mentions a person named Erra-bāni.[518] This incantation too turns specifically to a man, this time to a gentleman named Iddin-Damu. Iddin-Damu's body is described from top to bottom, and he is ordered – probably by a female lover, or a magician representing her – to be docile as a dog, and eager to be the lover of the one who desires him.

The colophon mentions the *maštakal*-plant (l. 108). I propose that this incantation revolves around a magic procedure which compares the man and a love-inducing plant. The *maštakal* is a well-known component in the Babylonian arsenal of *materia medica*, albeit not especially aphrodisiac. My proposition is that these lines describe the moment when the *maštakal* was pulled from the ground. The plant's parts were interpreted, by way of magical analogy, as representing the lover's body. Thus, "big-mouth" and "curled ears" (ll. 100–101) refer to the leaves and flowers of the plant, the "heart" (l. 102) to the central part of the plant, and the "heel" and "thighs" (ll. 103, 105) to the plant's roots. Plants with anthropomorphic features are known from other cultures, notably the *Mandragora autumnalis* (Heb.: *dūdā'im*, German: Gemeine Alraune) which serves in herbal and magical practices to influence and control amatory relations.[519]

Rev.

| | |
|---|---|
| 100 | *ra-ap-ša-am pī*(KA)-⌈*i-im*⌉ *la-wi-a-am uz-ni-in* $^{m}$*I*-⌈*din*-$^{d}$*Da*⌉-*mu* |
| 101 | *pi-te pī*(KA)-*i-ka ki-ma* KIN$^{ku6}$-*im* |
| 102 | *li-i*[*b-b*]*a-ka za-as-sà-ru-um* |
| 103 | *aš-lu-pa-am* [(x)] *i-qì-ib-ka* |
| 104 | *él-qè* [x x *b*]*i li-ib-bi-*[*i*]*m* |
| 105 | *e-si-ir p*[*u*?-*ri*]-⌈*di*⌉-*i-ka* |
| 106 | *ku-uz-zi-ba-an-ni k*[*i-ma mi*?]-*ra-ni-im* |
| 107 | *ki-ma ka-al-bi-im* ⌈*a-ta*⌉-*la*?-*ak*? ⌈*e*?-*li*?⌉-*ia* |

518 ZA 75, 198–204a 30 = № 27.
519 Among many different textbooks, see e.g., Birkhan 2010, 65–69.

----

108 KA-inim-ma ú-i[n-nu-uš]-[kam]

**Translation**

Rev.

100 Big-mouth, curled-ears, Iddin-Damu!

101 Open your mouth like a *K*.-fish,

102 Your heart is a *Z*.-plant,

103 I pulled out(?) your heel,

104 I took the [..]. of your heart,

105 I locked your thighs,

106 Fawn over me like a puppy,

107 Keep coming(?) on me like a dog.

----

108 Incantation of the *maštakal*-plant.

**Commentary**

100: *rapšam pīm lawiam uznīn*: On these two *Damqam-īnim* constructions,see Wasserman 2003, 48.

107: *atallak*: After *kīma kalbim* I suggest restoring a *alākum* Gtn-imp., "to go around, to keep going".

# № 34 I Have Opened for You My Seven Gates! (ZA 75, 198–204i)

Copy: -/-
Tablet Siglum: IB 1554
Photo: Wilcke 1985, 208–209
Edition: Wilcke 1985, 204: 109–121
Studies: Scurlock 1989–1990, Cooper 1996, 48, Cunningham 1997, Cat. No. 322, Wasserman 2003, Cat. No. 30, Foster 2005, 205–206 (l-m), Groneberg 2007, 103, 105
Collection: Iraq Museum, Baghdad
Provenance: Isin
Measurements: 25.5x8.0x2.5x4.5 cm (the entire tablet)
Period: OB

**Introduction**
This incantation is uttered by a woman addressing a man, first in a dominating voice (ll. 109–111), then in a yielding, perhaps even submissive tone (117–120). The section that follows (ll. 112–116) is in the 1 pers. so it is not clear whether a man or a woman is speaking. Cooper (1996, 47–48) assumes it is a "masturbating man […] taunting a love-hungry woman".

Rev.
109 *am-ta-ḫa-aṣ mu-úḫ-ḫa-ka ki-ma* x (x)]-KI-[x x] *ta-ap-ta-na-aš-ši-lam qá-aq-qá-*[*ra-am*]
110 *at-ta ki-ma ša-ḫi-i-im qá-aq-qá-ra-am* [x x x]
111 *a-di ki-ma ṣé-eḫ-ri-im e-le-eq-qú-ú er-ni-*[*it-ti*]
----
112 *ù šu?-mu-um i-na-ši pa-la ra-ma-ni-šu*
113 *ù al-pu-um i-na-ši pa-la ra-ma-ni-šu*
114 [*ki*]*-ma na-ru-um ir-ḫu-ú ki-ib-ri-i-ša*
115 [*a*]*-ra-aḫ-ḫi ra-ma-ni-ma*
116 *a-ra-aḫ-ḫi pa-ag-ri*

Up. Ed.
117 *up-te-et-ti-ku-um se-bé-et ba-bi-ia* $^{m}$*Èr-ra-ba-ni*
118 [*qá?-aq?-q*]*á?-ad?-sú ka ri ka ta am uš-ta-ad?-di?-ir*
119 [x (x) G]A-*am ap-ta-ša-ar ša-a-ti*
120 [*a-t*]*a-ku-ul li-ib-bi-ka šu-ta-aq-ti-a-am i-na ṣe-ri-ia*
----

Left Ed.
mu-šid 2.0;0 (= 120)
an mul ki mul-mul
an mul ki mul-mul

----

KA-inim-ma LA-e-sír-ka-limmú

**Translation**

Rev.

109 I have hit your(m.) head; you keep crawling on the ground towards me like ….

110 You, like a boar, [lay(?)] on the ground,

111 until I gain my victory like a child!

----

112 Indeed, even the garlic plant carries its own staff!

113 Indeed, even the bull carries its own staff!

114 Just like the river had flowed over its bank,

115 so I will engender myself!

116 (so) I will engender my body!

Up. Ed.

117 I have opened for you(m.) – Oh Erra-bāni – my seven gates!

118 His h[ead(?)]...

119 ... I have released him(?).

120 Let the constant consummation of your(m.) desire (lit. heart) come to completion in me!

----

Left Ed.

The line number (is) 120.

Sky, star, earth, stars!

Sky, star, earth, stars!

----

Incantation of the shred of the cross-road.

**Commentary**

112–113: *palûm*: For the metaphor "pole" or "rod", see Cooper 1996, 48, and Overview § 4.6.

117: *bābum*: For the "gate" as a euphemism for the female sex organ, see Moussaieff Love Song rev. 8 and Overview § 4.6.

# Bibliography


Abusch, Tz./Schwemer, D. 2011: Corpus of Mesopotamian Anti-Witchcraft Rituals (= Ancient Magic and Divintation 8/1).

Al-Rawi, F. N. H./Dalley, S. 2000: List of 70 birds, Edubba 7, 105–107.

Alster, B. 1991–1992: Early Dynastic Proverb and other Contributions to the Study of Literary Texts from Abū Ṣalābīkh, AfO 38–39, 1–51.

Alster, B. 1993: Marriage and Love in the Sumerian Love Songs, in: M. E. Cohen/D. C. Snell/D. B. Weisberg (ed.), The tablet and the scroll: Near Eastern studies in honor of William W. Hallo (Bethesda 1993), 15–27.

Alster, B. 1997: Proverbs of Ancient Sumer. The World's Earliest Proverb Collections, Bethesda: MA.

Anbar, M. 1975: Textes de l'époque babylonienne anciénne, RA 69, 109–136.

Arkhipov, I. 2012: Le Vocabulaire de la metallurgie et la nomenclature des objets en metal dans les textes de Mari: Materiaux pour le dictionnaire de Babylonien de Paris Tome III (= ARM 32).

Arberry, A. J. 1953: The Ring of the Dove, London.

Attinger, P. 1998: Un sicle la passe, NABU 1998/40.

Barton, J. 2005. The Canonicity of the Song of Songs, in: A. C. Hagedorn (ed.), Perspectives on the Song of Songs. Perspektiven der Hoheliedauslegung (= Beihefte zur Zeitschrift für die alttestamentliche Wissenschaft 346), 1–7.

Beckman, G. 1998: A Draft for an OB Seal Inscription, NABU 1998/72.

Biggs, R. D. 1967: ŠÀ.ZI.GA. Ancient Mesopotamian Potency Incantations (= TCS 2).

Birkhan, H. 2010: Magie im Mittelalter, München.

Black, J. A. 1983: Babylonian Ballads: A New Genre, JAOS 103, 25–34.

Black, J. A./Al-Rawi, F. N. H. 1987: A Contribution to the Study of Akkadian Bird Names, ZA 77, 117–126.

Böck, B. 2000: Die Babylonisch-Assyrische Morphoskopie (= AfO Beih. 27).

Bottéro, J. 1987: L'amour libre et ses désavantages, in: J. Bottéro, Mésopotamie: L'écriture, la raison et les dieux, Paris, 224–240.

Braungart, G. 1980–1981: *De Remedio Amoris*. Ein Motiv und seine Traditionen von der Antike bis Enea Silvio Piccolomini und Johannes Tröster, Archiv für Kulturgeschichte 62/63, 11–28.

Cancik-Kirschbaum, E. C. 1996: Die mittelassyrische Briefe aus Tall Šēḫ Ḥamad (Berichte der Ausgrabung Tall Šēḫ Ḥamad/Dūr Katlimmu 4).

Cavigneaux, A. 1996: Notes Sumérologiques, ASJ 18, 31–45.

Cavigneaux, A. 1998: YOS 11 n°29:19–21 // n°87:18–20 séduction et thérapie!, NABU 1998/74.

Cavigneaux, A. 1999: A Scholar's Library in Meturan?, in: T. Abusch/K. van der Toorn (ed.), Mesopotamian Magic: Textual, Historical, and interpretive Perspectives (= Ancient Magic and Divintation 1), 251–273.

Chambon, G. 2009: Les Archives du vin à Mari (= FM 11).

Chandezon, Ch. et al. 2014: Chandezon, Ch./Dasen, V./Wilgaux, J., Dream Interpretation, Physiognomy, Body Divination, in: Th. K. Hubbard (ed.), A Companion to Greek and Roman Sexualities (Malden: MA), 297–313.

Charpin, D. 1993–1994: Compte rende du CAD volume S (1984), AfO 40–41, 1–23.

Christiansen, B. 2008: Review of Dardano, Die hethitischen Tontafelkataloge aus Ḫattuša (CTH 276–282) (= StBoT 47), ZA 98, 302–308.

Civil, M. 1967: Remarks on "Sum. and Bilingual Texts", JNES 26, 200–211.

Civil, M./Biggs, R. D. 1966: Notes sur des textes sumériens archaïques, RA 60, 1–16.
Cohen, S. 2008: Animals as Disguised Symboles in Renaissance Art (= Brill's Studies in Intellectual History 169).
Cohen, Y. 2013: Wisdom from the Late Bronze Age (= Writings from the Ancient World 34).
Cohen, Y. 2015: The Wages of a Prostitute: Two Instructions from the Wisdom Composition 'Hear the Advice' and an Excursus on Ezekiel 16, Verse 33, Semitica 57, 43–55.
Cooper, J. S. 1996: Magic and M(is)use: Poetic Promiscuity in Mesopotamian Ritual, in: M. E. Vogelzang/H. L. J. Vanstiphout (ed.), Mesopotamian Poetic Language: Sum. and Akkadian (= CM 6), 47– 57.
Cooper, J. S. 2002: Buddies in Babylonia. Gilgamesh, Enkidu, and Mesopotamian Homosexuality, in: T. Abusch (ed.), Riches Hidden in Secret Places. Ancient Near Eastern Studies in Memory of Thorkild Jacobsen (Winona Lake: IN), 73–86.
Cooper, J. S. 2006–2008: Prostitution, RlA 11, 12–21.
Cooper, J. S. 2009: Free love in Babylonia? in: X. Faivre/B. Lion/C. Michel (ed.), Et il y eut un esprit dans l'Homme: Jean Bottéro et la Mésopotamie, Paris, 257–260.
Couto-Ferreira, E. 2010: It is the same for a man and a woman: melancholy and lovesickness in ancient Mesopotamia, Quaderni di Studi Indo-Mediterranei 3, 21–39.
Cunningham, G. 1997: 'Deliver me from Evil'. Mesopotamian Incantations 2500–1500 BC (= StPohl 17).

de Genouillac, H. 1924: Premières recherches archéologiques a Kich. Mission d'Henri de Genouillac 1911–1912. Rapport sur les travaux et inventaires, fac-similés, dessins, photographies et plans, Tome I (= PRAK I).
de Genouillac, H. 1925: Premières recherches archéologiques a Kich. Mission d'Henri de Genouillac 1911–1912. Notes archéologiques et inventaires, fac-similés, dessins et photographies, Tome II (= PRAK II).
Deller, K. 1983, STT 366. Deutungsversuch 1982, Assur 3, 139–153.
Deller, K./Mayer, W. R./Sommerfeld, W. 1987: Akkadische Lexikographie: CAD N, Or. 56, 176–218.
Draffkorn Kilmer, A. 1965: The Strings of Musical Instruments: Their Names, Numbers, and Significance, AS 16, 261–272.
Durand, J.-M. 2009: La nomenclature des habits et des textiles dans les textes de Mari. Matériaux pour le Dictionnaire de Babylonien de Paris, Tome 1 (= ARM 30).
Dyckhoff, Ch. 1998: Balamunamḫe von Larsa – eine altbabylonische Existenz zwischen Ökonomie, Kultus und Wirtschaft, in: CRRAI 43, 117–124.

Ebeling, E. 1922: Ein Hymnen-Katalog aus Assur ( = Berliner Beiträge zur Keilschriftforschung 1/3).
Edmonds, R. G. 2014: Bewitched, Bothered, and Bewildered. Erotic Magic in the Greco-Roman World, in: T. K. Hubbard (ed.), A Companion to Greek and Roman Sexualities (Malden: MA), 282–296.
Edzard, D. O. 1987: Zur Ritualtafel der sog. "Love Lyrics", in: F. Rochberg-Halton (ed.), Language, Literature and History: Philological and Historical Studies Presented to Erica Reiner (= AOS 67), 57–69.

Falkenstein, A. 1950: Sumerische religiöse Texte, ZA 49, 80–150.
Farber, W. 1981: Zur älteren akkadischen Beschwörungsliteratur, ZA 71, 57–58.
Farber, W. 2010: Ištar und die Ehekrise. Bemerkungen zu STT 257, RA 18, 21ff. ("Tisserant 17"), und STT 249, in: D. Shehata/F. Weiershäuser/K. V. Zand (ed.), Von Göttern und Menschen: Beiträge zu Literatur und Geschichte des Alten Orients: Festschrift für Brigitte Groneberg (= CM 41), 73–85.

Farber, W. 2014: Lamaštu. An Edition of the Canonical Series of Lamaštu Incantations and Rituals and Related Texts from the Second and First Millennia B.C. (= MC 17).
Farber-Flügge, G. 1973: Der Mythos "Inanna und Enki" (= StPohl 10).
Feingold, R. 2002: Texts from an Archive of a Seal Cutter, NABU 2002/44.
Fincke, J. C. 2000: Augenleiden nach keilschriftlichen Quellen (= Würzburger medizinihistorische Forschungen 70).
Fincke, J. C. 2013: Another fragment of the 'Love Lyrics' from Babylon (BM 47032), NABU 2013/76.
Finkel, I. L. 1988: A Fragmentary Catalogue of Lovesongs, ASJ 10, 17–18.
Foster, B. R. 1993: Before the Muses: An Anthology of Akkadian Literature, 1st Ed., Bethesda: MA.
Foster, B. R. 2005: Before the Muses: An Anthology of Akkadian Literature, 3rd Ed., Bethesda: MA.
Fox, M. V. 1985: The Song of Songs and the Ancient Egyptian Love Songs, Medison: WI.
Frahm, E. 2009: Historische und historisch-literarische Texte (= KAL 3).

Gabbay, U. 2008: The Akkadian Word for "Third Gender": the *kalû* (gala) Once Again, in: CRAAI 51, 49–65.
Gadotti, A. 2014: "Gilgamesh, Enkidu and the Netherworld" and the Sumerian Gilgamesh Cycle (= Untersuchungen zur Assyriologie und vorderasiatischen Archäologie 10).
Gehlken, E. 2012: Weather Omens of Enūma Anu Enlil. Thunderstorms, Wind and Rain (Tablets 44–49) (= CM 43).
Gelb, I. J. 1970: Sargonic Texts in the Ashmolean Museum, Oxford (= MAD 5).
Geller, M. J. 2010: Look to the Stars: Babylonian Medicine, Magic, Astrology and *Melothesia* (Max-Planck-Institut für Wissenschaftsgeschichte).
Geller, M. J. 2014: Melothesia in Babylonia. Medicine, Magic, and Astrology in the Ancient World (= Science, Technology, and Medicine in Ancient Cultures 2).
George, A. R. 2003: The Babylonian Gilgamesh Epic: Introduction, Critical Edition and Cuneiform Texts, Oxford.
George, A. R. 2009: Babylonian Literary Texts in the Schøyen Collection (= CUSAS 10).
George, A. R. 2010: The Assyrian Elegy: Form and Meaning, in: S. Melville/A. Slotsky (ed.), Opening the Tablet Box: Near Eastern Studies in Honor of Benjamin R. Foster (= CHANE 42), 203–216.
George, A. R. 2013: Babylonian Divinatory Texts Chiefly in The Schøyen Collection (= CUSAS 18).
George, A. R. forthcoming a: Mesopotamian Incantations and Related Texts in the Schøyen Collection.
George, A. R. forthcoming b: "Be My Baby" in Babylonia: an Akkadian poem of adolescent longing.
Goldhill, S. 2002: The Erotic Experience of Looking: Cultural Conflict and the Gaze in Empire Culture, in: M. C. Nussbaum/J. Sihvola (ed.), The Sleep of Reason: Erotic Experience and Sexual Ethics in Ancient Greece and Rome, Chicago/London, 374–399.
Goodnick Westenholz, J. 1987: A Forgotten Love Song, in: F. Rochberg-Halton (ed.), Language, Literature and History: Philological and Historical Studies Presented to Erica Reiner (= AOS 67), 415–425.
Goodnick Westenholz, J. 1992: Metaphorical Language in the Poetry of Love in the Ancient Near East, in: CRRAI 38, 381–387.
Goodnick Westenholz, J. 2005: Sing a Song for Šulgi, in: Y. Sefati et al. (ed.), "An Experienced Scribe Who Neglects Nothing": Ancient Near Eastern Studies in Honor of Jacob Klein (Bethesda: MA), 343–373.
Gordin, Sh. 2011: The Tablet and its Scribe: Between Archival and Scribal Spaces in Late Empire Period Ḫattusa, AoF 38, 177–198.
Groneberg, B. 1971: Untersuchungen zum hymnisch-epischen Dialekt der altbabylonischen literarischen Texte (Dissertation Münster University).

Groneberg, B. 1980: Zu den "gebrochenen Schreibungen", JCS 32, 151–167.

Groneberg, B. 1986: *ḫabābu-ṣabāru*, RA 80, 188–190.

Groneberg, B. 1987: Syntax, Morphologie und Stil der jungbabylonischen "hymnischen" Literatur (= FAOS 14).

Groneberg, B. 1999: "Brust" (*irtum*)-Gesänge, in: B. Böck/E. Cancik-Kirschbaum/Th. Richter (ed.), Munuscula Mesopotamica: Festschrift für Johannes Renger (= AOAT 267), 169–195.

Groneberg, B. 2001: Die Liebesbeschwörung MAD V 8 und ihr Literarischer Kontext, RA 94, 97–113.

Groneberg, B. 2002: The "Faithful Lover" Reconsidered: Towards Establishing a New Genre, in: CRRAI 47, 165–183.

Groneberg, B. 2003: Searching for Akkadian Lyrics: From Old Babylonian to the "Liederkatalog" KAR 158, JCS 55, 55–74.

Groneberg, B. 2007: Liebes- und Hundebeschwörungen im Kontext, in: M. T. Roth/W. Farber/M. W. Stolper/P. von Bechtolsheim (ed.), Studies Presented to Robert D. Biggs, June 4, 2004 (= From the Workshop of the Chicago Assyrian Dictionary 2 = AS 27), 91–107.

Guichard, M. 2014: L'Épopée de Zimrī-Lîm (= FM 14).

Guinan, A. 1997: Auguries of Hegemony: The Sex Omens of Mesopotamia, Gender & History 9, 462–479.

Gurney, O. R. 1956: The Sultantepe Tablets (V. The Tale of the Poor Man of Nippur), AnSt 6, 145–164.

Halperin, D. M. 1998: Forgetting Foucault: Acts, Identities, and the History of Sexuality, Representations 60, 93–120.

Hasselbach, R. 2005: Sargonic Akkadian. A Historical and Comparative Study of the Syllabic Texts, Wiesbaden.

Hecker, K. 1989: Akkadische Hymnen und Gebete. A. Texte der altbabylonischen Zeit, in: O. Kaiser (ed.), Lieder und Gebete I (= TUAT II/5), 718–752.

Hecker, K. 2005, "Kundbar werde mir deine Sehnsucht..." Eros und Lieber im Alten Orient, in: A. C. Hagedorn (ed.), Perspectives on the Song of Songs Perspektiven der Hoheliedauslegung (= Beihefte zur Zeitschrift für die alttestamentliche Wissenschaft 346), 163–179.

Hecker, K. 2008: Texte aus Mesopotamien: 2. Rituale und Beschwörungen, in: B. Janowski/G. Wilhelm (ed.), Omina, Orakel, Rituale und Beschwörungen (= TUAT NF 4), 61–127.

Hecker, K. 2013: Texte aus Mesopotamien: 1. "Ich zählte des Lieder", in: B. Janowski/D. Schwemer(ed.), Hymnen, Klagelieder und Gebete (= TUAT NF 7), 54–63.

Heeßel, N. 2000: Babylonisch-assyrische Diagnostik (= AOAT 43).

Heeßel, N. 2009: The Babylonian Physician Rabâ-ša-Marduk. Another Look at Physicians and Exorcists in the Ancient Near East, in: A. Attia/G. Buisson (ed.), Advances in Mesopotamian Medicine from Hammurabi to Hippocrates (= CM 37), 13–28.

Held, M. 1961: A Faithful Lover in an Old Babylonian Dialogue, JCS 15, 1– 26.

Held, M. 1962: A Faithful Lover in an Old Babylonian Dialogue (JCS 15 1–26) Addenda et Corrigenda, JCS 16, 37–39.

Hess, C. W. 2012: Untersuchungen zu den Literatursprachen der mittelbabylonischen Zeit (Dissertation Leipzig University).

Hilgert, M. 2002: Akkadisch in der Ur III-Zeit (= Imgula 5).

Holmberg, I. E. 2009: Sex in Ancient Greek and Roman Epic, in: T. K. Hubbard (ed.), A Companion to Greek and Roman Sexualities (Malden: MA), 314–334.

Horowitz, W. 1998: Mesopotamian Cosmic Geography (= MC 8).

Hrůša, I. 2010: Die akkadisceh Synonymenliste *malku* = *šarru* (= AOAT 50)

Hurowitz, V. A. 1995: An Old Babylonian Bawdy Ballad, in: Z. Zevit/S. Gitin/M. Sokoloff (ed.), Solving Riddles and Untying Knots: Biblical, Epigraphic, and Semitic Studies in Honor of Jonas C. Greenfield (Winona Lake: IN), 543–558.

Klein, J./Sefati, Y. 2008: "Secular" Love Songs in Mesopotamian Literature, in: C. Cohen et al. (ed.), Birkat Shalom: Studies in the Bible, Ancient Near Eastern Literature, and Postbiblical Judaism Presented to Shalom M. Paul on the Occasion of His Seventieth Birthday (Winona Lake: IN), 613–626.

Kogan, L./Markina, K. 2006: Review of R. Hasselbach, Sargonic Akkadian. A Historical and Comparative Study of the Syallabic Texts, Babel und Bibel 3, 555–588.

Kogan, L./Militarev, A. 2002: Akkadian Terms for Genitalia: New Etymologies, New Textual Interpretations, in: CRRAI 47, 311–319.

Kogan, L. 2011: Proto-Semitic Phonetics and Phonology, in: S. Weninger et al. (ed.), The Semitic Languages. An International Handbook, Berlin/Boston.

Kouwenberg, N. J. C. 2010: The Akkadian Verb and its Semitic Background (= LANE 2).

Kouwenberg, N. J. C. 2013: Review of N. Wasserman, Most Probably. Epistemic Modality in Old Babylonian, Babel und Bibel 7, 321–369.

Krebernik, M. 1996: Neue Beschwörungen aus Ebla, Vicino Oriente 10, 7–28.

Krebernik, M. 2009–2010: Šarrabu, RlA 12, 70–71.

Krecher, J. 1976–1980: Kataloge, literarische, RlA 5, 478–485.

Kwasman, Th./Parpola, S. 1991: Legal Transactions of the Royal Court of Nineveh, Part I. Tiglath-Pileser III through Esarhaddon (= SAA 6).

Lambert, W. G./Millard, A. R. 1969: Atra-Ḫasīs: The Babylonian Story of the Flood, Oxford.

Lambert, W. G. 1959–1960: Three Literary Prayers of the Babylonians, AfO 19, 47–66 (Taf. VII–XXIV).

Lambert, W. G. 1960: Babylonian Wisdom Literature, Oxford.

Lambert, W. G. 1962: A Catalogue of Texts and Authors, JCS 16, 59–77.

Lambert, W. G. 1966: Divine Love Lyrics from the Reign of Abi-ešuh, MIO 12, 41–51.

Lambert, W. G. 1970b: The Sultantepe Tablets (continued). IX. The Birdcall Text, AnSt 20, 111–117.

Lambert, W. G. 1975: The Problem of the Love Lyrics, in: H. Goedicke/J. J. M. Roberts (ed.) Unity and Diversity. Essays in the History, Literature, and Religion of the Ancient Near East (Baltimore: MD), 98–135.

Lambert, W. G. 1983: A New Verb: **ši'ālum*, RA 77, 190–191.

Lambert, W. G. 1987: Devotion: The Languages of Religion and Love, in: M. Mindlin/M. J. Geller/J. E. Wansbrough (ed.), Figurative Language in the Ancient Near East, London, 25–39.

Lambert, W. G. 1992: The Language of ARET V 6 and 7, QuadSem 18, 42–62.

Lambert, W. G. 2013: Babylonian Creation Myths (= MC 16).

Lapinkivi, P. 2004: The Sumerian Sacred Marriage in the Light of Comparative Evidence (= SAAS 15).

Laroche, E. 1971: Catalogue des Textes Hittites. Études et commentaires, Paris.

Limet, H. 1996: Le texte KAR 158, in: H. Gasche/B. Hrouda (ed.), Collectanea orientalia: histoire, arts de l'espace et industrie de la terre: études offertes en hommage à Agnès Spycket (= CPOA Série 1/3), 151–158.

Livingstone, A. 1989: Court Poetry and Literary Miscellanea (= SAA 3).

Livingstone, A. 1991: An enigmatic line in a mystical / mythological explanatory work as agriculture myth, NABU 19991/6.

Livingstone, A. 2013: Heberologies of Assyrian and Babylonian Scholars (= CUSAS 25).

Loretz, O. 1964: Zu Problem des Eros im Hohelied, Biblische Zeitschrift Neue Folge 8, 191–216.

Machinist, P. 1978: Epic of Tukulti-Ninurta I: A Study in Middle Assyrian Literature (Dissertation Yale University).
Marello, P. 1992: Vie Nomade, Florilegium marianum (= Mémoires de N.A.B.U. 1), 115–125.
Matuszak, J. 2012: Ka ḫulu-a. Der böse Mund. Ein sumerisches Lehrstück über die Konsequenzen des frevlerischen Fehlverhaltens einer Frau (MA thesis submitted to the university of Tübingen under the title "WB 169 und Duplikate - eine sumerische Diatribe").
Matuszak, J. forthcoming: "Und du willst eine Frau sein?" Ein sumerische Streitgespräch zwischen zwei Frauen (Dissertation Tübingen University).
Mayer, W. R. 1992: Das "gnomische Präteritum" im literarischen Akkadisch, Or. 61, 373–399.
Mayer, W. R. 1995: Zum Terminativ-Adverbialis im Akkadischen, Or. 64, 161–186.
Mayer, W. R. 2003: Akkadische Lexikographie: CAD R, Or. 72, 231–242.
Meinhold, W. 2009: Ištar in Aššur - Unterschung eines Lokalkultes von ca. 2500 bis 614 v. Chr. (= AOAT 367).
Michalowski, P. 2011: The Correspondence of the Kings of Ur. An Epistolary History of an Ancient Mesopotamian Kingdom (= MC 15).
Michel, C./Wasserman, N. 1997: Du nouveau sur šumma zikar a-li-da-ni šumma sinnišat na-ap-TA-ar-ta-ni, NABU 1997/64.
Michel, C. 1997: Un témoignage paléo-assyrien en faveur du port du voile par la femme mariée, NABU 1997/40.
Michel, C. 2004: Deux incantations paléo-assyriennes. Une nouvelle incantation pour accompagner la naissance, in: J. G. Dercksen (ed.), Assyria and beyond: studies presented to Mogens Trolle Larsen (= PIHANS 100), 395–420.
Mirelman, S./Sallaberger, W. 2010: The Performance of a Sumerian Wedding Song (CT 58, 12), ZA 100, 177–196.
Mirelman, S./Krispijn, T. J. H., 2009: The Old Babylonian Tuning Text UET VI/3 899, Iraq 71, 43–52.
Moren, S. M. 1977: A Lost "Omen" Tablet, JCS 29, 65–72.
Mulroy, D. 1992: Early Greek Lyric Poetry, (Ann Arbor: MI).

Nesbitt, M./Postgate, J. N. 1998–2001: "Nuss and Verwandtes", RlA 9, 633–635.
Neumann, H. 2008b: Eine Liebesbeschwörung, in: B. Janowski/G. Wilhelm (ed.), Omina, Orakel, Rituale und Beschwörungen (= TUAT NF 4), 9–11.
Nissinen, M. 2001: Akkadian Rituals and Poetry of Divine Love, in: R. M. Whiting (ed.), Mythology and Mythologies, Methodological Approaches to Intercultural Influences (= Melammu Symposia II), 93–136.

Ormand, K. 2009: Controlling Desires: Sexuality in ancient Greece and Rome, Westport: CT.
Ormand, K. 2014: Foucault's *History of Sexuality* and the Discipline of Classics, in: T. K. Hubbard (ed.), A Companion to Greek and Roman Sexualities (Malden: MA), 54–68.
Oshima, T. 2014: Babylonian Poems of Pious Sufferers. Ludlul Bēl Nēmeqi and the Babylonian Theodicy (= ORA 14).

Parpola, S. 1983: Letters from Assyrian Scholars to the King Esarhaddon and Assurbanipal (= AOAT 5/2).
Parpola, S. 1993: Letters from Assyrian and Babylonian Scholars (= SAA 10).
Paul, Sh. M. 1995: The "Plural of Ecstasy" in Mesopotamian and Biblical Love Poetry, in: Z. Zevit/S. Gitin/M. Sokoloff (ed.), Solving riddles and Untying Knots: Biblical, Epigraphic, and Semitic Studies in Honor of Jonas C. Greenfield (Winona Lake: IN), 585–597.

Paul, Sh. M. 1997: A Lover's Garden of Verse: Literal and Metaphorical Imagery in Ancient Near Eastern Love Poetry, in: M. Cogan/B. L. Eichler/J. H. Tigay (ed.), Tehillah Le-Moshe: Biblical and Judaic Studies in Honor of Moshe Greenberg (Winina Lake: IN), 99–110.
Paul, Sh. M. 2002: The Shared Legacy of Sexual Metaphors an Euphemism in Mesopotamian and Biblical Literature, in: CRRAI 47, 489–498.
Pedersén, O. 1986: Archives and Libraries in the City of Assur 2, Uppsala.
Peled, I. 2010a: *'Amore, more, ore, re...'* Sexual Terminology and Hittite Law, in: Y. Cohen/A. Gilan/J. L. Miller (ed.), Pax Hethitica: Studies on theHittites and Their Neighbours in Honour of Itamar Singer (= StBoT 51), 247–260.
Peled, I. 2010b: The Use of Pleasure, Constraints of Desire: Anniwiyani's Ritual and Sexuality in Hittite Magical Ceremonies, Acts of the VII International Congress of Hittitology, 623–636.
Peled, I. 2013: On the Meaning of the "Changing pilpilû", NABU 2013/3.
Peled, I. 2014: *assinnu* and the *kurgarrû* Revisited, JNES 73, 283–297.
Perry-Gal, L. et al. 2015: Earliest Economic Exploitation of Chicken Outside East Asia: Evidence from the Hellenistic Southern Levant, PNAS 112, 9849–9854.
Ponchia, S. 1996: La palma e il tamarisco e altri dialoghi mesopotamici, Venezia.
Panayotov, S. 2013 : A Ritual for a Flourishing Bordello, BiOr 70, 285–309.
Postgate, J. N. 2001: "Queen" in Middle Assyrian, NABU 2001/40.
Postgate, J. N./Hepper, F. N./Streck, M. P. 2011–2013: Tebernithe, RlA 13, 594–596.

Reid, N./Wagensonner, K. 2014: "My tooth aches so much", CDLB 2014/3.
Reiner, E. 1990: Nocturnal Talk, in: Tz. Abusch/J. Huehnergard/P. Steinkeller (ed.), Lingering Over Words: Studies in Ancient Near Eastern Literature in Honor of William L. Moran (= HSS 37), 421–424.
Römer, W. H. Ph. 1989: Review of F. Rochberg-Halton (ed.), Language, Literature and History: Philological and Historical Studies Presented to Erica Reiner (= AOS 67), BiOr 46, 630–637.
Römer, W. H. Ph./Hecker, K. 1989: Religiöse Texte: Lieder und Gebete I (= TUAT II/5).
Rothaus Caston, R. 2006: Love As Illness: Poets and Philosophers on Romantic Love, The Classical Journal 101, 271–298.
Rynearson, N. 2009: A Callimachean Case of Lovesickness: Magic, Disease, and Desire □In *Aetia* Frr. 67–75 PF., American Journal of Philology 130, 341–365.

Schuster-Brandis, A. 2008: Steine als Schutz- und Heilmittel Untersuchung zu ihrer Verwendung□in der Beschworungskunst Mesopotamiens im 1. Jt. v. Chr. (= AOAT 46).
Schwemer, D. 2004: Ein akkadischer Liebeszauber aus Ḫattuša, ZA 94, 59–79.
Scurlock, J. A. 1989–1990: Was There a "Love Hungry" Ēntu-priestess named Eṭirtum?, AfO 36–37, 107–112.
Scurlock, J. A. 2005–2006: Sorcery in the Stars: STT 300, BRM 4.19–20 and the Mandaic Book of the Zodiac, AfO 51, 125–145.
Sefati, Y. 1998: Love Songs in Sumerian Literature. Critical Edition of the Dumuzi-Inanna Songs, Ramat-Gan.
Shehata, D. 2009: Musiker und ihr vokales Repertoire (= Göttinger Beiträge zum Alten Orient 3).
Sigrist, M./Goodnick Westnholz, J. 2008: The Love Poem of Rim-Sîn and Nanaya, in: C. Cohen et al. (ed.), Birkat Shalom: Studies in the Bible, Ancient Near Eastern Literature, and Postbiblical Judaism Presented to Shalom M. Paul on the Occasion of His Seventieth Birthday (Winona Lake: IN), 667–704.
Sissa, G. 2008: Sex and Sensuality in the Ancient World, New Haven: CT.
Sjöberg, Å, 1977: Miscellaneous Sum. Texts II, JCS 29, 3–45.
Stadhouders, H. 2013: A Time to Rejoice: The Egalkura Rituals and the Mirth of Iyyar, in: CRRAI 56, 301–323.

Steinert, U. 2010: Der Schlaf im Licht der altmesopotamischer Überliefernung, in: D. Shehata/F. Weiershäuser/K. V. Zand (ed.), Von Göttern und Menschen: Beiträge zu Literatur und Geschichte des Alten Orients: Festschrift für Brigitte Groneberg (= CM 41), 237–285.
Stol, M. 1989: Old-Babylonian Ophthalmology, in: M. Lebeau/Ph. Talon (ed.), Reflets des deux fleuves: volume de mélanges offerts à André Finet (= Akkadica Suppl. 6), 163–166.
Stol, M. 1996: Suffixe bei Zeitangaben im Akkadischen, WZKM 86, 413–424.
Stol, M. 1998–2001: Nanaja, RlA 9, 146–151.
Stol, M. 2012a: Bitumen in Ancient Mesopotamia. The Textual Evidence, BiOr 69, 48–60.
Stol, M. 2012b: Renting the Divine Weapon as a Prebend, in: T. Boiy et al. (ed.), The Ancient Near East, A Life!: Festschrift Karel Van Lerberghe (= OLA 220), 561–583.
Stol, M. 2014: Masturbation in Babylonia, JMC 24, 39–40.
Stolarczyk, M. 1986: Akadyjski liryk milosny, Przeglad Orientalistyczny 1–2, 69–73.
Streck, M. P./Wasserman, N. 2008: The Old Babylonian Hymns to Papulegara, Or. NS 77, 335–358.
Streck, M. P./Wasserman, N. 2011: Dialogues and Riddles: Three Old Babylonian Wisdom Texts, Iraq 73, 117–125.
Streck, M. P./Wasserman, N. 2012: More Light on Nanāya, ZA 102, 183–201.
Streck, M. P. 1999: Die Bildersprache der akkadischen Epik (= AOAT 264).
Streck, M. P. 2006–2008: Salz, Versalzung. A., RlA 11, 592–599.
Streck, M. P. 2012a: The Pig and the Fox in Two Popular Sayings from Aššur, in: G. B. Lanfranchi/D. Morandi Bonacossi/C. Pappi/S. Ponchio (ed.), Leggo!: Studies Presented to Frederick Mario Fales on the Occasion of His 65th Birthday (= LAOS 2), 789–792.
Streck, M. P. 2012b: *tartāmū* "mutual love", the noun pattern taPtaRS in Akkadian and the classification of Eblaite, in: C. Mittermayer/S. Ecklin (ed.), Altorientalische Studien zu Ehren von Pascal Attinger: mu-ni u4 ul-li2-a-aš ĝa2-ĝa2-de3 (= OBO 256), 353–357.
Streck, M. P. 2014: Altbabylonisches Lehrbuch. Zweite, überabeitete Auflage (= Porta Linguarum Orientalium Neue Serie 23), Wiesbaden.
Steinkeller, P. 2013: An Arcahic "Prisoner Plaque" from Kiš, RA 107, 131–157.

Thureau-Dangin, F. 1925: Un hymne à Ištar, RA 22, 169–177.
Tinney, S. 1996: The Nippur Lament. Royal Rhetoric and Divine Legitimation in the Reign of Išme-Dagan of Isin (1953–1935 B.C.).

van der Toorn, K. 1995: The Significance of the Veil in the Ancient Near East, in: D. Wright/D. Freedman/A. Hurvitz (ed.), Pomegranates and Golden Bells: Studies in Biblical, Jewish, and Near Eastern Ritual, Law, and Literature in Honor of Jacob Milgrom (Winona Lake: IN), 327–339.
van Dijk, J. 1971: Nicht-kanonische Beschwörungen und sonstige literarische Texte (= VS 17).
van Dijk, J. 1982: Fremdsprachige Beschwörungstexte in der südmesöpotamischen literarischen Überlieferung, in: CRRA 25, 97–110.
van Gelder, G. J. 1982–1984: The Abstracted Self in Arabic Poetry", Journal of Arabic Literature 14, 22–30.
Veldhuis, N. 2004: Religion, Literature, and Scholarship: The Sum. Composition 'Nanše and the Birds' (= CM 22).
von Soden, W. 1931: Der hymnisch-epische Dialekt des Akkadischen, ZA 40, 163–227.
von Soden, W. 1933: Der hymnisch-epische Dialekt des Akkadischen (Schluß), ZA 41, 90–183.
von Soden, W. 1950: Ein Zwiegespräch Ḫammurabis mit einer Frau (Altbabylonische Dialektdichtungen Nr. 2), ZA 49, 151–194.
von Soden, W. 1972: Ergänzende Bemerkung zum "Liebeszauber"-Text MAD 5 Nr. 8., ZA 62, 273–274.
von Soden, W./Oelsner, J. 1991: Ein spät-altbabylonisches pārum-Preislied für Ištar, Or. NS 60, 339–343 (pl. CVI).

Walls, N. 2001: Desire, Discord and Death, Approaches to Ancient Near Eastern Myth 127–182.
Wasserman, N./Or, A. 1998: Babylonian Love Poetry, Helicon. Anthological Journal of Contemporary Poetry 27, 86–96. (Hebrew).
Wasserman, N. 1992: A New Reading in an Old Babylonian Literary Text, NABU 1992/80.
Wasserman, N. 1999: Sweeter than Honey and Wine... - Semantic Domains and Old Babylonian Imagery, in: L. Milano et al. (ed.), Landscapes. Territories, Frontiers and Horizons in the Ancient Near East. The 44 Rencontre Assyriologique Internationale (= HANE/M 3), 191–196.
Wasserman, N. 2003: Style and Form in Old Babylonian Literary Texts (= CM 27).
Wasserman, N. 2005: Review of B. Kienast, *iškar šēlebi*: Die Serie von Fuchs (= FAOS 22), ZA 95, 145–146.
Wasserman, N. 2008: On Leeches, Dogs, and Gods in Old Babylonian Medical Incantations, RA 102, 71–88.
Wasserman, N. 2010: From the Notebook of a Professional Exorcist, in: D. Shehata/F. Weiershäuser/K. V. Zand (ed.), Von Göttern und Menschen: Beiträge zu Literatur und Geschichte des Alten Orients: Festschrift für Brigitte Groneberg (= CM 41), 329–349.
Wasserman, N. 2012: Most Probably: Epistemic Modality in Old Babylonian (= LANE 3).
Wasserman, N. 2015: Piercing the Eyes: An Old Babylonian Love Incantation and the Preparation of Kohl, BiOr .
Wasserman, N. forthcoming: Fasting and Voluntary Not-Eating in Mesopotamian Sources, in: Fs. L. Milano.
Weidner, E. 1952–1953: Die Bibliothek Tiglatpilesers I., AfO 16, 197–215.
Weinstein, R. 2009: The Rise of the Body in Early Modern Jewish Society: The Italian Case, in: Diemling, M. /Veltri, G. (ed.), The Jewish Body: Corporeality, Society, and Identity in the Renaissance and Early Modern Period (= Studies in Jewish History and Culture 17), Leiden.
Westbrook, R. 1984: The Enforcement of Morals in Mesopotamian Law, JAOS 104, 753–756.
Westenholz, A./Westenholz, J. G. 1977: Help for Rejected Suitors. The Old Akkadian Love Incantation MAD V 8, Or. 46, 198–219.
Westenholz, A. 1972: Review of I. J. Gelb, MAD 4, JNES 31, 380–382.
Whiting, R. M. 1985: An Old Babylonian Incantation from Tell Asmar, ZA 75, 179–187.
Wiggermann, F. A. M. 2008: A Babylonian Scholar in Assur, in: R. J. van der Spek (ed.), Studies in Ancient Near Eastern World View and Society: Presented to Marten Stol on the Occasion of His 65th birthday, 10 November 2005, and His retirement from the Vrije Universiteit Amsterdam (Bethesda: MD), 203–234.
Wiggermann, F. A. M. 2010: Sexualtät, RlA 12, 410–426.
Wilcke, C. 1985: Liebesbeschwörungen aus Isin, ZA 75, 188–209.
Wilcke, C. 1991: Eine altakkadische Liebesbeschwörung, in: B. Hrouda, Der Alte Orient, 280–281.

# List of Figures

# Indices

## I. Texts (Besides of the Corpus)

### Akkadian and Sumerian

### Biblical



### Classical



### Arabic



### Egyptian



### Hebrew



## II. Personal and Divine Names (Selection)

## III. Words Discussed (Selection)



## IV. Grammatical, Literary and Other Terms